Dynamic Optimization and Control

A Variational Approach

M.I.T. PRESS RESEARCH MONOGRAPHS

Dynamic Optimization and Control: A Variational Approach
By Walerian Kipiniak

Iterative Arrays of Logical Circuits
By Frederick C. Hennie III

Sequential Decoding
By John M. Wozencraft and Barney Reiffen

The Control of Multivariable Systems
By Mihajlo D. Mesarović

Frequency-Power Formulas
By Paul Penfield, Jr.

Electronic Processing in Solids
By Pierre R. Aigrain

The Dynamic Behavior of Thermoelectric Devices
By Paul E. Gray

Hydromagnetic Channel Flows
By Lawson P. Harris

Processing Neuroelectric Data
By Walter A. Rosenblith and Members of the Communications Biophysics Group

Mathematical Programming and Electrical Networks
By Jack B. Dennis

Circuit Theory of Linear Noisy Networks
By Herman A. Haus and Richard B. Adler

Nonlinear Problems in Random Theory
By Norbert Wiener

by

WALERIAN KIPINIAK

Dynamic Optimization and Control

A Variational Approach

Published jointly by

The M.I.T. Press, *Massachusetts Institute of Technology*

and

John Wiley & Sons, Inc., *New York · London*

Library of Congress Catalog Card Number: 61-17104

PRINTED IN THE UNITED STATES OF AMERICA

ACKNOWLEDGMENT

This constitutes Technical Report Number 111 of the Electronic Systems Laboratory of the Massachusetts Institute of Technology. All the computations were carried out at the M.I.T. Computation Center, and the excellent cooperation of its staff is gratefully acknowledged. This work was supported in part by the U.S. Army Research Office under Contract No. DA-19-020-ORD-4637, M.I.T. DSR Project 7967. This report is published for technical information only and does not represent the recommendations or conclusions of the sponsoring agency.

FOREWORD

There has long been a need in science and engineering for systematic publication of research studies larger in scope than a journal article but less ambitious than a finished book. Much valuable work of this kind is now published only in a semiprivate way, perhaps as a laboratory report, and so may not find its proper place in the literature of the field. The present contribution is the twelfth of the M.I.T. Press Research Monographs, which we hope will make selected timely and important research studies readily accessible to libraries and to the independent worker.

J. A. Stratton

PREFACE

The term "control system" generally brings to mind a servomechanism or a simple temperature regulator. Such a device is characterized by the fact that it incorporates logic which detects when the output differs from the desired value and feeds back to the input a signal proportional to this difference, which in turn causes the output to change in the direction tending to decrease this difference. Thus – eventually – the output is made to approximate the desired value to an arbitrary tolerance. Such elementary application of the feedback principle is an adequate guide to the design of the simple control systems mentioned above, but in the more complex control problems such as arise in chemical process control, inventory control, and scheduling of manufacturing, as well as in stabilization and guidance of vehicles, a deeper theory is needed.

In the more general control situations the problem is still one of adjusting the inputs (adjustment based on the measurement of system outputs and the knowledge of the environment interacting with the system) so as to optimize a performance criterion. Now, however – in contrast to the servomechanism problem – it is no longer obvious when the optimum has been reached and what changes in the several inputs will result in an improvement. Thus there arises the need for developing a theory for the design of a controller to carry out optimization under such circumstances.

The second complication arises from the greater importance of system dynamics. Negative feedback can be counted on to null the error – eventually – possibly after a long time. But time is precious, and today's control system is required to optimize not just the steady state behavior – for steady state may never be reached since, generally, the desired outputs are stochastic time functions – but rather a time average or a time integral of the expected value of the performance criterion.

It is these two aspects of the design of complex control systems that give rise to the problem of dynamic optimizations which is the central theme of this monograph. The problem which is treated can be abstracted as follows: Given a description of the performance criterion, the dynamics of the element being controlled and its environment (the description may be only probabilistic); to find the control law expressing the control inputs as a function of system states and information about the environment, which optimizes the expected value of the performance criterion integrated over some future time. A general formulation of this problem is presented, and techniques for computing the control law and synthesizing the controller are developed. This formulation allows the solution of a number of problems not solvable by other means and improves the efficiency of solution in other cases. The wide variety of examples which are included bears witness to this.

This monograph does not represent a finished piece of research; a number of proofs lack rigor, and many questions are still left unanswered. It is rather a report on research in progress, marking only a change in the status of this researcher. A reader will find in it many techniques he can use on control problems at hand, as well as many topics for future research whose surface has barely been scratched.

This book is the outgrowth of the doctoral thesis research conducted by the author at the Massachusetts Institute of Technology. The work was done under the supervision of Professor Leonard A. Gould and the author wishes to express sincere gratitude for his advice and encouragement during the long years that this work was in progress. Special thanks are extended to Professors George C. Newton and Ronald A. Howard, also of M.I.T., for the careful reading of the manuscript and for suggestions with regard to practical problems on which the theories of this work could be tested. The writer also wishes to thank Dr. R. E. Kalman, whose suggestions and criticism spurred this research into many theoretical intricacies which otherwise would not have been explored. Finally, the author must thank the other graduate students at M.I.T., too many to mention by name, who gave their help and advice and listened patiently to the tales of the woes of large-scale numerical computation.

This work was carried out at the Electronic Systems Laboratory and the author wishes to thank all the members of the Laboratory staff for their help and cooperation during the conduct of the research and preparation of the manuscript. The patience and understanding of those who participated in the last minute changes and corrections is especially appreciated.

July, 1961 Walerian Kipiniak

CONTENTS

Chapter 1

INTRODUCTION

1.1. Statement of the Research Problem

The control of a given system can be viewed as the process of varying those of its parameters which can be manipulated by means external to it, so as to make its behavior in some sense best. In general, the ideal behavior is unachievable because of dynamic limitations of the element being controlled—henceforth to be called the plant—and because of uncertainty as to its characteristics and those of the external disturbances acting on it. Thus control is a matter of manipulating system inputs so as to optimize system performance, that is, to maximize the expected value of a preassigned performance criterion.

Within this broad definition all of engineering is a problem in control—an attempt to control the flow of materials, energy, or information. In all cases the solution proceeds in two steps: the development of a control policy and then its implementation. To develop a control policy one needs to define the performance criterion and establish a mathematical description of the plant and the surroundings interacting with it. On the basis of this description, one formulates the control law specifying the value of the optimum control inputs for every situation in which the system may find itself. Finally, one constructs the controller, that is, a device for generating the control inputs in accordance with the calculated control law.

This research is concerned with the problem of formulating and computing optimum control laws for the control of dynamic systems. It is assumed that the performance criterion and a mathematical description of the plant and its surroundings are all given, and the work is not concerned with implementation of the resultant laws.

There are already available a number of techniques for evaluating the optimum control laws, techniques which differ in their generality and ease of application.[2,3,4,8,13,36,43,47,59,66] Of course the most general approach is to try all possible control laws and by an exhaustive search pick the best one. Even when the number of possible laws is finite, this is seldom a practical approach. What this research (as well as that of the other workers in this field) seeks is a better, more efficient method—one that is practical. Therefore this work emphasizes not only the formulation of the methods of solution of optimization problems but also the development of practical means of calculating these solutions. Thus it concerns itself with the development of digital computer programs and analog devices for obtaining the solutions, to a large extent automatically. It is expected that the methods developed here will have some advantages over the other techniques now in existence.

The current growth in size and complexity of systems being placed under automatic control gave impetus to the development of dynamic optimization theory. With the increase in complexity, an appreciable economic gain can be expected from the application of more sophisticated, more nearly optimum control laws. It is therefore of interest to develop methods of finding the optimum control laws and determining how much can actually be gained by using them. Even if the optimum control laws so found turn out to be difficult to implement in practice, they may nevertheless suggest more easily realizable schemes. In any case, the designer would know how much is sacrificed in system performance for ease of constructing a controller. Thus it is hoped that the methods developed here will find application in practical control-system design.

1.2. Problem Background

A dynamic system is one whose future behavior depends on its past as well as on its present and future inputs. The influence of the past history on future behavior can be specified by a set of parameters which are termed the state variables. System behavior can therefore be described by the changes in system state caused by control inputs and external disturbances. The outputs can be expressed as functions of the state variables so that if $\underline{q}$ represents the system states, $\underline{m}$ the control inputs, $\underline{y}$ the outputs, and $\underline{u}$ the disturbances, every dynamic system can be described by differential equations*

* An underlined quantity, such as $\underline{m}$ or $\underline{G}$, denotes a vector or a vector function. Thus $\underline{m}$ is the input vector with components m_1, m_2, ... representing the individual inputs. The difference or differential equations 1.1 and 1.2 are vector equations and therefore represent scalar equations of order higher than one. The symbol $\triangleright$ denotes the forward difference operator so that $\triangleright \underline{q}(k)$ stands for $\underline{q}(k+\Delta)-\underline{q}(k)$. A more detailed explanation of nomenclature is presented in Appendix A.

$$\frac{d}{d\tau}\underline{q}(\tau) = \underline{G}(\tau, \underline{q}(\tau), \underline{m}(\tau), \underline{u}(\tau))$$

$$\underline{y}(\tau) = \underline{H}(\tau, \underline{q}(\tau), \underline{u}(\tau)) \qquad (1.1)$$

if changes of state occur continuously in time, or by difference equations[36,37]

$$\frac{\triangleright}{\Delta}\underline{q}(k) = \underline{G}(k, \underline{q}(k), \underline{m}(k), \underline{u}(k))$$

$$\underline{y}(k) = \underline{H}(k, \underline{q}(k), \underline{u}(k)) \qquad (1.2)$$

if they occur at discrete time $k = t,\ t+\Delta,\ t+2\Delta, \ldots$. The difference of differential equation representation of system behavior explained in Appendix C will be used almost exclusively in this work, although other representations are possible (see Appendix B) and sometimes useful.[16,28,68,75]

Control of a dynamic system is a matter of varying $\underline{m}$ so that in the presence of the disturbances $\underline{u}$, which generally are stochastic time functions, the behavior is in some sense best. Since the ideal behavior is unachievable, control becomes a matter of optimizing a specified performance criterion.

In the past, the commonly used performance criteria, such as error constants, related mainly to the steady-state behavior. Transient performance was treated only qualitatively.[18,69] More recently, it was accepted that a control system is subject to stochastic inputs and disturbances and so is forever in a transient mode.[13,34,66] In recognition of this fact the performance criterion must correspond to the expected value of a time integral of some function of the varying system outputs, the control inputs, and the disturbances, integrated over some future time interval. The control inputs are included because with the application of control effort there is usually associated a cost, and the performance criterion represents a balance between the cost of tolerating nonideal behavior and the cost of doing something about it. The performance criterion must be closely related to the particular task the system is to accomplish and must represent the accounting system by which the accomplishment is judged.

A generalized performance criterion which fits a majority of situations is

$$\mathcal{P} = E\left\{\int_t^T \hat{F}(\tau, T, \underline{y}(\tau), \underline{m}(\tau), \underline{u}(\tau))\, d\tau\right\} \qquad (1.3)$$

or in the discrete time case

$$\mathcal{P} = E\left\{ \sum_{k=t}^{T-\Delta} \Delta\hat{F}(k, T, \underline{y}(k), \underline{m}(k), \underline{u}(k)) \right\} \tag{1.4}$$

where $\hat{F}$ is an arbitrary function which is to be chosen so as to make this generalized performance criterion fit the problem at hand: The present time is t and T is the future time, possibly $+\infty$, after which system behavior is no longer of consequence. It is not necessary that T be fixed; it may rather be that time at which a condition of the form

$$\underline{g}(T, \underline{q}(\tau)) = \underline{0} \tag{1.5}$$

becomes satisfied. For example, this may represent the condition that control is terminated when the controlled vehicle meets with some prescribed trajectory. E is the expectation operator over the sample space of $\underline{u}$.

The disturbances $\underline{u}(\tau), t \leq \tau < T$ are stochastic time functions and therefore not fully known to the controlling intelligence. Those components of $\underline{u}$ which are arguments of $\underline{G}$ correspond to uncontrolled inputs, while those which enter into $\hat{F}$ but not $\underline{G}$ are the desired outputs. In any case, the inputs to the controller can be considered to be a set of parameters $\underline{v}(t)$ which are statistically related to $\underline{u}(\tau), t \leq \tau < T$. From $\underline{v}(t)$ the controller must infer the probable value of $\underline{u}(\tau)$, $t \leq \tau < T$ and make the control decision on that basis.*

Since system behavior, as characterized by $\underline{q}(\tau)$, $t \leq \tau < T$, depends on $\underline{q}(t)$ as well as $\underline{m}(\tau)$, $t \leq \tau < T$ and $\underline{u}(\tau)$, $t \leq \tau < T$, the control law $\mathcal{C}$ specifying $\underline{m}(t)$ must be a function of $\underline{q}(t)$ as well as $\underline{v}(t)$, t, and possibly T:

$$\underline{m}(\tau) = \underline{\mathcal{C}}(\tau, \underline{q}(\tau), \underline{v}(\tau), T) \tag{1.6}$$

One seeks the optimum control law $\underline{\mathcal{C}}$, i.e., that relation between $\underline{m}(\tau)$ and $\underline{v}(\tau)$, $\underline{q}(\tau)$, τ, T which if maintained along the entire trajectory $\underline{q}(\tau)$, $t \leq \tau < T$ would result in maximum $\mathcal{P}$. The controller is a device for generating $\underline{m}$ in accordance with the specified control law.

---

*For example, if $u(\tau)$, $t \leq \tau$ is a square wave of amplitude $\pm v(t)$, with Poisson-distributed zero crossings occurring with frequency α and $v(t) = u(t)$, then if one knows $v(t)$ one knows that the probability density of $u(\tau)$, $t \leq \tau$ is

$$\tfrac{1}{2}(1+\exp(-2\alpha(\tau-t)))\delta_0(u(\tau)-v(t)) + \tfrac{1}{2}(1-\exp(-2\alpha(\tau-t)))\delta_0(u(\tau)+v(t))$$

The generalized control problem described above is represented in Figure 1.1, and all the subsequent work refers to it. It represents the control of a nonlinear, time-varying multi-input, multi-output dynamic system subject to stochastic disturbances.

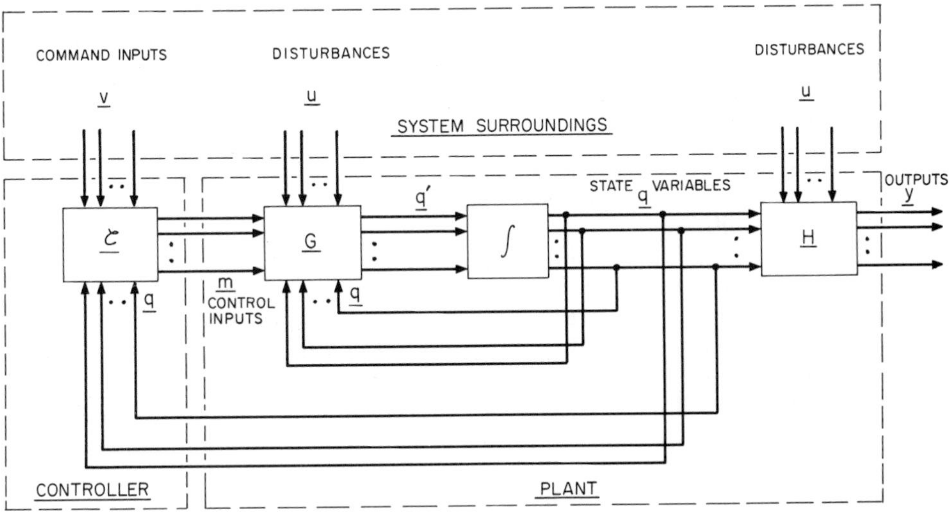

Fig. 1.1. The generalized control problem

There are essentially two approaches to the design of controllers. In the first case, a class of controllers is postulated, and the design procedure attempts to pick that member of the class which will maximize the performance criterion for the ensemble of disturbances considered. In the second approach, one calculates the optimum control law and then chooses whatever components are available to synthesize a controller to generate this control law or some approximation of it. If only an approximation must be settled for, the calculated law is a guide in the actual synthesis process and a performance standard.

In the first approach, it is virtually necessary to be able to express the system output analytically as a function of the input. This limits its applicability, for the most part, to linear systems and a limited class of performance criteria, of which the integral or the mean of the square of system error is the one most generally useful. Even then, the resultant controller is optimum only for the class considered, and there may be a controller outside of this class which is appreciably better. However, this approach does have the very important advantage of leading directly to the synthesis of an easily realizable control system.[13,14,34,54,66,68]

The second approach has been pioneered by researchers working on "ON-OFF" control and relay servomechanisms. In such cases there are only two or three possible values of control effort, and the controller is a device for choosing among them in accordance with a precalculated control law. In these situations the control law is relatively easy to calculate because the problems are usually limited to piecewise linear systems, a limited class of disturbances, and a limited class of performance criteria.[12,19,23,24,32,45,52,65]

Bellman combined this approach with the techniques of dynamic programming to develop a general numerical procedure for finding the optimum control law.[2,3,4,5,6,8,27] It is applicable to almost every conceivable type of dynamic system and performance criterion and, in addition, allows the setting of bounds on the range of the different variables. This computational procedure, while simple in principle, requires such an enormous amount of calculation that even with electronic digital computers only the very simplest cases can be solved.

More recently Merriam developed an analytical formulation of the control law based on Bellman's principle of optimality.[17,59,60,61,62] His method is applicable to systems described by Equation 1.1 and uses the performance criterion of Equation 1.3. The control law is presented as a solution of a partial differential equation in $\mathcal{P}^0(\tau, \underline{q}(\tau))$, $t \leq \tau < T$, subject to boundary conditions on $\mathcal{P}^0$ and $\underline{q}$ at $\tau = t$ and $\tau = T$, where $\mathcal{P}^0$ is the maximum achievable $\mathcal{P}$ starting at time τ from state $\underline{q}(\tau)$. In the special case when $\hat{F}$ is quadratic in $\underline{m}$ and $\underline{y}$ while $\underline{G}$ and $\underline{H}$ are linear in $\underline{q}$ and $\underline{m}$, the partial differential equation is solvable in terms of its characteristics obtainable as the solutions of a set of ordinary nonlinear differential equations of the Riccati type, solved as an initial value problem. Otherwise the partial differential equation must be solved numerically. A numerical procedure has been developed,[61] and although no precise computational algorithm has been suggested, this method may well require a smaller amount of computational effort than Bellman's procedure.

Problems in which the element being controlled is linear and $\hat{F}$ is quadratic in $\underline{m}$ and $\underline{y}$ have been treated rather thoroughly by Kalman.[36,37,38] His theory is based on Cartheodory's formulation of the variational calculus and on Pontriagin's "maximum" principle. For the problem treated, the optimum control law is shown to be linear and so specified by a matrix* of coefficients $[\mathcal{C}]$ as follows:

$$m] = [\mathcal{C}]\,q] \tag{1.7}$$

This matrix is shown to be a solution of a matrix differential equation of the Riccati type, solved as an initial value problem. (Thus, although differing in the theoretical derivation, this method is computationally similar to that of Merriam.) In situations in which it is applicable, this method yields an excellent way of solving the control problem, one that is computationally very convenient.

Another method of finding that value of the control input $\underline{m}$ which maximizes $\mathcal{P}$ is based on the classical calculus of variations. It has been applied to cases in which $\mathcal{P}$ is given by Equation 1.3 and the plant is described by a nonlinear differential equation:

$$m = G(t, q, q', \ldots q^{(n)}) \tag{1.8}$$

This procedure yields the optimum control law in terms of a solution of a two-point boundary-value problem associated with an ordinary differential equation in q. In special cases, including the one where G is linear in q and its derivatives and $\hat{F}$ is quadratic in m, q and the derivatives of q, analytic solutions are possible. In more general cases recourse to numerical techniques is necessary, but in many situations this method is computationally more efficient than the others.[1,15,43]

The methods of functional analysis and functional iteration have been applied to the control problem by Kulikowski.[47,48,49,50,51] This is a rather powerful approach and yields analytic answers to linear problems subject to power or distortion constraints and limits on the amplitude of the control effort. In many nonlinear problems the method offers iterative schemes for obtaining answers numerically. One such scheme has been applied recently to finding the control law for finite value controllers with amplitude-limited control effort.[32] Unfortunately, there is still no computational experience available by which to judge the effectiveness of these methods.

---

* Quantities in square brackets, such as $[\mathcal{C}]$, denote matrices. When it need be emphasized that a vector quantity such as $\underline{m}$ is to be treated as a column matrix, it is written as m] or as $\underbrace{m}$ if it is to be treated as a row matrix.

The theory of convex sets has given rise to still another optimization procedure that is interesting but applicable to a rather restricted class of systems and performance criteria. It treats the case in which the plant is described by linear differential equations and $\hat{F}$ is a linear function of $\underline{m}$ and $\underline{q}$ subject to constraints on $\underline{m}$ of the form:

$$b\ell_i(\tau) \leq m_i(\tau) \leq bu_i(\tau) \quad t \leq \tau \leq T, \; i = 1, 2, \ldots n$$
$$\int_t^T \underline{f}(\tau) \cdot \underline{m}(\tau)\, d\tau \leq M \tag{1.9}$$

It is shown that the optimum $m_i(\tau)$, $i = 1, 2, \ldots n$ is always either $bu_i(\tau)$ or $b\ell_i(\tau)$, and never an intermediate value. The switching points are determined through a solution of nonlinear algebraic equations.[4] The computational solution of this problem is relatively easy, but the method is applicable only in a very limited class of situations.

Many of the systems now being placed under automatic control are very complex and critically dependent for their success on limiting deviations from the prescribed performance to small values. Alternately, large improvements in the profitability of the operation can result from more precise control (for example chemical process control, missile guidance, inventory control, and scheduling of manufacturing). Yet in many cases the methods now available for dynamic optimization and the synthesis of such control systems are not entirely adequate. Either they are limited to a restricted class of systems and performance criteria or they involve an excessive amount of computation. Therefore it appears that further work on the development of design methods which overcome the limitations of the currently known synthesis procedures would be a worthwhile contribution to the art of control.

1.3. Control and Optimization of Dynamic Systems - the Variational Approach

The variational method of dynamic optimization to be developed in this work is one of those which attempt to define the optimum value of control effort for each situation in which the system may find itself. Consider that at time t the system is in state $\underline{q}(t)$, that the value of $\underline{u}(\tau), t \leq \tau < T$ is known, and that T or a relation defining T is specified. Given these quantities, which describe the situation in which the system finds itself, one can determine the time functions $\underline{q}(\tau), t \leq \tau < T$ and $\underline{m}(\tau), t \leq \tau < T$, subject to constraints between $\underline{q}(\tau)$ and $\underline{m}(\tau)$ imposed by the differential equations describing the system, and subject to the limitations imposed on the range of $\underline{q}(\tau)$ and $\underline{m}(\tau)$, which maximize the performance criterion

$$\mathscr{P} = \int_t^T F(\tau, T, \underline{q}(\tau), \underline{m}(\tau), \underline{u}(\tau))\, d\tau \tag{1.10}$$

If the system is described by difference equations, if T is finite, so that $\underline{q}$ and $\underline{m}$ change only at a finite number of points in time, and if one considers $\underline{m}$ to be quantized and requires that its range be bounded, then there is but a finite number of possible functions $\underline{q}$ and $\underline{m}$. By an exhaustive search one can pick the best ones. This search can be systematized in various ways, for example, by applying the principle of optimality as in dynamic programming, thereby reducing the number of functions which need be examined. If the problem specifies that the range of $\underline{m}$ is continuous, that the system is governed by differential equations, and that $T = \infty$, then one needs to take the limit as quantization becomes arbitrarily fine, as state transitions become continuous, and as T approaches infinity. It is not easy to ascertain, in a mathematically rigorous manner, under what conditions does such a limit indeed exist.[64] However, if the optimization problem is physically meaningful in the first place, one would expect these limiting processes to be valid. Then there remain only the questions pertaining to the computational schemes themselves; do they remain stable as the limits are approached, and what is the rate of convergence of the resulting solutions to their limit values?

If the range of $\underline{m}$ is continuous (but $\underline{m}$ still changes only at discrete instants of time), then by differentiating $\mathscr{P}$ with respect to $\underline{m}(k)$, $\underline{q}(k)$, $k = t, t+\Delta, t+2\Delta, \ldots$ and equating the partial derivatives to zero one can seek a maximum at the point of stationarity of $\mathscr{P}$. This yields a set of relations which must hold between neighboring values of $\underline{m}(k)$ and $\underline{q}(k)$, if they are to yield a maximum of $\mathscr{P}$. These relations are in the form of difference equations with n free parameters, where n is the order of the system, which need be so chosen that their solutions satisfy prescribed boundary conditions. In this way the search is systematized and the number of possible functions $\underline{m}$ and $\underline{q}$ greatly reduced. Loosely speaking, the degree of systematization is even greater than that achieved by the application of the principle of optimality, and the problem of quantization is avoided. At the same time, these relations yield what is only a necessary condition for a maximum, and require that $\mathscr{P}$ be differentiable with respect to $\underline{m}$ and $\underline{q}$. In the continuous time case, that is, in the limit as $\Delta \to 0$ the difference equations become differential equations, the so-called Euler or Euler-Lagrange equations of the classical calculus of variations.

Having determined the optimum $\underline{q}(\tau)$ and $\underline{m}(\tau)$, $t \leq \tau < T$, one has the value of $\underline{m}(t)$. For a given situation, that is, for a given t, $q(t)$, $\underline{u}(\tau), t \leq \tau < T$, and T or a relation specifying T, this $\underline{m}(t)$ is the optimum value of control effort. If the same calculations were repeated for all t, $\underline{q}(t)$, $\underline{u}(T), t \leq \tau < T$, and T of interest, this would define the optimum control law as

$$\underline{m}(t) = \underline{\mathscr{C}}(t, T, \underline{q}(t); \underline{u}(\tau), t \leq \tau < T) \tag{1.11}$$

Although one calculates the entire function $\underline{q}(\tau)$ and $\underline{m}(\tau), t \leq \tau < T$, only one point, $\underline{m}(t)$, is actually used in defining the control law. The remaining points on the computed trajectory, for example $\underline{m}(\tau_1)$, correspond to the values of control effort which would be used if the system was in state $\underline{q}(\tau_1)$ at time τ_1 with the same T and $\underline{u}(\tau), \tau_1 \leq \tau < T$ as in the original problem. In this way the information of the entire curve can be salvaged to define a set of points in the domain of $\underline{\mathscr{C}}$

$$\underline{m}(t_o) = \underline{\mathscr{C}}(t_o, T, \underline{q}(t_o); \underline{u}(\tau), t_o \leq \tau < T) \tag{1.12}$$

for $t \leq t_o \leq T$ and $\underline{q}(t_o)$ on the calculated trajectory. Furthermore, if T approaches infinity, for all t the end point looks infinitely far away so that $\underline{\mathscr{C}}$ is independent of T. Also, if the system description as well as the performance criterion do not involve time explicitly, then $\underline{\mathscr{C}}$ is independent of t.

In the preceding explanation, it was assumed that $\underline{u}(\tau), t \leq \tau \leq T$ is known. In practice $\underline{u}(\tau)$ is a stochastic time function specified only in a probabilistic sense by the inputs $\underline{v}(t)$. All the information that $\underline{v}(t)$ can convey about $\underline{u}(\tau), t \leq \tau < T$ is the conditional probability density $p(\underline{u}(\tau), t \leq \tau < T \mid \underline{v}(t))$. The conditional probability density assigns to each $\underline{v}(t)$ a probability density over the space of all possible $\underline{u}(\tau), t \leq \tau < T$ This implies that one does have a way of characterizing the possible functions $\underline{u}(\tau)$, $t \leq \tau < T$. In terms of mathematical rigor, this is a difficult problem,[14,16,73] but in the context of this work it is sufficient to rely on the intuitive notion that there is a set of coefficients, a set of properties which, for all engineering purposes, characterize $\underline{u}(\tau)$, $t \leq \tau < T$. The distribution considered is over the sample space of these coefficients. One must emphasize that $p(\underline{u}(\tau), t \leq \tau < T \mid v(t))$ is a deterministic function of $\underline{v}(t)$, which is assumed known. To each $\underline{v}(t)$ there corresponds a unique distribution. It is not proposed to study adaptive processes in which this conditional probability depends on $\underline{q}(\tau)$ or the adopted control policy.[8,46]

Because $\underline{v}(t)$ represents all that is known about $\underline{u}(\tau), t \leq \tau < T$, one wishes to maximize the expected value of $\mathscr{P}$ over the space of $\underline{u}(\tau), t \leq \tau < T$ conditional on $\underline{v}(t)$, that is

$$\underset{(\underline{u}(\tau),\, t\leq \tau < T) \,|\, \underline{v}(t)}{E}\left\{\mathscr{P}\right\} = \sum_{\substack{\text{all possible}\\ \text{functions}\\ \underline{u}(\tau),\, t\leq\tau<T}} \left\{ \mathscr{P} p(\underline{u}(\tau), t\leq \tau < T \,|\, \underline{v}(t))\right\} \qquad (1.13)$$

Since $E\{\mathscr{P}\}$ is a deterministic function of $\underline{v}(t)$, the optimum control law

$$\underline{m}(t) = \underline{\mathscr{C}}(t, T, \underline{q}(t), \underline{v}(t)) \qquad (1.14)$$

is also a deterministic function. The process of finding the optimum $\underline{m}$, it is shown, is—to a large extent—commutative with the expectation operator, so that in many cases optimization reduces to the solution of a deterministic problem involving parameters which are the conditional moments or some other statistical averages of the random time function $\underline{u}(\tau), t \leq \tau < T$, conditional on $\underline{v}(t)$.

Similarly, one can consider that the state variables $\underline{q}(t)$, whether measured directly or indirectly, are also subject to stochastic disturbances. Thus the expectation operator in Equation 1.13 should also be taken over the sample space of $\underline{q}(t)$, conditional on whatever information is available about $\underline{q}(t)$. Thus the control law is a function of $\underline{q}(t)$ and $\underline{v}(t)$, where $\underline{q}(t)$ corresponds to the actual measurement of the state of the plant:

$$\underline{m}(t) = \underline{\mathscr{C}}(t, T, \underline{q}(t), \underline{v}(t)) \qquad (1.15)$$

The theory of dynamic optimization deals with methods of calculating the control law. The methods of realizing the controller are of no concern except as they influence the methods of calculating and displaying this law. The control law is basically a no-memory function of many variables: t, $\underline{q}(t)$, $\underline{v}(t)$, and T. The controller is a device for generating it, or an approximation of it. However, if $\underline{\mathscr{C}}$ is a particularly complex function of many variables, it may be impractical to calculate and store the entire function. In such a case one might incorporate as part of the controller an "on-line" computing device that would calculate the optimum $\underline{m}(t)$ for the currently measured $\underline{q}(t)$ and $\underline{v}(t)$ and possibly for some neighborhood around them.

For example, it might calculate the coefficients of a Taylor series expansion of $\underline{\mathcal{C}}$ about $\underline{q}(t)$ and $\underline{v}(t)$. Such a self-computing controller could follow system operation, continually recalculating the control law about the most recent measurement of $\underline{q}(t)$ and $\underline{v}(t)$, thereby having to store comparatively little information.

In either case the result is a feedback control system with all the advantages which accrue from such operation. The outputs of the closed-loop system are bounded if unbounded outputs would not result in the optimum $\mathcal{P}$. The resultant system need not be asymptotically stable, and even if all inputs to it are constant it may command a periodic motion in a limit cycle. In any case this would be the optimum system.

In actual design, one would first attempt to compute the control law $\underline{\mathcal{C}}$ in the region of interest and approximate it in terms of easily realizable additions, multiplications, functions of a single variable, or switches. Only if the control law was so complex that every convenient approximation still yielded an appreciably lower $\mathcal{P}$ than the calculated ultimate optimum, would one go to a self-computing controller. This of course does not discount the usefulness of "on-line" computing devices for determining system description from operating data, compiling the distributions $p(\underline{u}(\tau), t \leq \tau < T \mid v(t))$, and periodically recomputing the control law as more information becomes available about the plant and its surroundings.

This work constitutes the development and exposition of the variational approach to the synthesis of feedback control systems. It formulates the theory, develops computational methods of solution, and illustrates these methods with a number of examples.

In this work the method of state transitions is used to describe the behavior of dynamic systems. This concept is reviewed in Appendix C and contrasted with the impedance concept presented in Appendix B. The numerical method of solution of the state transition equations is shown extended to the calculation of the coefficients of the Taylor series expansion of the solutions about an operating trajectory as a function of the initial system state.

The development of the fundamental necessary conditions for the optimum control law is carried out in Section 2.1. These take the form of two-point boundary-value problems associated with difference or differential equations, the so-called Euler-Lagrange equations. The optimum controller is shown to be a two-point boundary-value problem solver. Section 2.2 presents the sufficiency conditions for an optimum. The remaining sections extend the results of Section 2.1 to the treatment of systems with time delays and those described in other ways than by difference or differential equations and to cases in which the state or control variables are amplitude constrained. Some useful properties of the Euler-Lagrange equations are investigated, and analytic solutions are obtained for problems in which the controlled plant is described by linear constant coefficient equations, and an integral square performance criterion is used.

Chapter 3 deals with the methods of solution of two-point boundary-value problems which define the optimum control law. Methods applicable to the solution of linear problems are described in Section 3.1. Several flooding techniques are presented in Section 3.2 and compared with the methods of dynamic programming. Section 3.3 deals with methods of obtaining the solution for a single point in the state space. Section 3.4 presents a method of computing the control law in terms of a power series about a known solution point. Methods of obtaining solutions using spacial simulators of the boundary-value problems are discussed in Section 3.5. Throughout the chapter numerical examples are presented to support and illustrate the methods which were developed.

In Chapters 2 and 3 the solution of the deterministic problem is treated, tacitly assuming as correct the statements which appeared in this chapter that the expectation operator over the space of disturbance functions commutes with the process of optimization. Section 4.1 proves this statement, and shows what statistical properties of the disturbances need be known for the solution of the control problem. Section 4.2 illustrates a technique of obtaining the required statistical properties of the disturbances, which has been found useful in problems of this type.

An attempt has been made to keep the nomenclature and symbolism consistent throughout this work and in conformance with common usage and the recommendations of the AIEE Feedback Control Systems Committee. Uncommon or controversial nomenclature is described in Appendix A.

Chapter 2

DYNAMIC OPTIMIZATION THEORY

2.1. Basic Necessary Conditions

The philosophy of the variational approach to control system design has been described in Section 1.3. In this section the control problem will be abstracted in mathematical terms and the equations defining the optimum control law derived.

A description of the plant being controlled is given in terms of difference equations*

$$\frac{\triangleright}{\Delta}\, \underline{q}(k) = \underline{G}(k, \underline{q}(k), \underline{m}(k), \underline{u}(k))$$

$$\underline{y}(k) = \underline{H}(k, \underline{q}(k)) \qquad k = t,\ t+\Delta,\ t+2\Delta,\ \ldots\ T-\Delta \qquad (2.1)$$

or differential equations

$$\frac{d}{d\tau}\, \underline{q}(\tau) = \underline{G}(\tau, \underline{q}(\tau), \underline{m}(\tau), \underline{u}(\tau))$$

$$\underline{y}(\tau) = \underline{H}(\tau, \underline{q}(\tau)) \qquad t \leq \tau < T \qquad (2.2)$$

where $\underline{q}$ is the n-dimensional state vector (n is the order of the system) and $\underline{m}$ is the n_m-dimensional vector of controllable plant inputs, $1 \leq n_m \leq n$. The $\underline{y}$ are the plant outputs and the $\underline{u}$ are the externally generated disturbances.** The performance criterion $\mathcal{P}$ is specified for some future time interval, from the present time t to that future time T, possibly infinity, after which the performance is no longer of consequence. In the discrete time case, $\mathcal{P}$ is given as

$$\mathcal{P} = \sum_{k=t}^{T-\Delta} \Delta\, \hat{F}(k, T, \underline{y}(k), \underline{m}(k), \underline{u}(k)) + \hat{P}(T, \underline{y}(T)) \qquad (2.3)$$

---

* See Appendix C for a review of the difference and differential equations approach to describing the behavior of dynamic systems.

** Refer to Appendix A for a complete explanation of the nomenclature used.

or if the function $\underline{H}$ is incorporated with $\hat{F}$ into a function F and with $\hat{P}$ into a function P, then

$$\mathcal{P} = \sum_{k=t}^{T-\Delta} \Delta\, F(k, T, \underline{q}, (k), \underline{m}(k), \underline{u}(k)) + P(T, \underline{q}(T)) \tag{2.4}$$

and in the continuous time case,

$$\mathcal{P} = \int_{t}^{T} F(\tau, T, \underline{q}(\tau), \underline{m}(\tau), \underline{u}(\tau))\, d\tau + P(T, \underline{q}(T)) \tag{2.5}$$

The performance criterion may also require that at $\tau = T$ the system reach a certain prescribed state or that T be that value of τ for which the prescribed state is reached. In general it may specify a boundary condition

$$\underline{g}(T, \underline{q}(\tau)) = \underline{0} \tag{2.6}$$

where $\underline{g}$ has up to $n+1$ components specifying the values of any or all of $T, q_1(T), q_2(T), \dots q_n(T)$, or up to $n+1$ relations among them. Presence of the function P allows one to incorporate a valuation of the plant state reached at the end of the control period. The current system state $\underline{q}(t)$ is assumed known, and the controller input $\underline{v}(t)$ is considered to specify completely $\underline{u}(\tau), t \leq \tau < T$. The case in which $\underline{v}(t)$ and $\underline{u}(\tau), t \leq \tau < T$ are only statistically related is treated in Chapter 4, where it is shown that the stochastic nature of $\underline{u}$ introduces but minor modifications of the results derived here.

For a given $\underline{q}(t)$ and $\underline{v}(t)$ (therefore $\underline{u}(\tau), t \leq \tau < T$), it is required to find the function $\underline{m}(k), k = t, t+\Delta, \dots T-\Delta$, or $\underline{m}(\tau), t \leq \tau < T$ which maximizes $\mathcal{P}$. The function relating the optimum $\underline{m}(t)$ to $\underline{q}(t)$ and $\underline{v}(t)$ as well as possibly t and T is the optimum control law sought:

$$\underline{m}(t) = \underline{\mathcal{C}}(t, \underline{q}(t), \underline{v}(t), T) \tag{2.7}$$

Unless otherwise stated:

1. $\underline{m}(\tau)$ is to be a function of class* D^0.
2. $\underline{G}$ is to be of class C^1 with respect to $\underline{q}$ and $\underline{m}$ and of class D^0 with respect to τ, in the region $\mathcal{R}$ of interest in the $(\tau, \underline{q}, \underline{m})$ space.
3. F is to be of class C^1 with respect to $\underline{q}$ and $\underline{m}$ and D^0 with respect to τ, in $\mathcal{R}$.
4. The system is to be controllable** with respect to $\underline{m}$ in $\mathcal{R}$.

The solution of the optimization problem will be presented for a general dynamic system described by vector difference or differential equations. The fundamental necessary conditions for an optimum will be derived, first for a fixed and then for a variable T. Then under some additional restrictions on F and $\underline{G}$ further necessary and sufficient conditions will be obtained. Throughout, the discrete time case will be treated first and the continuous time case gotten in the limit as $\Delta \to 0$.

Consider the problem of finding the $\underline{m}(k)$, $k = t, t + \Delta, \ldots T-\Delta$ which maximizes $\mathcal{P}$ of Equation 2.4 subject to the constraint among $\underline{m}(k), k = t, t + \Delta, \ldots T-\Delta$ and $\underline{q}(k), k = t, t + \Delta, \ldots T-\Delta, T$ imposed by Equations 2.1 and 2.6. Consider that T itself is fixed.

Since F and $\underline{G}$ are functions of class C^1 with respect to $\underline{m}$ and $\underline{q}$, the maximum of $\mathcal{P}$ — if it exists — is for the set of values of $\underline{m}(k), k = t, t+\Delta, \ldots T-\Delta$ and $\underline{q}(k), k = t+\Delta, t+2\Delta, \ldots T$ satisfying Equation 2.1 for which $\mathcal{P}$ is stationary with respect to variations in these variables. To account for the constraint imposed by Equation 2.1 one introduces a set of auxiliary variables, the so-called Lagrange multipliers— $\underline{\lambda}(k)$, $k = t, t+\Delta, \ldots T-\Delta$ —and forms a new performance criterion $\mathcal{P}_1$:

$$\mathcal{P}_1 = \sum_{k=t}^{T-\Delta} \Delta \left\{ F(k, T, \underline{q}(k), \underline{m}(k), \underline{u}(k)) + \underline{\lambda}(k) \left(\frac{\triangleright}{\Delta} q(k)] - G(k, \underline{q}(k), \underline{m}(k), \underline{u}(k))] \right) \right\} + P(T, \underline{q}(T)) \tag{2.8}$$

and seeks its stationary point with respect to variations in $\underline{m}(k), \underline{q}(k), \underline{\lambda}(k)$, $k = t, t+\Delta, \ldots T-\Delta$ and $\underline{q}(T)$. $\mathcal{P}_1$ is stationary

---

* Refer to Appendix A for definition of classes of functions.

** This condition is explained in Appendix C.

with respect to variations in $\underline{\lambda}$ if and only if $\underline{m}(k), \underline{q}(k)$, $k = t$, $t+\Delta$, ... $T-\Delta$ and $\underline{q}(T)$ are related in such a way that Equation 2.1 is satisfied and so that the coefficients of $\underline{\lambda}(k)$, $k = t, t+\Delta$, ... $T-\Delta$ vanish. Then of course, $\mathcal{P}$ and $\mathcal{P}_1$ are equal so that finding a stationary point of $\mathcal{P}$ subject to the constraint of Equation 2.1 is equivalent to finding a stationary point of $\mathcal{P}_1$ with respect to $\underline{m}(k), \underline{q}(k), \underline{\lambda}(k)$, $k = t$, $t+\Delta$, ... $T-\Delta$ and $\underline{q}(T)$.

To find the stationary point, one forms the differential of $\mathcal{P}_1$ and requires that it vanish for all independent differentials $dm_i(k), dq_j(k), d\lambda_j(k)$, and $dq_j(T)$, $i=1, 2, \ldots n_m$, $j=1, 2, \ldots n$ $k=t, t+\Delta, \ldots T-\Delta$ subject to the constraints that $q(t)$ equal the current system state and $q(T)$ satisfy Equation 2.6. One forms $d\mathcal{P}_1$ as*

$$
\begin{aligned}
d\mathcal{P}_1 = {} & \sum_{k=t+\Delta}^{T-\Delta} \Delta\, d\underline{q}(k) \Big\{ \nabla_q F(k, T, \underline{q}(k), \underline{m}(k), \underline{u}(k))] + \frac{\lambda(k-\Delta)] - \lambda(k)]}{\Delta} \\
& \qquad - [\, J_q\big(\underline{G}(k, \underline{q}(k), \underline{m}(k), \underline{u}(k))\big)]^T \lambda(k)] \Big\} \\
& + \sum_{k=t}^{T-\Delta} \Delta\, d\underline{\lambda}(k) \Big\{ \frac{q(k+\Delta)] - q(k)]}{\Delta} - G(k, \underline{q}(k), \underline{m}(k), \underline{u}(k))] \Big\} \\
& + \sum_{k=t}^{T-\Delta} \Delta\, d\underline{m}(k) \Big\{ \nabla_m F(k, T, \underline{q}(k), \underline{m}(k), \underline{u}(k))] \\
& \qquad - [J_m\big(\underline{G}(k, \underline{q}(k), \underline{m}(k), \underline{u}(k))\big)]^T \lambda(k)] \Big\} \\
& + d\underline{q}(t) \Big\{ \nabla_q F(t, T, q(t), \underline{m}(t), \underline{u}(t))] - \frac{\lambda(t)]}{\Delta} \\
& \qquad - [\, J_q\big(\underline{G}(t, \underline{q}(t), \underline{m}(t), \underline{u}(t))\big)]^T \lambda(t)] \Big\} \\
& + d\underline{q}(T) \Big\{ \lambda(T-\Delta)] + \nabla_q P(T, q(T))] \Big\}
\end{aligned}
\tag{2.9}
$$

Since $d\mathcal{P}_1$ is to vanish for all independent differentials among $dm_i(k)$, $dq_j(k)$, $d\lambda_j(k)$ and $dq_j(T)$, $i=1, 2, \ldots n_m$, $j=1, 2, \ldots n$, $k=t, t+\Delta, \ldots T-\Delta$, the coefficient of each independent differential must be identically zero. The differentials $dq_j(t)$, $j = 1, 2, \ldots n$ are not independent. Since $\underline{q}(t)$ is the current system state and cannot be changed by the application of $\underline{m}(t)$, it follows

* The symbol $\nabla_q F$ signifies the gradient of F with respect to $\underline{q}$ and $\mathbf{J}_q(\underline{G})$ the jacobian of $\underline{G}$ with respect to $\underline{q}$, as explained in Appendix A.

that $dq_j(t)$, $j = 1, 2, \ldots n$ must all be zero. Similarly, $dq_j(T)$, $j = 1, 2, \ldots n$ are not all independent because of the constraint of Equation 2.6. Taking the differential of both sides of Equation 2.6, one obtains

$$dg(T, \underline{q}(T))] = 0] = [\,J_q\left(\underline{g}(T, \underline{q}(T))\right)]\; dq(T)] \tag{2.10}$$

If $g_i(T, \underline{q}(T)) = 0$, $i = 1, 2, \ldots n_g$ are mutually consistent and nonredundant conditions, $[J_q(\underline{g})]$ can be partitioned into a nonsingular $n_g \times n_g$ matrix $[\hat{J}_q(\underline{g})]$ and a remainder $[\check{J}_q(\underline{g})]$. The corresponding n_g components of $dq(T)$ are called $d\hat{q}(T)]$ and the remainder are denoted by $d\check{q}(T)]$, as illustrated in Figure 2.1.

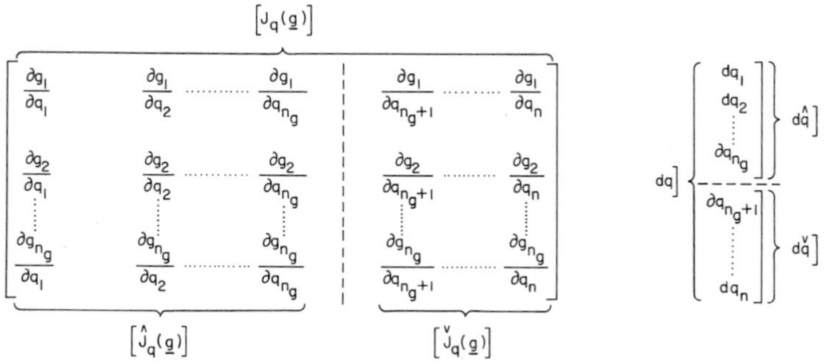

Fig. 2.1. Partitioning of the $[\,J_q(\underline{g})]$ matrix

Equation 2.10 can be rewritten as

$$[\,\hat{J}_q(\underline{g})]\; d\hat{q}(T)] = -\;[\,\check{J}_q(\underline{g})]\, d\check{q}(T) \tag{2.11}$$

and solved for $d\hat{q}(t)$ as

$$d\hat{q}(T)] = -\;[\,\hat{J}_q(\underline{g})^{-1}]\;\;[\,\check{J}_q(\underline{g})]\, d\check{q}(T)] \tag{2.12}$$

The last term of Equation 2.9 therefore becomes

$$\begin{aligned} \ldots + d\,\check{\underline{q}}\,(T)\Big\{&\check{\lambda}(T-\Delta)] + \nabla_{\check{q}}P(T, \underline{q}(T))] \\ &- [\,\check{J}_q(\underline{g})]^T\,[\,\hat{J}_q\,(\underline{g})^{-1}]^T\left(\hat{\lambda}(T-\Delta)] + \nabla_{\hat{q}}P(T, \underline{q}(T))]\right)\Big\} \end{aligned} \tag{2.13}$$

or, if it is written out component by component,

$$\ldots + \sum_{i=n_g+1}^{n} \left\{ \check{\lambda}_i + \nabla_{\check{q}} P_i - \sum_{j=1}^{n_g} \left(\hat{\lambda}_j + \nabla_{\hat{q}} P_j \right) \sum_{\ell=1}^{n_g} \left([\hat{J}_q(\underline{g})^{-1}] \right)_{j\ell} \left([\check{J}_q(\underline{g})] \right)_{\ell i} \right\} d\check{q}_i(T)$$

(2.14)

where $\hat{\lambda}_i$ and $\nabla_{\hat{q}} P_i$ are the components corresponding to $d\hat{q}]$ whereas $\check{\lambda}_i$ and $\nabla_{\check{q}} P_i$ are those corresponding to $d\check{q}]$. Now $d\check{q}_i(T)$, $i = n_g + 1, n_g + 2, \ldots n$ are independent. The vanishing of their coefficients requires that

$$\check{\lambda}(T-\Delta)] + \nabla_{\check{q}} P(T, \underline{q}(T))] = [\check{J}(\underline{g})]^T [\hat{J}(g)^{-1}]^T \left(\hat{\lambda}(T-\Delta)] + \nabla_{\hat{q}} P(T, \underline{q}(T))] \right)$$

(2.15)

This set of $n - n_g$ conditions, together with the n_g conditions expressed by Equation 2.6, specifies n relations on $\lambda_i(T-\Delta)$ or $q_i(T), i = 1, 2, \ldots n$ or on some combinations of these variables.

If $n_g = n$, Equation 2.6 uniquely specifies $\underline{q}(T)$, so that none of the $dq_i(T), i = 1, 2, \ldots n$ are independent. If $n_g=0$, $\underline{q}(T)$ is completely free; then

$$\lambda(T-\Delta)] = -\nabla_q P(T, \underline{q}(T))] \qquad (2.16)$$

and for any component q_i which does not enter P, $\lambda_i(T-\Delta)=0$. The cases where $0<n_g<n$ are intermediates between these two extremes.

All the remaining variables are not constrained, and therefore their differentials are independent. Equating their coefficients to zero, one obtains

$$\frac{\triangleright}{\Delta} q(k)] = G(k, \underline{q}(k), \underline{m}(k), \underline{u}(k))] \qquad k=t, t+\Delta, \ldots T-\Delta$$

$$\frac{\triangleleft}{\Delta} \lambda(k)] = \nabla_q F(k, T, \underline{q}(k), \underline{m}(k), \underline{u}(k))] - [J_q(\underline{G}(k, \underline{q}(k), \underline{m}(k), \underline{u}(k)))]^T \lambda(k)]$$

$$k=t+\Delta, t+2\Delta, \ldots T-\Delta$$

$$\nabla_m F(k, T, \underline{q}(k), \underline{m}(k), \underline{u}(k))] = [J_m(\underline{G}(k, \underline{q}(k), \underline{m}(k), \underline{u}(k)))]^T \lambda(k)]$$

$$k=t, t+\Delta, \ldots T-\Delta$$

(2.17)

In the limit as $\Delta \to 0$, $k \to \tau$ these equations become

$$\frac{d}{d\tau} \underline{q}(\tau)] = \underline{G}(\tau, \underline{q}(\tau), \underline{m}(\tau), \underline{u}(\tau))] \qquad t \le \tau < T$$

$$\frac{d}{d\tau} \underline{\lambda}(\tau)] = \nabla_q F(\tau, T, \underline{q}(\tau), \underline{m}(\tau), \underline{u}(\tau))] - [J_q(\underline{G}(\tau, \underline{q}(\tau), \underline{m}(\tau), \underline{u}(\tau)))]^T \underline{\lambda}(\tau)]$$
$$t < \tau < T$$

$$\nabla_m F(\tau, T, \underline{q}(\tau), \underline{m}(\tau), \underline{u}(\tau))] = [J_m(\underline{G}(\tau, \underline{q}(\tau), \underline{m}(\tau), \underline{u}(\tau)))]^T \underline{\lambda}(\tau)]$$
$$t \le \tau < T \qquad (2.18)$$

Equations 2.17 are difference equations and Equations 2.18 are differential equations defining the functions $\underline{q}(\tau)$, $\underline{m}(\tau)$, and $\underline{\lambda}(\tau)$ subject to the boundary conditions at $\tau=t$ specifying $\underline{q}(t)$ and at $\tau=T$ as expressed by Equations 2.6 and 2.15. These are the so-called Euler or Euler-Lagrange difference or differential equations. Together with the boundary conditions they form a two-point boundary-value problem. For $\mathcal{P}_1$ to be optimum, it is necessary that $\underline{q}(\tau)$ and $\underline{m}(\tau)$ be a solution of this two-point boundary-value problem.

It should be noted that as $\Delta \to 0$ only the forward (right-hand) limit was required to exist in the case of $\underline{q}(\tau)$ and only the backward (left-hand) limit in the case of $\underline{\lambda}(\tau)$. Therefore $\underline{q}'$ and $\underline{\lambda}'$ may well be discontinous. Thus there was no need to require the continuity of

$\underline{G}$, F, $[J_q(\underline{G})]$, $[J_m(\underline{G})]$, $\nabla_q(F)]$, and $\nabla_m(F)]$ with respect to τ.

However, $\underline{\lambda}'$ has to exist and be bounded so that $\underline{\lambda}$ is a differentiable function.

The above solutions are for the case when T is fixed. If T is variable and is contrained only by Equation 2.6, in constructing the differential of $\mathcal{P}_1$ one must take into account possible variations in the termination time T. It will be assumed that $\underline{g}(T, \underline{q}(T))$ is a differentiable function of $\underline{q}(T)$. In some physically meaningful situations $\underline{g}(T, \underline{q}(T))$ may be a continuous function of T, whereas in others it may be defined only for discrete values of T, $T=t, t+\Delta, \ldots$ so that the trajectories are allowed to terminate only at these time instants. If $\underline{g}(T, \underline{q}(T))$ is a discrete function of T, then there are no techniques available for solving the problem beyond evaluating the optimum $\mathcal{P}_1$ for successive values of T and choosing the most optimum optimum. Only if $\underline{g}(T, \underline{q}(T))$ is differentiable in T can some progress be made towards an analytic formulation of the solution.

If $\underline{g}(T, \underline{q}(T))$ is differentiable in T and T is variable, then in forming the differential of $\mathcal{P}_1$ one must also consider the differential of T. We shall proceed with a discrete time description of the problem by considering the number of time steps N, $N=\frac{T-t}{\Delta}$, to be fixed and all the Δ's except the last one to be constant, so that as T is varied by dT the last Δ, to be designated Δ*, is given as

$$\Delta^* = T - t - (N-1)\Delta + dT \tag{2.19}$$

In this way $d\mathcal{P}_1$ will contain all the terms of Equation 2.9 and in addition the following ones, as shown here;

$d\mathcal{P}_1$=(terms of Equation 2.9)

$$+\Big\{F(T-\Delta, T, \underline{q}(T-\Delta), \underline{m}(T-\Delta), \underline{u}(T-\Delta)) + \sum_{k=t}^{T-\Delta} \Delta \frac{\partial F}{\partial T}(k, T, q(k), m(k), \underline{u}(k))$$

$$+\frac{\partial P}{\partial T}(T, q(T)) + \frac{\partial}{\partial T}\underline{q}(T)\nabla_q P(T, q(T))\Big]\Big\} dT \tag{2.20}$$

This time, however, the requirement that $d\underline{g}(T, \underline{q}(T)) = \underline{0}$ implies

$$dg_i(T, \underline{q}(T)) = \sum_{j=1}^{n} \Big([\;_q(\underline{g})]\Big)_{i,j} dq_i(T) + \Bigg\{\frac{\partial}{\partial T} g_i + \sum_{j=1}^{n} \Big([J_q(\underline{g})]\Big)_{i,j} \frac{\partial}{\partial T} q_j(T)\Bigg\} dT =$$

$$i = 1, 2, \ldots n_g \tag{2.21}$$

Breaking this up into the (∧) and (∨) parts as before and solving for $d\hat{q}(T)]$ yields

$$d\hat{q}(T)] = -[\hat{J}_q(\underline{g})^{-1}]\Big\{[\check{J}_q(\underline{g})]\, d\check{q}(T)] + dT\Big([J_q(\underline{g})]\frac{\partial}{\partial T} q(T)] + \frac{\partial}{\partial T} g(T)]\Big)\Big\}$$

$$= -dT\frac{\partial}{\partial T}\hat{q}(T)] - [\hat{J}_q(\underline{g})^{-1}]\Big\{dT\Big([\check{J}_q(\underline{g})]\frac{\partial}{\partial T}\check{q}(T)] + \frac{\partial}{\partial T} g(T)]\Big)$$

$$+ [\check{J}_q(\underline{g})]\, d\check{q}]\Big\} \tag{2.22}$$

The terms corresponding to Equation 2. 14 become

$$\ldots + \sum_{i=n_g+1}^{n} \Bigg\{ \check{\lambda}_i(T-\Delta) + \nabla_{\check{q}} P_i(\,T, \underline{q}(T)\,)$$

$$- \sum_{j=1}^{n_g} \Big(\hat{\lambda}_j(T-\Delta) + \nabla_{\hat{q}} P_j(\,T, \underline{q}(T)\,) \Big) \sum_{\ell=1}^{n_g} \Big([\hat{J}_q(\underline{g})]^{-1} \Big)_{j,\ell} \Big([\check{J}_q(\underline{g})] \Big)_{\ell,i} \Bigg\} d\check{q}_i(T)$$

$$+ \Bigg\{ F(\,T-\Delta, T, \underline{q}(T-\Delta), \underline{m}(T-\Delta), \underline{u}(T-\Delta)\,) + \sum_{k=t}^{T-\Delta} \Delta \frac{\partial F}{\partial T}(k,\ T,\ \underline{q}(k), \underline{m}(k), u(k)\,)$$

$$+ \frac{\partial P}{\partial T}(\,T, \underline{q}(T)\,) + \sum_{i=1}^{n} \Big(\nabla_q P_i(\,T, \underline{q}(T)\,) \frac{\partial q_i(T)}{\partial T} \Big)$$

$$- \sum_{i=1}^{n_g} \Big(\hat{\lambda}_i(T-\ \Delta) + \nabla_{\hat{q}} P_i(\,T, \underline{q}(T)) \Big) \Big(\frac{\partial \hat{q}_i(T)}{\partial T} + \sum_{j=1}^{n_g} \Big([\hat{J}_q(\underline{g})]^{-1} \Big)_{i,j} \Big(\frac{\partial g_j}{\partial T}$$

$$+ \sum_{\ell=n_g+1}^{n} \Big([\check{J}_q(\underline{g})] \Big)_{j,\ell} \frac{\partial \check{q}_\ell(T)}{\partial T} \Big) \Big) \Bigg\} dT \qquad (2.23)$$

And the total set of boundary conditions is

$$\check{\lambda}(T-\Delta)] + \nabla_{\check{q}} P(\,T, \underline{q}(T)\,)] = [\check{J}_q(\underline{g})]^{T} [\hat{J}_q(\underline{g})^{-1}]^{T} \Big(\hat{\lambda}(T-\Delta)] + \nabla_{\hat{q}} P(\,T, \underline{q}(T)\,)] \Big)$$

$$F(T-\Delta, T, \underline{q}\ (T-\Delta), \underline{m}(T-\Delta), \underline{u}(T-\Delta)\,) + \sum_{k=t}^{T-\Delta} \Delta \frac{\partial F}{\partial T}(\ k, T, \underline{q}(k), \underline{m}(k), \underline{u}(k)\,)$$

$$+ \frac{\partial P}{\partial T}(\,T, \underline{q}(T)\,) + \frac{\partial}{\partial T} \underline{q}(T) \nabla_q P(\,T, \underline{q}(T)\,)]$$

$$= \Big(\hat{\underline{\lambda}}(T-\Delta) + \nabla_{\hat{\underline{q}}} P(\,T, \underline{q}(T)\,) \Big) \Big(\frac{\partial \hat{q}(T)}{\partial T}] + [\hat{J}_q(\underline{g})]^{-1} \Big(\frac{\partial g}{\partial T}] + [\check{J}_q(\underline{g})] \frac{\partial}{\partial T} \check{q}(T)] \Big) \Big)$$

(2.24)

The Euler equations and the boundary conditions at $\tau = t$ are of course unchanged. Allowing the end point to vary does not change the structure of the problem. It affects only the boundary conditions by making them more complex, especially if $\frac{\partial F}{\partial T} \neq 0$.

That the introduction of a variable end point should affect only the boundary condition can be seen from the following consideration. If T was fixed and the optimum trajectory found, then it would satisfy the Euler equations. If this was now repeated for a number of fixed values of T, then each of the optimum trajectories would satisfy the same Euler equation, and therefore so would the one corresponding to the value of T yielding the most optimum optimum.

From the general boundary conditions expressed in Equation 2.24, one can deduce the following property of the optimum trajectories. Consider trajectory abc in Figure 2.2.

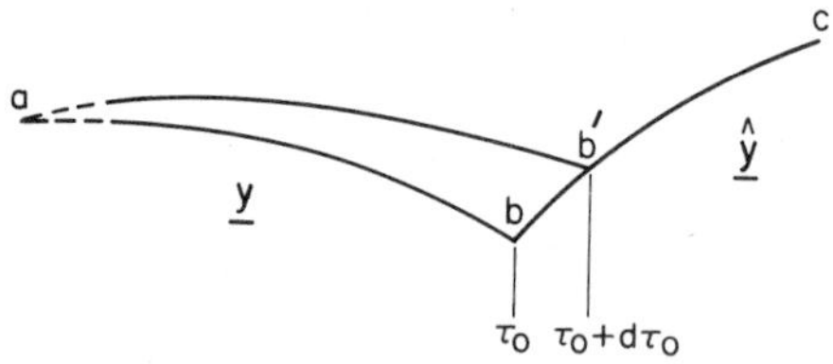

Fig. 2.2. Conditions at a corner of an optimum trajectory

It is a solution of the Euler equations and therefore continuous but possibly with a discontinuity in slope at b. Let $\underline{y}$ and $\hat{\underline{y}}$ be the ab and bc portions of the trajectory, respectively, and let b' be a point on bc such that if b occurs at τ_o, b' is at $\tau_o + d\tau_o$. If the abc trajectory yields a stationary point of $\mathcal{P}$, then $\mathcal{P}$ along abc is equal to the first approximation to $\mathcal{P}$ along ab'c. The difference between $\mathcal{P}$ along ab'c and abc is given by Equation 2.23, where one considers $\hat{\underline{y}}$ as a fixed trajectory which $\underline{y}$ is to meet. In this case the constraint $\underline{g} = \underline{0}$ is the requirement that

$$\underline{y}(\tau_o) - \hat{\underline{y}}(\tau_o) = \underline{0} \tag{2.25}$$

so that

$$[\hat{J}_q(\underline{g})] = [0], \quad [\check{J}_q(\underline{g})] = [I], \quad \frac{\partial}{\partial \tau_o} \underline{g}] = -\frac{d}{d\tau_o} \hat{\underline{y}}(\tau_o)] \tag{2.26}$$

and

$$P = \int_{\tau_o}^{T} \left\{ F(\tau, \hat{\underline{y}}(\tau), \hat{\underline{m}}(\tau), \underline{u}(\tau)) + \hat{\underline{\lambda}}(\tau) . \left(\dot{\hat{y}}(\tau)] - G(\hat{\underline{y}}(\tau), \hat{\underline{m}}(\tau))] \right) \right\} d\tau \tag{2.27}$$

This yields

$$\frac{\partial P}{\partial \tau_o} = - F(\tau_o, \hat{\underline{y}}(\tau_o), \hat{\underline{m}}(\tau_o), \underline{u}(\tau_o)) \quad \nabla_y P] = 0] \tag{2.28}$$

Equation 2.24 therefore requires that

$$F(\tau_o - \Delta, \underline{y}(\tau_o - \Delta), \underline{m}(\tau_o - \Delta), \underline{u}(\tau_o - \Delta)) - F(\tau_o, \hat{\underline{y}}(\tau_o), \hat{\underline{m}}(\tau_o), \underline{u}(\tau_o))$$

$$= \underset{\smile}{\lambda}(\tau_o - \Delta)\left(\hat{y}'(\tau_o)] - \hat{y}(\tau_o)]\right) \tag{2.29}$$

In the limit as $\Delta \to 0$, because $\underline{y}$ and $\underline{\lambda}$ are both continuous on a b c

$$F(\tau_o, \underline{y}(\tau_o), \underline{m}(\tau_o), \underline{u}(\tau_o)) - \underset{\smile}{\lambda}(\tau_o)\underline{y}'(\tau_o)] = F(\tau_o, \underline{y}(\tau_o), \hat{\underline{m}}(\tau_o), \underline{u}(\tau_o))$$

$$- \underset{\smile}{\lambda}(\tau_o)\hat{y}'(\tau_o)] \tag{2.30}$$

This together with the requirement that $\underline{\lambda}$ be continuous, as implied by Equation 2.18, form the so-called Weierstrass-Erdman corner conditions. They must hold on every trajectory defining a stationary point so that if there is a unique solution of the Euler conditions, the Weierstrass-Erdman relation holds everywhere on that solution. If there are several possible solutions of the Euler conditions (see Section 2.6), Equation 2.30 may be used to choose from among the various possibilities. Also, if the functions F or $\underline{G}$ are discontinuous in time, the Weierstrass-Erdman conditions may be used to simplify the solution of the boundary-value problems.

The **ba**sic necessary condition for an optimum trajectory is that it satisfy the Euler equations, Equation 2.17 or 2.18, and the boundary conditions at $\tau = t$ and $\tau = T$, the end-point conditions being expressed in their most general form by Equations 2.24 and 2.6. Several special cases of Equation 2.24 are of particular importance, and these will now be discussed.

1. If T is fixed and $\underline{q}(T)$ is prescribed, then dT and $dq_i(T)$, $i = 1, 2, \ldots n$ are all zero; thus their coefficients need not vanish for $d\wp$ to be zero. The end-point boundary conditions then are just the specifications on T and q(T)].
2. If T is fixed but $\underline{q}(T)$ is unspecified, then [J(g)] is of rank 0 and Equation 2.24 becomes

$$\lambda(T - \Delta)] = -\nabla_q P(T, \underline{q}(T))] \tag{2.31}$$

This is the so-called "natural" boundary condition. If P is independent of $\underline{q}(T)$, as it often is, then

$$\lambda(T - \Delta)] = 0] \tag{2.32}$$

3. When T is variable, $\underline{g}$ usually has the simple form

$$g(T, \underline{q}(T)) = q_\ell(T) - i(T) \tag{2.33}$$

In such a case Equation 2.24 becomes

$$\lambda_j(T-\Delta) = -\frac{\partial P(T, \underline{q}(T))}{\partial q_j(T)} \qquad \ell \neq j$$

$$F(T-\Delta, T, \underline{q}(T-\Delta), \underline{m}(T-\Delta), \underline{u}(T-\Delta)) + \sum_{k=t}^{T-\Delta} \Delta \frac{\partial F(k, T, \underline{q}(k), \underline{m}(k), \underline{u}(k))}{\partial T}$$

$$+ \frac{\partial P(T, \underline{q}(T))}{\partial T} + \frac{\partial \underline{q}(T)}{\partial T} \nabla_q P(T, \underline{q}(T))]$$

$$= \left(\lambda_\ell(T-\Delta) + \frac{\partial P(T, \underline{q}(T))}{\partial q_\ell(T)}\right)\left(\frac{\partial q_\ell(T)}{\partial T} - \frac{di(T)}{dT}\right) \tag{2.34}$$

and if P is independent of $\underline{q}(T)$

$$\lambda_j = 0 \quad \text{for } j \neq \ell$$

$$\sum_{k=t}^{T-\Delta} \Delta \frac{\partial F}{\partial T}(k, T, \underline{q}(k), \underline{m}(k), \underline{u}(k)) + F(T-\Delta, T, \underline{q}(T-\Delta), \underline{m}(T-\Delta), \underline{u}(T-\Delta))$$

$$+ \frac{dP}{dT} = \lambda_\ell(T-\Delta)\left(\frac{\partial q_\ell(T)}{\partial T} - \frac{di(T)}{dT}\right) \tag{2.35}$$

4. In many control situations $T \to \infty$ and

$$\lim_{\tau \to \infty} \left\{ \frac{\partial F}{\partial \tau}(\tau, T, \underline{q}(\tau), \underline{m}(\tau), \underline{u}(\tau)) + \nabla_{\underline{u}} F(\tau, T, \underline{q}(\tau), \underline{m}(\tau), \underline{u}(\tau)) \frac{du(\tau)}{d\tau}]\right\} = 0$$

$$\lim_{\tau \to \infty} \left\{ \frac{\partial G}{\partial \tau}(\tau, \underline{q}(\tau), \underline{m}(\tau), \underline{u}(\tau))] + [J_u\left(\underline{G}(\tau, \underline{q}(\tau), \underline{m}(\tau), \underline{u}(\tau)\right)] \frac{du(\tau)}{d\tau}]\right\} = \underline{0} \tag{2.36}$$

and furthermore as $\tau \to \infty$ the optimum values of $\underline{q}$ and $\underline{m}$ are such as to cause the system to be in steady state. In that case

$$\lim_{\tau\to\infty} \frac{dq(\tau)}{d\tau}] = 0] = \lim_{\tau\to\infty} \nabla_q F(\Delta, T, \underline{q}(\tau), \underline{m}(\tau), \underline{u}(\tau))] \qquad (2.37)$$

so that the system approaches a steady-state optimum. The requirement that Equation 2.24 be satisfied corresponds to the requirement that

$$\lim_{\tau\to\infty} \frac{d}{d\tau} \underline{q}(\tau) = \underline{0} = \frac{d}{d\tau} \underline{\lambda}(\tau) \qquad (2.38)$$

The steady-state optimum is therefore an equilibrium point of the Euler equations. It will be shown subsequently that on an incremental basis the Euler equations always have n stable and n unstable solutions so that each equilibrium point, and in particular the steady-state optimum, is a saddle-type singularity. Therefore in these circumstances the end-point boundary condition is that the solution as viewed in the phase space approach and terminate at the saddle type equilibrium point as $\tau \to T \to \infty$. This is probably the most important type of boundary condition and it will be treated further in later chapters. However, one must not forget that there are situations in which even though Equation 2.37 holds the optimum policy may be to operate the system in a limit cycle and never reach a steady state. This is treated further in Section 3.2.

2.2. Basic Sufficiency Conditions

The Euler equations and the appropriate boundary restrictions are the basic necessary conditions for an optimum. In many physical situations this is enough, for one can deduce on physical grounds whether the stationary point found is indeed an extremum. However, with further assumptions about the system and the performance criterion, certain sufficiency conditions for the existence of an optimum can be derived, and further insight can be gained into the structure of the Euler equations.

In addition to the previously stated restrictions on the form of F and $\underline{G}$, let us also require that $[J_q(\underline{G})]$, $[J_m(\underline{G})]$, $[J_q(\nabla_q F)]$, $[J_q(\nabla_m F)]$, $[J_m(\nabla_q F)]$, and $[J_m(\nabla_m F)]$ all exist and be of class C^1 with respect to $\underline{q}$ and $\underline{m}$ and of the class D^0 with respect to τ in the region $\mathcal{R}$ which is of interest in the $(\underline{q}, \underline{m}, \tau)$ space. Under these conditions for anv trajectory $\underline{q}^*(\tau)$, $\underline{m}^*(\tau)$ in $\mathcal{R}$ the total solutions $\underline{q}_T(\tau)$, $\underline{m}_T(\tau)$ in the neighborhood of this trajectory can be expressed as $\underline{q}_T = \underline{q}^* + \underline{q}$ and $\underline{m}_T = \underline{m}^* + \underline{m}$ where $\underline{q}$ and $\underline{m}$ are now 'he incremental solutions.

The incremental Euler difference equations about $\underline{q}^*(\tau)$ and $\underline{m}^*(\tau)$ are

$$\frac{\triangleright}{\Delta}\, q(k)] = [J_q(\underline{G}(\, k, \underline{q}^*(k), \underline{m}^*(k), \underline{u}(k)\,)\,)]\, q(k)]$$

$$+\, [J_m(\underline{G}(\, k, \underline{q}^*(k), \underline{m}^*(k), \underline{u}(k)\,)\,)]\, m(k)]$$

$$k=t,\, t+\Delta,\, \ldots\, T-\Delta$$

$$\frac{\triangleleft}{\Delta}\, \lambda(k)] = [J_q(\nabla_q F(\, k, T, \underline{q}^*(k), \underline{m}^*(k), \underline{u}(k)\,)\,)]\, q(k)]$$

$$+\, [J_m(\nabla_q F(\, k, T, \underline{q}^*(k), \underline{m}^*(k), \underline{u}(k)\,)\,)]\, m(k)]$$

$$-\, [J_q(\underline{G}(\, k, \underline{q}^*(k), \underline{m}^*(k), \underline{u}(k)\,)\,)]^T \lambda(k)]$$

$$k=t+\Delta,\, t+2\Delta,\, \ldots\, T-\Delta$$

$$[J_m(\underline{G}(\, k, \underline{q}^*(k), \underline{m}^*(k), \underline{u}(k)\,)\,)]^T \lambda(k)]$$

$$= \; [J_m(\nabla_m F(\, k, T, \underline{q}^*(k)\underline{m}^*(k), \underline{u}(k)\,)\,)]\, m(k)]$$

$$+ \; [J_q(\nabla_m F(\, k, T, \underline{q}^*(k)\underline{m}^*(k), \underline{u}(k)\,)\,)]\, q(k)$$

$$k=t,\, t+\Delta,\, \ldots\, T-\Delta \qquad (2.39)$$

This is the result of the standard linearization procedure. The equations are linear in the new incremental variables but with coefficients which depend on the trajectory about which linearization is done and therefore vary with time. Letting

$$[G_q(k)] = [J_q(\underline{G}(k, \underline{q}^*, \underline{m}^*, \underline{u})\,)] \qquad [G_m(k)] = [J_m(\underline{G}(k, \underline{q}^*, \underline{m}^*, \underline{u})\,)]$$

$$[F_{mq}(k)] = [J_q(\nabla_m F(k, T, \underline{q}^*, \underline{m}^*, \underline{u})\,)] \qquad [F_{qm}(k)] = [J_m(\nabla_q F(k, T, \underline{q}^*, \underline{m}^*, \underline{u})$$

$$[F_{qq}(k)] = [J_q(\nabla_q F(k, T, \underline{q}^*, \underline{m}^*, \underline{u})\,)] \qquad [F_{mm}(k)] = [J_m(\nabla_m F(k, T, \underline{q}^*, \underline{m}^*, \underline{u})$$

$$(2.40)$$

the incremental equations can be rewritten as

$$\frac{\triangleright}{\triangle} q(k) \Big] = \Big[\begin{array}{c} G_q(k) \end{array} \Big] q(k) \Big] + \Big[G_m(k) \Big] \quad m(k) \Big]$$

$$\frac{\triangleleft}{\triangle} \lambda(k) \Big] = \Big[\begin{array}{c} F_{qq}(k) \end{array} \Big] q(k) \Big] + \Big[F_{qm}(k) \Big] \quad m(k) \Big] - \Big[G_q^T(k) \Big] \lambda(k) \Big]$$

$$\Big[F_{mm}(k) \Big] m(k) \Big] = \Big[G_m^T(k) \Big] \lambda(k) \Big] - \Big[\quad F_{mq}(k) \quad \Big] q(k) \Big]$$

$$(2.41)$$

where the size of the brackets is used to indicate the relative
dimensionality of the various matrices.

At this point a second necessary condition for an optimum in
the continuous time problem becomes apparent. If $\mathcal{D}$ is to have
a minimum or a maximum, $[F_{mm}]$ must be positive semidefinite
or negative semidefinite respectively, everywhere along the
trajectory $\underline{q}^*$, $\underline{m}^*$.

To show this, let us assume that a maximum of $\mathcal{D}$ is sought.
If $[F_{mm}]$ is not negative semidefinite, then for every $\epsilon_1 > 0$
there is an $\epsilon > 0$ and an $\underline{m}$ with $0 < \| m \| < \epsilon_1$ such that

$$\underline{m} \, [F_{mm}] m] < -\epsilon \qquad (2.42)$$

Thus there is some combination of components of $\underline{m}$ which if made
to oscillate about zero would make

$$\int_t^T (\underline{m}^* + \underline{m})[F_{mm}](m^*] + m])d\tau < \int_t^T \underline{m}^* [F_{mm}]m^*]d\tau - \epsilon$$

$$(2.43)$$

But if one causes m] to oscillate about zero rapidly enough, q]
will be affected sufficiently little so that the change in $\mathcal{D}$ due to
these variations in q] will be less in magnitude than $\epsilon / 2$. Thus
there is an $m^*] + m]$ such that

$$\mathcal{D} (\underline{m}^* + \underline{m}, \underline{q}^* + \underline{q}) < \mathcal{D} (\underline{m}^*, \underline{q}^*) \qquad (2.44)$$

Therefore, in order that the solution of the Euler equations
yield a minimum, $[F_{mm}]$ must be positive semidefinite; an
analogous argument shows that $[F_{mm}]$ must be negative semidefinite for the solution of the Euler equations to yield a maximum.
(This necessary condition corresponds to the Legendre conditions
in the classical variational problem.[9,26,64]) The above consideration also shows that if $[F_{mm}]$ is semidefinite, the optimum $\underline{m}^*$

trajectory is not unique. Therefore, for ease of computation, it is customary to choose F such that $[F_{mm}]$ is positive definite or negative definite.

With this additional strengthening of the second necessary conditions, m] can be eliminated from Equation 2.41. Defining

$$[P] = [G_q] - [G_m][F_{mm}^{-1}][F_{mq}] \qquad [\hat{P}] = [I] + \Delta [P]$$

$$[Q] = [F_{qq}] - [F_{qm}][F_{mm}^{-1}][F_{mq}] \qquad [\hat{Q}] = \Delta [Q]$$

$$[R] = [G_m][F_{mm}^{-1}][G_m^T] \qquad [\hat{R}] = \Delta [R] \qquad (2.45)$$

and making use of the fact that $[F_{qm}] = \left([F_{mq}]\right)^T$, Equation 2.41 can be rewritten as

$$q(k+\Delta)] = [\hat{P}(k)]q(k)] + [\hat{R}(k)]\lambda(k)] \qquad k=t, t+\Delta, \ldots T-\Delta$$

$$\lambda(k-\Delta)] = -[\hat{Q}(k)]q(k)] + [\hat{P}^T(k)]\lambda(k)] \qquad k=t+\Delta, t+2\Delta, \ldots T-\Delta \qquad (2.46)$$

or in terms of differences

$$\frac{\triangleright}{\Delta} q(k)] = [P(k)]q(k)] + [R(k)]\lambda(k)] \qquad k=t, t+\Delta, \ldots T-\Delta$$

$$\frac{\triangleleft}{\Delta} \lambda(k)] = [Q(k)]q(k)] - [P^T(k)]\lambda(k)] \qquad k=t+\Delta, t+2\Delta, \ldots T-\Delta \qquad (2.47)$$

In the continuous time case this becomes

$$\frac{d}{d\tau} q(\tau)] = [P(\tau)]q(\tau)] + [R(\tau)]\lambda(\tau)] \qquad t \leq \tau < T$$

$$\frac{d}{d\tau} \lambda(\tau)] = [Q(\tau)]q(\tau)] - [P^T(\tau)]\lambda(\tau)] \qquad t < \tau < T \qquad (2.48)$$

It should be noted that $[Q]$ and $[R]$ are both symmetric and semidefinite; whereas $[P]$ and $[\hat{P}]$ are in general not symmetric, but for sufficiently small Δ, $[\hat{P}]$ is nonsingular. In the majority of cases $[R]$ will be singular—in particular, whenever $[G_m]$ is not square, that is, whenever there are fewer control inputs than states.

The two n-dimensional first-order Euler equations can be reduced to a single n-dimensional second-order difference or differential equation, which in turn corresponds to a simultaneous set of linear equations. The matrix of these equations, being positive or negative definite, will be shown to be a sufficient condition for the Euler equations to define a minimum or a maximum, respectively.

To begin with, let us assume that $[R(k)]$ is nonsingular. By solving Equation 2.46 for $\lambda(k)]$ and substituting back one obtains

$$-\left([\hat{R}^{-1}(k-\Delta)][\hat{P}(k-\Delta)]\right)q(k-\Delta)] + \left([\hat{Q}(k)] + [\hat{P}^T(k)][\hat{R}(k)^{-1}][\hat{P}(k)] + [\hat{R}^{-1}(k-\Delta)]\right)q(k)] - \left([\hat{R}^{-1}(k)][\hat{P}(k)]\right)^T q(k+\Delta)] = 0]$$

$$k = t+\Delta, t+2\Delta, \ldots T-\Delta \qquad (2.49)$$

and in the continuous time case, there results

$$[R^{-1}(\tau)]\frac{d^2}{d\tau^2}q(\tau)] - \left([R^{-1}(\tau)][P(\tau)] - \left([R^{-1}(\tau)][P(\tau)]\right)^T\right)\frac{d}{d\tau}q(\tau)]$$

$$-\left([Q(\tau)] + [P^T(\tau)]\,[R^{-1}(\tau)][P(\tau)]\right)q(\tau)]$$

$$+\left(\frac{d}{d\tau}[R^{-1}(\tau)]\right)\frac{d}{d\tau}q(\tau)]$$

$$-\left(\frac{d}{d\tau}\left([R^{-1}(\tau)][P(\tau)]\right)\right)q(\tau)] = 0] \qquad t < \tau < T \qquad (2.50)$$

The initial conditions enter as a specification of $q(t)]$ and the final conditions, if they involve only $q(T)]$, as a specification of $q(T)]$. If the final conditions involve $\lambda(T-\Delta)]$, then Equation 2.49 for $k = T-\Delta$ becomes modified so as to express these end-point boundary conditions. In the continuous time case the end boundary condition will involve a linear combination of $q(T)]$ and $\frac{dq(T)]}{dT}$.

Considering the case in which $q(T)]$ is prescribed, and defining

$$[B(\ell)] = -[\hat{R}(k-\Delta)]^{-1}[P(k-\Delta)] \qquad \ell = 1, 2, \ldots N$$

$$[A(\ell)] = [B(\ell+1)]^T[\hat{R}(k)][B(\ell+1)] + [\hat{Q}(k)] + [\hat{R}(k-\Delta)]^{-1} \qquad \ell = 1, 2, \ldots N$$

where

$$\ell = \frac{k-t}{\Delta} \qquad N = \frac{T-t}{\Delta}$$

the set of equations represented by Equation 2.49 can be combined into a compound matrix:

$$\begin{bmatrix} [A(1)] & [B(2)]^T & & & & & \\ [B(2)] & [A(2)] & [B(3)]^T & & & & \\ & [B(3)] & [A(3)] & [B(4)]^T & & & \\ & \cdots & \cdots & \cdots & & & \\ & & [B(\ell)] & [A(\ell)] & [B(\ell+1)]^T & & \\ & & & \cdots & \cdots & \cdots & \\ & & & & [B(N-2)] & [A(N-2)] & [B(N-1)]^T \\ & & & & & [B(N-1)] & [A(N-1)] \end{bmatrix} \begin{bmatrix} q(1)] \\ q(2)] \\ q(3)] \\ \cdots \\ q(\ell)] \\ \cdots \\ q(N-2)] \\ q(N-1)] \end{bmatrix} = \begin{bmatrix} -[B(1)]q(0)] \\ 0] \\ 0] \\ \cdots \\ 0] \\ \cdots \\ 0] \\ -[B(N)]^T q(N)] \end{bmatrix} \tag{2.51}$$

For brevity, this will be written as

$$[M]q] = \Gamma] \tag{2.52}$$

where q] now corresponds to the entire compound vector of $\underline{q}(t+\Delta), \underline{q}(t+2\Delta), \ldots \underline{q}(T-\Delta)$.

Similarly, if $[Q(k)]$ is nonsingular, the equations can be expressed as

$$\begin{aligned} &-\left([\hat{P}(k)][\hat{Q}^{-1}(k)]\right)\lambda(k-\Delta)] \\ &+\left([\hat{P}(k)][\hat{Q}^{-1}(k)][\hat{P}(k)^T] + [\hat{R}(k)] + [\hat{Q}^{-1}(k+\Delta)]\right)\lambda(k)] \\ &-\left([\hat{P}(k+\Delta)][\hat{Q}^{-1}(k+\Delta)]\right)^T \lambda(k+\Delta)] = 0] \end{aligned} \tag{2.53}$$

and in the continuous time case as

$$
\begin{aligned}
[Q^{-1}(\tau)]\frac{d^2}{d\tau^2}\lambda(\tau)] &- \left([P(\tau)][Q^{-1}(\tau)] - ([P(\tau)][Q^{-1}(\tau)])^T\right)\frac{d}{d\tau}\lambda(\tau)] \\
&- \left([R(\tau)]+[P(\tau)][Q^{-1}(\tau)][P^T(\tau)]\right)\lambda(\tau)] \\
&+ \left(\frac{d}{d\tau}[Q^{-1}(\tau)]\right)\frac{d}{d\tau}\lambda(\tau)] - \left(\frac{d}{d\tau}[P(\tau)][Q^{-1}(\tau)]\right)^T\lambda(\tau)] = 0]
\end{aligned}
$$

$$t < \tau < T \qquad (2.54)$$

At the initial boundary, $q(t)]$ and not $\lambda(t)]$ is prescribed so that the initial condition on Equation 2.54 involves both $\lambda(t)]$ and $\frac{d}{dt}\lambda(t)]$; in like manner, the condition at $\tau=T$ may involve $\lambda(T)]$ and $\frac{d}{d\tau}\lambda(T)]$. The difference equation 2.53 is affected in that a linear combination of $\lambda(t)]$ and $\lambda(t+\Delta)]$ is specified as the initial condition, and similarly, a linear combination of $\lambda(T-\Delta)]$ and $\lambda(T-2\Delta)]$ may be specified as the final condition. Thus considering again the case in which $q(T)]$ is specified and defining

$$[B(\ell)] = -[\hat{Q}^{-1}(k)][\hat{P}(k)] \qquad \ell = 1, 2, \ldots N-1$$

$$[A(\ell)] = [B(\ell)][\hat{Q}(k)][B(\ell)]^T + [\hat{R}(k)] + [\hat{Q}^{-1}(k+\Delta)] \qquad \ell = 1, 2, \ldots N-2$$

$$[A(0)] = [\hat{Q}^{-1}(t+\Delta)] + [\hat{R}(t)]$$

$$[A(N-1)] = [B(N-1)][\hat{Q}(T-\Delta)][B(N-1)]^T + [\hat{R}(T-\Delta)] \qquad (2.55)$$

the compound matrix equation in terms of $\lambda(k)]$ can be written:

$$
\begin{bmatrix}
[A(0)] & [B(1)]^T & & & & \\
[B(1)] & [A(1)] & [B(2)]^T & & & \\
& [B(2)] & [A(2)] & [B(3)]^T & & \\
& \cdots & \cdots & \cdots & & \\
& & [B(\ell)] & [A(\ell)] & [B(\ell+1)]^T & \\
& & \cdots & \cdots & \cdots & \\
& & & [B(N-2)] & [A(N-2)] & [B(N-1)]^T \\
& & & & [B(N-1)] & [A(N-1)]
\end{bmatrix}
\begin{bmatrix}
\lambda(0)] \\ \lambda(1)] \\ \lambda(2)] \\ \cdots \\ \lambda(k)] \\ \cdots \\ \lambda(N-2)] \\ \lambda(N-1)]
\end{bmatrix}
=
\begin{bmatrix}
-\Delta([1]+\Delta[P(0)])q(0)] \\ 0 \\ 0 \\ \cdots \\ 0 \\ \cdots \\ 0 \\ \Delta q(N)]
\end{bmatrix}
$$

$$(2.56)$$

Let us consider the matrix [M] of Equation 2.52. It should be noted that [M] is symmetric, and the quadratic form $\underline{q}[M]q]$ represents the incremental $\mathcal{P}$ due to the incremental variations of q] and m] about the trajectory q* and m*, satisfying the Euler equations. This can be checked by expanding $\Delta\mathcal{P}$, the incremental $\mathcal{P}$, as

$$\Delta\mathcal{P} = \sum_{k=t}^{T-\Delta} \Delta\Big\{\underline{q(k)}[F_{qq}(k)]q(k)] + \underline{q(k)}[F_{qm}(k)]m(k)] + \underline{m(k)}[F_{mq}(k)]q(k)] + \underline{m(k)}[F_{mm}(k)]m(k)]\Big\} \quad (2.57)$$

and substituting for m(k)] from Equation 2.41 to obtain

$$\Delta\mathcal{P} = \sum_{k=t}^{T-\Delta} \Delta\Big\{\underline{q(k)}[Q(k)]q(k)] + \underline{\lambda(k)}[R(k)]\lambda(k)]\Big\} \quad (2.58)$$

using the terms defined in Equation 2.45,

$$\Delta\mathcal{P} = \sum_{k=t}^{T-\Delta} \Delta\Big\{\underline{q(k)}\big([\hat{Q}(k)] + [\hat{P}(k)^T][\hat{R}^{-1}(k)][\hat{P}(k)]\big)q(k)] + \underline{q(k)}[\hat{P}(k)^T][\hat{R}^{-1}(k)]q(k+\Delta)] + \underline{q(k+\Delta)}[\hat{R}^{-1}(k)][\hat{P}(k)]q(k)] + \underline{q(k+\Delta)}[\hat{R}^{-1}(k)]q(k+\Delta)]\Big\} \quad (2.59)$$

which differs from $\underline{q}[M]q]$ only by constant terms involving q(0)] and q(T)].

If [M] is positive definite, then $\underline{q}[M]q]$ is smallest for q]=0 so that the trajectory $\underline{q}$*, $\underline{m}$* yields a smaller $\mathcal{P}_1$ than any other trajectory in its immediate neighborhood. Thus it represents a local minimum. Similarly, if [M] is negative definite, $\underline{q}$*, $\underline{m}$* is a local maximum. If [M] is neither of these, the trajectory $\underline{q}$*, $\underline{m}$*, although it satisfies the Euler equation, yields neither a maximum nor a minimum but a saddle point. (A similar development shows the definiteness of the matrix of Equation 2.56 as an alternate sufficiency condition for q* and m* to define an optimum.) It is therefore imperative to investigate what conditions on F and $\underline{G}$ guarantee that [M] will be positive or negative definite.

The definiteness of [M] can be tested as follows. Equation 2.51 can be successively reduced, row by row, to a block triangular form

$$[A(1)]q(1)] + [B^T(2)]q(2)] = - [B(1)]q(0)]$$

$$\left([A(2)] - [B(2)][A^{-1}(1)][B^T(2)]\right)q(2)] + [B^T(3)]q(3)] = - [B(2)][A^{-1}(1)][B(1)]q(0)]$$

$$\left([A(3)] - [B(3)]\left([A(2)] - [B(2)][A^{-1}(1)][B^T(2)]\right)^{-1}[B^T(3)]\right)q(3)] + [B^T(4)]q(4)]$$

$$= - [B(3)]\left([A(2)] - [B(2)][A^{-1}(1)][B^T(2)]\right)^{-1}[B(2)][A^{-1}(1)][B(1)]q(0)]$$

$$\cdots\cdots\cdots\cdots\cdots\cdots\cdots\cdots \tag{2.60}$$

The component matrices on the principal diagonal $[M_i]$, $i = 1, 2, \ldots N-1$ are seen to satisfy the recursion relation

$$[M_i] = [A(i)] - [B(i)][M^{-1}_{i-1}][B^T(i)] \tag{2.61}$$

and $[M]$ is definite if and only if $[M_i]$, $i = 1, 2, \ldots N-1$ are all definite of the same sign.

A still more useful test follows from the expansion in Equation 2.60. The solution of Equation 2.46 or 2.47 can be expressed as

$$q(\ell)] = [\phi_A(\ell)]q(1)] + [\phi_B(\ell)]q(0)] \tag{2.62}$$

Setting $q(0)] = 0$, one obtains from Equation 2.60 an expression for $[\phi_A(\ell)]$ as follows:

$$q(2)] = - [B^T(2)]^{-1}[M_1]q(1)]$$

$$q(3)] = - [B^T(3)]^{-1}[M_2]q(2)] = - [B^T(3)]^{-1}[M_2]\left(- [B^T(2)]^{-1}[M_1]\right)q(1)]$$

$$\cdots\cdots\cdots\cdots\cdots\cdots\cdots\cdots$$

$$q(\ell)] = \left\{\prod_{i=1,\ell-1} -\left([B^T(i+1)]^{-1}[M_i]\right)\right\}q(1)] \tag{2.63}$$

For sufficiently small Δ, $-[B^T(i)]$ is always positive definite so that $[\phi_A(\ell)]$ is definite of constant sign if and only if $[M_i]$ $i = 1, 2, \ldots \ell-1$ is definite of constant sign.

This test is particularly useful because $[\phi_A(\ell)]$ can be determined from the incremental Euler equations (Equation 2.41) without the necessity of constructing matrix $[M]$. If $[\phi_A(\ell)]$, $\ell = 1, 2, \ldots N$ is definite of constant sign, then $[M]$ is definite and the trajectory $\underline{q}^*$, $\underline{m}^*$, which is the solution of the Euler equations (Equation 2.17), does indeed represent an optimum. It should be pointed out that $[\phi_A(N)]$ involves $[A(N-1)]$, which depends on the end-point boundary conditions, so that $[M]$ may well be definite for one set of end-point boundary conditions and not for others. Thus for one set of end-point boundary conditions the solution of the Euler conditions may represent an optimum, whereas for other boundary conditions it may be just a saddle point.

Alternately, one can consider a representation

$$q(\ell)] = [\phi_{A'}(\ell)] \frac{\triangleright}{\Delta} q(0)] + [\phi_{B'}(\ell)] q(0)] \tag{2.64}$$

It is seen that $[\phi_{B'}(\ell)] \neq [\phi_B(\ell)]$ but $[\phi_{A'}(\ell)] = \Delta[\phi_A(\ell)]$ so that testing $[\phi_{A'}(\ell)]$ is equivalent to testing $[\phi_A(\ell)]$. This allows one to extend the test to the continuous time case since as $\Delta \rightarrow 0$,

$$q(\tau)] = [\phi_{A'}(\tau)] q'(t)] + [\phi_{B'}(\tau)] q(t)] \tag{2.65}$$

Thus if, in the solution of the incremental Euler equations (Equations 2.48), $[\phi_{A'}(\tau)]$ is definite of constant sign on the interval $t \leq \tau \leq T$, then the trajectory $\underline{q}^*$, $\underline{m}^*$ defines an optimum. Since $[\phi_{A'}(\tau)]$ is continuous, it cannnot cease being definite without its determinant passing through zero. Therefore in the continuous time case it is sufficient to look for the points where $[\phi_{A'}(\tau)]$ becomes singular, the so-called conjugate points. The above tests therefore require that there be no conjugate points on the interval $t \leq \tau < T$. (This corresponds to the strengthened Jacobi condition of the variational calculus.)

In the case that both $[Q]$ and $[R]$ are singular, but provided that the system is controllable, it is still possible to convert the incremental Euler equations (Equation 2.46) into a single equation in $q(k)]$, $k = t+\Delta, t+2\Delta, \ldots T-\Delta$ of higher order and find the corresponding $[M]$ matrix. The quadratic form associated with this matrix represents the incremental $\mathscr{P}$, and the definiteness of $[M]$ is a sufficient condition for the Euler equations to define an extremum. $[M]$ has additional significance in that it specifies the form of a spatial analog which may be used for the solution of the two-point boundary-value problem (see Section 3.5). If both $[Q]$ and $[R]$ are singular, to express Equation 2.46 in terms of a single variable one has to solve it, component by component, so that the elegance of the matrix formulation is lost. For this reason a somewhat different approach will now be presented which has the advantage that it retains matrix notation and displays the sufficiency conditions for an optimum in terms of general end-point boundary conditions (T is assumed fixed) but which does not display the $[M]$ matrix.

The incremental Euler equations (Equation 2.46) can be manipulated into the form

$$q(k+\Delta)] = [\hat{P}(k)]q(k)] + [\hat{R}(k)]\lambda(k)]$$

$$\lambda(k+\Delta)] = [\hat{P}^T(k+\Delta)]^{-1}[\hat{Q}(k+\Delta)][\hat{P}(k)]q(k)]$$

$$+ [\hat{P}^T(k+\Delta)]^{-1}\Big([I] + [\hat{Q}(k+\Delta)][R(k)]\Big)\lambda(k)] \qquad (2.66)$$

and the solution of Equation 2.66 represented as

$$q(k)] = [\phi_{11}(k,t)]q(t)] + [\phi_{12}(k,t)]\lambda(t)]$$

$$\lambda(k)] = [\phi_{21}(k,t)]q(t)] + [\phi_{22}(k,t)]\lambda(t)] \qquad (2.67)$$

The general end-point boundary conditions which the solution of the Euler equations is to satisfy can be represented on an incremental basis as

$$[A_A]q(T-\Delta)] + [A_B]\lambda(T-\Delta)] = 0] \qquad (2.68)$$

One should note that this allows the inclusion of specifications on $q(T)]$ as well, since

$$q(T)] = [\hat{P}(T-\Delta)]q(T-\Delta)] + [\hat{R}(T-\Delta)]\lambda(T-\Delta)] \qquad (2.69)$$

By substituting in Equation 2.68 the expressions for $q(T-\Delta)]$ and $\lambda(T-\Delta)]$ from Equation 2.67 and solving for $\lambda(t)]$, one obtains

$$\lambda(t)] = -\Big([A_A][\phi_{12}(T-\Delta,t)] + [A_B][\phi_{22}(T-\Delta,t)]\Big)^{-1}$$

$$\Big([A_A][\phi_{11}(T-\Delta,t)] + [A_B][\phi_{21}(T-\Delta,t)]\Big)q(t)] \qquad (2.70)$$

Letting

$$[\mathcal{C}(T-\Delta,t)] = -\Big([A_A][\phi_{12}(T-\Delta,t)] + [A_B][\phi_{22}(T-\Delta,t)]\Big)^{-1}$$

$$\Big([A_A][\phi_{11}(T-\Delta,t)] + [A_B][\phi_{21}(T-\Delta,t)]\Big) \qquad (2.71)$$

one can relate $\lambda]$ and $q]$ everywhere on the optimum trajectory as

$$\lambda(k)] = [\mathcal{C}(T-\Delta,k)]q(k)] \qquad (2.72)$$

On substituting this into Equation 2.58, one obtains for the incremental $\mathcal{P}$:

$$\Delta\mathcal{P} = \sum_{k=t}^{T-\Delta} \Delta\left\{\underline{q}(k)\left([Q(k)] + [\mathcal{E}(T-\Delta, k)^{T}][R(k)][\mathcal{E}(T-\Delta, k)]\right)q(k)]\right\}$$

(2.73)

Thus the trajectory $\underline{q}^*$, $\underline{m}^*$ specifies a maximum of $\mathcal{P}$ only if $\Delta\mathcal{P}$ is nonpositive for all incremental $\underline{q}(k)$ $k = t, t+\Delta, t+2\Delta, \ldots T-\Delta$ which can be altered through application of $\underline{m}$. A sufficient condition for $\underline{q}^*$, $\underline{m}^*$ to specify a maximum is that

$$[Q(k)] + [\mathcal{E}^{T}(t-\Delta, k)]\,[R(k)][\mathcal{E}(T-\Delta, k)] \tag{2.74}$$

be negative definite for $k = t+\Delta, t+2\Delta, \ldots T-\Delta$. If there is a component $\hat{q}(\ell)]$ of $q(\ell)]$ such that $q(\ell+\Delta)]$, $q(\ell+2\Delta)]$, $\ldots q(T-\Delta)]$ is independent of $\hat{q}(\ell)]$, then $\underline{q(\ell)}\left([Q(\ell)] + [\mathcal{E}^{T}(T-\Delta, \ell)][R(\ell)][\mathcal{E}(T-\Delta, \ell)]\right)q(\ell$ may be zero with respect to variations in $\hat{q}(\ell)]$. In particular, if the end-point boundary conditions are $\lambda(T-\Delta)] = 0]$, it is sufficient that $[Q(T-\Delta)] + [\mathcal{E}^{T}(T-\Delta, \quad \Delta)][R(T-\Delta)][\mathcal{E}(T-\Delta, T-\Delta)]$ be semidefinite.

The above represents general sufficiency conditions for an optimum. These tests are also applicable in the continuous time case as $\Delta \to 0$. Then, however, if the end conditions specify $q(T)]$, $[\mathcal{E}(T, T)]$ is infinite (see Section 2.1), and in carrying out the test one must consider whether

$$\lim_{\Delta \to 0}\left([Q(T-\Delta)] + [\mathcal{E}^{T}(T-\Delta, T-\Delta)]\,[R(T-\Delta)][\mathcal{E}(T-\Delta, T-\Delta)]\right)$$

is or is not positive or negative definite.

All of the sufficiency conditions derived require the generation of the solutions of the Euler equations. It would have been desirable to express the sufficiency conditions in terms of restrictions on F and $\underline{G}$ alone. It has not been possible to do this in any significant class of cases. The following examples illustrate the difficulties and at the same time demonstrate the selectiveness of the tests.

As an example, consider a problem in which the plant is described by

$$q' + \alpha q = m \tag{2.75}$$

and the performance criterion is

$$\mathcal{P} = \int^{T} \left\{m^2 + \gamma(q-1)^2\right\} d\tau \tag{2.76}$$

The Euler condition as expressed in terms of a single second-order difference equation is

$$-q(\ell-1)+2\left(1+\frac{\Delta^2(a^2+\gamma)}{2(1-a\Delta)}\right)q(\ell)-q(\ell+1)=\Delta\gamma i(\ell) \qquad (2.77)$$

which in the limit as $\Delta \rightarrow 0$ becomes

$$\frac{d^2}{d\tau^2}q(\tau)=(a^2+\gamma)q(\tau)-\gamma i(\tau) \qquad (2.78)$$

For generation of the [M] matrix, one defines

$$[B(\ell)] = -1 \qquad \ell=1,2,\ \ldots\ N-1$$

$$[A(\ell)] = 2\left(1+\frac{\Delta^2(a^2+\gamma)}{2(1-a\Delta)}\right)=2(1+\rho) \qquad \ell=1,2,\ \ldots\ N-2$$

(2.79)

If the end boundary conditions are fixed—that is, if $q(T)$ is specified—then [B(N)] and [A(N-1)] are the same as above; but if the end point is completely free, then $\lambda(N-1)=0$ and

$$[B(N)] = -1 \qquad [A(N-1)] = 1+\Delta\left(\frac{a+\Delta\gamma}{1-\Delta a}\right)=1+\rho'$$

(2.80)

To test for definiteness of [M], one considers

$$[M_i] = 2(1+\rho)-[M_{i-1}^{-1}] \qquad i=1,2,\ \ldots\ N-1$$

$$[M_N] = (1+\rho')-[M_{N-1}^{-1}] \qquad (2.81)$$

In this special case because $[M_i]$ is a scalar Equation 2.81 can be reduced to

$$D_{i+1}=2(1+\rho)D_i-D_{i-1} \qquad (2.82)$$

where

$$D_i=\prod_{j=1,i}M_j \qquad (2.83)$$

In the case of a fixed end boundary condition, Equation 2.82 is a constant coefficient difference equation. After transforming this equation into the Z transform domain, the root locus of its characteristic equation can be plotted as a function of ρ, as in Figure 2.3. With the initial conditions $D_1 = 2(1+\rho)$, $D_2 = (2(1+\rho))^2 - 1$, the solution of Equation 2.82 is monotonic increasing if $\rho > 0$, and so a minimum of $\mathcal{P}$ exists. If $\rho < 0$, the solution is oscillatory about 0; thus for sufficiently small N there will be a maximum, but for sufficiently large N there will be a saddle point. The solution of Equation 2.82 is

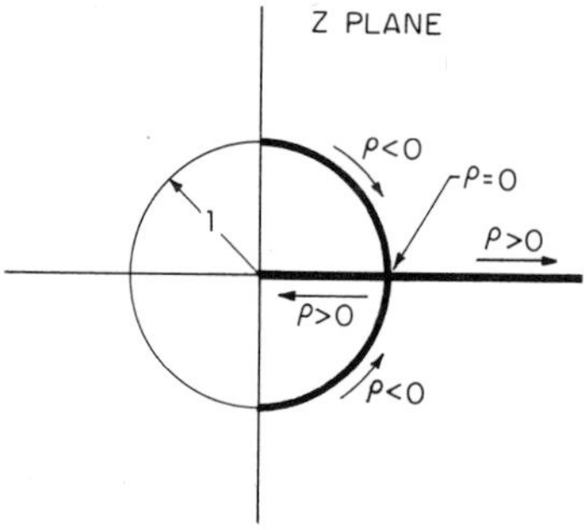

Fig. 2.3 The locus of the roots of Equation 2.82

$$D_\ell = \frac{1}{2}\left\{\left(D_1 - \frac{(1+\rho)D_1 - D_2}{\sqrt{\rho^2 + 2\rho}}\right)\left(1 + \rho + \sqrt{\rho^2 + 2\rho}\right)^{\ell - 1} + \left(D_1 + \frac{(1+\rho)D_1 - D_2}{\sqrt{\rho^2 + 2\rho}}\right)\left(1 + \rho - \sqrt{\rho^2 + 2\rho}\right)^{\ell - 1}\right\} \tag{2.84}$$

and in the limit as $\Delta \to 0$, $N\Delta \to T$,

$$D_\ell = 2\cosh\left(\frac{(\ell-1)}{N} T\sqrt{a^2 + \gamma}\right) + \frac{1}{\Delta\sqrt{a^2+\gamma}} \sinh\left(\frac{(\ell-1)}{N} T\sqrt{a^2+\gamma}\right) \tag{2.85}$$

or

$$\Delta D_\ell = \frac{1}{\sqrt{-(a^2+\gamma)}} \sin\left(\frac{(\ell-1)}{N} T\sqrt{-(a^2+\gamma)}\right) \tag{2.86}$$

Therefore an optimum exists only for

$$T \le \frac{\pi}{\sqrt{-(a^2+\gamma)}} \tag{2.87}$$

If ρ is strictly zero, that is, if $\gamma = -a^2$, then the solution of Equation 2.82 is simply a rising ramp, and so an optimum does exist for all T. Thus for fixed end-point boundary conditions the above results can be combined by asserting that an optimum exists for

$$T \le \frac{\pi}{\mathcal{R}e\sqrt{-(\alpha^2 + \gamma)}} \tag{2.88}$$

On the other hand, if q(T) is free and $\lambda(T-\Delta) = 0$, then D_ℓ is given by Equation 2.82 for $\ell = 1, 2, \ldots N-1$, but

$$D_N = (1 + \rho')D_{N-1} - D_{N-2} \tag{2.89}$$

For sufficiently small Δ, $\rho' < 1 + 2\rho$ so that if an optimum does not exist for a fixed end condition, it will not exist for a free end condition. Also, if ρ' is positive and an optimum exists for fixed end conditions (this implies $\alpha \geq 0$ and thus a stable element), then it will also exist for a free end condition. However, a free end point may not allow an optimum when a fixed end does. In this case in the limit as $\Delta \to 0$

$$D_\ell = \cosh\left(\frac{(\ell - 1)}{N} T\sqrt{\alpha^2 + \gamma}\right) + \frac{\alpha}{\sqrt{\alpha^2 + \gamma}} \sinh\left(\frac{(\ell - 1)}{N} T\sqrt{\alpha^2 + \gamma}\right) \tag{2.90}$$

Thus if $\gamma = -\alpha^2$ and $\alpha < 0$, for example, an optimum will exist only if $T < \frac{1}{-\alpha}$.

These examples are anything but typical. They are shown to indicate the sensitivity of the tests presented and demonstrate why simpler tests are not possible.

At this point it is worth noting the difference between the control problem treated here and the multidimensional variational problem treated in classical texts.[64] In the classical treatment certain continuity properties are required of the state vector $\underline{q}(\tau)$. For example, it is to be of Class D^1. In the control problem some components of the state vector have their derivatives influenced directly by the control vector and need be of class D^1; but others may have only their second, third, or n^{th} derivatives so affected and therefore need be of class D^2, D^3, or D^n, respectively. It is this lack of uniformity of the continuity properties that distinguishes the control problem and is a direct consequence of the presence of externally applied control inputs. Thus both the necessary and sufficient conditions are somewhat different.

The basic necessary conditions are the Euler equations. The equivalent of the strengthened Legendre necessary conditions is the requirement that $[F_{mm}]$ be positive definite for there to be a minimum of $\mathscr{P}$ and that it be negative definite for there to be a maximum. The requirement that $[\phi_A(\ell)]$ $\ell = 1, 2, \ldots N$ be definite of the same sign or that $[\phi_A(\tau)]$, $t \le \tau \le T$ be nonsingular corresponds to the strengthened Jacobi conditions. As in the classical variational calculus, the Euler and the strengthened Legendre and Jacobi conditions are sufficient conditions for the existence of an optimum with respect to all possible "weak" variations.[9,10,25,26,64,71]

Both the necessary and the sufficiency conditions are local in nature. Of course if the local necessary conditions are not satisfied anywhere, then no optimum can exist, and if the local sufficiency conditions are satisfied for several trajectories, the global optimum must correspond to one of them. Furthermore, all the necessary and sufficient conditions are subject to the previously described restrictions on differentiability of F and $\underline{G}$, with respect to $\underline{q}$ and $\underline{m}$. In addition, optima may exist on the boundaries of the region $\mathcal{R}$ within which F and $\underline{G}$ have the required differentiability properties. Thus one should not try to use the sufficiency conditions presented here in place of an engineering analysis to ascertain on physical grounds whether the stationary point found is indeed an optimum.

The fundamental condition for the solution of a dynamic optimization problem is the Euler condition, and the most effort is expended in satisfying it. The Legendre conditions are usually obvious, and if the Jacobi conditions are violated, the fact becomes evident during an attempt to solve the Euler conditions. Whether the solution of the Euler conditions is indeed an optimum is best ascertained on physical grounds.

2.3. Stability Properties of Euler Equations

The symmetry properties of the matrices in the incremental Euler difference or differential equations imply the instability of these equations. It will be shown that the equations have no stable equilibrium points and that every equilibrium point is a saddle-type singularity to which there converge n stable solutions and from which there diverge n other unstable solutions.

Consider the incremental Euler differential equations

$$q'] = [P]q] + [R]\lambda]$$

$$\lambda'] = [Q]q] - [P^T]\lambda] \qquad (2.91)$$

If there is an equilibrium point, then in its neighborhood $[P]$, $[Q]$, and $[R]$ are constants. Therefore, to investigate stability in the vicinity of the equilibrium point one can make use of transform methods. On taking the Laplace transform of Equation 2.91 one obtains

$$\left([P] - [I]s\right)q(s)] \qquad + [R]\lambda(s)] = \text{const.}$$

$$[Q]q(s)] \quad \left([P^T + [I]s\right)\lambda(s)] = \text{const.} \tag{2.92}$$

The stability of the solutions is governed by the location of the roots of the polynomial

$$p(s) = \left\| \begin{bmatrix} [P] - [I]s & [R] \\ [Q] & -[P]^T - [I]s \end{bmatrix} \right\| \tag{2.93}$$

in the complex s plane. Roots in the right half-plane correspond to unstable characteristic solutions (growing exponentials), and roots in the left half-plane correspond to stable characteristic solutions (decaying exponentials).

Since the determinant of a matrix equals the determinant of its transpose

$$\left\| \begin{bmatrix} [P] - [I]s & [R] \\ [Q] & -[P^T] - [I]s \end{bmatrix} \right\| = \left\| \begin{bmatrix} [P^T] - [I]s & [Q] \\ [R] & -[P] - [I]s \end{bmatrix} \right\| \tag{2.94}$$

where use has been made of the fact that [Q] and [R] are symmetric. By interchanging columns, then rows, one obtains successively

$$\left\| \begin{bmatrix} [P^T] - [I]s & [Q] \\ [R] & -[P] - [I]s \end{bmatrix} \right\| = \left\| \begin{bmatrix} -[Q] & -[P^T] + [I]s \\ -[P] - [I]s & [R] \end{bmatrix} \right\|$$

$$= \left\| \begin{bmatrix} [P] + [I]s & [R] \\ [Q] & -[P^T] + [I]s \end{bmatrix} \right\| \tag{2.95}$$

so that

$$\left\| \begin{bmatrix} [P] - [I]s & [R] \\ [Q] & -[P^T] - [I]s \end{bmatrix} \right\| = \left\| \begin{bmatrix} [P] - [I](-s) & [R] \\ [Q] & -[P^T] - [I](-s) \end{bmatrix} \right\| \tag{2.96}$$

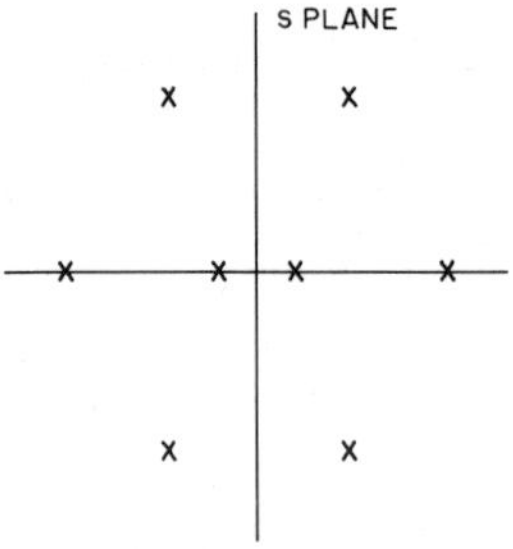

Fig. 2.4. Location of the characteristic roots of the Euler differential equations

Therefore, the characteristic polynomial of Equation 2.93 contains only even powers of s, and so its roots must be located symmetrically about the imaginary axis in the s plane, as illustrated in Fig. 2.4. Thus for each stable characteristic solution of Equation 2.91 there is a corresponding unstable characteristic solution with the same time constant.

In a similar manner the Euler difference equation

$$\begin{aligned} q(k+\Delta)] &= [\hat{P}]q(k)] + [\hat{R}]\ \lambda(k)] \\ \lambda(k-\Delta)] &= -[\hat{Q}]q(k)] + [\hat{P}]^T \lambda(k)] \end{aligned} \tag{2.97}$$

in terms of Z transforms becomes

$$\begin{aligned} \left([\hat{P}] - [I]z\right)q(z)] + \qquad [\hat{R}]\lambda(z)] &= \text{const.} \\ -[\hat{Q}]\ q(z)] + \left([\hat{P}]^T - [I]z^{-1}\right)\lambda(z)] &= \text{const.} \end{aligned} \tag{2.98}$$

and its characteristic solutions are stable or unstable depending on whether the corresponding roots of

$$p(z) = \left\|\begin{bmatrix} [\hat{P}] - [I]z & [\hat{R}] \\ -[\hat{Q}] & [\hat{P}] - [I]z^{-1} \end{bmatrix}\right\| \tag{2.99}$$

are outside or inside of the unit circle in the z plane. By equating the determinant of the matrix to the determinant of its transpose, interchanging columns, then rows, one obtains

$$\left\| \begin{bmatrix} [\hat{P}] - [I]\,z & [\hat{R}] \\ -[\hat{Q}] & [\hat{P}]^T - [I]\,z^{-1} \end{bmatrix} \right\| = \left\| \begin{bmatrix} [\hat{P}]^T - [I]\,z & -[\hat{Q}] \\ [\hat{R}] & [\hat{P}] - [I]\,z^{-1} \end{bmatrix} \right\|$$

$$= \left\| \begin{bmatrix} -[\hat{Q}] & -[\hat{P}]^T + [I]\,z \\ [\hat{P}] - [I]\,z^{-1} & -[\hat{R}] \end{bmatrix} \right\|$$

$$\left\| \begin{bmatrix} [\hat{P}] - [I]\,z & [\hat{R}] \\ -[\hat{Q}] & [\hat{P}]^T - [I]\,z^{-1} \end{bmatrix} \right\| = \left\| \begin{bmatrix} [\hat{P}] - [I]\,z^{-1} & -[\hat{R}] \\ -[\hat{Q}] & [\hat{P}]^T - [I]\,z \end{bmatrix} \right\| \tag{2.100}$$

which shows that the polynomial of Equation 2.99 is invariant under the transformation of z into z^{-1} so that for each root within the unit circle there is another root, a reciprocal of the first, outside of the unit circle, as illustrated in Figure 2.5.

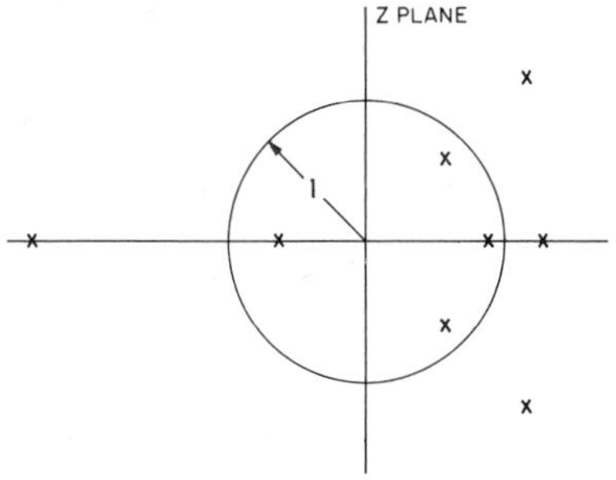

Fig. 2.5 Location of the characteristic roots of the Euler difference equations

Thus it has been shown that both the difference and the differential Euler equations contain n stable and n unstable characteristic solutions about the equilibrium point. Therefore, every equilibrium point is a saddle-type singularity from which there radiate n stable and n unstable characteristic solutions.

At the equilibrium point of the Euler equations (looking now at the original Euler equations, Equation 2.17), the following conditions are satisfied:

$$\underline{G}(\tau, \underline{q}(\tau), \underline{m}(\tau), \underline{u}(\tau)) = \underline{0} \tag{2.101}$$

$$\nabla_q F(\tau, T, \underline{q}(\tau), \underline{m}(\tau), \underline{u}(\tau))] = [J_q(\underline{G}(\tau, \underline{q}(\tau), \underline{m}(\tau), \underline{u}(\tau)))]^T \lambda(\tau)] \tag{2.102}$$

$$\nabla_m F(\tau, T, \underline{q}(\tau), \underline{m}(\tau), \underline{u}(\tau))] = [J_m(\underline{G}(\tau, \underline{q}(\tau), \underline{m}(\tau), \underline{u}(\tau)))]^T \lambda(\tau)] \tag{2.103}$$

But these are the conditions that $F(\tau, T, \underline{q}, \underline{m}, \underline{u})$ be stationary with respect to variations in $\underline{q}$ and $\underline{m}$ subject to the constraint that

$$\underline{G}(\tau, \underline{q}, \underline{m}, \underline{u}) = 0 \tag{2.104}$$

In other words, this is the condition for a steady-state optimum of $\mathcal{P}$.

Therefore if there is a steady-state $\underline{q}$ and $\underline{m}$, then the optimum steady-state $\underline{m}$ and the resultant steady-state $\underline{q}$ yield an equilibrium point of the Euler equations and so can be used to find that point. Having found the optimum $\underline{m}$, the resultant steady-state $\underline{q}$ is found from Equation 2.101, and then $\lambda]$ is obtained from Equations 2.102 and 2.103. Since $[J_m(\underline{G})]$ is of rank n_m, n_m components of $\lambda]$ can be defined from 2.103. If $\underline{G}$ is controllable, $[J_q(\underline{G})]$ is of rank $n-n_m$, and the remaining components of $\lambda]$ can thus be obtained from Equation 2.102.

Conversely, one might wish to use the Euler equations to calculate the steady-state optimum. Since the equilibrium point of Equation 2.91 is unstable, it cannot be obtained by solving the Euler equations towards the "steady state." One may suspect that the unstable Euler equation can be changed into another equation that has the same equilibrium point but is stable. Unfortunately, there is no simple way of manipulating the matrices to achieve this.

If

$$\frac{d}{d\tau} q] = [P]\, q] \tag{2.105}$$

is stable, then very often

$$\begin{aligned} \frac{d}{d\tau} q] &= [P] q] + [R]\, \lambda] \\ \frac{d}{d\tau} \lambda] &= -[Q] q] + [P]^T \lambda] \end{aligned} \tag{2.106}$$

will also be stable. However, this is not necessarily so; indeed, nonpathological examples were met when it was unstable. Nevertheless, because of its simplicity it is often worth trying.

2.4. Treatment of Special Forms of System Description

In the optimizing procedures of Section 2.2 the general nonlinear dynamic system was considered as being described by equations of the form

$$\frac{\triangleright}{\Delta}\underline{q}(k) = \underline{G}(\,\tau, \underline{q}(k), \underline{m}(k), \underline{u}(k)\,) \tag{2.107}$$

in the discrete time case, and in the continuous case by

$$\frac{d}{d\tau}\underline{q}(\tau) = \underline{G}(\,\tau, \underline{q}(\tau), \underline{m}(\tau), \underline{u}(\tau)\,) \tag{2.108}$$

This is general enough to describe any lumped parameter system; however, other descriptions are often more convenient to use. This became apparent in Section 2.2 during attempts to construct the [M] matrix and express the Euler equations in terms of a single vector variable.

In that connection it was argued that if the system is controllable, the incremental Euler equations can be transformed into the form

$$\underline{m}(k)] = \sum_{i=0}^{r} [C_i(k)]q(k+i\Delta)] \tag{2.109}$$

or in the continuous case

$$\underline{m}(\tau)] = \sum_{i=0}^{r} [C_i(\tau)]q^{(i)}(\tau)] \tag{2.110}$$

where $[C_r(k)]$ and $[C_r(\tau)]$ are nonsingular.
If in a region $\mathcal{R}$ in the $(\underline{q}, \underline{m}, \tau)$ space $\underline{G}$ is of class C^1 with respect to $\underline{q}$ and $\underline{m}$, and if the incremental equation, as evaluated about every trajectory in $\mathcal{R}$, is controllable, then the $[C_i(k)]$'s can be pieced together and the system described in the form

$$\underline{m}(k) = \underline{G}(\,\tau,\ q(k+i\Delta),\ i = 0, 1, 2, \ldots r,\ \underline{u}(k)\,) \tag{2.111}$$

or in terms of differences

$$\underline{m}(k) = \underline{G}(\,\tau,\ \overset{i}{\triangleright} q(k),\ i = 0, 1, 2, \ldots r,\ \underline{u}(k)\,) \tag{2.112}$$

Similarly, in the continuous time case Equation 2.108 is reducible to

$$\underline{m}(\tau) = \underline{G}(\,\tau,\ q^{(i)}(\tau),\ i = 0, 1, 2, \ldots r,\ \underline{u}(\tau)\,) \tag{2.113}$$

Although possible in principle, such reductions may of course be difficult to carry out in practice; but on the other hand, system description may be given in this form in the first place.

Still another commonly used description of the behavior of a system is in terms of its impulse response and the convolution integral. It is generally used with linear systems, although it may sometimes be useful in nonlinear situations.[75] In such a case the description takes the form

$$q(\tau)] = [\phi(t,\tau)]q(t)] + \int_t^{\tau} [\phi(t,\xi)]m(\xi)]d\xi \qquad (2.114)$$

where $[\phi(t,\tau)]$ is the system impulse response matrix.

If system description in terms of Equations 2.111, 2.112, 2.113, or 2.114 is used, the performance criterion can be expressed in terms of a single variable as

$$\mathscr{P} = \sum_{k=t}^{T-\Delta} \Delta F\Big((k, T, \underline{q}(k+i\Delta), i = 0,1,2, \ldots r, \underline{G}(k, \underline{q}(k+i\Delta), i = 0,1,2,\ldots r, \underline{u}(k)), \underline{u}(k)\Big) \qquad (2.115)$$

$$\mathscr{P} = \sum_{k=t}^{T-\Delta} \Delta F\Big((k, T, \overset{i}{\triangleright}\underline{q}(k), i = 0,1,2, \ldots r, \underline{G}(k, \overset{i}{\triangleright}\underline{q}(k), i = 0,1,2,\ldots r, \underline{u}(k)), \underline{u}(k)\Big) \qquad (2.116)$$

$$\mathscr{P} = \int_t^T F\Big(\tau, T, \underline{q}^{(i)}(\tau), i = 0,1,2, \ldots r, \underline{G}(\tau, q^{(i)}(\tau), i = 0,1,2, \ldots r, \underline{u}(\tau))\ \underline{u}(\tau)\Big)d\tau \qquad (2.117)$$

$$\mathscr{P} = \int_t^T F\Big(\tau, T, [\phi(\tau,t)]q(t)] + \int_t^{\tau} [\phi(\tau,\xi)]m(\xi)]d\xi, \underline{m}(\tau), \underline{u}(\tau)\Big)d\tau \qquad (2.118)$$

respectively. It will be shown how the Euler equations in terms of a single variable can be derived from each of these descriptions.

The differential of $\mathscr{P}$ in Equation 2.115 contains terms of the form

$$\sum_{k=t}^{T-\Delta} \ldots \underline{dq}(k+\ell)\nabla_{q(k+\ell)}F(k, T, \underline{q}(k+i\Delta), i = 0,1, \ldots r, \underline{G}(k), \underline{u}(k))] \ldots \qquad (2.119)$$

which is equivalent to

$$\sum_{k=t+\ell\Delta}^{T+(\ell-1)\Delta} \ldots \underline{dq}(k)\nabla_{q(k+(i-\ell)\Delta)}F(k-\ell\Delta, T, \underline{q}(k+(i-\ell)\Delta), i = 0,1, \ldots r, \underline{G}(k-\ell\Delta), \underline{u}(k-\ell\Delta))] \qquad (2.120)$$

If we define Z as the delay operator such that

$$Z^i(\underline{y}(k)) = \underline{y}(k+i\Delta) \qquad (2.121)$$

then the contribution of the above term to the coefficient of $\underline{dq(k)}$ is

$$Z^{-\ell}\left\{\nabla_{q(k+\ell\Delta)} F(\, k, T, \underline{q}(k+i\Delta),\ i = 0,1, \ldots r, \underline{G}(k),\ \underline{u}(k)\,)]\right\} \tag{2.122}$$

so that

$$\underline{dZ^{\ell}\ (\, q(k)\,)}f(k)] \rightarrow \underline{dq(k)}\ Z^{-\ell}(\, f(k)\,)] \tag{2.123}$$

Therefore the Euler equation resulting from $\mathcal{P}$ in Equation 2.115 is

$$\sum_{\ell=0}^{r} Z^{-\ell}\Big\{\nabla_{q(k+\ell\Delta)} F(\, k, T,\ \underline{q}(k+i\Delta),\ i = 0,1,\ \ldots\ r,\ \underline{G},\ \underline{u}(k)\,)]$$

$$+ [J_{q(k+\ell\Delta)}\big(\underline{G}(\, k,\ \ \underline{q}(k+i\Delta),\ i = 0,1,\ \ldots\ r\ ,\underline{u}(k))\big)]^{T}$$

$$\nabla_G F(\, k,\ T,\ \underline{q}(k+i\Delta),\ i=0,\ 1,\ \ldots\ r,\ \ \underline{G}(k),\ \underline{u}(k)\,)]\Big\} = 0] \tag{2.124}$$

Since the operators Z and $\triangleright$ are related by

$$\overset{\ell}{\triangleright} = (Z-1)^{\ell} \tag{2.125}$$

it follows that

$$\underline{d\ \overset{\ell}{\triangleright}q(k)}\ f\ (k)] = \underline{d(Z-1)^{\ell}\ (\, q(k)\,)}\, f\ \ (k)] \rightarrow \underline{dq(k)}\ (Z^{-1}\ -\ 1)^{\ell}(\, f(k)\,)] \tag{2.126}$$

but since

$$\overset{\ell}{\triangleleft} = (1\ -\ Z^{-1})^{\ell} \tag{2.127}$$

this becomes

$$\underline{d\ \ \overset{\ell}{\triangleright}q(k)}\ \ f(k)] \rightarrow \underline{dq(k)}(\ -\triangleleft\,)^{\ell}\ (f(k)\,)] \tag{2.128}$$

This relation can then be used to write down the Euler equation for $\mathcal{P}$ of Equation 2.116.

$\mathcal{P}$ in Equation 2.117 is the limiting case of the $\mathcal{P}$ in Equation 2.116 as $\Delta \rightarrow 0$. Since the differential operators are defined as

$$\lim_{\Delta \to 0} \left(\frac{\triangleleft}{\Delta}\right)^{\ell} = \frac{d}{d\tau} = \lim_{\Delta \to 0} \left(\frac{\triangleright}{\Delta}\right)^{\ell} \tag{2.129}$$

the relation expressed by Equation 2.128 becomes in the limit as $\Delta \to 0$

$$\underline{d\left(\frac{d^{\ell}}{d\tau^{\ell}} q(\tau)\right)} f(\tau)] \to \underline{dq(\tau)} (-1)^{\ell} \frac{d^{\ell}}{d\tau^{\ell}} \left(f(\tau)\right)] \tag{2.130}$$

allowing one to derive the Euler equation for the $\mathcal{P}$ of Equation 2.117. In Equations 2.123, 2.128, and 2.130 the symbol $\to$ meaning "corresponds to" rather than the = sign was used because the process of differentiating with respect to each of the variables at successive time instants forms not only the Euler equation but also the appropriate boundary conditions.

To consider $\mathcal{P}$ of Equation 2.118 one again replaces the integrals by sums. Then on taking the differential, one obtains

$$d\mathcal{P} = \sum_{k=t}^{T-\Delta} \Delta \left\{ \underline{dm(k)} \nabla_m F(k)] + \left(\sum_{\ell=t}^{k-\Delta} \Delta \underline{dm(\ell)}, [\phi(k, \ell+\Delta)]^T\right) \nabla_q F(k)]\right\} \tag{2.131}$$

On collecting the coefficients of $\underline{dm(k)}$,

$$d\mathcal{P} = \sum_{k=t}^{T-\Delta} \Delta \, \underline{dm(k)} \left\{\nabla_m F(k)] + \sum_{\ell=k+\Delta}^{T-\Delta} \Delta\left([\phi(\ell, k+\Delta)]^T \nabla_q F(\ell)]\right)\right\} \tag{2.132}$$

so that the Euler equation becomes

$$\nabla_m F(k, T, \underline{q}(k), \underline{m}(k), \underline{u}(k))] + \sum_{\ell=k+\Delta}^{T-\Delta} \Delta [\phi(\ell, k+\Delta)]^T \nabla_q F(\ell, T, \underline{q}(\ell), \underline{m}(\ell), \underline{u}(\ell))] = 0 \tag{2.133}$$

and in the continuous time case

$$\nabla_m F(\tau, T, \underline{q}(\tau), \underline{m}(\tau), \underline{u}(\tau)) + \int_{\tau}^{T} [\phi(\xi, \tau)]^T \nabla_q F(\xi, T, \underline{q}(\xi), \underline{m}(\xi), \underline{u}(\xi))] d\xi = 0] \tag{2.134}$$

Thus

$$d\left(\sum_{\ell=t}^{k-\Delta} \Delta \underline{m(\ell)}\, [\phi(k, \ell+\Delta)]^T\right) f(k)] \rightarrow \underline{dm(k)} \left(\sum_{\ell=k+\Delta}^{T-\Delta} \Delta [\phi(\ell, k+\Delta)]^T f(\ell)]\right) \tag{2.135}$$

and

$$d\left(\int_t^{\tau} \underline{m(\xi)}\, [\phi(\tau, \xi)]^T d\xi\right) f(\tau)] \rightarrow \underline{dm(\tau)} \int_{\tau}^{T} [\phi(\xi, \tau)]^T f(\xi)] d\xi \tag{2.136}$$

In this way, using the rules expressed by Equations 2.123, 2.128, 2.130, and 2.136, one can write down the Euler equation when the system description is in terms of Equations 2.111, 2.112, 2.113, and 2.114, respectively, as well as any combination thereof.

2.5. Time Delays and Distributed Parameter Systems

The systems treated so far have been those describable by ordinary difference or differential equations the state of which was defined by n parameters, that is, by a finite dimensional vector. Systems which require an infinite set of parameters to describe their state, the distributed parameter systems, represent a more difficult problem. Indeed, the presently known techniques are capable of dealing with only a limited number of cases from this general class. The most important subclass of solvable problems includes systems containing pure time delays. This subclass will be discussed first; then it will be shown how the subclass can be expanded to include systems describable by partial differential equations of the convection type.

In the discrete time case, time delays are not a new problem. Indeed, the difference equation itself is a description of a system the dynamics of which are made up entirely of time delays of length Δ. It is only in the limit as $\Delta \rightarrow 0$ that a new phenomenon appears.

Consider an element with a transfer function $\frac{e^{-sT_o}}{s}$, described by the differential equation

$$\frac{d}{d\tau} q(\tau + T_o) = m(\tau) \tag{2.137}$$

In terms of a finite difference approximation, this would be

$$q(k+(K+1)\Delta) - q(k+K\Delta) = \Delta m(k) \tag{2.138}$$

where $\Delta K = T_o$.

To specify the solution for $q(k)$, $k = t, t+\Delta, \ldots,$ one needs not only $m(k)$, $k = t, t+\Delta, \ldots$ but also K+1 parameters $q(t), q(t+\Delta)$, $q(t+2\Delta), \ldots q(t+K\Delta)$ so that the system is of order K+1. Letting $\Delta \to 0$ so that Equation 2.138 approaches Equation 2.137, one makes $K \to \frac{T_o}{\Delta}$ so that the order of the system becomes unbounded and in the limit it becomes a distributed parameter system, while the state vector $q(t), q(t+\Delta), \ldots q(t+K\Delta)$ becomes a state function $q(\xi), t \leq \xi < T_o$.

Consider the general dynamic system with time delays described by the differential equations

$$\begin{aligned} \frac{d}{d\tau} q_i(\tau + T_{i0}) = G_i \Big(&\tau, q_1(\tau + T_{i,1,1}), q_1(\tau + T_{i,1,2}), \ldots, q_1(\tau + T_{i,1,K_{i1}}), \\ &q_2(\tau+T_{i,2,1}), q_2(\tau+T_{i,2,2}), \ldots, q_2(\tau+T_{i,2,K_{i2}}), \\ &\ldots\ldots\ldots\ldots\ldots\ldots\ldots\ldots\ldots\ldots \\ &q_n(\tau+T_{i,n,1}), q_n(\tau+T_{i,n,2}), \ldots, q_n(\tau+T_{i,n,K_{in}}), \\ &m_1(\tau), m_2(\tau), \ldots m_{n_m}(\tau), \underline{u}(\tau) \Big) \qquad i = 1, 2, \ldots n \end{aligned} \tag{2.139}$$

These equations represent the following causal relationships: Application of $\underline{m}$ at time τ causes a delayed response in $\frac{d}{d\tau} q_i$ at time $\tau + T_{i0}$ $i = 1, 2, \ldots n$ the magnitude of which depends on the state of the system at times $\tau + T_{i,j,\ell}$ $j = 1, 2, \ldots n$; $\ell = 1, 2, \ldots K_{i,j}$, the accumulation of $\frac{d}{d\tau} q_i$, the term $\int_{-\infty}^{\tau} \frac{d}{d\xi} q_i(\xi) d\xi$ is $q_i(\tau)$. For these causal relations to hold, that is, for the system to be physically realizable, it is necessary that

$$T_{i0} \geq 0 \quad i = 1, 2, \ldots n \tag{2.140}$$

and

$$T_{i,j,\ell} \leq T_{i0} \quad i = 1, 2, \ldots n; \; j = 1, 2, \ldots n; \; \ell = 1, 2, \ldots K_{ij} \tag{2.141}$$

In the interest of conciseness of notation, Equation 2.139 will be written as

$$\frac{d}{d\tau}\underline{q}(\tau+T_{i0}) = \underline{G}(\ \tau, \underline{q}(\tau+T_{i,j,k}), \underline{m}(\tau), \underline{u}(\tau)\ ) \tag{2.142}$$

where T_{i0} and $T_{i,j,k}$ represent the various time delays involved in Equation 2.139.

If the performance criterion for a problem is

$$\mathcal{P} = \int_t^T F(\ \tau, T, \underline{q}(\tau), \underline{m}(\tau), \underline{u}(\tau)\ )d\tau \tag{2.143}$$

then expressing it and Equation 2.142 in terms of finite differences and introducing the Lagrange multipliers, one obtains

$$\mathcal{P}_1 = \sum_{k=t}^{T-\Delta} \Delta \Big\{ F(\ k, T, \underline{q}(k), \underline{m}(k), \underline{u}(k)\ ) + \underline{\lambda}(k)\Big(\frac{q(k+\Delta(K_{i0}+1)\ )\ ] - q(k+\Delta K_{i0})]}{\Delta}$$

$$- \underline{G}(\ k, \underline{q}(k+\Delta\, K_{i,j,k}), \underline{m}(k), \underline{u}(k)\ )\Big)\Big\} \tag{2.144}$$

where

$$\Delta K_{i0} = T_{i0}$$

$$\Delta K_{i,j,\ell} = T_{i,j,\ell} \tag{2.145}$$

In Equation 2.144, as in Equation 2.142, K_{i0} and $K_{i,j,k}$ stand for the various possible time delays as spelled out in detail in Equation 2.139. The differential of $\mathcal{P}_1$ is

$$d\mathcal{P}_1 = \sum_{k=t}^{T-\Delta} \Delta \Big\{ \underline{dq(k)}\ \nabla_q F(\ k, T, \underline{q}(k), \underline{m}(k), \underline{u}(k)\ )]$$

$$+ \underline{dm(k)}\ \nabla_m F(\ k, T, \underline{q}(k), \underline{m}(k), \underline{u}(k)\ )]$$

$$+ \underline{dq(k+\Delta(1+K_{i0}))}\ \frac{1}{\Delta}\lambda(k)] - \underline{dq(k+\Delta K_{i0})}\ \frac{1}{\Delta}\lambda(k)]$$

$$- \underline{dq(k+\Delta K_{i,j,\ell})}[J_q\Big(\underline{G}(\ k, \underline{q}(k+\Delta K_{i,j,\ell}), \underline{m}(k),\ \underline{u}(k))\Big)\ ]^T\lambda(k)]$$

$$- \underline{dm(k)}\ [J_m\Big(\underline{G}(\ k, \underline{q}(k+\Delta K_{i,j,\ell}), \underline{m}(k), \underline{u}(k)\ )\Big)]^T\lambda(k)]$$

$$+ \underline{d\lambda(k)}\ \Big(\frac{\triangleright}{\Delta}q(k+\Delta K_{i0})] - G(\ k, \underline{q}(k+\Delta K_{i,j,\ell}), \underline{m}(k), \underline{u}(k)\ )]\Big)\Big\}$$

$$\tag{2.146}$$

or if one changes the limits of the summations,

$$
\begin{aligned}
d\mathcal{P}_1 = & \sum_{k=t}^{T-\Delta} \Delta \Big\{ \underbrace{d\lambda(k)} \Big(\frac{\triangleright}{\Delta} q(k+\Delta K_{i0})\big] - G(k, \underline{q}(k+\Delta K_{i,j,\ell}), \underline{m}(k), \underline{u}(k)\,)\big]\Big)\Big\} \\
& + \sum_{k=t}^{T-\Delta} \Delta \Big\{ \underbrace{dq(k)} \nabla_q F(k, T, \underline{q}(k), \underline{m}(k), \underline{u}(k)\,)\big]\Big\} \\
& + \sum_{k=t+T_{i0}+\Delta}^{T+T_{i0}} \Delta \left\{ \underbrace{dq(k)} \frac{1}{\Delta} \lambda\,(k-\Delta(K_{i0}+1)\,)\,\big] \right\} \\
& - \sum_{k=t+T_{i0}}^{T+T_{i0}-\Delta} \Delta \left\{ \underbrace{dq(k)} \frac{1}{\Delta} \lambda\,(k-\Delta K_{i0})\,\big] \right\} \\
& - \sum_{k=t+T_{i,j,k}}^{T+T_{i,j,k}-\Delta} \Delta \Big\{ \underbrace{dq(k)} \big[J_q \Big(\underline{G}(k, \underline{q}(k-\Delta(K_{i,j,\ell} - K'_{i,j,\ell}), \underline{m}(k-\Delta K_{i,j,\ell}), \\
& \qquad \underline{u}(k)\,)\Big)\big]^T \lambda(k-\Delta K_{i,j,\ell})\big]\Big\} \\
& + \sum_{k=t}^{T-\Delta} \Delta \Big\{ \underbrace{dm(k)} \Big(\nabla_m F(k, T, \underline{q}(k), \underline{m}(k), \underline{u}(k)\,)\big] \\
& - \big[J_m \Big(G(k, T, \underline{q}(k+\Delta K_{i,j,\ell}), \underline{m}(k), \underline{u}(k)\,)\Big)\big]^T \lambda(k)\big]\Big)\Big\}
\end{aligned}
$$

(2.147)

where $K'_{i,j,k}$ was used to indicate that not all time delays in $\underline{G}$ are of the same length. The necessary condition for an optimum is that the coefficients of each of the differentials vanish. If

$$K = \text{Max}\,(K_{i0}+1,\ K_{i,j,\ell},\ i, j = 1, 2, \ldots n;\ \ell = 1, 2, \ldots K_{ij})$$

(2.148)

then the Euler equations become

$$\frac{\triangleright}{\Delta}\, q(k+\Delta K_{i0})] = G(\, k, \underline{q}(k+\Delta K_{i,j,k}), \underline{m}(k), \underline{u}(k)\,)]$$

$$\frac{\triangleleft}{\Delta}\, \lambda(k-\Delta K_{i0})] = [J_q\Big(\underline{G}(\, k, \underline{q}(k-\Delta(K_{i,j,\ell} - K'_{i,j,\ell})), \underline{m}(k-\Delta K_{i,j,\ell}), \underline{u}(k)\,)\Big)]^T \lambda(k-\Delta K_{i,j,\ell})]$$

$$- \nabla_q F(\, k, T, \underline{q}(k), \underline{m}(k), \underline{u}(k)\,)]$$

$$\nabla_m F(\, k, T, \underline{q}(k), \underline{m}(k), \underline{u}(k)\,)] = [J_m\Big(\underline{G}(\, k, T, \underline{q}(k+\Delta K_{i,j,\ell}), \underline{m}(k), \underline{u}(k))\Big)]^T \lambda(k)]$$

$$k = t+\Delta K, t+\Delta(K+1), \ldots \; T-\Delta \qquad (2.149)$$

The vanishing of the coefficients of the remaining differentials constitutes the boundary condition. In the limit as $\Delta \to 0$ the Euler equations become

$$\frac{d}{d\tau} q(\tau+T_{i0})] = G(\, \tau, \underline{q}(\tau+T_{i,j,\ell}), \underline{m}(\tau), \underline{u}(\tau)\,)]$$

$$\frac{d}{d\tau} \lambda(\tau-T_{i0})] = [J_q\Big(\underline{G}(\, \tau, \underline{q}(\tau-T_{i,j,\ell}+T'_{i,j,\ell}), \underline{m}(\tau-T_{i,j,\ell}), \underline{u}(\tau))\Big)]^T \lambda(\tau-T_{i,j,\ell})]$$

$$- \nabla_q F(\, \tau, T, \underline{q}(\tau), \underline{m}(\tau), \underline{u}(\tau)\,)]$$

$$\nabla_m F(\, \tau, T, \underline{q}(\tau), \underline{m}(\tau), \underline{u}(\tau)\,)] = [J_m\Big(\underline{G}(\, \tau, \underline{q}(\tau+T_{i,j,\ell}), \underline{m}(\tau), \underline{u}(\tau))\Big)]^T \lambda(\tau)]$$

$$\mathrm{Max}(T_{i0}, T_{i,j,\ell}) < \tau < T \qquad (2.150)$$

In general, it is not possible to generate the solution of these Euler equations numerically, as described in Appendix C. Whereas the solution of the first equation of Equation 2.15 can be generated forward in time, the solution of the second equation can be propagated only backward in time. Only then does it represent a causal generation of $\underline{\lambda}$ from $\frac{d}{d\tau}\underline{\lambda}$. Thus, in general, the Euler equations cannot be integrated simultaneously, either forward or backward in time. One cannot generate their solution on an electronic analog computer, for there is no physically realizable system whose behavior is governed by such equations.

An alternate to dealing with the system description of Equation 2.139 is to consider the representation

$$\underline{m}(\tau) = \underline{G}\left(\tau, \frac{d^i}{d\tau^i} q(\tau+T_{ij}), i = 0, 1, 2, \ldots r; j = 1, 2, \ldots K_i, \underline{u}(\tau) \right) \tag{2.151}$$

where for physical realizability it is necessary that

$$T_{r,j} = T_r \geq 0 \qquad j = 1, 2, \ldots K_r$$

$$T_r \geq T_{i,j,} \quad i = 1, 2, \ldots r-1; \; j = 1, 2, \ldots K_i \tag{2.152}$$

The expression for $\wp$ can then be written as

$$\wp = \int_t^T \Big\{ F\big(\tau, T, \underline{q}^{(i)}(\tau), i = 0, 1, \ldots r, \; \underline{G}(\tau, q^{(i)}(\tau+T_{ij}), i = 0, 1, \ldots r; \; j = 1, 2, \ldots K_i, \; \underline{u}(\tau)), \; \underline{u}(\tau) \big) \Big\} d\tau$$

The differential of $\wp$ contains terms of the form

$$\int_t^T \Big\{ \ldots \underbrace{dq^{(i)}(\tau+T_{ij})} \, \nabla_{q^{(i)}(\tau+T_{ij})} F(\tau)] \ldots \Big\} d\tau \tag{2.153}$$

or with changes of variables,

$$\int_{t+T_{ij}}^{T+T_{ij}} \Big\{ \ldots \underbrace{dq^{(i)}(\tau)} \; \nabla_{q^{(i)}(\tau+T_{ij})} F(\tau - T_{ij})] \ldots \Big\} d\tau \tag{2.154}$$

Terms of this kind have been treated in Section 2.4. Thus if we define the continuous delay operator Z^{T_o} as

$$Z^{T_o}(\underline{q}(\tau)) = \underline{q}(\tau+T_o) \tag{2.155}$$

then

$$\underline{dZ^{T_{ij}}\left(\frac{d^i}{d\tau^i} q(\tau)\right)f(\tau)]} = \underline{dq(\tau)}\, (-1)^i Z^{-T_{ij}}\left(\frac{d^i}{d\tau^i} f(\tau)]\right) \qquad (2.156)$$

which completes the set of rules listed in Section 2.4 for deriving Euler equations.

An Euler equation derived this way may still be "physically unrealizable" and not solvable sequentially. In accordance with the rule expressed by Equation 2.152, the highest derivative is $\underline{q}^{(2r)}$, and the longest possible time delay associated with it is zero since $T_r \geq T_{i,j}$. On the other hand, if the coefficient of $dq^{(i)}(\tau+T_{i,j})]$ is $q^{(i*)}(\tau+T_{i*,j})]$, then this gives rise to a term in the Euler equations $(-1)^i q(i+i*)(\tau+T_{i*,j}-T_{i,j})]$. Therefore its delay can be either positive or negative, and in two such terms both cases may occur. Thus once more the possibility arises that it may be impossible to solve it sequentially.

Of course, the Euler equations do not always turn out to be physically unrealizable. Consider the system represented by the transfer function $\frac{e^{-sT_o}}{s}$, described by the equation

$$m(\tau) = \frac{d}{d\tau} q(\tau+T_o) \qquad (2.157)$$

and let it be required to optimize the performance criterion

$$\mathcal{D} = \int_0^T \left\{\gamma\left(q(\tau) - i(\tau)\right)^2 + \left(m(\tau) - \rho q(\tau)\right)^2\right\} d\tau \qquad (2.158)$$

Introducing a Lagrange multiplier and rewriting in terms of finite differences, one obtains

$$\mathcal{D}_1 = \sum_{k=t}^{T-\Delta} \Delta \left\{\gamma\left(q(k) - i(k)\right)^2 + \left(m(k) - \rho q(k)\right)^2 + 2\lambda(k)\left(\frac{1}{\Delta} q(k+(K_o+1)\Delta) - \frac{1}{\Delta} q(k+K_o\Delta) - m(k)\right)\right\} \qquad (2.159)$$

where $\Delta K_o = T_o$.

Forming the differential of $\mathcal{D}_1$, one obtains

$$d\mathcal{P}_1 = \sum_{k=t}^{T-\Delta} \Delta 2 \Big\{\Big((\gamma + \rho^2)q(k) - \gamma i(k) - \rho m(k)\Big)dq(k) + \Big(m(k) - \rho q(k) - \lambda(k)\Big)dm(k)$$

$$+ \frac{1}{\Delta}\lambda(k)dq(k+(K_o+1)\Delta) - \frac{1}{\Delta}\lambda(k)dq(k+K_o\Delta)$$

$$+\Big(\frac{1}{\Delta}q(k+(K_o+1)\Delta) - \frac{1}{\Delta}q(K_o\Delta+k) - m(k)\Big)d\lambda(k)\Big\} \qquad (2.160)$$

or

$$\tfrac{1}{2}d\mathcal{P}_1 = \sum_{k=t}^{T-\Delta}\Delta\Big\{\Big(\frac{\triangleright}{\Delta}q(k+K_o\Delta) - m(k)\Big)d\lambda(k) + \Big(m(k) - \rho q(k) - \lambda(k)\Big)dm(k)$$

$$+ \Big((\gamma + \rho^2)q(k) - \rho m(k) - \gamma i(k)\Big)dq(k)\Big\} + \sum_{k=t+(K_o+1)\Delta}^{T+\Delta K_o}\Delta\Big\{\frac{1}{\Delta}\lambda(k-(1+K_0)\Delta)dq(k)\Big\}$$

$$- \sum_{k=t+K_o\Delta}^{T+(K_o-1)\Delta}\Delta\Big\{\frac{1}{\Delta}\lambda(k-K_o\Delta)dq(k)\Big\} \qquad (2.161)$$

Since $m(t)$ cannot affect $q(k)$ for $t \leq k < t + (K_o+1)\Delta$, then, $dq(k) = 0$ for $t \leq k < (K_o+1)\Delta$, and there remains

$$\tfrac{1}{2}d\mathcal{P}_1 = \sum_{k=t}^{T-\Delta}\Delta\Big\{\Big(\frac{\triangleright}{\Delta}q(k+K_o\Delta) - m(k)\Big)d\lambda(k) + \Big(m(k) - \rho q(k) - \lambda(k)\Big)dm(k)\Big\}$$

$$+ \sum_{k=t+(K_o+1)\Delta}^{T+K_o\Delta}\Delta\Big\{\Big(-\frac{\triangleleft}{\Delta}\lambda(k-K_o\Delta) + (\gamma + \rho^2)q(k) - \rho m(k) - \gamma i(k)\Big)dq(k)\Big\}$$

$$(2.162)$$

which in the limit as $\Delta \to 0$ leads to the Euler differential equations

$$\frac{d}{d\tau} q(\tau+T_o) = m(\tau)$$

$$\frac{d}{d\tau} \lambda(\tau) = (\gamma + \rho^2)q(\tau+ T_o) - \rho m(\tau+T_o) - \gamma i(\tau+T_o)$$

$$\lambda(\tau) = m(\tau) - \rho q(\tau) \qquad (2.163)$$

and after eliminating $m(\tau)$,

$$\frac{d}{d\tau} q(\tau+T_o) = \rho q(\tau) + \lambda(\tau)$$

$$\frac{d}{d\tau} \lambda(\tau) = \gamma q(\tau+T_o) - \rho\lambda(\tau+T_o) - \gamma i(\tau+T_o) \qquad (2.164)$$

The solution of the first equation of Equation 2.164 can be propagated forward in time, and the solution of the second equation can be propagated backward. However, there is no way of propagating the two solutions simultaneously. One cannot solve these equations on an analog computer. This becomes more apparent if one eliminates $\lambda(\tau)$ to form

$$\frac{d^2}{d\tau^2} q(\tau) + \rho\left(\frac{d}{d\tau} q(\tau+T_o) - \frac{d}{d\tau} q(\tau- T_o)\right) - (\gamma + \rho^2)q(\tau) + \gamma i(\tau) = 0 \qquad (2.165)$$

On the other hand, if $\rho = 0$, which is a physically meaningful situation, then the Euler equation becomes

$$\frac{d^2}{d\tau^2} q(\tau) = \gamma\left(q(\tau) - i(\tau)\right) \qquad (2.166)$$

and is now solvable on an analog computer.

If the Euler equations are not physically realizable, then they cannot be solved sequentially; but it is still possible to construct the $[M]$ matrix and using it solve simultaneously for $q(k)$, $k = t, t+\Delta, \ldots T-\Delta$. However, in doing so one approximates the continuous problem by a finite difference formulation, and in that case it becomes the basic problem treated in Sections 2.1 and 2.2. Indeed, the most generally applicable method of dealing with time delays is to approximate the continuous time problem by a discrete time formulation.

The Euler equation resulting from the system description of Equation 2.151, if it is physically realizable, is of the form

$$\underline{q}^{(2r)}(\tau) = \underline{f}(\tau, \underline{q}^{(i)}(\tau+T^*_{i,j}), i = 0, 1, \ldots 2r-1; j = 1, 2, \ldots K_i, \underline{m}(\tau - T_r))$$

$$t+T_r \leq \tau < T \qquad (2.167)$$

where $T^*_{i,j} \leq 0$, for $i = 0, 1, \ldots 2r-1$; $j = 1, 2, \ldots K_i$. It is solvable sequentially and differs from the Euler equations treated in Section 2.4 only through the way in which boundary conditions enter.

System description in terms of Equation 2.151 represents the following causal relation: Application of $\underline{m}$ at time τ causes a delayed response in $\frac{d^r}{d\tau^r}\underline{q}$ at time $\tau + T_r$ the magnitude of which depends on the state of the system at times $\tau+T_{i,j}$ and $\underline{q}^{(i)}(\tau)$, $i = 0, 1, 2, \ldots r-1$ are generated as the integrals of $\frac{d^r}{d\tau^r}\underline{q}$. Thus the application of control effort at time t cannot affect $\underline{q}(\tau)$ or any of its derivatives for $t \leq \tau < t+T_r$. Consequently the differentials of $\underline{q}(\tau)$ for $t \leq \tau < t+T_r$ are zero, and so the Euler equations defining $\underline{q}(\tau)$ need hold only for $t+T_r \leq \tau$. At the same time this defines $\underline{m}(\tau)$ for $t \leq \tau$. The values of $\underline{q}(\tau)$ for $\tau < t+T_r$ (this includes the derivatives of $\underline{q}$) are the initial conditions for the Euler equation. The initial conditions are no longer a finite set of parameters but rather an entire function, hence an infinite set of values. In such a case, rather than there being a set of state variables, there is a state function. It may well be that Equation 2.167 is an ordinary differential equation not involving delays as is the case in Equation 2.166 (Equation 2.165 in the case that $\rho = 0$). Then the initial condition of the Euler equation for determination of $\underline{m}(t)$ is $\underline{q}(t+T_r)$, which is a vector. However, $\underline{q}(t+T_r)$ is not measurable at time t, and it is only calculable from $\underline{q}(t)$ and $\underline{m}(\tau)$, $t-T_r \leq \tau < t$, so that in the last analysis it is still a function which determines the state of the system and the initial conditions for the Euler equations. Similarly, the end-point conditions may specify a final state function $\underline{q}(\tau)$ for $T \leq \tau < T+T_r$

There are a number of distributed parameter systems, the control of which is equivalent to the control of a system with time lag As an example (Problem 5 of Appendix E) let us consider the control of a plant described by the partial differential equations

$$\frac{\partial q(\tau, x)}{\partial x} + \frac{1}{V_o}\frac{\partial q(\tau, x)}{\partial \tau} = f_1(q(\tau, x))$$

$$m(\tau) = \frac{\partial q(\tau, 0)}{\partial \tau} \qquad (2.168)$$

to optimize the performance criterion

$$\mathcal{P} = \int_t^T \left\{ F_1(\, m(\tau)\,) + F_2(\, q(\tau, X)\,) \right\} d\tau \tag{2.169}$$

or

$$\mathcal{P} = \int_t^T \left\{ F_1(\, m(\tau)\,) + \int_0^X F_2(\, q(\tau, x)\,)\, dx \right\} d\tau \tag{2.170}$$

If $q(\tau, x)$ corresponds to a temperature distribution, then the first part of Equation 2.168 may be describing the behavior of a heat exchanger or a fixed-bed chemical reactor. In the first case the performance criterion of Equation 2.169 may refer to the outlet fluid temperature, and in the second case the criterion of Equation 2.170 may deal with the conversion achieved in the bed, that is, outlet stream composition.

If one defines f_2 as

$$f_2(y) = \int f_1(y)\,dy \tag{2.171}$$

then the general solution of Equation 2.168 is

$$f_2(\, q(\tau, x)\,) = \tfrac{1}{2}(x + V_o\tau) + g(x - V_o\tau) \tag{2.172}$$

and if

$$q(\tau, 0) = \rho(\tau) \tag{2.173}$$

then

$$q(\tau, x) = f_2^{-1}\left\{ x + f_2\left(\rho(\tau - \frac{x}{V_o})\right)\right\} \tag{2.174}$$

Defining still another function

$$F_3(x, y) = F_2\left(f_2^{-1}(\, x + f_2(y)\,)\right) \tag{2.175}$$

$\mathcal{P}$ of Equation 2.169 becomes

$$\mathcal{P} = \int_t^T \left\{ F_1\left(\frac{d\rho(\tau)}{d\tau}\right) + F_3\left(X, \rho(\tau - \frac{x}{V_o})\right)\right\} d\tau \tag{2.176}$$

which is a member of a class of problems treated above.

Similarly, $\mathcal{D}$ of Equation 2.170 becomes

$$\mathcal{D} = \int_t^T \left\{ F_1\left(\frac{d\rho(\tau)}{d\tau}\right) + \int_0^X F_3\left(x, \rho(\tau - \frac{x}{V_o})\right) dx \right\} d\tau \tag{2.177}$$

However, now the time delay is variable, and the problem is somewhat different.

Formulating Equation 2.177 in terms of a finite difference approximation and taking the differential, there results

$$d\mathcal{D} = \sum_{k=t}^{T-\Delta} \Delta \left\{ \frac{\partial F_1\left(\frac{\triangleright}{\Delta}\rho(k)\right)}{\partial\left(\frac{\triangleright}{\Delta}\rho(k)\right)} \left(\frac{d\rho(k+\Delta) - d\rho(k)}{\Delta}\right)\right.$$

$$\left. + \sum_{\ell=0}^{M-1} \Delta \left\{ \frac{F_3\left(\ell\Delta', \rho(k - \frac{\ell\Delta'}{V_o})\right)}{\partial \rho\left(k - \frac{\ell\Delta'}{V_o}\right)} d\rho(k - \frac{\ell\Delta'}{V_o}) \right\}\right\} \tag{2.178}$$

where $\Delta' = \frac{X}{M}$ and the time scale is chosen so that $\Delta = \frac{\Delta'}{V_o}$.
After collecting terms involving $d\rho(k)$, Equation 2.178 becomes

$$d\mathcal{D} = \Delta \left\{ - \frac{\partial F_1(0)}{\partial \rho'} \frac{d\rho(0)}{\Delta} + \sum_{\ell=0}^{M-1} \sum_{k=t}^{\ell\Delta} \Delta' \frac{\partial}{\partial \rho} F_3(\ell\Delta', \rho(-k)) \, d\rho(-k) \right.$$

$$+ \sum_{k=t}^{T-\Delta} \left\{ \frac{1}{\Delta} \left(\frac{\partial}{\partial \rho'} F_1(k-\Delta) - \frac{F_1(k)}{\partial \rho'} \right) + \sum_{\ell=0}^{K} \Delta' \frac{\partial F_3}{\partial \rho}(\ell\Delta', \rho(k)) \right\} d\rho(k)$$

$$\left. + \frac{\partial F_1(T-\Delta)}{\partial \rho'} \frac{d\rho(T)}{\Delta} \right\} = 0 \tag{2.179}$$

where $K = \text{Min}(M-1, \frac{T-k}{\Delta})$ so that in the limit as $\Delta \to 0$ the Euler equation becomes

$$\frac{d}{d\tau}\left(\frac{\partial F_1(\rho'(\tau))}{\partial \rho'}\right) = \int_0^X \frac{\partial}{\partial \rho} F_3(x, \rho(\tau)) \, dx \qquad (2.180)$$

This is but a simple example of how distributed parameter systems may be treated. There are no general rules for treating general distributed parameter systems, but the above example is indicative of what can be achieved and what techniques are to be used.

2.6. Constraints in Variational Problems

In the procedures developed so far no account has been made of possible limitations on the allowable range of the state or control variables, their derivatives or integrals. Requirements that certain relations between variables be maintained were treated only with regard to the difference or differential equations governing the behavior of the plant. In this section a general treatment of constraints will be attempted.

If the variables $\underline{m}$ and $\underline{q}$ are constrained such that

$$\underline{f}(\tau, \underline{q}(\tau), \underline{m}(\tau)) = 0 \qquad (2.181)$$

then one can introduce a new set of Lagrange multipliers $\underline{\mu}(\tau)$, add to the performance criterion a term

$$\int_t^T \underline{\mu(\tau)}\, f(\tau, \underline{q}(\tau), \underline{m}(\tau))]\, d\tau \qquad (2.182)$$

and require that it be stationary with respect to $\underline{\mu}(\tau)$ as well as the other variables. The modified performance criterion will be stationary only if Equation 2.181 is satisfied; then the value of the modified criterion will be equal to the original $\mathcal{P}$. This procedure will introduce into the Euler conditions an extra set of algebraic equations, Equation 2.181, and an extra set of variables $\underline{\mu}$.

Another possible constraint is a requirement that a condition of the form

$$\int_t^T f_i(\tau, \underline{q}(\tau), \underline{m}(\tau))\, d\tau \le \Gamma_i \qquad i = 1, 2, \ldots n \qquad (2.183)$$

be satisfied. One can again introduce a set of constant Lagrange multipliers $\underline{\rho}$, add to the performance criterion a term

$$\int_t^T \underline{\rho}\, f(\tau, \underline{q}(\tau), \underline{m}(\tau))]\, d\tau \qquad (2.184)$$

and carry out the optimization for a range of values of the multipliers $\underline{\rho}$, expressing the optimum $\mathcal{D}$ as a function of $\underline{\rho}$. One then performs what is but static optimization with respect to $\underline{\rho}$ subject to the constraint of Equation 2.183.

Most important of all are the inequality constraints, that is, requirements of the form

$$m_{\ell_i}(\tau) \leq m_i(\tau) \leq m_{u_i}(\tau)$$

$$q_{\ell_i}(\tau) \leq q_i(\tau) \leq q_{u_i}(\tau) \qquad (2.185)$$

and there are several ways of incorporating them. The simplest and often the most convenient approach is to subtract from $\mathcal{D}$ terms of the form

$$\int_t^T \mathcal{P}_{m_i}(m_i(\tau))d\tau, \quad \text{and} \quad \int_t^T \mathcal{P}_{q_i}(q_i(\tau))d\tau$$

respectively, where $\mathcal{P}_{m_i}$ and $\mathcal{P}_{q_i}$ are penalty functions such that they contribute a large penalty to $\mathcal{D}$ if their arguments are about to violate the bounds expressed by Equation 2.185, but little if their arguments are within bounds. The exact form of $\mathcal{P}$ is not crucial. It must have the continuity properties required of the integrand of $\mathcal{D}$, but within this requirement it can take on any convenient form and incorporate as sharp a constraint as may be desired. The most convenient function of this kind has been found to be

$$\mathcal{P}_{m_i}(m_i) = \begin{cases} k_2\hat{m}^2 + (k_2 - k_1)(1 + 2\hat{m}) & \hat{m} < -1 \\ k_1\hat{m}^2 & |\hat{m}| < 1 \\ k_2\hat{m} + (k_2 - k_1)(1 - 2\hat{m}) & \hat{m} > 1 \end{cases} \qquad (2.186)$$

or

$$\mathcal{P}_{m_i}(m_i) = (\hat{m})^r \qquad (2.187)$$

where

$$\hat{m} = \left(\frac{m_i - \frac{1}{2}(m_{u_i} + m_{\ell_i})}{m_{u_i} - m_{\ell_i}}\right)$$

$k_2 > k_1$, and r is as high an even power as is necessary to achieve a sharp enough constraint. Values of r of anywhere from 8 to 128 have been found useful.

For example, the control of a system described by the equation

$$m = q^{(n)} + \sum_{i=0}^{n-1} a_i q^{(i)} \tag{2.188}$$

to maximize a performance criterion

$$\mathcal{P} = -\int_t^{\infty} \left(q(\tau) - i(\tau)\right)^2 d\tau \tag{2.189}$$

subject to the constraint

$$|m| \leq 1 \tag{2.190}$$

may be considered in this formulation as the maximization of

$$\mathcal{P} = -\int_t^{\infty} \left\{\left(q(\tau)-i(\tau)\right)^2 + \left(m(\tau)\right)^r\right\} d\tau \tag{2.191}$$

The resultant Euler equations are

$$q_1' = -\sum_{i=1}^{n} a_{n-i} q_i + \mathrm{sign}(\lambda_1) \left|\frac{2}{r} \lambda_1\right|^{\frac{1}{r-1}}$$

$$q_j' = q_{j-1} \qquad j = 2, 3, \ldots n$$

$$\lambda_j' = a_{n-j} \lambda_j - \lambda_{j+1} \qquad j = 1, 2, \ldots n-1$$

$$\lambda_n' = a_o \lambda_1 + q_n - i(\tau)$$

$$m = \mathrm{sign}(\lambda_1) \left|\frac{2}{r} \lambda_1\right|^{\frac{1}{r-1}} \tag{2.192}$$

The function $\text{sign}(x)\left|\frac{2}{r}x\right|^{\frac{1}{r-1}}$ is shown plotted in Figure 2.6, where it is seen to approach the function sign(x) as $r \to \infty$. This would cause $m(\tau)$ to be ± 1. The exact solution to the problem

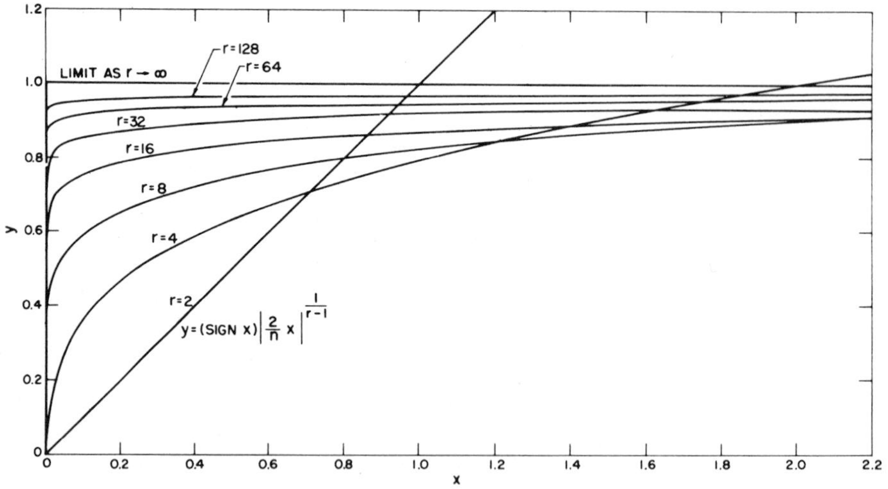

Fig. 2.6. Function $\text{sign}(x)\left|\frac{2x}{r}\right|^{\frac{1}{r-1}}$

specified in Equations 2.188, 2.189, and 2.190 is known, and indeed $m(\tau)$ always equals plus or minus one.

It must be emphasized that the above is only an approximate solution, and in each case in which it is applied further analysis is necessary to determine just how good an approximation it is. On the other hand, it has the advantage that it is easy to apply in complicated problems and can be used to constrain both the state and the control variables. Furthermore, if the constraints are imposed in this way, the derivatives of the variables generated by the Euler equations remain continuous, which will be seen to be a significant computational advantage.

Another way of handling inequality constraints which leads to an exact solution is through a change of variables. If $x(\tau)$ is the variable to be constrained between $x_u(\tau)$ and $x_\ell(\tau)$, one introduces a variable $y(\tau)$ given by

$$x(\tau) = f(\tau, y(\tau)) \tag{2.193}$$

where f is such that $f(\tau, y)$ is a differentiable function which is always between the limits of $x_u(\tau)$ and $x_\ell(\tau)$ for all y. Substituting $f(\tau, y)$ for x, one then performs the optimization with respect to y. Thus for any $y(\tau)$ that may result, $x(\tau)$ will remain within the constraint limits.

For example, if a system described by the equation

$$m(\tau) = q''(\tau) \tag{2.194}$$

is to be controlled so as to minimize a performance criterion

$$\mathcal{P} = \int_t^T \left\{\left(q(\tau) - i(\tau)\right)^2 + \left(m(\tau)\right)^2\right\} d\tau \tag{2.195}$$

subject to the constraint of Equation 2.190, then a suitable change of variable is

$$m(\tau) = \sin\left(\Theta(\tau)\right) \tag{2.196}$$

With this transformation and after incorporating the Lagrange multipliers, one obtains

$$\mathcal{P} = \int_t^T \left\{\left(q_2(\tau) - i(\tau)\right)^2 + \sin^2\Theta(\tau) + 2\lambda_1(\tau)\left(q_1(\tau) - \sin\Theta(\tau)\right) + 2\lambda_2(\tau)\left(q_2(\tau) - q_1(\tau)\right)\right\} d\tau \tag{2.197}$$

so that the Euler equations are

$$q_1' = \sin\Theta = m \qquad \lambda_1' = -\lambda_2$$

$$q_2' = q_1 = q \qquad \lambda_2' = q_2 - i$$

$$\sin\Theta \cos\Theta = \lambda_1 \cos\Theta \tag{2.198}$$

For the same example, if the constraint was on the state rather than the control variable, for instance

$$q(\tau) \geq 0 \tag{2.199}$$

then a suitable substitution might be

$$q(\tau) = y^2(\tau) \tag{2.200}$$

The performance criterion would become

$$\wp = \int_t^T \left\{ \left(y^2(\tau) - i(\tau)\right)^2 + \left(\frac{d^2}{d\tau^2}\left(y^2(\tau) \right)\right)^2 \right\} d\tau \qquad (2.201)$$

and the resultant Euler equation is

$$y\left\{2y''''y + 8y'''y' + 6(y'')^2 + y^2 - i\right\} = 0 \qquad (2.202)$$

However, the first three terms are but the fourth derivative of y^2, so that Equation 2.202 reduces to

$$\sqrt{q(\tau)}\left\{q''''(\tau) + q(\tau) - i(\tau)\right\} = 0 \qquad (2.203)$$

One should note that there are several ways in which the Euler equations, Equation 2.198, can be satisfied. If one chooses m such that the last relation of Equation 2.198 is satisfied in the form

$$m(\tau) = \sin\Theta(\tau) = \lambda_1(\tau) \qquad (2.204)$$

(this can be done whenever $|\lambda_1(\tau)| \leq 1$), then the Euler equation becomes the same as for the case when $m(\tau)$ is unconstrained. However, one can also choose

$$m(\tau) = \sin\Theta(\tau) = \pm 1 \qquad (2.205)$$

in which case the last relation is satisfied since

$$\cos\Theta(\tau) = \cos\left(\sin^{-1}(\pm 1) \right) = 0 \qquad (2.206)$$

Furthermore, the Euler equations will be satisfied if one switches $m(\tau)$ arbitrarily between the values of +1 and -1 and in the event that $|\lambda_1(\tau)| \leq 1$ between the values of +1, $\lambda_1(\tau)$ and -1. Thus it is possible to satisfy the Euler equations with various discontinuous functions $m(\tau)$ and trajectories $q(\tau)$ with discontinuous second derivatives.

Similarly, the Euler equation, in the case in which a constrained state variable is involved (Equation 2.203), factors into two equations, the unconstrained Euler equation and an equation specifying the solution on the constraint boundary, in this case

$$\sqrt{q(\tau)} = 0 \qquad (2.207)$$

Thus if i = 0 and the initial and final conditions are

$$q(t) = 1 \qquad q'(t) = 1 \qquad q(T) = 0 = q'(T) \tag{2.208}$$

any ony of the trajectories illustrated in Figure 2.7 may satisfy Equation 2.203.

In a similar way, Equation 2.198 factors into the unconstrained Euler equation and an equation defining a solution on the constraint boundary.

This factoring property of the Euler equations subject to inequality constraints follows from what is a generalization of the chain rule of differentation. If the original performance criterion is

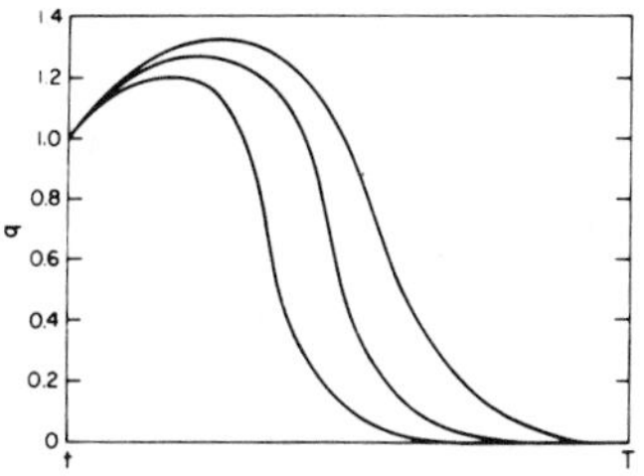

Fig. 2.7. Trajectories with a constrained state variable

$$\mathcal{P} = \int_t^T F(\tau, q(\tau), q'(\tau))d\tau \tag{2.209}$$

then the Euler equation resulting from a variation of $q(\tau)$ is

$$\delta q(\tau)\left(\frac{\partial F}{\partial q} - \frac{d}{d\tau}\frac{\partial F}{\partial q'}\right) = 0 \tag{2.210}$$

but if

$$q(\tau) = f(y(\tau)) \tag{2.211}$$

then since

$$\delta q(\tau) = \delta y(\tau)\frac{\partial f}{\partial y} \tag{2.212}$$

the Euler equation resulting from a variation of $y(\tau)$ is

$$\delta y(\tau)\frac{\partial f}{\partial y}\left(\frac{\partial F}{\partial q} - \frac{d}{d\tau}\frac{\partial F}{\partial q'}\right) = 0 \tag{2.213}$$

Since at the constraint f(y) remains equal to $q_u(\tau)$ or $q_\ell(\tau)$ for a range of y, then at the constraints

$$\frac{\partial f}{\partial y} = 0 \tag{2.214}$$

Thus Equation 2.213 is satisfied either by the solution of the unconstrained equation or by the solutions on the constraint boundary:

$$q(\tau) = q_u(\tau) \text{ or } q_\ell(\tau) \tag{2.215}$$

When such factoring of the Euler equations is possible, additional properties of the optimum trajectory must be invoked to choose the desired solution. In continuous time problems one can use the Weierstrass-Erdman conditions and the fact that $\underline{q}$, $\underline{m}$, and $\underline{\lambda}$ must satisfy the Euler equations to specify the condition

$$\lim_{\Delta \to 0} F(\tau - \Delta, \underline{q}(\tau), \underline{m}(\tau - \Delta), \underline{u}(\tau - \Delta)) - \underbrace{\frac{d}{d\tau} q(\tau - \Delta)\lambda(\tau)}] =$$

$$F(\tau + \Delta, \underline{q}(\tau), \underline{m}(\tau + \Delta), \underline{u}(\tau + \Delta)) - \underbrace{\frac{d}{d\tau} q(\tau + \Delta)\lambda(\tau)}] \tag{2.216}$$

Equation 2.216 together with the equations describing the system serve to determine which branch of the Euler equations constitutes the optimum trajectory.

Thus in the example of Equation 2.198,

$$\left(q_2(\tau) - i(\tau - \Delta)\right)^2 + \left(m(\tau - \Delta)\right)^2 - 2q_1'(\tau - \Delta)\lambda_1(\tau) = \left(q_2(\tau) - i(\tau + \Delta)\right)^2$$
$$+ \left(m(\tau + \Delta)\right)^2 - 2q_1'(\tau + \Delta)\lambda_1(\tau) \tag{2.217}$$

and

$$q_1'(\tau) = m(\tau) \tag{2.218}$$

so that

$$m^2(\tau + \Delta) - 2m(\tau + \Delta)\lambda_1(\tau) = \left(q(\tau) - i(\tau - \Delta)\right)^2 - \left(q(\tau) - i(\tau + \Delta)\right)^2$$
$$+ m^2(\tau - \Delta) - 2m(\tau - \Delta)\lambda_1(\tau) \tag{2.219}$$

If i is continuous at τ, then there are two ways of satisfying Equation 2.219, either $m(\tau+\Delta) = m(\tau-\Delta)$ or $m(\tau+\Delta) + m(\tau-\Delta) = 2\lambda_1(\tau)$ Thus $m(\tau)$ is either continuous or else switches between +1 and -1 when $\lambda_1(\tau)$ changes sign. By the same token, if $i(\tau)$ is discontinuous, $m(\tau)$ will in general also be discontinuous at that point. The same result could also have been deduced by introducing a penalty function of the form shown in Equation 2.187 and considering the limit as $r \to \infty$.

As was pointed out in Section 2.2, in the discrete time case there is no analytic analog to the Weierstrass-Erdman conditions.

Thus it is not possible to choose the correct branch of the Euler equations. By analogy with the continuous time case, one would expect that, for sufficiently small Δ anyway, m(k) would remain on one or the other of the constraint boundaries and switch only by passing through the continuous range. The difficulty of course is that the passage through the continuous range may all happen in one Δ.

When one is using a penalty function to incorporate effect of amplitude constraints, these difficulties are not encountered. Furthermore, the decisions involved in applying the Weierstrass-Erdman conditions which may be awkward to implement in an automatic computational scheme are avoided. For these reasons it has usually been found most convenient to account for inequality constraints by introducing the penalty functions.

2.7. Constant-Coefficient Linear Systems

A class of control problems for which dynamic optimization has been carried out by methods other than those presented here and for which considerable design experience has been accumulated is that in which the system is described by linear constant-coefficient differential equations and the performance criterion is quadratic and is to be weighed over the semi-infinite future time interval. It is therefore desirable to show how the approach presented in this work applies to that class of problems so that the methods may be compared. Furthermore, the behavior of the Euler equations deduced here will carry over in a qualitative way to more complicated problems.

A general linear constant-coefficient system can be described by the equation

$$q'] = [G_q]q] + [G_m]m] + [G_u]u] \tag{2.220}$$

where $[G_q]$, $[G_m]$, and $[G_u]$ are matrices of constant coefficients. The performance criterion to be treated is

$$\mathcal{P} = \lim_{T \to \infty} \int_t^T F(\underline{q}, \underline{m}, \underline{u})d\tau \tag{2.221}$$

subject to general end-point boundary conditions of the form

$$[A_A]q(T)] + [A_B]\lambda(T)] = B] \tag{2.222}$$

where F is a quadratic function of $\underline{q}$, $\underline{m}$, and $\underline{u}$ with constant coefficients and T is fixed.

Given the current value of the state vector $\underline{q}(t)$ and the values of the functions $u(\tau), t \leq \tau < T$, one seeks the current value of the control effort $\overline{m(t)}]$ such that $m(\tau)], t \leq \tau < T$ optimizes $\mathcal{P}$ and the resultant trajectory satisfies the prescribed end-point boundary conditions.

By introducing Lagrange multipliers $\underline{\lambda}$, one derives the Euler equations as

$$
\begin{aligned}
q'] &= [G_q]q] + [G_m]m] + [G_u]u] \\
\lambda'] &= [F_{qq}]q] + [F_{qm}]m] - [G_q]^T\lambda] + [F_{qu}]u] \\
[G_m]^T\lambda] &= [F_{mm}]m] + [F_{mq}]q] + [F_{mu}]u]
\end{aligned}
\tag{2.223}
$$

where

$$[F_{xy}] = [J_y(\nabla_x F)] \tag{2.224}$$

Since $[F_{mm}]$ is assumed to be nonsingular, $m]$ can be eliminated to yield

$$
\begin{aligned}
q'] &= [P]q] + [R]\lambda] + \hat{u}] \\
\lambda'] &= [Q]q] - [P]^T\lambda + \check{u}]
\end{aligned}
\tag{2.225}
$$

where

$$
\begin{aligned}
[P] &= [G_q] - [G_m][F_{mm}^{-1}][F_{mq}] \qquad & \hat{u}] &= [G_u]u] - [G_m][F_{mu}]u] \\
[Q] &= [F_{qq}] - [F_{qm}][F_{mm}^{-1}][F_{mq}] \qquad & \check{u}] &= [F_{qu}]u] - [F_{qm}][F_{mm}^{-1}][F_{mu}]u] \\
[R] &= [G_m][F_{mm}^{-1}][G_m^T]
\end{aligned}
\tag{2.226}
$$

so that $[Q]$ and $[R]$ are both symmetric.

One can find a matrix $[U]$ such that

$$[U]\begin{bmatrix}[P] & [R] \\ [Q] & [-P]^T\end{bmatrix}[U]^{-1} = [D] \tag{2.227}$$

where $[D]$ is the diagonal matrix of characteristic roots. As shown in Section 2.3, $\begin{bmatrix}[P] & [R] \\ [Q] & [-P]^T\end{bmatrix}$ has n characteristic roots in the right half s plane and n roots of opposite sign in the left half s plane. One can further require of [U] that [D] be of the form

$$[D] = \begin{bmatrix} [D_r] & [0] \\ [0] & [D_\ell] \end{bmatrix} \tag{2.228}$$

where $[D_r]$ contains only the roots with positive real parts and $[D_\ell]$ only those with negative real parts (imaginary roots are assumed to have real parts of $\pm\ \epsilon$) and that

$$[D_r] = -[D_\ell] \tag{2.229}$$

Thus if we define $[\phi_\ell(\tau, t)]$ and $[\phi_r(\tau, t)]$ by

$$\frac{\partial [\phi_\ell(\tau, t)]}{\partial \tau} = [D_\ell][\phi_\ell(\tau, t)] \qquad [\phi_\ell(t, t)] = [I]$$

$$\frac{\partial [\phi_r(\tau, t)]}{\partial \tau} = [D_r][\phi_r(\tau, t)] \qquad [\phi_r(t, t)] = [I] \tag{2.230}$$

then $[\phi_\ell(\tau, t)]$ decays to 0, whereas $[\phi_r(\tau, t)]$ grows unbounded as $\tau \to \infty$.

Defining

$$y_A] = [U_{AA}]q] + [U_{AB}]\lambda] \qquad \hat{\omega}] = [U_{AA}]\hat{u}] + [U_{AB}]\check{u}]$$

$$y_B] = [U_{BA}]q] + [U_{BB}]\lambda] \qquad \check{\omega}] = [U_{BA}]\hat{u}] + [U_{BB}]\check{u}] \tag{2.231}$$

where

$$\begin{bmatrix} [U_{AA}] & [U_{AB}] \\ [U_{BA}] & [U_{BB}] \end{bmatrix} = [U] \qquad [U]^{-1} = \begin{bmatrix} [U^-_{AA}] & [U^-_{AB}] \\ [U^-_{BA}] & [U^-_{BB}] \end{bmatrix} \tag{2.232}$$

the general solution of Equation 2.225 can be written as

$$y_A(T)] = [\phi_r(T,t)]y_A(t)] + \int_t^T [\phi_r(T,\xi)]\hat{\omega}(\xi)]d\xi$$

$$y_B(T)] = [\phi_\ell(T,t)]y_B(t)] + \int_t^T [\phi_\ell(T,\xi)]\check{\omega}(\xi)]d\xi \tag{2.233}$$

In terms of the new variables the end boundary conditions become

$$\left([A_A][U^-_{AA}] + [A_B][U^-_{BA}]\right)y_A(T)] + \left([A_A][U^-_{AB}] + [A_B][U^-_{BB}]\right)y_B(T)] = B] \tag{2.234}$$

and after substituting into Equation 2.234 from Equation 2.233, one obtains

$$\left([K_A][\phi_r(T,t)][U_{AA}] + [K_B][\phi_\ell(T,t)][U_{BA}]\right)q(t)] + \left([K_A][\phi_r(T,t)][U_{AB}] + [K_B][\phi_\ell(T,t)][U_{BB}]\right)\lambda(t)] = B] - [K_A]\int_t^T [\phi_r(T,\xi)]\hat{\omega}(\xi)]d\xi - [K_B]\int_t^T [\phi_\ell(T,\xi)]\check{\omega}(\xi)]d\xi \tag{2.235}$$

where

$$[K_A] = [A_A][U_{AA}] + [A_B][U_{BA}]$$

$$[K_B] = [A_A][U_{AB}] + [A_B][U_{BB}] \tag{2.236}$$

Thus the control law becomes

$$m(t)] = \mathcal{E}_c] - [\mathcal{E}_s]q(t)] + L_A(\underline{\hat{u}}(\tau))] + L_B(\underline{\check{u}}(\tau))] \tag{2.237}$$

where

$$\mathcal{E}_c] = [F^{-1}_{mm}][K_o]B]$$

$$[\mathcal{E}_s] = [F^{-1}_{mm}]\left\{[F_{mq}] + [K_o]\left([K_A][\phi_r(T,t)][U_{AA}] + [K_B][\phi_\ell(T,t)][U_{BA}]\right)\right\}$$

$$L_A(\hat{\underline{u}}(\tau))] = -[F_{mm}^{-1}][K_o]\left\{[K_A]\int_t^T [\phi_r(T,\xi)][U_{AA}][G_u]\hat{u}(\xi)]\,d\xi + [K_B]\int_t^T [\phi_\ell(T,\xi)][U_{BA}][G_u]\hat{u}(\xi)]\,d\xi\right\}$$

$$L_B(\check{\underline{u}}(\tau))] = [F_{mm}^{-1}]\left\{[F_{mu}] + [K_o]\left([K_A]\int_t^T [\phi_r(T,\xi)][U_A]\check{u}(\xi)\,d\xi + [K_B]\int_t^T [\phi_\ell T,\xi)][U_B]\check{u}(\xi)]\,d\xi\right)\right\} \qquad (2.238)$$

and

$$[K_o] = [G_m]^T\left([K_A][\phi_r(T,t)][U_{AB}] + [K_B][\phi_\ell(T,t)][U_{BB}]\right)^{-1}$$

$$[U_A] = [U_{AA}][G_m][F_{mu}] - [U_{AB}][F_{qu}] + [U_{AB}][F_{qm}][F_{mm}^{-1}][F_{mu}]$$

$$[U_B] = [U_{BA}][G_m][F_{mu}] - [U_{BB}][F_{qu}] + [U_{BB}][F_{qm}][F_{mm}^{-1}][F_{mu}] \qquad (2.239)$$

As $T \to \infty$, Equations 2.238 simplify to

$$[\mathscr{C}_c] = [0]$$

$$[\mathscr{C}_s] = [F_{mm}^{-1}]\left\{[F_{mq}] + [G_m]^T[U_{AB}]^{-1}[U_{AA}]\right\}$$

$$L_A(\hat{\underline{u}}(\tau))] = -[F_{mm}^{-1}]\left([U_{AB}]^{-1}\int_t^\infty [\phi_r(t,\xi)][U_{AA}][G_u]\hat{u}(\xi)]\,d\xi\right)$$

$$L_B(\check{\underline{u}}(\tau))] = [F_{mm}^{-1}]\left([F_{mu}] + [U_{AB}^{-1}]\int_t^\infty [\phi_r(t,\xi)][U_A]\check{u}(\xi)]\,d\xi\right) \qquad (2.240)$$

It should be noted that $L_A(\hat{\underline{u}}(\tau))]$ and $L_B(\check{\underline{u}}(\tau))]$ will exist only if $\hat{\underline{u}}(\tau)$ and $\check{\underline{u}}(\tau)$ increase not faster than $e^{\sigma\tau}$ where σ is the greatest lower bound on the real parts of the diagonal elements of $[D_r]$. Since σ will always be positive, L_A and L_B will converge for all $\underline{u}$ and $\underline{\omega}$, which grow as some finite power of τ.

Equation 2.237 illustrates the fact that the control law resulting from a linear control problem separates into the feedback and the director portions. The feedback part comprising $[\mathscr{C}_s]$ and $[\mathscr{C}_c]$

depends on the parameters of the system, the performed criterion, and the end-point boundary conditions but is completely independent of the functions $\hat{u}$ and $\check{u}$. Similarly, the director portion, that is, the operators $L_A(\ )]$ and $L_B(\ )]$, depends only on the system being controlled; $\hat{\underline{u}}(\tau)$ and $\check{\underline{u}}(\tau)$ enter only as the arguments of these linear integral operators. Thus in a system meant to adapt to varying characteristics of the desired outputs and disturbances, the feedback portion is not required to change. The director portion must have information about $\hat{\underline{u}}(\tau)$ and $\check{\underline{u}}(\tau)$ for $t \leq \tau < T$ and operate on it by the nonadapting operators $L_A(\ )]$ and $L_B(\ )]$ to generate $L_A(\ \hat{\underline{u}}(\tau)\ )]$ and $L_B(\ \check{\underline{u}}(\tau)\ )]$

As $T \to \infty$, the influence of the end-point boundary conditions on the controller vanishes, $\mathcal{C}_c]$ becomes zero, and the other portions of the controller approach constant values. As seen from Equation 2.238, the rate of approach is of the form

$$\frac{e^{\sigma T} + k_1 e^{-\sigma T}}{e^{\sigma T} + k_2 e^{-\sigma T}} \tag{2.241}$$

where σ is the real part of the smallest characteristic root of the Euler equations, so that the influence of the end conditions diminishes as $e^{-2\sigma T}$ For a trajectory which differs from the optimum trajectory by a norm ϵ at the end-point boundary conditions, the value of $m(t)]$ differs from the optimum by a norm of approximately $\epsilon k e^{-2\sigma T}$ Knowing σ and two suboptimum trajectories, one can compute k and estimate the error in $m(\tau)]$. By the same token, the error committed by solving the optimization problem for a finite instead of an infinite T decreases as $e^{-2\sigma T}$.

It is of interest to note that if one starts the solution of the constant-coefficient Euler equations from an arbitrary set of conditions at $\tau = T$ and propagates it backward in time, then the solution is unstable, and $q]$ and $\lambda]$ both grow without bound. However, the "ratio" of these two quantities, that is, the matrix $[\mathcal{C}_s]$ where

$$\lambda] = [\mathcal{C}_s]q] + \mathcal{C}_r] \tag{2.242}$$

does converge to a limit. This limit is the optimum control law, as expressed in the second relation of Equation 2.240, since the effect of the conditions at $\tau = T$ on $[\mathcal{C}_s]$ vanishes as $T - t \to \infty$. As shown in Chapter 3, this offers a relatively attractive way of computing $[\mathcal{C}_s]$.

The above discussion is not meant to imply that as $T \to \infty$ there ceases to exist a two-point boundary-value problem. Nothing could be further from the truth. As T increases, the influence of the error at the end boundary decreases; but at the same time the likelihood of a large error increases. In the limit as $T \to \infty$ any boundary condition can be replaced by the condition of boundedness of the error at $\tau = T$ because any departure from the optimum trajectory at a finite τ causes an infinite error at T as $T \to \infty$. This behavior is a direct consequence of the instability of the Euler equations. It will be seen in Chapter 3 that this has both advantages and disadvantages from the computational standpoint.

The possibility of replacing the end-point boundary conditions with a requirement on the boundedness of the error at T as $T \to \infty$ can be used to express in another form the solution to the single-input linear constant-coefficient problem. As shown in Section 2.2, any single-input system of the type described by Equation 2.220 can be reduced to the form

$$m = \sum_{i=0}^{n} a_i q^{(i)} + u \tag{2.243}$$

where u now includes all the functions u_1 and their derivatives (of order up to n-1) which resulted from the reduction of Equation 2.220 to Equation 2.243. Introducing Equation 2.243 into the performance criterion of Equation 2.221 and operating on it by the methods of Section 2.4, one obtains an Euler equation

$$\sum_{i=0}^{n} b_i q^{(2i)} = \omega \tag{2.244}$$

where ω now includes all the forcing terms, in general ω will involve the derivatives of the original functions of orders up to 2n-1 and therefore possibly impulses of up to that order.

On taking the Laplace transform of Equation 2.244, there results

$$\left(\sum_{i=0}^{n} s^{2i} b_i\right) q(s) = \omega(s) + \sum_{i=1}^{n} b_i \sum_{j=1}^{2i} s^{2i-j} q^{(j-1)}(t) \tag{2.245}$$

If one lets

$$\sum_{i=0}^{n} s^{2i} b_i = W(s)W(-s) \tag{2.246}$$

then

$$q(s) = \frac{1}{W(s)W(-s)}\left\{\omega(s) + \sum_{j=1}^{2n} \frac{1}{(j)!}\left\{\frac{d^j}{d\xi^j}\left(W(\xi)W(-\xi)\right)\Bigg|_{\xi=0}\right\}\sum_{i=1}^{j} s^{j-i}\overset{(i-1)}{q(t)}\right\} \tag{2.247}$$

or if one interchanges the order of summation

$$q(s) = \frac{1}{W(s)W(-s)}\left\{\omega(s) + \sum_{i=1}^{2n}\left\{\sum_{j=i}^{2n} \frac{1}{j!}\frac{d^j}{d\xi}\left(W(\xi)W(-\xi)\right)\Bigg|_{\xi=0}\right\}s^{j-i}\overset{(i-1)}{q(t)}\right\} \tag{2.248}$$

Once more one wishes to find the values of $q^{(i)}(t)$, $i = n, n+1, \ldots 2n-1$ such that for a given state $q^{(i)}(t)$, $i = 0, 1, \ldots n-1$ the solution of the Euler equations satisfies the end-point boundary conditions. These will be taken to be the requirement that the error be bounded, that is, that the coefficients of the partial fraction expansion of q(s) with poles corresponding to the roots of $W(s)W(-s)$ in the right half of the s plane all be zero. If the roots of $W(s)W(-s)$ are $\pm r_1, \pm r_2, \ldots, \pm r_n$ where the real part of each r_i is greater than zero and no roots are repeated, then this requirement is that

$$\sum_{i=n+1}^{2n}\left\{\sum_{j=i}^{2n} \frac{1}{j!}\frac{d^j}{d\xi^j}\left(W(\xi)W(-\xi)\right)\Bigg|_{\xi=0}\right\}r_k^{j-i}\overset{(i-1)}{q(t)}$$

$$= -\left\{\omega(r_k) + \sum_{i=1}^{n}\left\{\sum_{j=1}^{2n} \frac{1}{j!}\frac{d^j}{d\xi^j}\left(W(\xi)W(-\xi)\right)\Bigg|_{\xi=0}\right\} r_k^{j-i}\overset{(i-1)}{q(t)}\right\}$$

$$k = 1, 2, \ldots n \tag{2.249}$$

This represents a set of linear equations which can be solved to yield $q^{(n)}(t)$ as a function of $q^{(i)}(t)$, $i = 0, 1, \ldots n-1$ and the Laplace transform of $\omega(\tau)$, $t \leqslant \tau < \infty$.

Thus

$$q^{(n)}(t) = \sum_{i=0}^{n-1} C_i q^{(i)}(t) + \sum_{i=1}^{n} C_i^* \int_t^{\infty} e^{-r_i \tau} \omega(\tau) d\tau \tag{2.250}$$

and

$$m(t) = \sum_{i=0}^{n-1} (C_i + a_i) q^{(i)}(t) + \sum_{i=1}^{n} C_i^* \int_t^{\infty} e^{-r_i \tau} \omega(\tau) d\tau \tag{2.251}$$

In both of the techniques just presented it was necessary to factor an nth-degree polynomial to find the characteristic roots of the Euler equation. This corresponds exactly to the spectral factorization required in the analytic design theory. It is not suggested that these methods be used for computational purposes. More efficient computational schemes will be presented in the next chapter.

Chapter 3

CONTROL LAW COMPUTATIONS

3.1. Solution of Linear Two-Point Boundary Value Problems

It has been shown in Chapter 2 that, for a given dynamic system and a prescribed performance criterion, the optimum control law is specified as a solution of a two-point boundary value problem associated with the Euler difference or differential equations. This boundary value problem represents the basic necessary conditions, and the bulk of the work involved in finding the optimum control law is in obtaining its solution. This solution then has to be tested either by using the techniques outlined in Section 2.2 or by relying on the knowledge of the physical situation involved in order to ascertain that it indeed represents an optimum rather than merely a stationary point.

In the general control problem the solution of the two-point boundary value problem is difficult, and no systematic techniques are available. Therefore a major concern of this work has been the development of practically useful ways of computing solutions. These resolve into two classes: flooding techniques which attempt to specify the control law over a region in the space of $\underline{q}$ and $\underline{v}$ and point techniques which compute the optimum value of control effort for a single specified value of $\underline{q}$ and $\underline{v}$. The first class is useful for precalculating a control law, the second for use by an on-line control computer. An intermediate class is one in which one attempts to develop the control law in a Taylor series expansion about a point solution. In the case of a linear boundary value problem the control law is linear in $\underline{q}$ so that the Taylor series terminates with the linear terms which then specify the control law over the entire state space.

Analytic solutions of nonlinear two-point boundary value problems are available only in very special cases. For example, if

$$m(\tau) = G(\, q'(\tau), q(\tau)\,) \tag{3.1}$$

and

$$\mathcal{P} = \int_t^{\infty} F(\, q'(\tau), q(\tau), m(\tau)\,)d\tau \tag{3.2}$$

where neither G nor F involve time explicitly, the optimum control law is given implicitly by the relations

$$m(t) = G(\, q'(t), q(t)\,)$$

$$q'(t) = \frac{F(\, q'(t), q(t), m(t)\,) + C}{\dfrac{\partial F(q'(t), q(t), m(t)\,)}{\partial q'(t)} + \dfrac{\partial F(\, q'(t), q(t), m(t)\,)}{\partial m(t)} \dfrac{\partial G(\, q'(t), q(t)\,)}{\partial q'(t)}} \tag{3.3}$$

where C is to be chosen so that the solution satisfies the end-point boundary conditions.[43] Reference 72 lists a majority of the remaining nonlinear boundary value problems solvable analytically, none of which, however, correspond to a practically significant control situation.

On the other hand, linear boundary value problems can be solved in a systematic manner by what are at least quasi-analytic techniques and this in an even more general class of cases than that treated in Section 2.7. These techniques are the concern of the present section.

Consider the linear boundary value problem associated with the Euler differential equations

$$q'(\tau)] = [P(\tau)]q(\tau)] + [R(\tau)]\lambda(\tau)] + \hat{u}(\tau)]$$

$$\lambda'(\tau)] = [Q(\tau)]q(\tau)] - [P^T(\tau)]\lambda(\tau)] + \check{u}(\tau)] \qquad t \leq \tau < T \tag{3.4}$$

and the boundary conditions

$$q(t)] = q(t)]$$

$$[A_A]q(T)] + [A_B]\lambda(T)] = B] \tag{3.5}$$

It would have arisen from the optimization problem of the type described in Section 2.7 except that all the coefficients both in the plant description and in the performance criterion are now allowed to be functions of time. Thus Equations 3.4 and 3.5 correspond to Equations 2.225 and 2.222 except that all the coefficients depend on time so that the diagonalization procedure of Equation 2.227 cannot be carried out. However, one can still express the solution of Equation 3.4 as

$$q(T)] = [\phi_{11}(T,t)]q(t)] + [\phi_{12}(T,t)]\lambda(t)] + \hat{\omega}(T,t)]$$

$$\lambda(T)] = [\phi_{21}(T,t)]q(t)] + [\phi_{22}(T,t)]\lambda(t)] + \check{\omega}(T,t)] \tag{3.6}$$

where

$$\frac{\partial[\phi(\tau,t)]}{\partial \tau} = [G_E(\tau)][\phi(\tau,t)] \qquad [\phi(t,t)] = [I]$$

$$[G_E(\tau)] = \begin{bmatrix} [P(\tau)] & [R(\tau)] \\ [Q(\tau)] & -[P^T(\tau)] \end{bmatrix} \qquad [\phi(\tau, t)] = \begin{bmatrix} [\phi_{11}(\tau, t)] & [\phi_{12}(\tau, t)] \\ [\phi_{21}(\tau, t)] & [\phi_{22}(\tau, t)] \end{bmatrix}$$

$$\begin{bmatrix} \hat{\omega}(T, t)] \\ \check{\omega}(T, t)] \end{bmatrix} = \int_t^T \begin{bmatrix} \phi(\tau, t) \end{bmatrix} \begin{bmatrix} \hat{u}(\tau)] \\ \check{u}(\tau)] \end{bmatrix} d\tau \tag{3.7}$$

so that the boundary conditions can be rewritten as

$$\left([A_A][\phi_{12}(\tau, t)] + [A_B][\phi_{22}(T, t)]\right)\lambda(t)] = B] - [A_A]\hat{\omega}(T, t)] - [A_B]\check{\omega}(T, t)]$$

$$- \left([A_A][\phi_{11}(T, t)] + [A_B][\phi_{21}(T, t)]\right) q(t)] \tag{3.8}$$

If $m(t)]$ and $\lambda(t)]$ are related as in Equation 2.223 by

$$m(t)] = [F_{mm}(t)]^{-1}\left([G_m(t)]\lambda(t)] - [F_{mq}(t)]q(t)] - [F_{mu}(t)]u(t)]\right) \tag{3.9}$$

then from Equation 3.8 it follows that the control law is

$$m(t)] = [\mathcal{E}(T, t)]q(t)] + \mathcal{D}(T, t)] \tag{3.10}$$

where

$$[\mathcal{E}(T, t)] = -[F_{mm}(t)]^{-1}\Big\{[G_m^T(t)]\left([A_A][\phi_{12}(T, t)]\right.$$

$$\left. + [A_B][\phi_{22}(T, t)]\right)^{-1}\left([A_A][\phi_{11}(\tau, t)] + [A_B][\phi_{21}(T, t)]\right) + [F_{mq}(t)]\Big\}$$

$$\mathcal{D}(T, t)] = [F_{mm}(t)]^{-1}\Big\{[G_m^T(t)]\left([A_A][\phi_{12}(T, t)]\right.$$

$$\left. + [A_B][\phi_{22}(T, t)]\right)^{-1}\left(B] - [A_A]\hat{\omega}(T, t)] - [A_B]\check{\omega}(T, t)]\right)$$

$$- [F_{mu}(t)]u(t)]\Big\} \tag{3.11}$$

One should note that if the end-point boundary conditions specify $q(T)]$, then $[A_A] = [I]$ and $[A_B] = [0]$. But because $[\phi_{12}(t,t)] = [0]$, with this boundary condition $[\mathcal{E}(T, t)]$ grows unbounded as $T-t \to 0$. This implies that as the time to go becomes infinitesimal and there remains some error, then the control effort asked for becomes unbounded in an attempt to satisfy the end boundary conditions. On the other hand, if the specified end conditions are the natural boundary conditions then $[A_A] = [0]$ and $[A_B] = [I]$ so that $[\mathcal{C}(T,t)]$ approaches $[0]$ as $T-t \to 0$, since $[\phi_{22}(t,t)] = [I]$ and $[\phi_{21}(t,t)] = [0]$. This implies that as the time to go becomes infinitesimally small and there remains an error (but it is immaterial what the error is at the boundary), then the control effort is independent of system state and maximizes only the instantaneous rate of return.

The optimum control law, that is $[\mathcal{C}(T,t)]$ and $\mathcal{D}(T,t)]$, can be calculated by computing $[\phi(T,t)]$ and evaluating Equation 3.11. $[\phi(T,t)]$ is obtained by solving 2n sets of 2n-dimensional vector equations

$$\frac{\partial}{\partial \tau}\left(\phi(\tau,t)\right)_{i,j} = \sum_{\ell=1}^{2n} \left(G_E(\tau)\right)_{i,\ell}\left(\phi(\tau,t)\right)_{\ell,j} \quad t \le \tau \le T \quad \begin{matrix} i=1,2,\ldots 2n \\ j=1,2,\ldots 2n \end{matrix} \tag{3.12}$$

with the initial conditions

$$\left(\phi(t,t)\right)_{i,j} = \delta^{i}_{j} \tag{3.13}$$

The term

$$\int_t^T \left[\phi(\tau,\xi)\begin{matrix} u(\xi)\,] \\ \\ u(\xi)\,] \end{matrix}\right] d\xi = \begin{matrix} \hat{\omega}(\tau,t)] \\ \\ \check{\omega}(\tau,t)] \end{matrix}\Bigg] = \psi(\tau,t)\,] \tag{3.14}$$

is gotten by solving

$$\frac{\partial \psi(\tau,t)]}{\partial \tau} = [G_E(\tau)]\psi(\tau,t)] + \begin{matrix} \hat{u}(\tau)] \\ \check{u}(\tau)] \end{matrix}\Bigg] \quad t \le \tau \le T \quad \psi(t,t)] = 0] \tag{3.15}$$

Once $[\phi(\tau,t)]$ and $\psi(\tau,t)]$ have been generated for $t \le \tau \le T$ it is possible to obtain more than a solution to just a single boundary value problem. It may well be that one wishes to solve a problem for the case when $T \to \infty$. It is then of interest to solve it for a fixed value of t and successive values of T to observe how $[\mathcal{C}(T,t)]$ and $\mathcal{D}(T,t)]$ approach their limits as $T \to \infty$.

If $[\phi(T,t)]$ and $\psi(T,t)]$ were computed for $t < T \leq T_o$, then using Equation 3.11, $[\mathscr{C}(T,t)]$ and $\mathscr{D}(T,t)]$ can be calculated for the whole range of values of T, $t < T \leq T_o$ and so the limit of $[\mathscr{C}(T,t)]$ and $\mathscr{D}(T,t)]$ as T approaches infinity can be observed. When $[\mathscr{C}(T,t)]$ and $\mathscr{D}(T,t)]$ for a finite value of T are used as an approximation to $[\mathscr{C}(\infty,t)]$ and $\mathscr{D}(\infty,t)]$, the system is said to be optimized for a "floating time to go", T-t. In such a case one considers the interval T-t over which $\mathscr{P}$ is to be weighed to be fixed in length but T to be moving with t.

In a different problem the termination time T may be fixed and the control law may be required for successive values of t as t increases towards T. In this case one requires $[\phi(T,t)]$ and $\psi(T,t)]$ on some interval $t_o \leq t < T$. To obtain this, one generates $[\hat{\phi}(t,T)]$ by solving

$$\frac{\partial}{\partial t}\left(\hat{\phi}(t,T)\right)_{i,j} = \sum_{\ell=1}^{2n} \left(G_E(t)\right)_{i,\ell}\left(\hat{\phi}(t,T)\right)_{\ell,j} \qquad i = 1, 2, \ldots 2n$$

$$\left(\hat{\phi}(T,T)\right)_{i,j} = \delta^i_j \qquad (3.16)$$

for $j = 1, 2, \ldots 2n$, backwards in time, that is, for t running from T to t_o. Thus one can express $\underline{q}(t)$ and $\underline{\lambda}(t)$ as

$$\begin{bmatrix} q(t) \\ \\ \lambda(t) \end{bmatrix} = \begin{bmatrix} \\ \hat{\phi}(t,T) \\ \\ \end{bmatrix} \begin{bmatrix} q(T) \\ \\ \lambda(T) \end{bmatrix} + \int_T^t \begin{bmatrix} \\ \hat{\phi}(t,\xi) \\ \\ \end{bmatrix} \begin{bmatrix} \hat{u}(\xi) \\ \\ \check{u}(\xi) \end{bmatrix} d\xi$$

and

$$\begin{bmatrix} q(T) \\ \\ \lambda(T) \end{bmatrix} = \begin{bmatrix} \\ \hat{\phi}(t,T) \\ \\ \end{bmatrix}^{-1} \begin{bmatrix} q(t) \\ \\ \lambda(t) \end{bmatrix} - \begin{bmatrix} \\ \hat{\phi}(t,T) \\ \\ \end{bmatrix}^{-1} \int_T^t \begin{bmatrix} \\ \hat{\phi}(t,\xi) \\ \\ \end{bmatrix} \begin{bmatrix} u(\xi) \\ \\ u(\xi) \end{bmatrix} d\xi$$

$$(3.18)$$

The comparison of Equation 3.18 to Equations 3.6 and 3.14 defines $[\phi(T,t)]$ and $\psi(T,t)]$ for a fixed T and successive values of t. Using these functions in conjunction with $[F_{mm}(t)]$, $[G_m(t)]$, $[F_{mq}(t)]$, and $[F_{mu}(t)]$ for $t_o \leq t < T$, one can calculate $[\mathscr{C}(T,t)]$ and $\mathscr{D}(T,t)]$ for $t_o \leq t \leq T$. This solves the so-called "shrinking time to go" control problem in which the termination time is fixed and the interval over which $\mathscr{P}$ is considered decreases as t approaches T. The differences between this and the "floating time to go" problem are illustrated in Figure 3.1

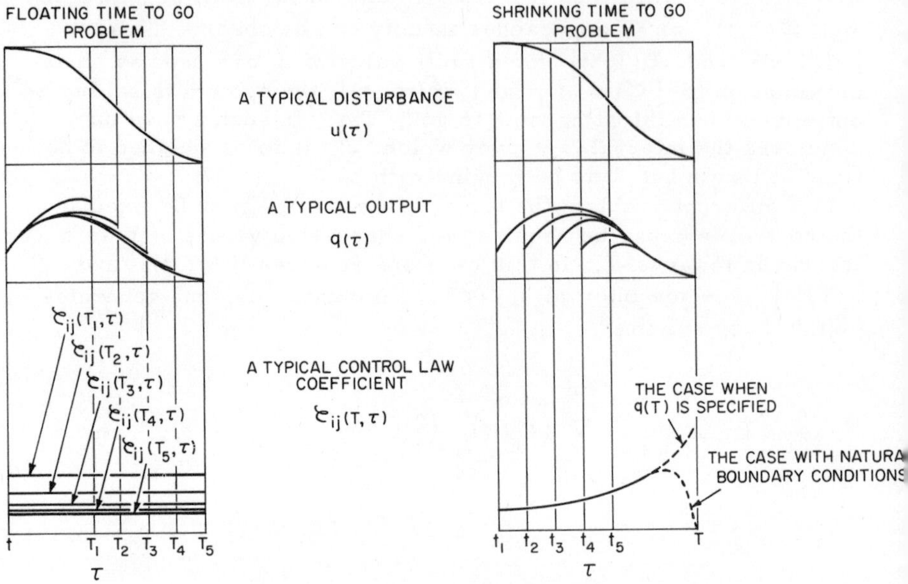

Fig. 3.1. Comparison between the "floating time to go" and the "shrinking time to go" problems

The values of $[\mathcal{C}(T,t)]$ and $\mathcal{D}(T,t)]$, as calculated above, specify the control law over the entire space of $\underline{q}(t)$. If, however, it is required to evaluate just the value of control effort $\underline{m}(t)$ for a particular $\underline{q}(t)$ the above computations can be shortened. Combining Equations 3.9 and 3.11, one obtains for the value of the optimum control effort

$$\begin{aligned} m(t)] = &- [F_{mm}(t)]^{-1}[G_m^T(t)]\Big([A_A][\phi_{12}(\tau,t)] + [A_B][\phi_{22}(T,t)]\Big)^{-1} \\ &\Big\{[A_A]\Big([\phi_{11}(\tau,t)]q(t)] + \hat{\omega}(\tau,t)]\Big) + [A_B]\Big([\phi_{21}(T,t)]q(t)] \\ &+ \check{\omega}(T,t)]\Big)\Big\} + [F_{mm}(t)]^{-1}\Big\{[G_m^T(t)]\Big([A_A][\phi_{12}(T,t)] \\ &+ [A_B][\phi_{22}(T,t)]\Big)^{-1}B] - [F_{mq}(t)]q(t)] - [F_{mu}(t)]u(t)]\Big\} \end{aligned} \tag{3.19}$$

Thus it is seen that one need not evaluate the entire matrix $[\phi(T,t)]$. It is sufficient to compute $[\phi_{12}(T,t)]$ and $[\phi_{22}(T,t)]$ by solving Equations 3.12 for $j = n+1, n+2, \ldots 2n$ since $[\phi_{11}(T,t)]q(t)] + \hat{\omega}(T,t)]$ and $[\phi_{21}(T,t)]q(t)] + \check{\omega}(T,t)]$ can be obtained by solving Equation 3.15 with the initial conditions

$$\psi(t,t)] = q(t)] \tag{3.20}$$

Of course this shortcut is not possible when a "shrinking time to go" problem is to be solved.

The above methods were designed to yield an efficient computational scheme for solving linear two-point boundary value problems. They are characterized by the fact that they make the fullest possible use of a single computation of $[\phi]$. These methods have been programmed for use on an IBM 709 computer in a subroutine LNS, which is a part of the BVPS group of programs which have been developed for the solution of boundary value problems and which are described in Appendix G. The program is capable of solving either the "floating time to go" or the "shrinking time to go" problem yielding $[\mathcal{C}(T,t)]$ and $\mathcal{D}(T,t)]$ as a function of T or t, respectively. It can also compute $m]$ without calculating $[\mathcal{C}]$ and $\mathcal{D}]$ using the shortened formula of Equation 2.19.

To illustrate the above method of solution and the capabilities of the LNS subprogram the following linear two-point boundary value problem was solved. The Euler equations for the first problem presented in Appendix E using a penalty function

$$\mathcal{P}(m) = \gamma m^2 \tag{3.21}$$

turn out to be

$$
\begin{bmatrix} q_1' \\ q_2' \\ q_3' \\ \lambda_1' \\ \lambda_2' \\ \lambda_3' \end{bmatrix}
=
\begin{bmatrix}
k_{11} & k_{12} & 0 & k_{10}/\gamma & 0 & 0 \\
k_{21} & k_{22} & 0 & 0 & 0 & 0 \\
0 & 1 & 0 & 0 & 0 & 0 \\
0 & 0 & 0 & -k_{11} & -k_{21} & 0 \\
0 & 0 & 0 & -k_{12} & -k_{22} & -1 \\
0 & 0 & 1 & 0 & 0 & 0
\end{bmatrix}
\begin{bmatrix} q_1 \\ q_2 \\ q_3 \\ \lambda_1 \\ \lambda_2 \\ \lambda_3 \end{bmatrix}
\pm
\begin{bmatrix} 0 \\ 0 \\ 0 \\ 0 \\ 0 \\ -i(\tau) \end{bmatrix}
$$

$$m = \lambda_1/\gamma \tag{3.22}$$

The problem was solved for the numerical values of the constants

$$k_{10} = 1.0 \qquad k_{11} = -1.5 \qquad k_{12} = -3.0$$

$$\gamma = .0625 \qquad k_{21} = .75 \qquad k_{22} = -.50 \tag{3.23}$$

and for a desired output function

$$i(\tau) = \frac{1}{1 + \tau^2} \tag{3.24}$$

Figure 3.2 shows the solution of the "floating time to go" problem, subject to natural boundary conditions at $\tau = T$.

In Figure 3.2 there are shown $\mathcal{C}_1(T,t)$, $\mathcal{C}_2(T,t)$, $\mathcal{C}_3(T,t)$, and $\mathcal{D}(T,t)$, the elements of $[\mathcal{C}(T,t)]$ and $\mathcal{D}(T,t)]$ where

$$m(t) = \mathcal{C}_1(T,t)q_1(t) + \mathcal{C}_2(T,t)q_2(t) + \mathcal{C}_3(T,t)q_3(t) + \mathcal{D}(T,t) \tag{3.25}$$

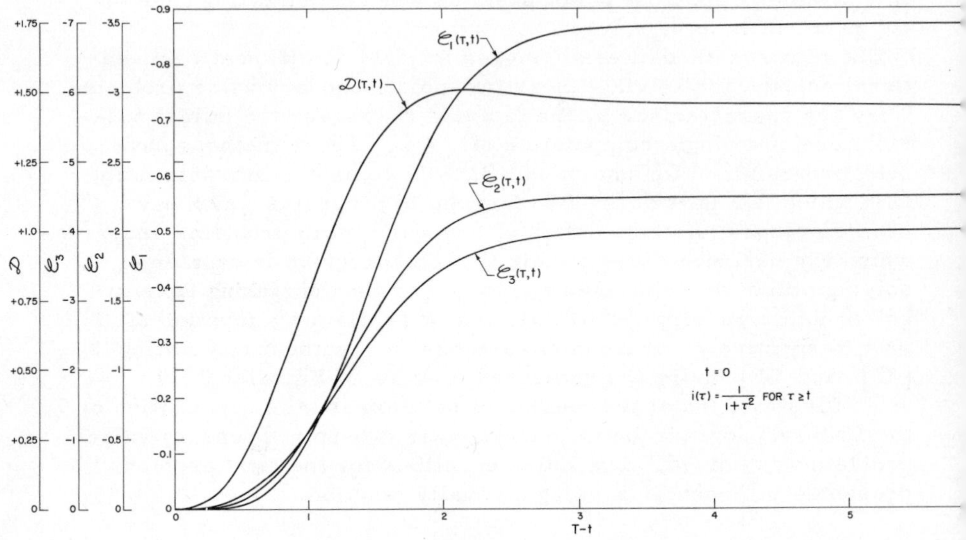

Fig. 3.2. The control law coefficients--linear constant coefficient problem, natural boundary conditions, floating time to go

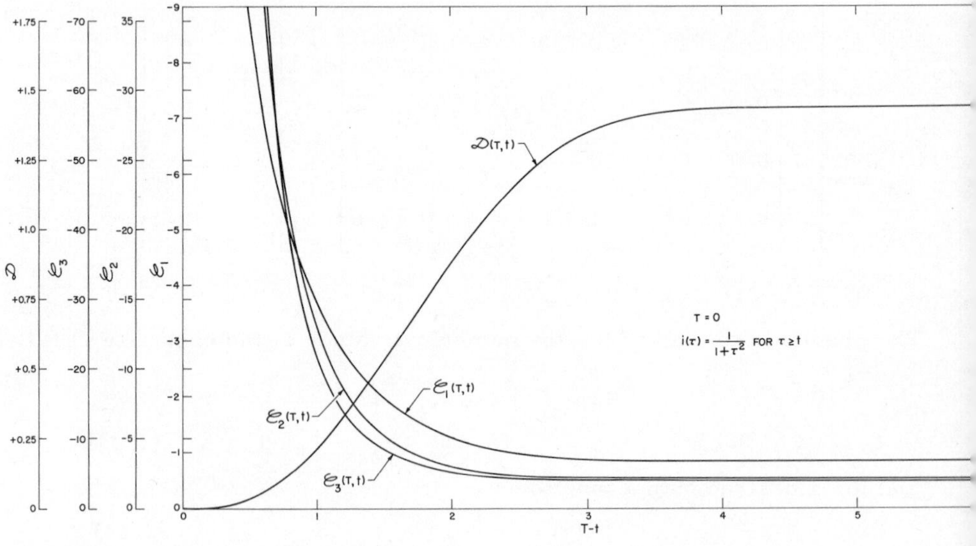

Fig. 3.3. The control law coefficients--linear constant coefficient problem, boundary conditions specifying $q_3(T) = 0$, floating time to go

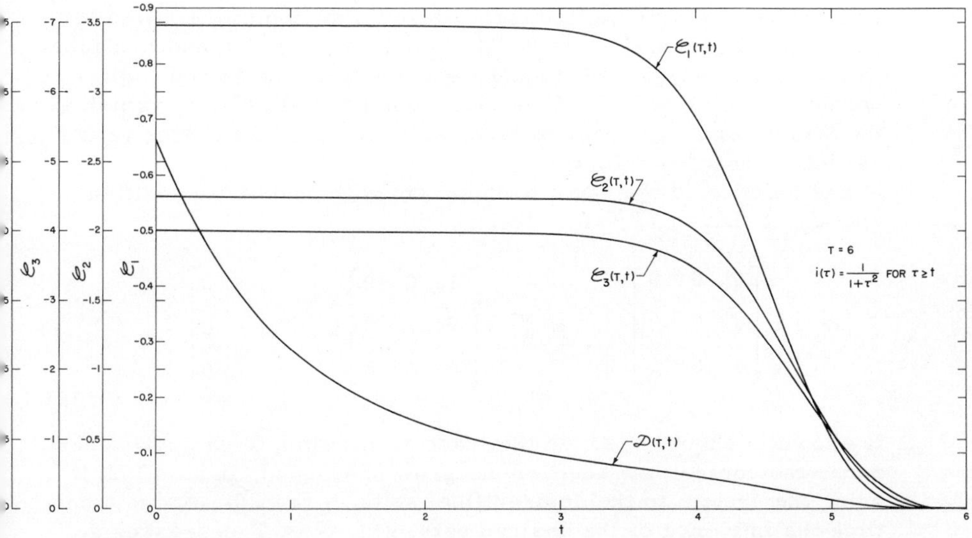

Fig. 3.4. The control law coefficients—linear constant coefficient problem, natural boundary conditions, shrinking time to go

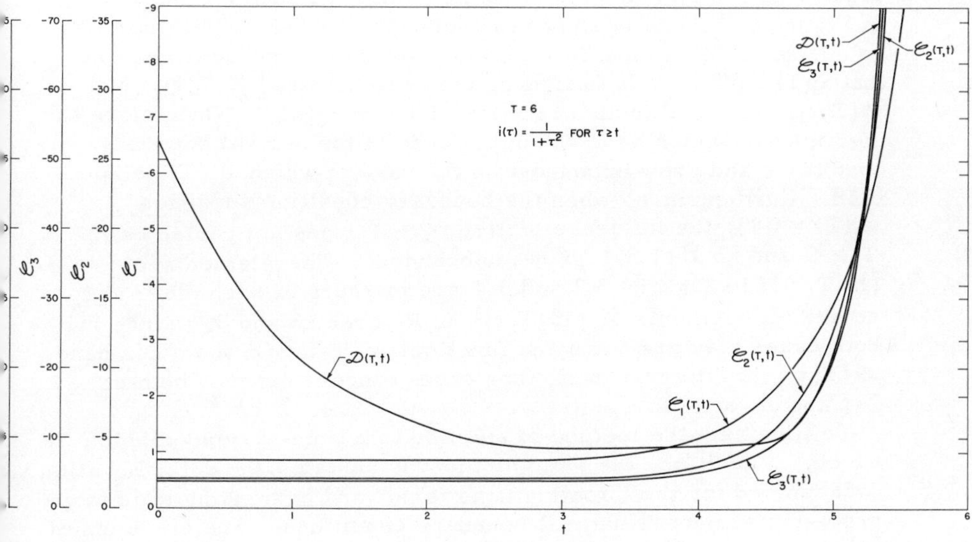

Fig. 3.5. The control law coefficients—linear constant coefficient problem, boundary conditions specifying $q_3(T) = i(T)$, shrinking time to go

The coefficients are plotted for $t=0$ as a function of the "time to go" $T-t$. The matrix $[\mathcal{C}(T,t)]$ is independent of t and is a function only of $T-t$, but $\mathcal{B}(T,t)]$ is a function of t as well, since it depends on $i(\tau)$, $t \leq \tau < T$. The coefficients are all seen to vanish as the "time to go" approaches zero, and converge to limiting values as T-t approaches infinity.

The solution to the same problem but with boundary conditions specifying that $q_3(T) = 0$, , that is, with

$$[A_A] = \begin{bmatrix} 0 & 0 & 0 \\ 0 & 0 & 0 \\ 0 & 0 & 1 \end{bmatrix} \qquad [A_B] = \begin{bmatrix} 1 & 0 & 0 \\ 0 & 1 & 0 \\ 0 & 0 & 0 \end{bmatrix} \qquad B] = \begin{bmatrix} 0 \\ 0 \\ 0 \end{bmatrix} \tag{3.26}$$

is shown in Figure 3.3. In this case as the time to go approaches zero, the control law coefficients grow unbounded, in an effort to bring the system to the desired final state $q_3(T) = 0$. At the same time the influence of the desired path $i(\tau)$, $t \leq \tau < T$ decreases so that $\mathcal{B}(T,t)$ vanishes as T-t approaches zero. As the time to go becomes very large the coefficients approach constant values, the same constant values as in the problem with natural boundary conditions. (Note the difference in scales of Figures 3.2 and 3.3.)

Figure 3.4 illustrates the solution to a "shrinking time to go" problem for $T=6$ and subject to the natural boundary conditions. In Figure 3.5 there is shown the solution of a "shrinking time to go" problem for a case in which the boundary conditions require that $q(T) = i(T)$. In both figures the coefficients $[\mathcal{C}(T,t)]$ and $\mathcal{B}(T,t)]$ are plotted as a function of t for $0 \leq t < T$. Once more the coefficients vanish as $t \to T$ in the case of the natural boundary conditions and grow unbounded in the case in which $q_3(T)$ is specified. Furthermore, when the boundary condition specifies $q_3(T) = i(T)$, the influence of $i(\tau)$, $t \leq \tau \leq T$ does not vanish as $T-t \to 0$ and so $\mathcal{D}(T,t)]$ grows unbounded. The elements of $[\mathcal{C}(T,t)]$ in Figures 3.2 and 3.4 are mirrors of each other and so are the elements of $[\mathcal{C}(T,t)]$ in Figures 3.3 and 3.5 since in both cases they are the same functions of T-t. On the other hand, $\mathcal{B}(T,t)]$ is different in all four cases since it depends both on T-t and on t.

To illustrate the method of solution to a time-varying problem in which, in addition, the fixed element is unstable, the Euler Equation 3.2 was solved for the "floating time to go" and "shrinking time to go" problems subject to natural boundary conditions. The elements of $[\mathcal{C}(T,t)]$ and $\mathcal{B}(T,t)]$ are shown in Figures 3.6 and 3.7 for the two cases. Figure 3.6 is for $t=0$ and Figure 3.7 is for $T=6$. $[\mathcal{C}(T,t)]$ and $\mathcal{B}(T,t)]$ are now functions of both T-t and t so that the curves look appreciably different in the two drawings.

$$\begin{bmatrix} q_1' \\ q_2' \\ \lambda_1' \\ \lambda_2' \end{bmatrix} = \begin{bmatrix} \frac{1}{1+\tau^2} & 0 & 1 & 0 \\ 1 & 0 & 0 & 0 \\ 0 & 0 & \frac{-1}{1+\tau^2} & -1 \\ 0 & 1 & 0 & 0 \end{bmatrix} \begin{bmatrix} q_1 \\ q_2 \\ \lambda_1 \\ \lambda_2 \end{bmatrix} + \begin{bmatrix} 0 \\ 0 \\ 0 \\ \frac{-1}{1+\tau^2} \end{bmatrix}$$

$$m = \lambda_1 \tag{3.27}$$

For the solution of the "shrinking time to go" problem there is available a somewhat more elegant method of computing $[\mathcal{C}(T,t)]$ and $\mathcal{B}(T,t)]$. To apply this technique it is convenient to change Equation 3.4 into the form

$$q'^*(\tau)] = [P^*(\tau)]q^*(\tau)] + [R^*(\tau)]\lambda^*(\tau)]$$

$$\lambda'^*(\tau)] = [Q^*(\tau)]q^*(\tau)] - [P^*(\tau)]^T \lambda^*(\tau)] \tag{3.28}$$

This is done by adding an extra component to $q(\tau)]$ and $\lambda(\tau)]$ and augmenting the matrices such that

$$\underline{q}^*(\tau) = \underbrace{\underline{q}(\tau),\ q_o(\tau)} \qquad \underline{\lambda}^*(\tau) = \underbrace{\underline{\lambda}(\tau),\ \lambda_o(\tau)}$$

$$[P^*(\tau)] = \begin{bmatrix} [P(\tau)] & \hat{u}(\tau)] \\ \underline{0} & 0 \end{bmatrix} \qquad [G_m^*(\tau)] = \begin{bmatrix} [G_m(\tau)] \\ \underline{0} \end{bmatrix}$$

$$[R^*(\tau)] = \begin{bmatrix} [R(\tau)] & 0] \\ \underline{0} & 0 \end{bmatrix} \qquad [Q^*(\tau)] = \begin{bmatrix} [Q(\tau)] & \hat{\omega}(\tau)] \\ \underline{\hat{\omega}}(\tau) & 0 \end{bmatrix} \tag{3.29}$$

Since in the above $q_o'(\tau) = 0$, if the initial condition $q_o = 1$ is imposed, then $q_o(\tau)$ remains equal to 1 and so all the components of $q^*(\tau)$ and $\lambda^*(\tau)$, except $q_o(\tau)$ and $\lambda_o(\tau)$ are governed by the same relations as in Equation 3.4. $q_o(\tau)$ remains equal to 1 while $\lambda_o(\tau)$ goes through some bounded, but otherwise unspecified gyrations which do not affect the behavior of the other components. In terms of these new variables the control law is specified as

$$m(t)] = [F_{mm}(t)]^{-1}\left([G_m^*(t)]^T\lambda^*(t)] - [F_{mq}(t)]q(t)] - [F_{mu}(t)]u(t)]\right) \tag{3.30}$$

where

$$\lambda^*(t)] = [\mathscr{C}^*(T,t)]q^*(t)] \tag{3.31}$$

One can now derive a differential equation governing $[\mathscr{C}^*(T,t)]$. On substituting Equation 3.31 into the second equation of Equation 3.28 there results

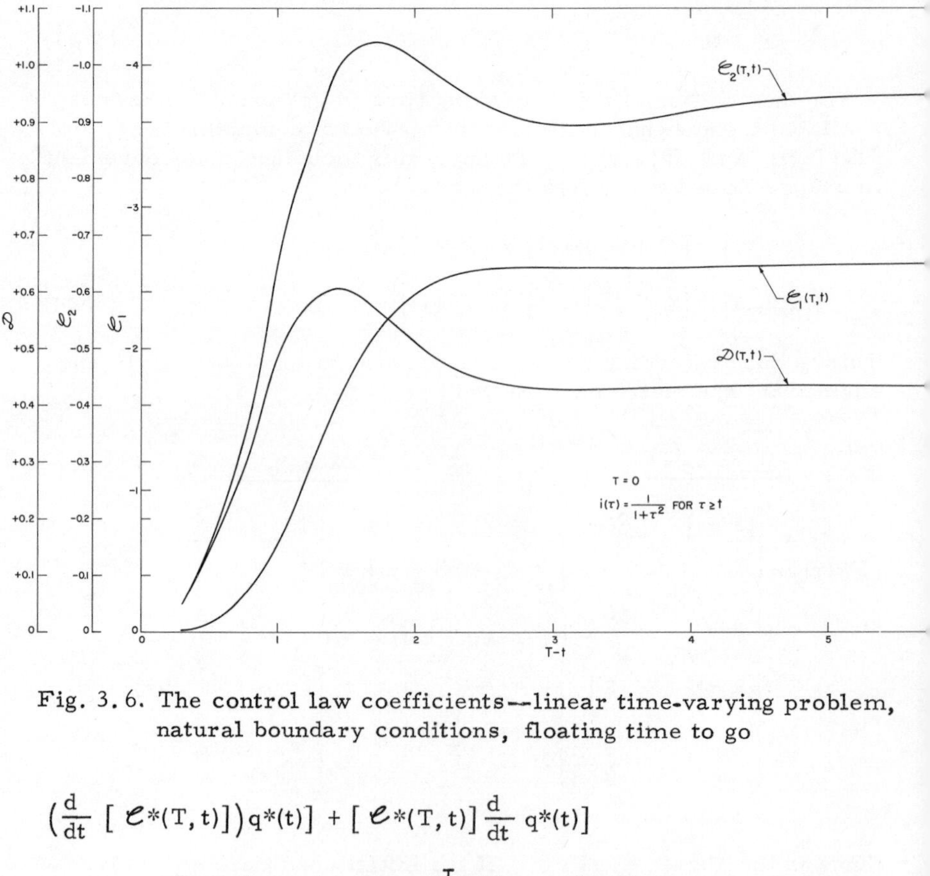

Fig. 3.6. The control law coefficients—linear time-varying problem, natural boundary conditions, floating time to go

$$\left(\frac{d}{dt}[\mathscr{C}^*(T,t)]\right)q^*(t)] + [\mathscr{C}^*(T,t)]\frac{d}{dt}q^*(t)]$$

$$= [Q^*(t)]q^*(t)] - [P^*(t)]^T[\mathscr{C}^*(T,t)]q(t)] \tag{3.32}$$

By substituting Equation 3.31 into the first part of Equation 3.28 and then replacing $\frac{d}{dt}q^*(t)]$ in Equation 3.32 by the right-hand side of the first equation of Equation 3.28 one obtains

$$\left(\frac{d}{dt}\left[\mathcal{C}^*(T,t)\right]q^*(t)\right] + \left[\mathcal{C}^*(T,t)\right]\left[P^*(t)\right]q^*(t)\right]$$
$$+ \left[\mathcal{C}^*(T,t)\right]\left[R^*(t)\right]\left[\mathcal{C}^*(T,t)\right]q^*(t)\right]$$
$$= \left[Q^*(t)\right]q^*(t)\right] - \left[P^*(t)\right]^T\left[\mathcal{C}^*(T,t)\right]q^*(t)\right] \qquad (3.33)$$

The above has to hold for all $q^*(t)] \neq 0]$. Therefore $[\mathcal{C}^*(T,t)]$ satisfies the nonlinear matrix differential equation

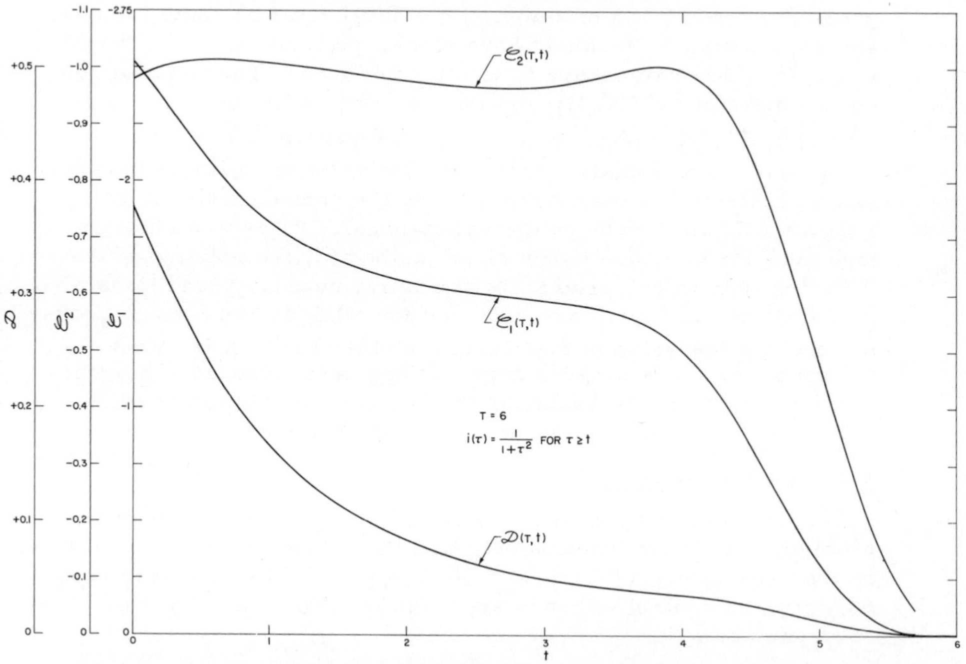

Fig. 3.7. The control law coefficients--linear time-varying problem, natural boundary conditions, shrinking time to go

$$\frac{d}{dt}\left[\mathcal{C}^*(T,t)\right] + \left[\mathcal{C}^*(T,t)\right]\left[R^*(t)\right]\left[\mathcal{C}^*(T,t)\right] + \left[\mathcal{C}^*(T,t)\right]\left[P^*(t)\right]$$
$$+ \left[P^*(t)\right]^T\left[\mathcal{C}^*(T,t)\right] = \left[Q(t)\right] \qquad (3.34)$$

If $[\mathcal{C}^*(T,T)]$ is known, Equation 3.34 can be solved backwards in time, that is, for $t_o \leq t < T$. When the boundary conditions at T are the natural boundary conditions then $[\mathcal{C}^*(T,T)]$ equals $[0]$ as explained above, but if the conditions specify $q(T)]$ then $[\mathcal{C}^*(T,T)]$ is unbounded and so undefined. Thus Equation 3.34 can be used in some but not all linear control problems.

Equation 3.34 is a nonlinear matrix differential equation of the Riccati type. Such equations are known to have a finite escape time, that is, there is some finite value of the independent variable, determined by the initial conditions, at which the solution becomes unbounded. Thus for the boundary conditions specifying $q(T)]$ the escape time of Equation 3.34 is for $t = T$. However, if the control problem does have an optimum, $[\mathcal{C}^*(T,t)]$ must be finite for $t < T$, and so Equation 3.34 cannot have an escape time for $t < T$. It will, in general, have an escape time for some $t > T$. The condition on boundedness of $[\mathcal{C}^*(T,t)]$ implies non-singularity of $([A_A][\phi_{12}(T,t)] + [A_B][\phi_{22}(T,t)])$ in Equation 3.8.

The use of the Riccati equation for the solution of linear boundary value problems has been introduced to the control problem by Kalman. From the computational standpoint it has a slight advantage over the previously described method for the solution of the "floating time to go" problem with natural boundary conditions when $[\mathcal{C}(T,t)]$ and $\mathcal{D}(T,t)]$ are required for all t, $t_o \leq t < T$ since it does not require inversion of matrices. In other cases it is either inapplicable or loses its advantage. It has been introduced here because it will form the basis for the calculation of a power series expansion of the control law in nonlinear problems.

3.2 Flooding Techniques

The control law specified by a linear two-point boundary-value problem is a linear function of $\underline{q}$ and therefore completely described by the matrices $[\mathcal{C}(T,t)]$ and $\mathcal{D}(T,t)]$. In the nonlinear case the optimum control effort is specified by a nonlinear function of the state variables

$$\underline{m}(t) = \underline{\mathcal{C}}\,(T, t, \underline{q}(t), \underline{v}(t)) \tag{3.35}$$

One way of specifying this function is by tabulating it on a grid of points of $\underline{q}(t)$, T, t and $\underline{v}(t)$. Thus to compute the control law, one needs to solve a set of boundary-value problems for a single end-point condition and a set of initial conditions in the $(\underline{q}(t), T, t, \underline{v}(t))$ space.

To compute the solution of a boundary-value problem out of this set, one starts a solution of the Euler equations at $\tau = T$ with the n end-point boundary conditions as n of its 2n initial conditions and the remaining n initial conditions set to some essentially arbitrarily chosen set of values and propagates it backward in time, for τ running from T toward t. (The n arbitrarily chosen initial conditions at $\tau = T$ shall henceforth be referred to as $\underline{\eta}(T)$.) At $\tau = t$ the resultant $\underline{q}(t)$ is a point in the $(\underline{q}(t), T, t, \underline{v}(t))$ space for which the generated trajectory is a solution of the boundary-value problem.

Thus for each choice of $\underline{\eta}(T)$ imposed on the Euler equations at $\tau = T$, there is computed the optimum control law for a point in the domain of $\underline{\mathcal{E}}$. By choosing a number of values of $\underline{\eta}(T)$ and generating the corresponding solutions of the Euler equations, $\underline{\mathcal{E}}$ is evaluated at a grid of points in the space of ($\underline{q}(t), T, t, \underline{v}(t)$), as illustrated in Figure 3.8. This yields the control law specifying $\underline{m}$ as a function of $\underline{q}$ for a particular T, t, and $\underline{v}(t)$ The above procedure needs then to be repeated for the various values of T, t, and $\underline{v}(t)$ that are of interest, to yield the complete control law of Equation 3.35.

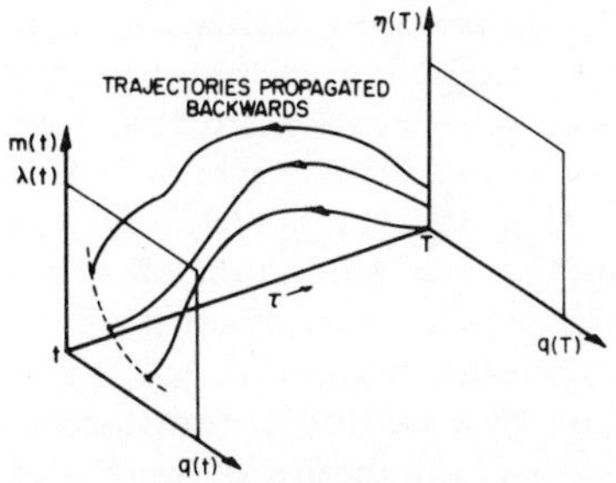

Fig. 3.8. Computation of the optimum control law by flooding

Of course, the grid of points generated by the above procedure is not uniform over the space of $\underline{q}(t)$. This may be both an advantage and a source of difficulties. On the one hand, it is possible to evaluate $\underline{\mathcal{E}}$ at a more densely spaced set of points in the region where it changes radically and at fewer points where $\underline{\mathcal{E}}$ is well behaved. On the other hand, until one obtains a good idea of the mapping from the space of $\underline{\eta}(T)$ into the space of $\underline{q}(t)$ by computing a number of points, it is impossible to predict the value of $\underline{\eta}(T)$ needed to yield the solution at a particular point in the domain of $\underline{\mathcal{E}}$.

It may well happen that two sets of values of $\underline{\eta}(T)$ yield the same $\underline{q}$ at $\tau = t$ and different values of the control effort $\underline{m}(t)$. In such a case only one of the solutions corresponds to a global optimum, and it can be chosen from among the others by comparing the values of $\mathcal{P}$ computed along the corresponding trajectories.

The flooding technique, just described, yields the solution in essentially the same form as the fundamental computational algorithm of dynamic programming. It is of interest, therefore, to compare the two techniques with respect to the number of computations involved.

If n is the number of state variables and r is the number of levels into which each is quantized, then at each stage in the algorithm, for each of r^n possible points in the state space one needs to evaluate and compare r^n transitions into each of the r^n possible points in the state space at the next stage. If there are n_t stages, then a total of $n_t(r^n)^2$ computation units are required. The number of calculations involved in evaluating a transition between two points in the state space is comparable to the number required to propagate the solution of the Euler equations a single step in time. Under this assumption, to generate $\underline{\mathcal{E}}$ at r^n points of its domain using the variational technique, only $n_t r^n$ computation units are required.

The above comparison reflects unfavorably on dynamic programming. Of course, there are a number of special techniques[33] and shortcuts possible within the general framework of the dynamic programming approach which are more efficient than the fundamental algorithm, but then the above variational scheme can also be improved upon.

A major simplification in the procedure for the calculation of the control law comes about when T is fixed and T - t is very large with respect to the time scale of the Euler equations, so that T - t approaches infinity. If as τ approaches infinity, $\underline{G}(\tau, \underline{q}(\tau), \underline{m}(\tau), \underline{u}(\tau))$, $F(T, \tau, \underline{q}(\tau), \underline{m}(\tau), \underline{u}(\tau))$, and $\underline{u}(\tau)$ approach functions independent of τ and T, then the optimum trajectory approaches a "steady-state optimum." This may correspond either to constant values of all the components of $\underline{q}(\tau)$ and $\underline{m}(\tau)$ entering F or to a periodic oscillation of $\underline{q}(\tau)$ and $\underline{m}(\tau)$. (Some cases in which components of $\underline{q}(\tau)$ and $\underline{u}(\tau)$ do not approach constant values for large τ can also be included after a suitable change of variables, for example, by considering the error rather than the output as a state variable.)

If the optimum steady-state trajectory is a constant, then in the vicinity of the steady-state optimum the Euler equations can be considered as being linear with constant coefficients. In that case, as shown in Section 2.3, the steady-state optimum corresponds to an equilibrium point of the Euler equations, and that equilibrium point is a saddle-type singularity. From it there radiate 2n independent solutions, n of them growing and n decaying. The optimum trajectory for $\tau \to \infty$ must be composed of the solutions which decay when propagated forward in time, for any one of the growing components would become unbounded as $\tau \to \infty$, preventing the trajectory from reaching the steady-state optimum. By the same token, looking backward in time, the optimum trajectory is composed of the diverging solutions. If one were to start the Euler equations with initial conditions corresponding to the equilibrium state and propagate them backward, then ideally the variables would remain constant and not reach any other state, except possibly after infinite time. However, if the Euler equations were perturbed from the equilibrium and the solutions propagated backward, they would diverge, reaching a state $\underline{q}(t)$ after a finite time. The solution would be composed of the optimum trajectory joining $\underline{q}(t)$ with the steady-state optimum and a transient due to the initial perturbation which decays when propagated backward.

This situation is illustrated in Figure 3.9 for linear Euler equations

$$q'(\tau) = m(\tau) \qquad m(\tau) = \lambda(\tau) \qquad \lambda'(\tau) = q(\tau) \tag{3.36}$$

arising from optimization of

$$\mathscr{P} = -\int_{t}^{\infty} \left\{ \left(q(\tau)\right)^2 + \left(m(\tau)\right)^2 + 2\lambda(\tau)\left(q'(\tau) - m(\tau)\right) \right\} d\tau \tag{3.37}$$

and in Figure 3.10 for nonlinear equations

$$q'(\tau) = m(\tau) \qquad m = \text{sign}(\lambda) \left| \frac{\lambda}{4} \right|^{1/7} \qquad \lambda'(\tau) = q(\tau) \tag{3.38}$$

which follow from the optimization of

$$\mathscr{P} = -\int_{t}^{\infty} \left\{ \left(q(\tau)\right)^2 + \left(m(\tau)\right)^8 + 2\lambda(\tau)\left(q'(\tau) - m(\tau)\right) \right\} d\tau \tag{3.39}$$

In the figures are shown the trajectories in the phase space of q and λ, obtained by perturbing λ from the equilibrium and propagating the solutions backward. The curve to which they converge is the optimum trajectory for $T \to \infty$. The corresponding m as a function of q is the optimum control law.

Thus to compute the control law for the case in which $T \to \infty$, one need not solve the Euler equations for an infinite time. Solutions perturbed from the equilibrium point converge to the optimum trajectory in finite time and generate the optimum control law by computing the optimum $\underline{m}$ for values of $\underline{q}$ on the trajectory $q(\tau)$, $\lambda(\tau)$ for $t \leq \tau < \tau_0$. In the above, τ_0 is the value of τ past which the solutions are deemed to have converged sufficiently close to the optimum trajectory for the infinite T case. Unfortunately, it is not possible to predict the rate of convergence. The easiest and most useful test of convergence is to try perturbations of different magnitudes and start the solutions at different values of T and then compare the trajectories. The linear case of Section 2.7 can also serve as a guide by suggesting that the rate of convergence is exponential with an exponent which is twice the smallest characteristic root of the Euler equations treated on a quasi-linear, quasi-stationary basis. One may note in passing that if the Euler equations are linear, then in this case it is sufficient to generate solutions for $n+1$ perturbations and from these $[\mathscr{C}(T,t)]$ and $\mathscr{D}(T,t)]$ can be calculated by evaluating the coefficients of the hyperplanes passing through the solution points at $\tau = t$.

If the steady-state optimum trajectory is an oscillatory motion, then the Euler equations may still have an equilibrium point. It would correspond to the optimum operation subject to the constraints that $\underline{q}'(\tau) = 0$. However, the oscillating trajectory would yield a higher value of $\mathscr{P}$ than the best constant values of $\underline{q}$. The Euler equations can be linearized about the optimum limit cycle to yield a linear, but time-varying set of equations. One would expect their behavior to be qualitatively similar to that of the constant coefficient equations in that there are n independent solutions decaying toward the optimum limit cycle and n solutions diverging from

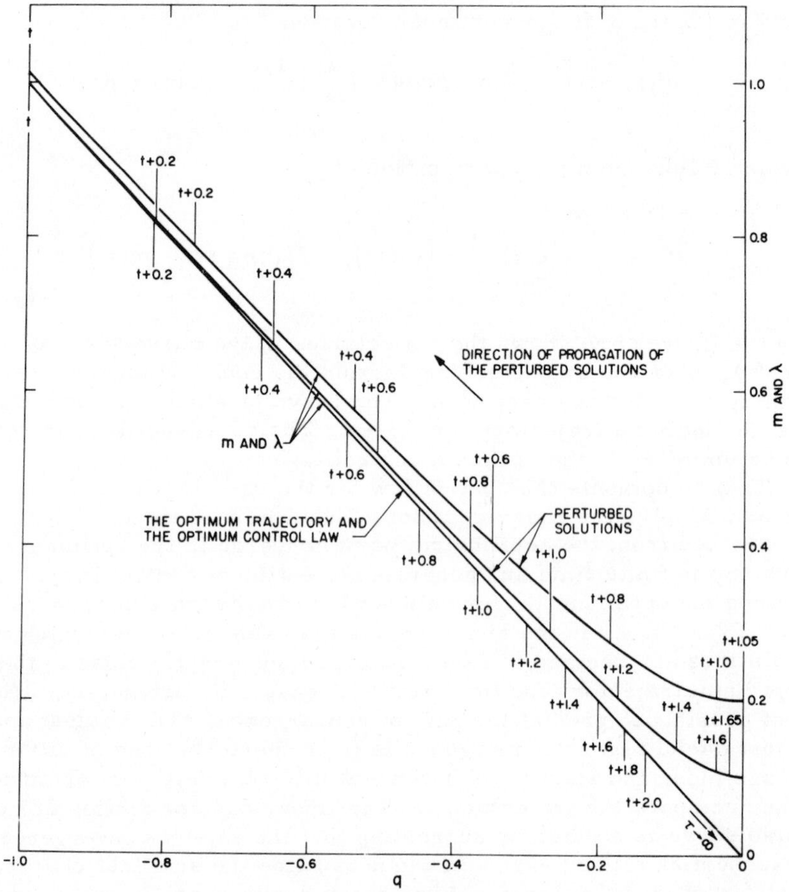

Fig. 3.9. Convergence of the perturbed solutions to the optimum control law in a linear problem

it. If that was indeed the case, the optimum control could be gotten by perturbing the solutions away from the limit cycle and propagating them backward.

In view of the fact that the time-varying Euler equations, if treated as quasi-stationary equations with movable characteristic roots, have at each value of time both stable and unstable roots, the above seems plausible. However, a proof is lacking. The same considerations would indicate that for the Euler equations to exhibit a limit cycle, the roots of the quasi-stationary equation must move across the $j\omega$ axis, and this in turn might imply that a limit cycle as an optimum steady-state condition requires that there be regions in the state space in which the integrand of the

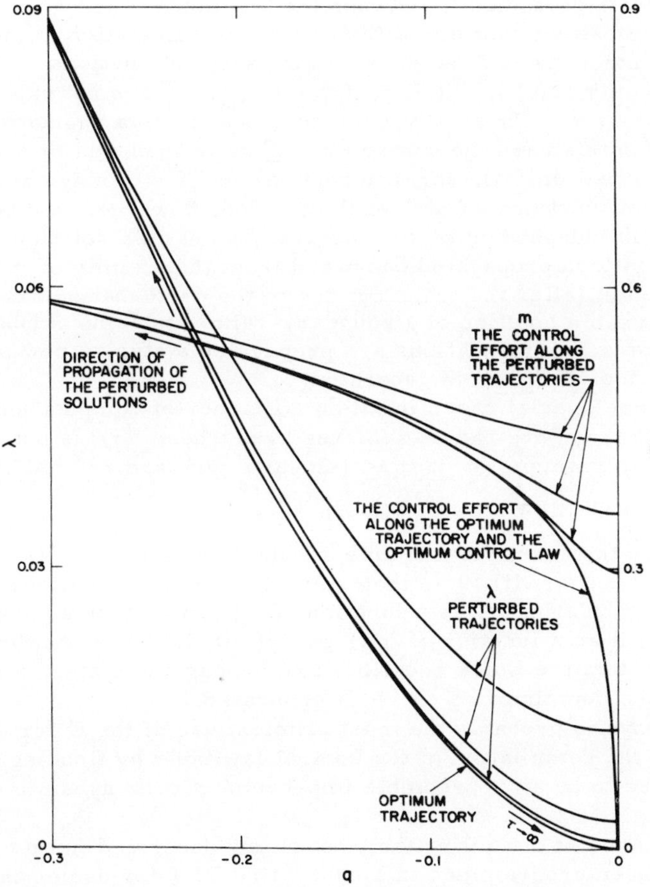

Fig. 3.10. Convergence of the perturbed solutions to the optimum control law in a nonlinear problem

performance criterion is concave and regions in which it is convex in m.

The above hypotheses are unproven, although supported by some first-order examples. They should provide fascinating subjects for future research. One should point out that there are many physical situations in which the optimum "steady-state" mode of operation is known to be a limit cycle. As an example, consider the operation of a plant to which is charged a fixed cost whenever it is used, plus a variable cost depending on the rate of production. Let us assume the plant is to be operated so as to maintain a specified average production rate at the smallest production cost. Clearly, the optimum policy is to operate it at peak efficiency for a period and then to have the plant shut down for another period and alternate periodically between the two modes.

A further significant simplification in the calculation of the optimum control law occurs when $T = \infty$ and the functions $\underline{G}(\tau, \underline{q}(\tau), \underline{m}(\tau), \underline{u}(\tau))$, $F(T, \tau, \underline{q}(\tau), \underline{m}(\tau), \underline{u}(\tau))$ are not explicitly dependent on τ. Physically, this corresponds to a regulator problem, and in this case the control law $\underline{\mathcal{C}}$ is independent of t. It is still dependent on $\underline{v}(t)$, for different values of $\underline{v}(t)$ may correspond to different functions of $\underline{u}(\tau)$ each of which, however, is a constant. Since $\underline{\mathcal{C}}$ is independent of t, then every point on a solution of the Euler equations propagated backward from the vicinity of the equilibrium point (after the transient due to the perturbation has died out) is a usable solution of a boundary-value problem. Thus every time that the Euler equations are propagated a step, a new point in the domain of $\underline{\mathcal{C}}(\underline{q}, \underline{v})$ is generated.

There are special cases in which efficiency of computation comparable to the above can be achieved even when $\underline{u}(\tau)$ is not a constant. For example, if $\underline{u}(\tau), t \leq \tau < T$ and $\underline{v}(t)$ are related by

$$\underline{u}(\tau) = \underline{f}(\tau - t - g(\underline{v}(t))) \tag{3.40}$$

as is often the case, for example if $u(\tau) = v(t)\exp(-\tau + t) = \exp\left(-\tau + t + \ln(v(t))\right)$, then solving the Euler equations backward and tabulating $\underline{\mathcal{C}}$ as a function of $\underline{q}(t)$ and t is equivalent to tabulating it as a function of $\underline{q}(t)$ and $g(\underline{v}(t))$. Thus once more, each time that the Euler equations are propagated a step, a new point in the domain of $\underline{\mathcal{C}}(\underline{q}, \underline{v})$ is generated.

The above is probably the most efficient use of the Euler equations for the compilation of the control law table by flooding. It is considered to be an appreciable improvement over dynamic programming.

The method of compiling the control law described in this section has been programmed in a subroutine BPT for use on the IBM 709 computer in connection with the BVPS group of programs described in Appendix G. BPT generates a set of solutions backward in time from a specified point in the $(\underline{q}(T), \underline{\lambda}(T))$ space for various perturbations of $\underline{\lambda}(T)$. Values of the $\underline{\mathcal{C}}$ function which are generated are tabulated and processed to generate contours of constant $\underline{m}$, constant $\underline{\lambda}$, and constant $\mathscr{P}$, in the space of $\underline{q}$. This program was prepared so as to automate as far as possible the control law calculations. The above methods of computing the control law and the use of the BPT subprogram are demonstrated below on several examples.

Euler equations defining the optimum control law for a first-order system described by

$$q'(\tau) = m(\tau) \tag{3.41}$$

according to the performance criterion

$$\mathcal{P} = \int_t^{\infty} \left\{ (q(\tau))^2 + \mathcal{P}(m(\tau)) \right\} d\tau \tag{3.42}$$

are

$$q'(\tau) = m(\tau) \qquad \lambda'(\tau) = q(\tau) \qquad \mathcal{P}'(m) = \lambda \tag{3.43}$$

This problem may be considered as a gross simplification of Problem 1 of Appendix E. Equation 3.43 has been solved backward from the equilibrium point by perturbing $\lambda(T)$. Figures 3.11 and 3.12 show the trajectories in the phase plane of λ and q or m and q for various forms of $\mathcal{P}(m)$ corresponding to penalty functions simulating an amplitude constraint on m. Since $\mathcal{C}$ is independent of t, these trajectories represent the optimum control law except in the neighborhood of the equilibrium point where it is distorted by the perturbation transients. Since the control law is known to be an antisymmetric function of q, only one half of it, that for negative q, is shown here. Figure 3.11 shows the solutions using high-power penalty function

$$\mathcal{P}(m) = (m)^{n_c} \tag{3.44}$$

for $n_c = 2, 4, 8, 16$, and 32 . The dotted lines indicate the perturbation transients. The effects of the perturbations are shown in more detail in Figure 3.13 for $n_c = 4, 8, 16$, and 32 . Figure 3.12 shows the effect of using a piecewise quadratic penalty function

$$\mathcal{P}(m) = \begin{cases} \gamma(m)^2 & \text{for } |m| \leq 1 \\ \gamma(k(m)^2 - (2|m| - 1)(k-1)) & \text{for } |m| > 1 \end{cases} \tag{3.45}$$

It should be noted that in this case the control is linear in the segment about the equilibrium point, but it is pronouncedly nonlinear in the second segment.

To demonstrate the solution for a higher-order case, the boundary-value problems associated with the Euler equations

$$q_1'(\tau) = -q_1(\tau) + m(\tau) \qquad \lambda_1'(\tau) = \lambda_1(\tau) - \lambda_2(\tau)$$

$$q_2'(\tau) = q_1(\tau) \qquad \lambda_2'(\tau) = q_2(\tau)$$

$$\mathcal{P}'(m) = 2\lambda_1 \tag{3.46}$$

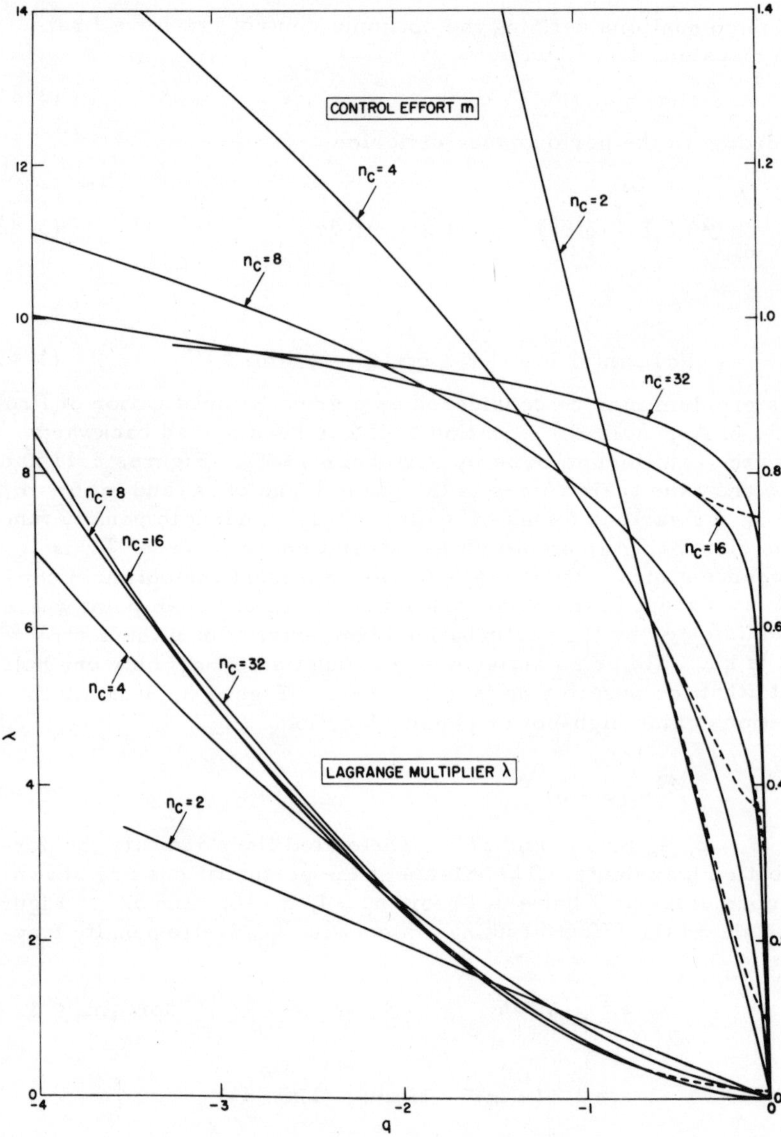

Fig. 3.11. The effect of a high-power penalty function on the control law

arising from the optimization of

$$\mathscr{P} = \int_t^{\infty} \left\{ (q_2(\tau))^2 + P(m(\tau)) + 2\lambda_1(\tau)\left(q_1'(\tau) + q_1(\tau) - m(\tau)\right) + 2\lambda_2(\tau)\left(q_2'(\tau) - q_1(\tau)\right)\right\} d\tau \tag{3.47}$$

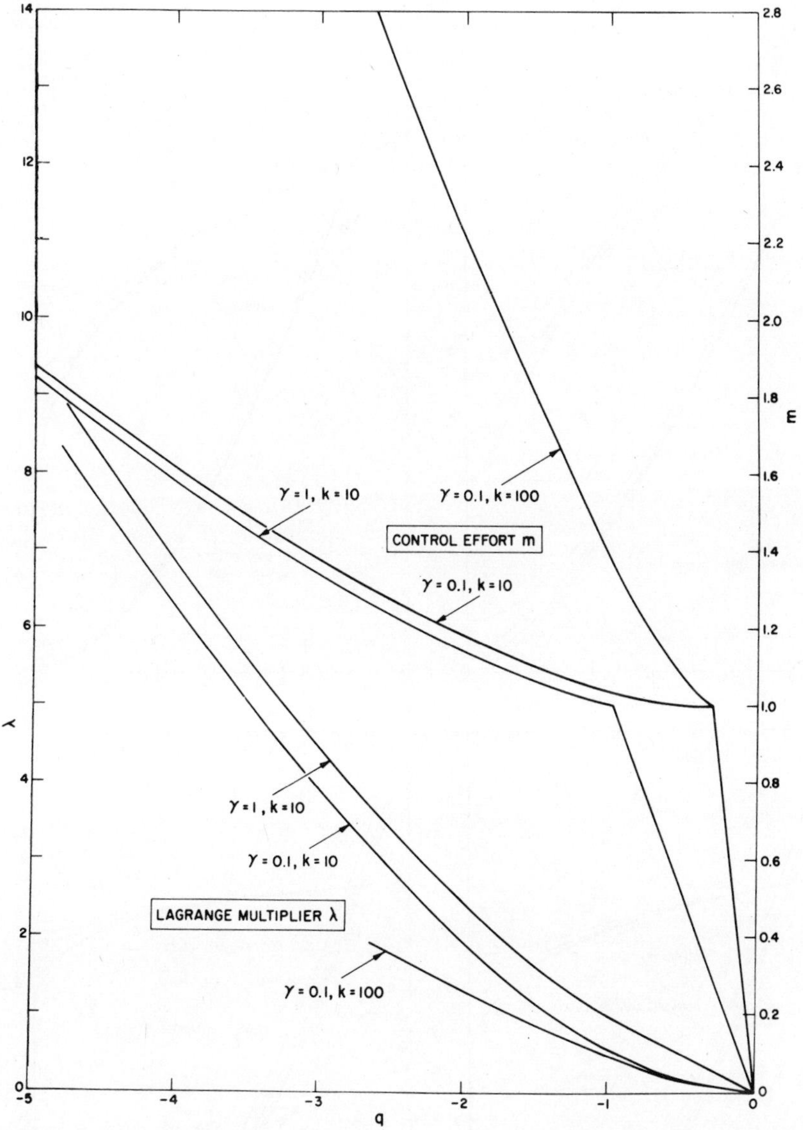

Fig. 3.12. The effect of a piecewise quadratic penalty function on the control law

were solved by using the BPT subprogram. For the case in which $\mathcal{P}(m) = m^2$, Figure 3.14 shows the trajectories propagated backward from the vicinity of the equilibrium point in the state space of (q_1, q_2), and Figure 3.15 shows the contours of constant λ_1, λ_2, and m. All the solutions which were tried are shown in Figure 3.14. The fact that some areas of the state space are less thoroughly explored than others illustrates the difficulty of choosing the appropriate perturbations of $\underline{\lambda}(T)$ to direct the trajectories

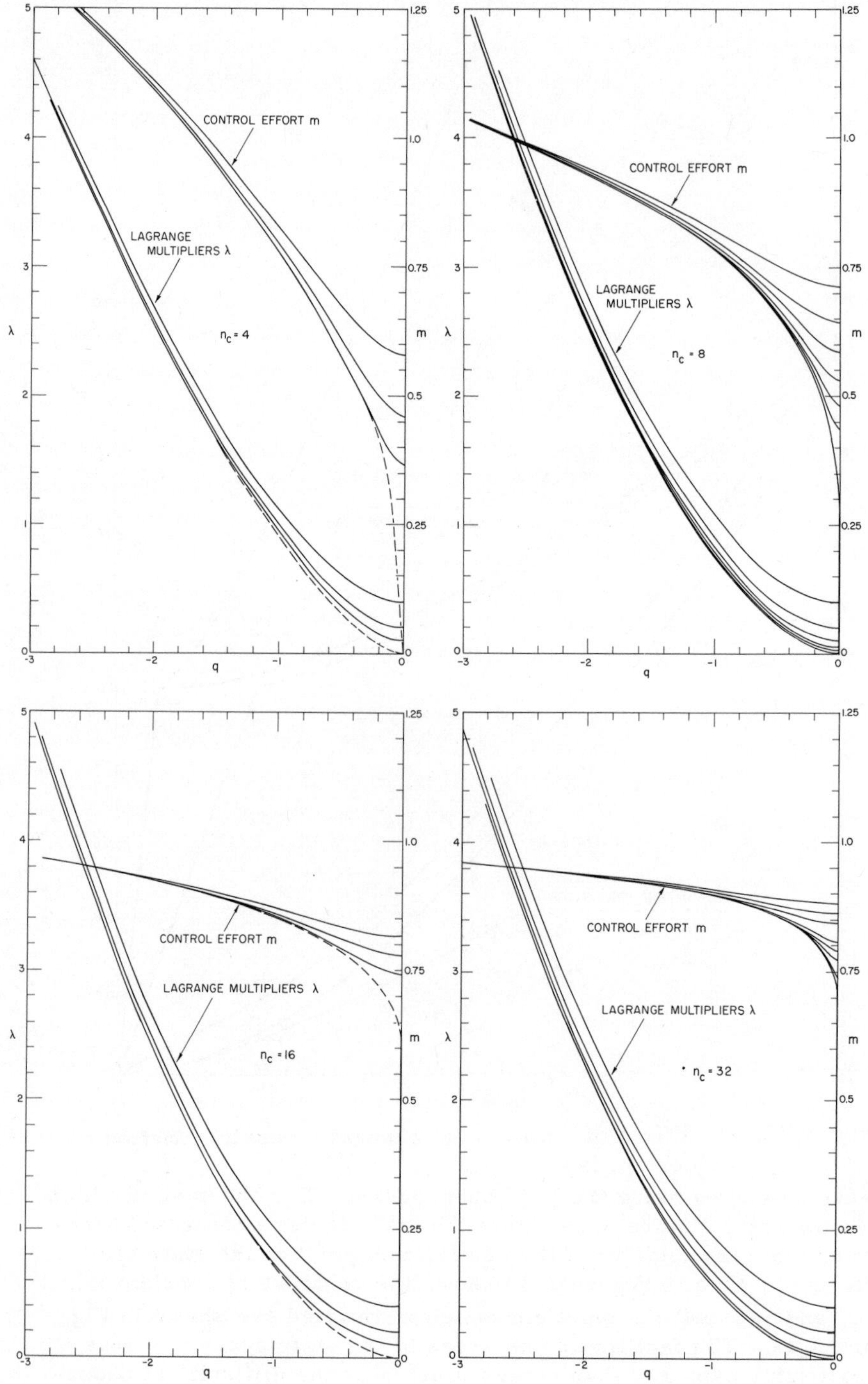

Fig. 3.13. Convergence of the perturbed solutions to the optimum control law

Table 3.1
The Relationship between Trajectories and the Initial Perturbations

$n_c = 2$			$n_c = 32$		
Trajectory Number	$\Delta\lambda_1$	$\Delta\lambda_2$	Trajectory Number	$\Delta\lambda_1$	$\Delta\lambda_2$
1	-.10	+.10	1	-.10	+.10
2	-.05	+.15	7	-.10	+.15
3	+.10	+.15	9	-.05	+.10
4	+.05	+.15	8	-.05	+.15
5	-.05	+.10	10	+.05	+.15
6	+.10	+.10	15	+.05	+.15
19	0	+.10	11	+.10	+.15
7	+.15	+.05	12	+.15	+.10
8	+.10	+.05	3	+.10	+.10
18	+.05	+.05	13	+.15	+.05
9	+.15	0	2	0	+.10
10	+.10	0	4	+.05	+.05
11	+.15	-.05	5	+.10	0
12	+.10	-.05	20	+.20	-.05
13	+.15	-.10	19	+.15	-.05
14	+.15	-.15	14	+.05	0
15	+.10	-.10	17	+.10	-.05
16	+.05	-.05	18	+.15	-.10
17	-.05	-.05	22	+.14	-.10
			26	+.15	-.12
			23	+.13	-.10
			27	+.15	-.13
			24	+.12	-.10
			25	+.11	-.10
			21	+.15	-.15
			6	+.10	-.10
			16	+.05	-.05

Note: Trajectories are ordered in a counterclockwise direction on Figure 3.14 and Figure 3.18, respectively.

into the unexplored areas of the (q_1, q_2) space. The trajectories are numbered, and the perturbations corresponding to each are compiled in Table 3.1 to indicate the complexity of the $\underline{\lambda}(T)$ to $\underline{q}(t)$ mapping. Since the trajectories and the control law have rotational symmetry in the (q_1, q_2) space, only half of the trajectories shown were actually computed; the remainder were obtained from symmetry considerations, and these are not numbered. In the case shown in Figure 3.15, the control law is linear and time-invariant.

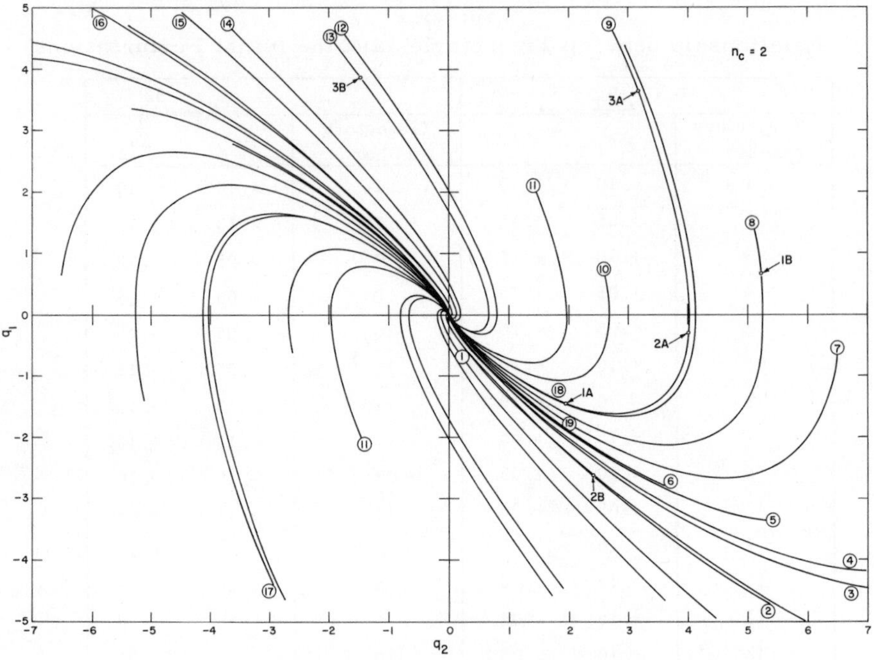

Fig. 3.14. The perturbed trajectories - $n_c = 2$

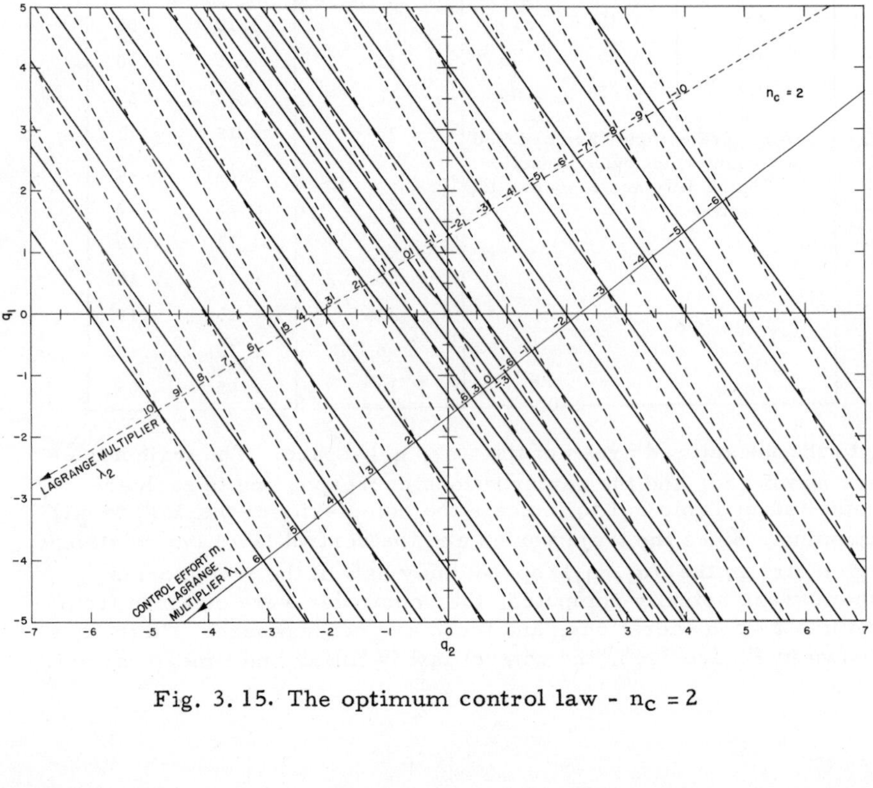

Fig. 3.15. The optimum control law - $n_c = 2$

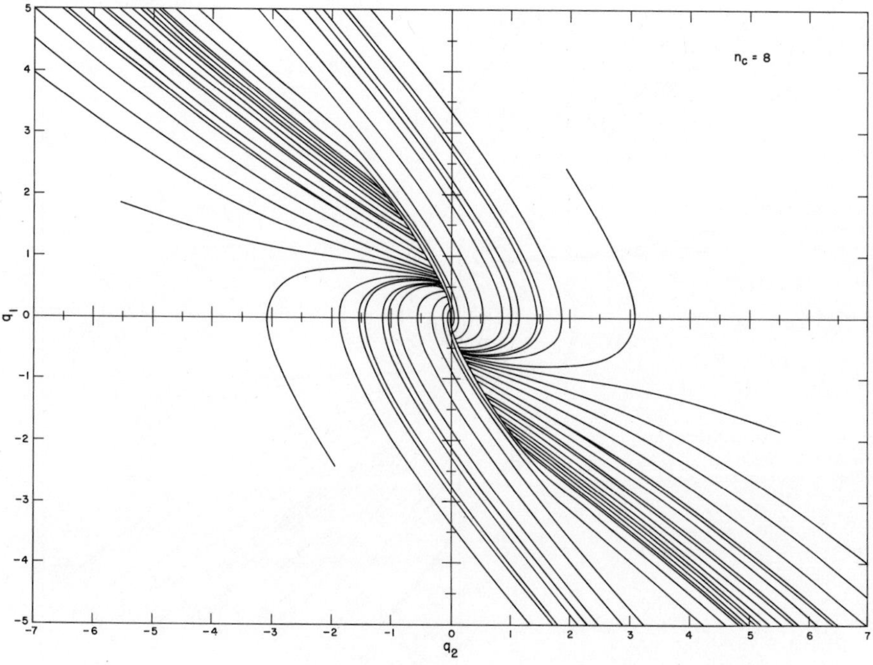

Fig. 3.16. The perturbed trajectories - $n_c = 8$

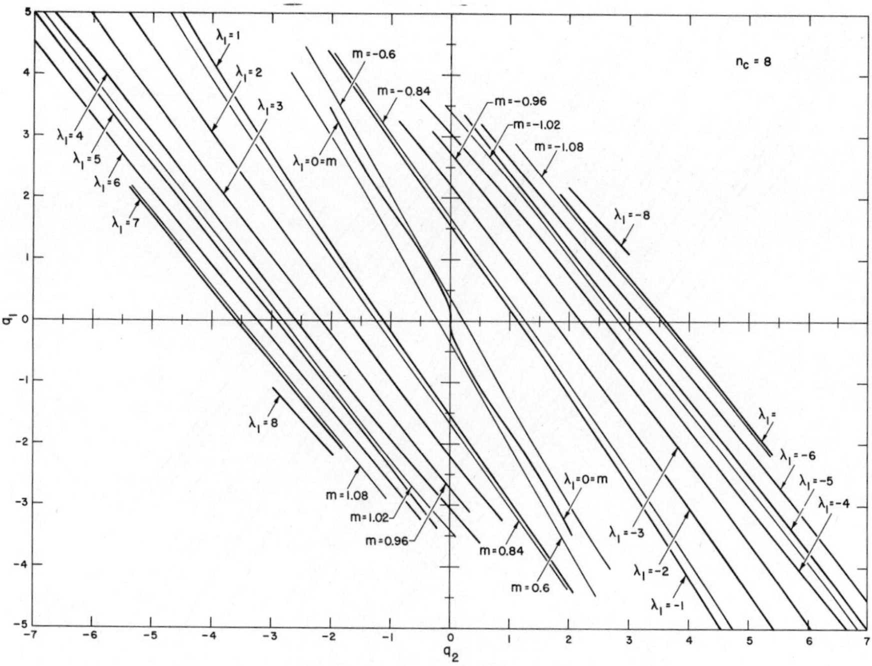

Fig. 3.17. The optimum control law - $n_c = 8$

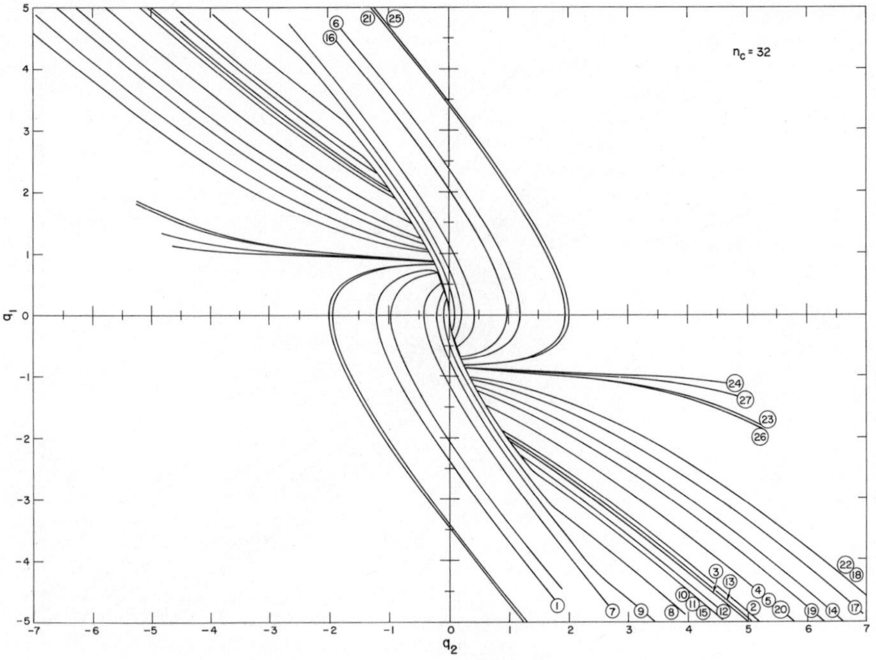

Fig. 3.18. The perturbed trajectories - $n_c = 32$

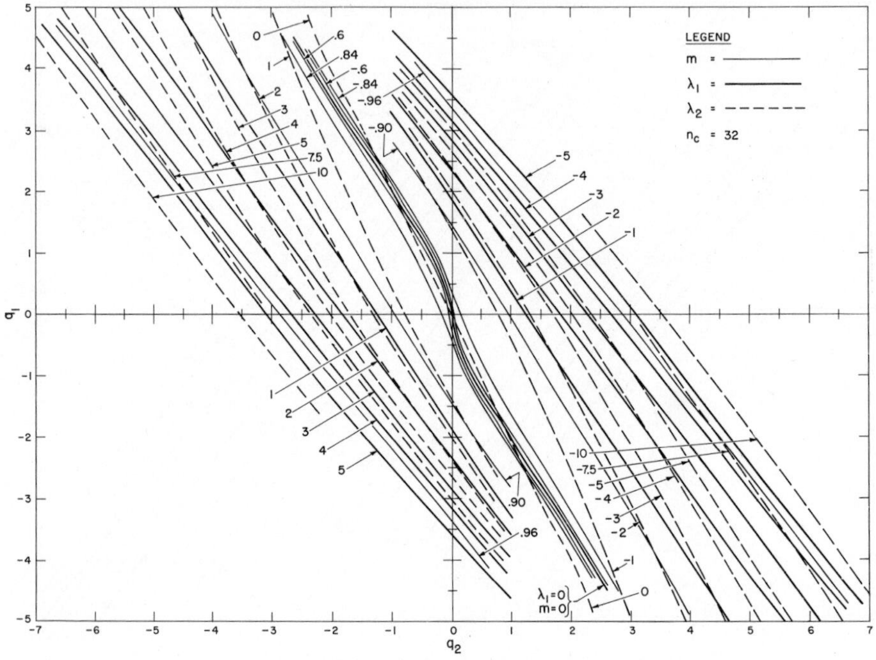

Fig. 3.19. The optimum control law - $n_c = 32$

Therefore it could also have been calculated from any three points on the trajectories of Figure 3.14, such as A1, A2, and A3, or B1, B2, and B3, by solving the equations

$$\begin{aligned} -1.444a + 1.933b + c &= -\ .889 \\ -\ .299a + 4.024b + c &= -\ 3.807 \\ +3.642a + 3.155b + c &= -\ 5.822 \end{aligned} \quad \text{or} \quad \begin{aligned} +\ .068a + 5.241b + c &= -\ 5.739 \\ -2.660a + 2.458b + c &= -\ .511 \\ +3.865a - 1.452b + c &= -\ 1.380 \end{aligned} \tag{3.48}$$

to evaluate the coefficients a, b, and c of the control law

$$m = aq_1 + bq_2 + c \tag{3.49}$$

The entire map of the control law has been computed and plotted in Figure 3.15 to demonstrate that the distortion due to the initial perturbations is negligible. Figures 3.16 and 3.18 show the trajectories, while Figures 3.17 and 3.19 display the contours of constants λ_1, λ_2, and m for the cases in which $\mathcal{P}(m)$ equals m^8 and m^{32}, respectively.

As a more difficult and practically more significant example, the calculation of the control law for a simplified version of the Williams' stirred-tank reactor, described as Problem 4 of Appendix E, was attempted. Assuming that $T \to \infty$, taking the variation of the performance criterion defined for this problem in Equation E.23 yields the Euler equations

$$\mathcal{P}'(m) = -\lambda_1$$

$$q_1' = H_A q_3 r_A + H_B(1 - q_2 - q_3) r_B + f_A(T_A - q_1) + f_B(T_B - q_1) + m$$

$$q_2' = (1 - q_2 - q_3) r_B - (f_A + f_B) q_2$$

$$q_3' = f_A - (f_A + f_B) q_3 - q_3 r_A$$

$$\lambda_1' = \left(f_A + f_B - H_A \beta_A \frac{q_3}{(q_1)^2} r_A - H_B \beta_B \frac{(1 - q_2 - q_3)}{(q_1)^2} r_B\right) \lambda_1 + \left(\frac{-(1 - q_2 - q_3)}{(q_1)^2} \beta_B r_B\right) \lambda_2 + \left(\frac{q_3}{(q_1)^2} \beta_A r_A\right) \lambda_3$$

$$\lambda_2' = (H_B r_B) \lambda_1 + (f_A + f_B + r_B) \lambda_2 - (f_A + f_B)(P_B^o - P_C^o)$$

$$\lambda_3' = (H_B r_B - H_A r_A) \lambda_1 + r_B \lambda_2 + (f_A + f_B + r_A) \lambda_3 - P_B^o (f_A + f_B) \tag{3.50}$$

where

$$r_A = \exp(a_A - \frac{\beta_A}{q_1})$$

$$r_B = \exp(a_B - \frac{\beta_B}{q_1})$$

$$\mathcal{P}(m) = (m)^8 \tag{3.51}$$

At the equilibrium point of the Euler equations

$$q_2 = \frac{r_A r_B}{(1+r_A)(1+r_B)} \qquad q_3 = \frac{1}{1+r_A}$$

$$\lambda_1 = \frac{2}{r_B}\Big((1+r_B)\lambda_2 - 50\Big) = \frac{100 r_A(11 r_A r_B + r_B - 10)}{(q_1)^2(r+r_A)^2(1+r_B)^2 + r_A(11 r_A r_B - 19 r_B - 10 r_B^2 - 20)}$$

$$\lambda_2 = \frac{\lambda_1 r_B + 100}{2 + 2r_B} = \frac{50\Big(q_1^2(1+r_A)^2(1+r_B) + r_A(11 r_A r_B - 9 r_B - 20)\Big)}{(q_1)^2(Hr_A)^2(1+r_B)^2 + r_A(11 r_A r_B - 19 r_B - 10 r_B^2 - 20)}$$

$$\lambda_3 = \frac{50 + (r_A + .5 r_B + r_A r_B)\lambda_1}{(1 + r_A)(1 + r_B)} \tag{3.52}$$

where q_1 has to satisfy

$$\frac{r_A(1 + .5 r_B)}{(1+r_A)(1 + r_B)} + 1 - q_1 - (\mathcal{P}')^{-1}(\lambda_1) = 0 \tag{3.53}$$

In Equation 3.52 and in subsequent work the numerical values for the parameters used are

$$\begin{array}{lllll} a_A = 23.0 & a_B = 25.0 & P_A^o = 0 & P_A^i = 5 & f_A = 1.0 \\ \beta_A = 20.0 & \beta_B = 22.0 & P_B^o = 50 & P_B^i = 50 & f_B = 0 \\ H_A = 1.0 & H_B = -.5 & P_C^o = 0 & P_C^i = 5 & T_A = 1.0 \end{array} \tag{3.54}$$

Solving Equation 3.53 numerically, one obtains for the steady-state optimum the conditions

$$q_1 = .871736 \qquad q_2 = .226824 \qquad q_3 = .485688$$

$$\lambda_1 = .092954 \qquad \lambda_2 = 27.9693 \qquad \lambda_3 = 13.6322 \tag{3.55}$$

To evaluate the control law, a number of solutions of the Euler equations were generated, starting from the neighborhood of the equilibrium point and propagating the solutions backward in time. Typical trajectories are shown in Figure 3.20.

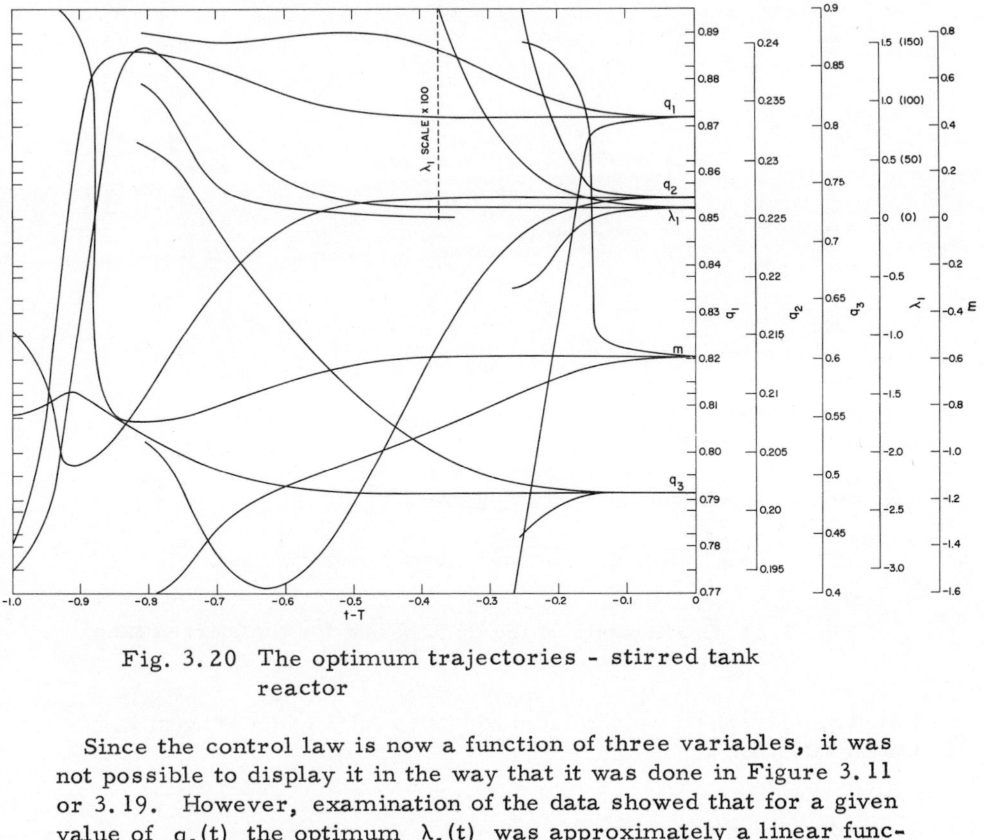

Fig. 3.20 The optimum trajectories - stirred tank reactor

Since the control law is now a function of three variables, it was not possible to display it in the way that it was done in Figure 3.11 or 3.19. However, examination of the data showed that for a given value of $q_1(t)$ the optimum $\lambda_1(t)$ was approximately a linear function of $q_2(t)$ and $q_3(t)$ in the region of interest. Therefore it was possible to express the control law as

$$m = -\operatorname{sign}(\lambda_1)\left|\frac{\lambda_1}{4}\right|^{1/7}$$

$$\lambda_1 = a(q_1) + \left(q_2 - .226824\right) b(q_1) + \left(q_3 - .485688\right) c(q_1) \tag{3.56}$$

and determine $a(q_1)$, $b(q_1)$, and $c(q_1)$ by a least squares fit. The coefficients a, b, and c, are shown plotted in Figure 3.21 as a function of q_1. This example illustrates the fact that it is next to impossible to display, much less generate, a "general" function of n variables. In the end the optimum control law as calculated by the flooding technique has to be approximated by some easily generated functional forms.

The following example illustrates the calculation of the optimum control law as a function of $\underline{q}$ and $\underline{v}$ in a case when T approaches

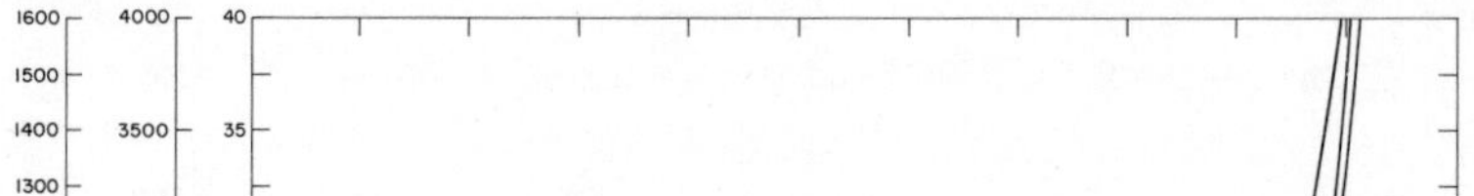

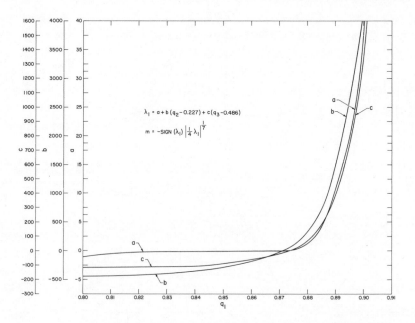

Fig. 3.21 Coefficients of the control law for the stirred tank reactor

infinity and $\underline{u}(\tau), t \leq \tau$ is related to $\underline{v}(t)$ as $\underline{u}(\tau) = \underline{f}(\tau - t - g(\underline{v}))$. Optimization of

$$\mathcal{P} = -\int_t^{\infty} \left\{ \left(q(\tau) - i(\tau)\right)^2 + \left(m(\tau)\right)^8 + 2\lambda(\tau)\left(q'(\tau) - m(\tau)\right) \right\} d\tau \qquad (3.57)$$

was carried out for a situation in which $i(\tau)$ is a delayed step

$$i(\tau) = \delta_{-1}(\tau - t - g(\underline{v})) - 1 \qquad (3.58)$$

The equilibrium point corresponding to the steady-state optimum is

$$q = 0 = \lambda = m \qquad (3.59)$$

The trajectories were propagated backward from its vicinity for various perturbations of $\lambda(T)$ and various values of $T - t - g(v)$ In Figure 3.22 the trajectories are plotted as a function of τ or equivalently as a function of $g(\underline{v})$, for $g(\underline{v})$ in Equation 3.58 represents the time to go before the occurrence of the step. The optimum control law is displayed in Figure 3.22 by the contours of constant m and constant λ in the $(q, g(\underline{v}))$ plane. It specifies the value of the control effort as a function of the state and the time to go before the occurrence of the step. For $g(\underline{v}) < 0$ the control law is the same as that obtained from optimization of $\mathcal{P}$ in Equation 3.39. For $g(v) \to \infty$ the control law is the same as for $g(\underline{v}) < 0$ except that it is shifted by one along the q axis. Figure 3.22 displays the transition between these two extremes. In Figure 3.22 there is shown a solution to the same example but with

$$i(\tau) = \exp(-\tau + t + g(\underline{v})) \tag{3.60}$$

or equivalently

$$i(\tau) = \hat{g}(\underline{v})e^{-(\tau - t)} \tag{3.61}$$

In both cases the control law is highly nonlinear because of the high-power penalty function on m, and in both cases the control law is seen to require application of control effort in anticipation of $i(\tau)$.

Solution of Problem 3 of Appendix E demonstrates a case in which there may be several different trajectories which satisfy the Euler equation and the prescribed boundary conditions. For the example, the demand curve $f(q)$ and the cumulative demand $F(q)$ were taken as

$$\begin{array}{lll} f = 5q & 0.0 < q < 0.2 & F(q) = 2.5q^2 \\ f = 3 - 10q & 0.2 < q < 0.3 & F(q) = -.3 + 3q - 5q^2 \\ f = 20q - 6 & 0.3 < q < 0.4 & F(q) = 1.05 - 6q + 10q^2 \\ f = 4 - 5q & 0.4 < q < 0.6 & F(q) = -.95 + 4q - 2.5q^2 \\ f = 1 & 0.6 < q < 1.0 & F(q) = -.05 + q \end{array} \tag{3.62}$$

These are plotted in Figure 3.24. The Euler equations become

$$f(q(\ell)) \triangleleft q(\ell) = \triangleright F(q(\ell)) \qquad \ell = 1, 2, \ldots N-1 \tag{2.63}$$

where

$$\Delta N = T - t \tag{3.64}$$

and the boundary conditions are

$$q(0) = 0 \qquad q(N) = 1.0 \tag{3.65}$$

Letting $j = N - \ell$ and $y(j) = q(N - \ell)$ Equation 3.63 can be rewritten as

$$y(j+1) = y(j) - \frac{F(\,y(j-1)\,) - F(\,y(j)\,)}{f(\,y(j)\,)} \qquad j = 1, 2, \ldots N-1 \tag{3.66}$$

where $y(0) = 1.0$, $F(\,y(0)\,) = .95$. By choosing a value of $y(1)$, one can generate $y(2)$, $y(3)$, ... $y(N)$. Since $y(N)$ is the same as $q(0)$, it should equal 0, but if it is generated this way, then in general it will not. One then has to search for a value of $y(1)$ for which $y(N)$ does equal 0. It may be that there are several values

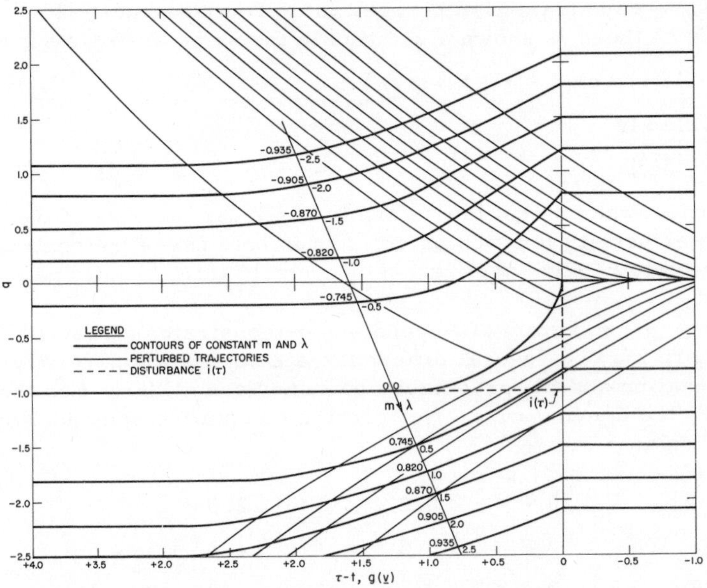

Fig. 3.22. The optimum control law when the desired output is a delayed step

of $y(1)$ for which $y(N) = 0$; one then has to compute $\mathcal{P}$ to choose between the candidates.

Figure 3.25 displays the computed values of $y(j)$, $j = 1, 2, \ldots$ as a function of $y(1)$, and in Figure 3.26 is shown $\mathcal{P}_p$ as a function of $y(1)$ where

$$\mathcal{P}_p = \sum_{i=0}^{\ell} F(\,y(i)\,)\,\bigl(y(i) - y(i+1)\bigr) \tag{3.67}$$

and i^{ℓ} is the largest value of i for which $q(i) > 0$. (The value of $q(i^{\ell} + 1)$ is taken as 0.) In Table 3.2 there are listed the values of $y(1)$ for which $y(j)$, $j = 2, 3, \ldots$ equal 0 and the corresponding values of $\mathcal{D}_p$. The optimum trajectories for $N = 3, 4, \ldots 10$ are underlined. Thus if $N = 4$, the optimum ordering times are $\tau = 0$, .3428, .5258, .7629 yielding a $\mathcal{D}_p$ of .5363 rather than $\tau = 0$, .1786, .3944, .6972 with a $\mathcal{D}_p$ of .5493 or $\tau = 0$, .2255, .4206, .7103 with a $\mathcal{D}_p$ of .5505 or any other set of ordering times. The cumulative order curve $F^*(q)$ for the optimum ordering times, for $N = 4$ is shown in Figure 3.24. The optimum ordering times for $N = 4$ are shown in Figure 3.25.

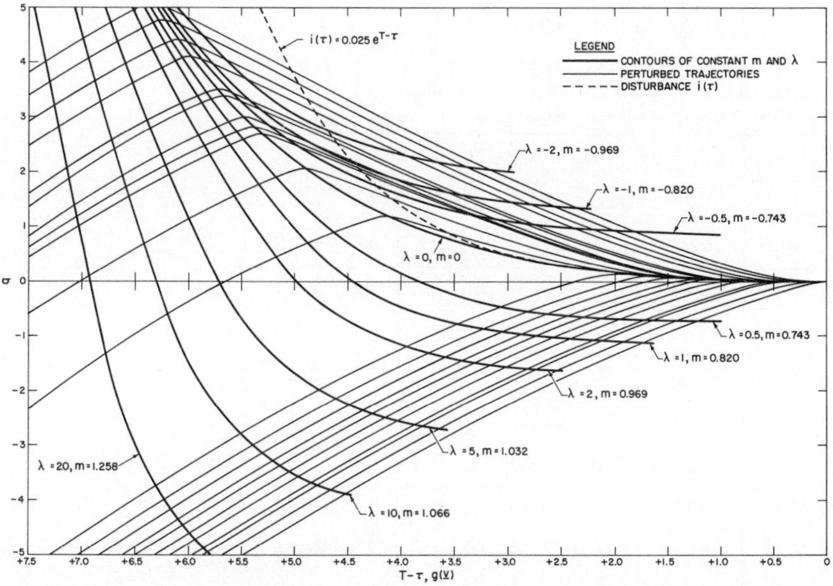

Fig. 3.23. The optimum control law when the desired output is a decaying exponential

All of the above examples were solved on an IBM 709 computer. It is difficult to give a reliable estimate of the computing time involved since in almost all cases appreciably more data was read out of the computer than was necessary for the solution of the problem itself. As a rough guide, solutions at about 500 points could be generated in a minute, although in solving the more complicated Euler equations only about 100 solution points could be obtained, processed, and read out in a minute.

The flooding technique for the evaluation of the optimum control law has been developed and demonstrated in this section. It has been used successfully on a variety of problems, as the examples indicate.

Table 3.2

Possible Ordering Policies

$\mathscr{D}_p$	y(1)	y(2)	y(3)	y(4)	7(5)	7(6)	y(7)	y(8)	y(9)	y(10)
.5722	.6807	.3614	0							
.5493	.6972	.3944	.1786	0						
.5505	.7103	.4206	.2255	0						
.5363	.7629	.5258	.3428	0						
.5177	.7795	.5590	.3725	.1642	0					
.5218	.8010	.6020	.4030	.2539	0					
.5142	.8218	.6436	.4656	.3318	0					
.4983	.8285	.6570	.4855	.3556	.1561	0				
.5046	.8385	.6770	.5155	.3894	.2677	0				
.5019	.8506	.7012	.5519	.4264	.3223	0				
.4865	.8587	.7174	.5762	.4482	.3442	.1500	0			
.4817	.8657	.7313	.5970	.4646	.3584	.2001	.1154	0		
.4817	.8682	.7364	.6057	.4728	.3674	.2292	.1291	0		
.4948	.8715	.7430	.6145	.4860	.3835	.2733	0			
.4918	.8758	.7516	.6273	.5032	.4037	.3167	0			
.4780	.8790	.7580	.6370	.5160	.4184	.3332	.1463	0		
.4735	.8810	.7620	.6430	.5240	.4273	.3431	.1877	.1020	0	
.4736	.8858	.7716	.6574	.6432	.4480	.3658	.2540	.1371	0	
.4858	.8883	.7766	.6646	.5531	.4582	.3764	.2785	0		
.4864	.8925	.7850	.6775	.5700	.4746	.3931	.3134	0		
.4708	.8943	.7886	.6829	.5772	.4811	.3995	.3257	.1454	0	
.4673	.8973	.7946	.6919	.5892	.4915	.4092	.3357	.1876	.1669	0
.4681	.9030	.8060	.7090	.6120	.5150	.4343	.3624	.2610	.1416	0
.4799	.9044	.8087	.7131	.6175	.5218	.4421	.3699	.2800	0	
.4745	.9070	.8140	.7210	.6280	.5350	.4568	.3836	.3140	0	
.4658	.9077	.8156	.7234	.6312	.5390	.4610	.3927	.3154	.1499	0
.4275	.9143	.8286	.7429	.6572	.5715	.4946	.4274	.3665	.4844	0
.4776	.9175	.8350	.7525	.6700	.5875	.5095	.4419	.3808	.3101	0

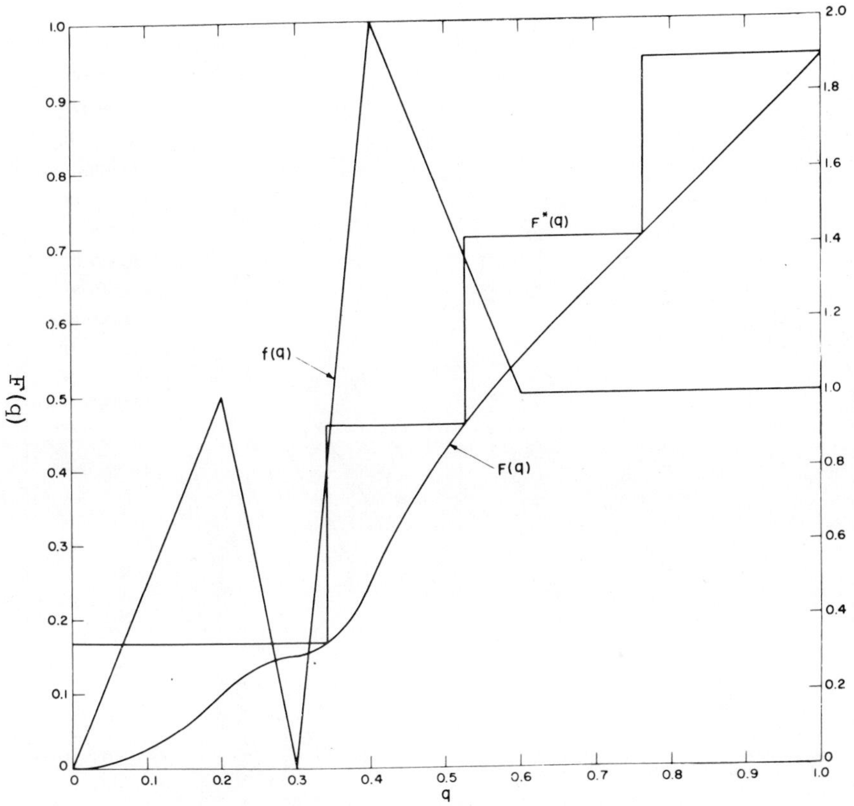

Fig. 3.24. Predicted demand and cumulative demand curves, and the optimum order curve for $N = 4$

3.3. Single-Point Solutions

When one is required to calculate the value of the optimum control effort for a single specified value of the state vector rather than to tabulate the entire control law, the flooding techniques become grossly inefficient and other methods must be devised. This becomes of particular importance when one attempts to use an on-line computing device to calculate the optimum control input for the currently measured value of the state variables.

The original problem of optimizing $\mathcal{P}$ requires choosing an entire function $\underline{m}(\tau), t \leq \tau < T$, a quantity with infinitely many degrees of freedom. The derivation of Euler equations immediately reduces the problem to one of only n degrees of freedom. For a specified state $\underline{q}(t)$, one needs to choose the n remaining initial conditions $\underline{\lambda}(t)$, such that the resultant trajectory satisfies the end-point

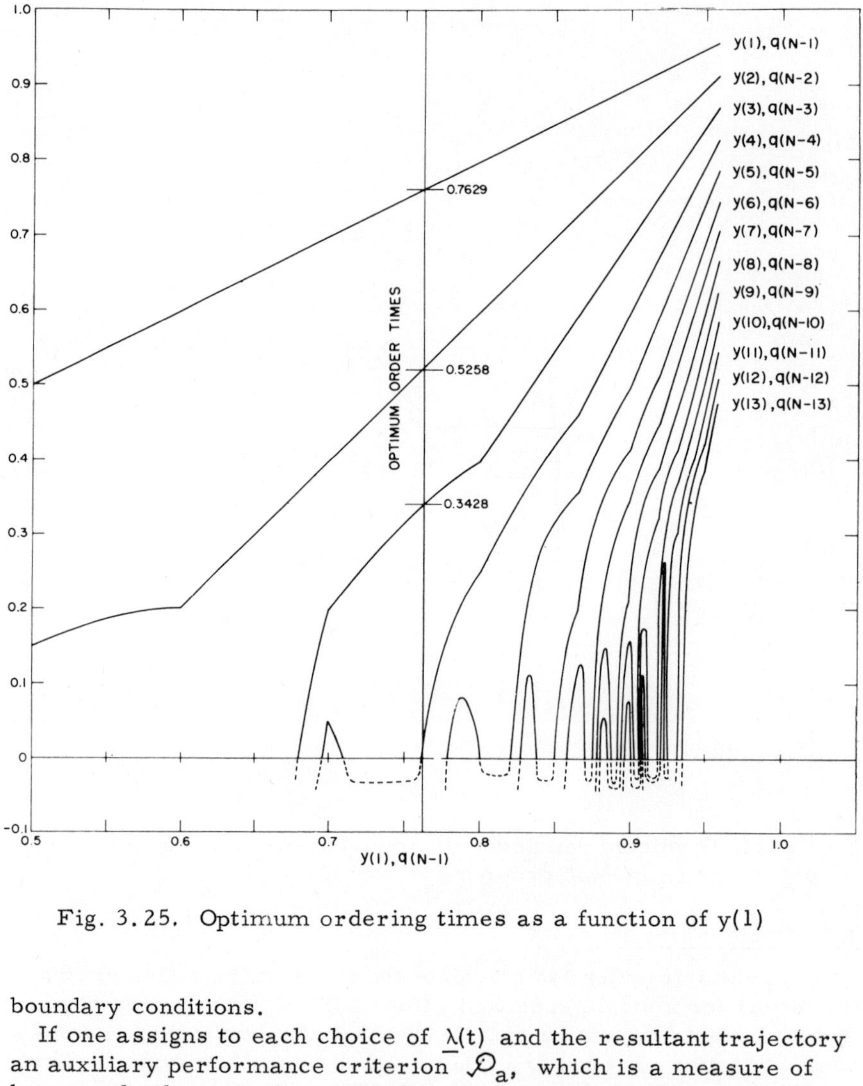

Fig. 3.25. Optimum ordering times as a function of y(1)

boundary conditions.

If one assigns to each choice of $\underline{\lambda}(t)$ and the resultant trajectory an auxiliary performance criterion $\mathcal{P}_a$, which is a measure of how nearly the trajectory satisfies the end-point boundary conditions, then one can use any one of the hill-climbing or gradient procedures to choose $\underline{\lambda}(t)$ so as to optimize $\mathcal{P}_a$. The function $\mathcal{P}_a$ should be unimodal and must take on its maximum value when the prescribed boundary conditions are satisfied. Its actual form is to a large extent arbitrary, and some forethought is needed in choosing a form which will induce the most rapid convergence of the process. Of course, in the case that the natural boundary conditions are prescribed, the most logical choice for $\mathcal{P}_a$ is $\mathcal{P}$ itself.

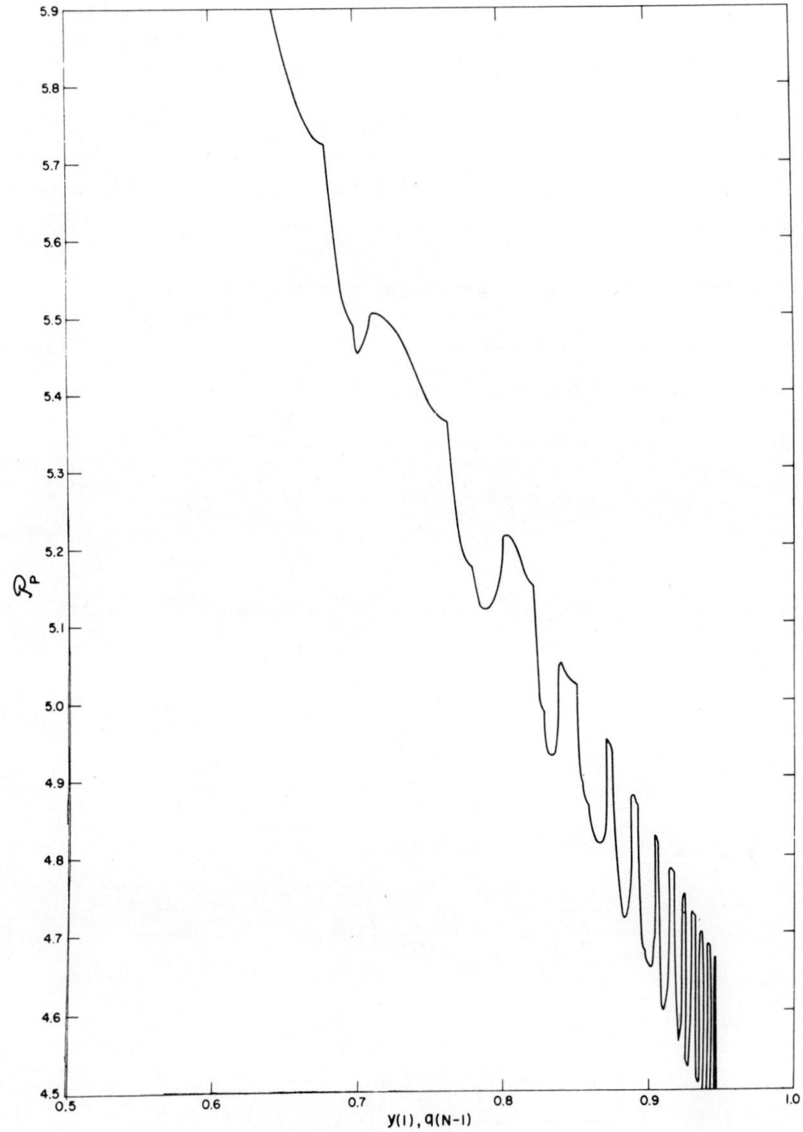

Fig. 3.26 $\mathcal{P}_p$ as a function of y(1)

Unlike the techniques of the previous two sections, this method can be used when the end-point boundary conditions are a function of T. It can therefore be used to find the optimum trajectory to meet a given path or hypersurface.

As an example, Problem 2 of Appendix E will be solved in this way. Using the following functions to describe the change of missile mass, aerodynamic drag, and the pull of gravity

$$M(\tau) = 1 + e^{-10\tau} \qquad D(q_1, q_2) = \frac{(2q_1(\tau))^7}{(1 + 10q_2(\tau))^8} \qquad G = \frac{9.8(1 + e^{-10\tau})}{(1 + q_2(\tau))^2} \tag{3.68}$$

and considering the aimed-for trajectory $i(\tau)$ as

$$i(\tau) = \tau^2 - \tau + .35 \tag{3.69}$$

the performance criterion $\mathcal{P}$ becomes

$$\mathcal{P} = \int_t^T \Bigg|_{\substack{q_2(T) = i(T) = T^2 - T + .35 \\ q_1(T) = i(T) = 2T - 1}} \Big\{ \big(m(\tau)\big)^2 + \lambda_1(\tau)\Big(q_1'(\tau)(1 + e^{-10\tau}) - 10q_1(\tau)e^{-10\tau} + \frac{(2q_1(\tau))^7}{(1 + 10q_2(\tau))^8} + \frac{9.8(1 + e^{-10\tau})}{(1 + q_2(\tau))^2} - m(\tau)\Big) + \lambda_2(\tau)\big(q_2'(\tau) - q_1(\tau)\big)\Big\} d\tau \tag{3.70}$$

The Euler equations are derived as

$$q_1'(\tau) = \frac{-9.8}{(1 + q_2)^2} + \frac{1}{1 + e^{-10\tau}}\left(10q_1e^{-10\tau} - \frac{(2q_1)^7}{(1 + 10q_2)^8} + m\right)$$

$$q_2'(\tau) = q_1$$

$$\lambda_1'(\tau) = \frac{1}{1 + e^{-10\tau}}\left(\frac{14(2q_1)^6}{(1 + 10q_2)^8}\lambda_1 - \lambda_2\right)$$

$$\lambda_2'(\tau) = -\left(\frac{19.6(1 + e^{-10\tau})}{(1 + q_2)^3} + \frac{80(2q_1)^7}{(1+10q_2)^8}\right)\lambda_1$$

$$m(\tau) = \frac{1}{2}\lambda_1 \tag{3.71}$$

and the boundary conditions are

$$q_1(T) = 2T - 1$$

$$q_2(T) = T^2 - T + .35$$

$$m^2(T) = \lambda_1(T)\left(q_1'(T) - 2\right) + \lambda_2(T)\left(q_2'(T) - 2T + 1\right) \qquad (3.72)$$

A suitable auxiliary performance criterion is

$$\mathcal{P}_a = \gamma_3\left\{m(T)^2 - \lambda_1(T)\left(\frac{1}{1+e^{-10T}}\left(10q_1(T)e^{-10T} - \frac{(2q_1(T))^7}{(1+10q_2(T))^8} + m(T)\right)\right.\right.$$

$$\left.\left. - \frac{9.8}{(1+q_2(T))^2} - 2\right)\right\}^2 + \gamma_1\left(q_1(T) - 2T + 1\right)^2 + \gamma_2\left(q_2(T) - T^2 + T - .35\right)^2$$

(3.73)

The maximum value of $\mathcal{P}_a$ is 0, and this is when the boundary conditions are satisfied exactly. Thus the achievable maximum is independent of the actual form of $\mathcal{P}_a$ although the form can affect markedly the rate of convergence of the process. Thus in Equation 3.73 the relative importance of the terms of Equation 3.72 is determined by the weighting factors γ_1, γ_2, and γ_3, and some experimentation is needed to determine the values of γ_1, γ_2, and γ_3, which induce the most rapid convergence.

In the solution of this problem, γ_3 was taken to be 1.111×10^{-9}, while γ_1 and γ_2 were taken equal to 1. The optimization was carried out using a subprogram HCL, described in Appendix G, which performs the optimization using a relatively unsophisticated hill-climbing technique. The search was started with an initial guess of $\lambda_1(t) = 45.0$, $\lambda_2(t) = 270$, and the final optimum was reached for $\lambda_1(t) = 43.933$ and $\lambda_2(t) = 276.69$, at which time $\mathcal{P}_a$ was -6.40×10^{-6}, a value less than a prescribed tolerance. The value of $\mathcal{P}$ at these conditions was -64.822. The optimum trajectory and several of the trial trajectories leading to it are shown in Figure 3.27. The initial portions of all of the trajectories are seen to be very similar, but the final stages are rather sensitive to changes in $\lambda_1(t)$ and $\lambda_2(t)$. This behavior is characteristic and is a direct consequence of the instability of the Euler equations. As a result, the finding of the optimum trajectory is more difficult, but for the same reason it can yield a very accurate determination of $\underline{\lambda}(t)$ and $\underline{m}(t)$.

The above method of solution amounts to choosing from among trajectories which satisfy Euler equations the one which satisfies the boundary conditions. Alternately one can choose from among

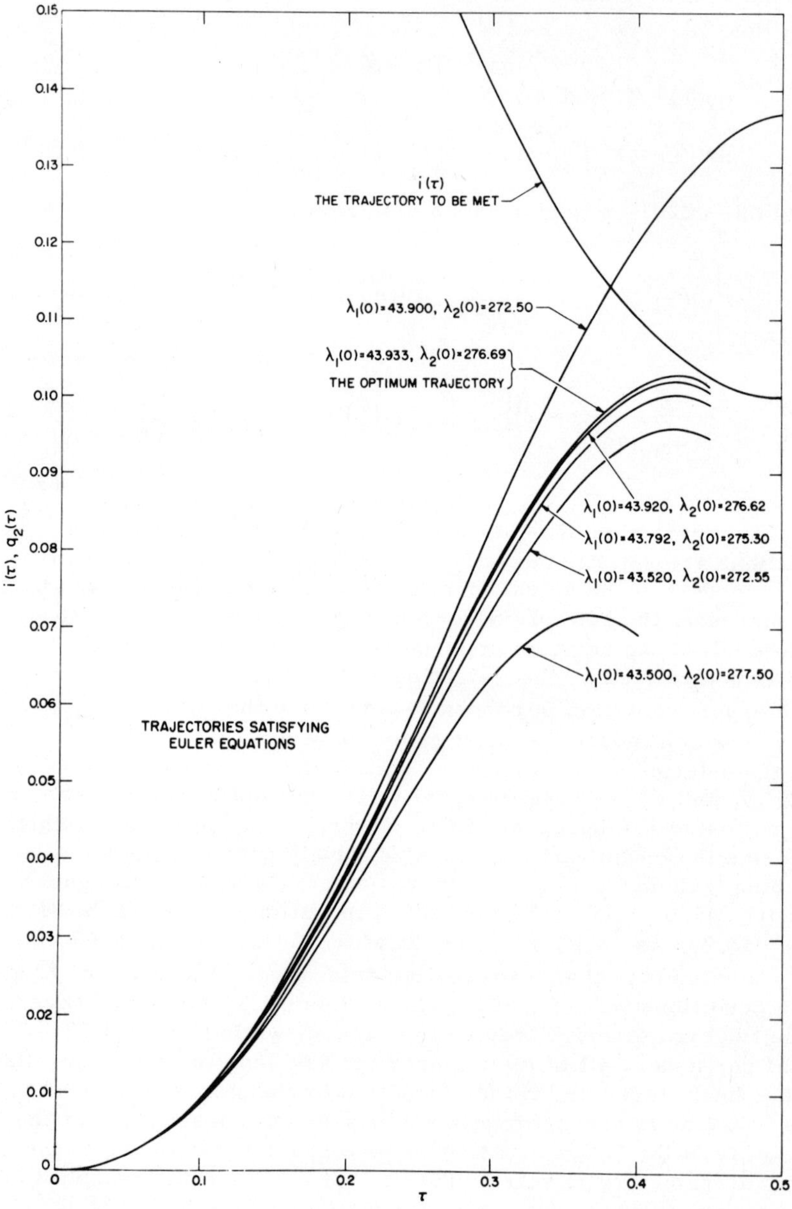

Fig. 3.27. The optimum trajectory to reach an orbiting vehicle

trajectories which satisfy the boundary conditions the one which satisfies the Euler equations.

Consider a trajectory $\underline{q}^*(\tau), \underline{\lambda}^*(\tau), t \leq \tau < T$ satisfying the boundary conditions

$$\underline{q}^*(t) = \underline{q}^*(t)$$
$$\underline{f}(\underline{q}^*(T), \underline{\lambda}^*(T)) = \underline{0} \tag{3.74}$$

(T is considered fixed) but not satisfying the Euler equations. One seeks functions $\underline{q}(\tau), \underline{\lambda}(\tau), t \leq \tau < T$ with

$$q(t)] = 0\,]$$

$$[\,J_{q^*}(\underline{f}(\underline{q}^*(T), \underline{\lambda}^*(T)))\,]q(T)] + [\,J_{\lambda^*}(\underline{f}(\underline{q}^*(T), \lambda^*(T)))]\,\lambda(T)\,] = 0\,] \tag{3.75}$$

for which the Euler equation

$$\underline{q}^{*\prime}(\tau) + \underline{q}'(\tau) = \underline{G}_1(\tau, \underline{q}^*+q, \lambda^*+\lambda)$$
$$\underline{\lambda}^{*\prime}(\tau) + \underline{\lambda}'(\tau) = \underline{G}_2(\tau, \underline{q}^* + q, \lambda^*+\lambda) \tag{3.76}$$

is satisfied. (In Equation 3.76 $\underline{m}^*$ has been replaced by the corresponding function of $\underline{\lambda}^*$ and $\underline{q}^*$.) If $\underline{q}$, $\underline{\lambda}$ is but a perturbation of $\underline{q}^*$, $\underline{\lambda}^*$, then it satisfies the incremental Euler equation

$$q'(\tau)] = [\,P(\tau, \underline{q}^*, \underline{\lambda}^*)]\,q] + [\,R(\tau, \underline{q}^*, \underline{\lambda}^*)]\,\lambda\,] - q^*] + G_1(\tau, \underline{q}^*, \underline{\lambda}^*)]$$
$$\lambda'(\tau)] = [\,Q(\tau, \underline{q}^*, \underline{\lambda}^*)]\,q] - [\,P^T(\tau, \underline{q}^*, \underline{\lambda}^*)\,]\,\lambda\,] - \lambda^*\,] + G_2(\tau, \underline{q}^*, \underline{\lambda}^*)\,] \tag{3.77}$$

Therefore there is some $\epsilon > 0$ for which

$$\mathcal{D}(\underline{q}^*, \underline{\lambda}^*) \leq \mathcal{D}(\underline{q}^* + \epsilon\, \underline{q}, \underline{\lambda}^* + \epsilon\, \underline{\lambda}) \tag{3.78}$$

where $\underline{q}(\tau), \underline{\lambda}(\tau), t \leq \tau \leq T$ is a solution of Equation 3.77 with the boundary conditions of Equation 3.75. By setting $\underline{q}^*$, λ^* equal to $\underline{q}^* + \epsilon\,\underline{q}$, $\underline{\lambda}^* + \epsilon\underline{\lambda}$ and repeating the process, one obtains an iterative scheme for obtaining solutions of two-point boundary-value problems. If the equations were indeed linear, the procedure would converge in one step for $\epsilon = 1$.

No computational experience has been acquired by which to judge the effectiveness of this method. It would seem to be particularly useful when the Euler equations are only weakly nonlinear or when the trajectory from which the iterations are started is already close to being an optimum.

3.4. Taylor Series Expansion of the Control Law

The nonlinear control law

$$\underline{m}(t) = \underline{\mathcal{C}}(\, t, T, \underline{q}(t), \underline{v}(t)\,) \tag{3.79}$$

was represented in Section 3.2 by a table of values. Alternately, if the control law function is analytic in some neighborhood about a point $\underline{q}^*(t)$ in the state space, it can be represented in that neighborhood by a power series expansion about $\underline{q}^*(t)$. If it is only differentiable $K+1$ times, it can be approximated at a point $\underline{q}(t)$ in the neighborhood of $\underline{q}^*(t)$ by a truncated Taylor series of $K+2$ terms*

$$\begin{aligned} m^{\underline{i}_o}(\, t, \underline{q}(t)) = {} & \mathcal{D}^{\underline{i}_o}(\, t, \underline{q}^*(t)\,) + \mathcal{C}^{\underline{i}_o}_{j_1}(\, t, \underline{q}^*(t)\,)\left(q^{\underline{j}_1}(t)\right) \\ & + \mathcal{C}^{\underline{i}_o}_{j_1, j_2}(\, t, \underline{q}^*(t)\,)\left(q^{\underline{j}_1}(t) - q^{*\underline{j}_1}(t)\right)\left(q^{\underline{j}_2}(t) - q^{*\underline{j}_2}(t)\right) \\ & + \ldots + \mathcal{C}^{\underline{i}_o}_{j_1, j_2, \ldots j_k}(\, t, \underline{q}^*(t)\,) \prod_{\ell=1}^{K}\left(q^{\underline{j}_\ell}(t) - q^{*\underline{j}_\ell}(t)\right) \\ & + \mathcal{C}^{\underline{i}_o}_{j_1, j_2 \ldots j_{K+1}}(\, t, \underline{\eta}(t)\,) \prod_{\ell=1}^{K+1}\left(q^{\underline{j}_\ell}(t) - q^{*\underline{j}_\ell}(t)\right) \end{aligned} \tag{3.80}$$

for some $\underline{\eta}$ such that $\eta_i = a q^*_i + (1 - a) q_i$ for some $0 < a < 1$. If the first $K+1$ terms are used to evaluate $\underline{m}(t)$, the last term represents an error bound. It will be shown how one can derive a differential equation defining the successive terms in this expansion in the same manner that the Riccati equation defining $\mathcal{C}^{\underline{i}}_{j}$ in the linear case was derived in Section 3.1.

Such a power series expansion is of interest in representing a precalculated control law, for the first several coefficients can represent the control function in a given neighborhood more efficiently than a table of values—especially if the control law $\underline{\mathcal{C}}$ is a well-behaved function of $\underline{q}(t)$. It is also of interest for on-line computer control, for if the control law is known in a sizable

---

* The abbreviated notation for higher-order partial derivatives, which was introduced in Appendices A and C, is being used here.

neighborhood about the currently measured state, then it need not be recomputed until the system state is about to leave this neighborhood, thereby reducing the required computation rate.

In what follows it will be assumed that $\underline{m}(t)$ is a known function of $\underline{\lambda}(t)$, and the tensor expansion for $\underline{\lambda}(t)$ will be derived. The optimum control law, the relation between $\underline{\lambda}(t)$ and $\underline{q}(t)$:

$$\underline{\lambda}(t) = \underline{S}(\, t, \underline{q}(t)\,) \tag{3.81}$$

specifies that value of the initial conditions of the Euler equations $\underline{\lambda}(t)$, which for a given initial system state $\underline{q}(t)$ at time t generate the solution that satisfies the end-point boundary conditions at $\tau = T$. Let us consider that for a given value of $\underline{q}^*(t)$, the $\underline{\lambda}^*(t)$ which solves the two-point boundary-value problem and the entire optimum trajectory $\underline{q}^*(\tau), \underline{\lambda}^*(\tau), t \leq \tau < T$ are known. It may be the constant trajectory corresponding to a steady-state optimum or some other trajectory satisfying the Euler equations, which might have been obtained by one of the techniques of Section 3.3. One seeks the expansion of the control law of Equation 3.81 about the trajectory $\underline{q}^*(\tau), \underline{\lambda}^*(\tau), t \leq \tau < T$.

Using the abbreviated notation introduced in Appendices A and C, the Euler equations can be written as

$$\frac{d}{d\tau} S^{\underline{x}^{i_o}}(\tau, \underline{q}(t), \underline{\lambda}(t)\,) = G^{\underline{x}^{i_o}}(\,\tau, \underline{q}(\tau), \underline{\lambda}(\tau)\,) \tag{3.82}$$

where $x^{\underline{i}_o}$ takes on values $q^{\underline{i}_o}$ and $\lambda^{\underline{i}_o}$ and where

$$S^{\underline{q}^{i_o}}(\,\tau, \underline{q}(t), \underline{\lambda}(t)\,) = q^{\underline{i}_o}(\,\tau, q(t), \underline{\lambda}(t)\,) \text{ and}$$

$$S^{\underline{\lambda}^{i_o}}(\,\tau, \underline{q}(t), \underline{\lambda}(t)\,) = \lambda^{\underline{i}_o}(\,\tau, \underline{q}(t), \underline{\lambda}(t)\,)$$

representing solutions at time τ propagated from the state $\underline{q}(t), \underline{\lambda}(t)$ at $\tau = t$. The symbol $G^{\underline{x}^{i_o}}(\,\tau, \underline{q}(\tau), \underline{\lambda}(\tau)\,)$ represents the entire right-hand side of the Euler equations, that is, $G^{\underline{q}^{i_o}}$ expresses the rate of change of $q^{\underline{i}_o}(\tau)$, and $G^{\underline{\lambda}^{i_o}}$ the rate of change of $\lambda^{\underline{i}_o}(\tau)$. The solutions of the Euler equations for initial conditions in the neighborhood of $q^*(t)$, $\underline{\lambda}^*(t)$ can be expressed in terms of a Taylor series

$$q^{i_o}(\tau, \underline{q}^*(t)+\Delta\underline{q}(t), \underline{\lambda}^*(t)+\Delta\underline{\lambda}(t)) = \Big(S^{q^{i_o}}(\tau, \underline{q}^*(t), \underline{\lambda}^*(t))$$

$$+ S^{q^{i_o}}_{a_{j_1}}(\tau, \underline{q}^*(t), \underline{\lambda}^*(t))\Delta a^{j_1}(t) + S^{q^{i_o}}_{a_{j_1}, b_{j_2}}(\tau, \underline{q}^*(t), \underline{\lambda}^*(t))\Delta a^{j_1}(t)\Delta b^{j_2}(t) + \ldots \Big)$$

$$\lambda^{i_o}(\tau, \underline{q}^*(t)+\Delta\underline{q}(t), \underline{\lambda}^*(t)+\Delta\underline{\lambda}(t)) = \Big(S^{q^{i_o}}(\tau, \underline{q}^*(t), \underline{\lambda}^*(t))$$

$$+ S^{q^{i_o}}_{a_{j_1}}(\tau, \underline{q}^*(t), \lambda^*(t))\Delta a^{j_1}(t) + S^{q^{i_o}}_{a_{j_1}, b_{j_2}}(\tau, \underline{q}^*(t), \underline{\lambda}^*(t))\Delta a^{j_1}(t)\Delta b^{j_1}(t) + \ldots \Big)$$

(3.83)

where $\Delta x^i(t) = x^i(t) - x^{*i}(t)$ and the dummy variables such as "a" and "b" when they appear within the brackets as both subscripts and superscripts indicate that one is to sum over their possible values, q and λ. In this, the symbol Δa^{j_1} counts as a superscript. Thus

$$\Big(S^{q^{i_o}}_{a_{j_1}, b_{j_2}}(\tau)\,\Delta a^{j_1}\Delta b^{j_2} \Big) = \Big(S^{q^{i_o}}_{q_{j_1}, q_{j_2}}(\tau)\Delta q^{j_1}\Delta q^{j_2} + S^{q^{i_o}}_{q_{j_1}, \lambda_{j_2}}(\tau)\Delta\lambda^{j_1}\Delta\lambda^{j_2}$$

$$+ S^{q^{i_o}}_{\lambda_{j_1}, q_{j_2}}(\tau)\Delta q^{j_1}\Delta\lambda^{j_2} + S^{q^{i_o}}_{\lambda_{j_1}, \lambda_{j_2}}(\tau)\Delta\lambda^{j_1}\Delta\lambda^{j_2} \Big)$$

$$= \sum_{j_1=1}^{n} \sum_{j_2=1}^{n} \left\{ \frac{\partial^2 q_{i_o}(\tau)}{\partial q_{j_1}(t)\partial q_{j_2}(t)} + 2\, \frac{\partial^2 q_{i_o}(\tau)}{\partial q_{j_1}(t)\partial \lambda_{j_2}(t)} + \frac{\partial^2 q_{i_o}(\tau)}{\partial \lambda_{j_1}(t)\partial \lambda_{j_2}(t)} \right\}$$

(3.84)

As shown in Appendix C, the first two coefficients in the expansion of Equation 3.83 are defined by the equations

$$\frac{d}{d\tau} S^{\underline{x}^{i_0}}_{y_{i_1}}(\tau) = \left(G^{\underline{x}^{i_0}}_{a_{j_1}}(\tau, \underline{q}^*(\tau), \underline{\lambda}^*(\tau))\, S^{\underline{a}^{j_1}}_{y_{i_1}}(\tau) \right) \qquad S^{\underline{x}^{i_0}}_{y_{i_1}}(t) = \delta^{\underline{x}^{i_0}}_{y_{i_1}}$$

$$\frac{d}{d\tau} S^{\underline{x}^{i_0}}_{y_{i_1}, y_{i_2}}(\tau) = \left(G^{\underline{x}^{i_0}}_{a_{j_1}}(\tau, \underline{q}^*(\tau), \underline{\lambda}^*(\tau))\, S^{\underline{a}^{j_1}}_{y_{i_1}, y_{i_2}}(\tau) \right.$$

$$\left. + \, G^{\underline{x}^{i_0}}_{a_{j_1}, b_{j_2}}(\tau, \underline{q}^*(\tau), \underline{\lambda}^*(\tau))\, S^{\underline{a}^{j_1}}_{y_{i_1}}(\tau)\, S^{\underline{b}^{j_1}}_{y_{i_2}}(\tau) \right)$$

$$S^{\underline{x}^{i_0}}_{y_{i_1}, y_{i_2}}(t) = 0 \qquad (3.85)$$

Let the expansion of the control law of Equation 3.81 be represented as

$$\lambda^{i_0}(\tau, \underline{q}(t), \underline{\lambda}(t)) = \left(S^{\underline{\lambda}^{i_0}}(\tau, \underline{q}^*(t), \underline{\lambda}^*(t)) + C^{\underline{\lambda}^{i_0}}_{q_{j_1}}(\tau, \underline{q}^*(t), \underline{\lambda}^*(t))\, S^{\underline{q}^{j_1}}_{a_{j_2}}(\tau)\, \Delta \underline{a}^{j_2} \right.$$

$$+ \, D^{\underline{\lambda}^{i_0}}_{q_{j_1}}(\tau, \underline{q}^*(t), \underline{\lambda}^*(t))\, S^{\underline{q}^{j_1}}_{a_{j_2}, b_{j_3}}(\tau)\, \Delta \underline{a}^{j_2}\, \Delta \underline{b}^{j_3}$$

$$\left. + \, E^{\underline{\lambda}^{i_0}}_{q_{j_1}, q_{j_2}}(\tau, \underline{q}^*(t), \underline{\lambda}^*(t))\, S^{\underline{q}^{j_1}}_{a_{j_3}}(\tau)\, S^{\underline{q}^{j_2}}_{b_{j_4}}(\tau)\, \Delta \underline{a}^{j_3}\, \Delta \underline{b}^{j_4} + \ldots \right) \qquad (3.86)$$

In this expression $C^{\underline{\lambda}^{i_0}}_{q_{j_1}}$ represents the coefficients of the linearized control law about the trajectory $\underline{q}^*(\tau), \underline{\lambda}^*(\tau), t \leq \tau < T$. The coefficients $\overset{\lambda^{i_o}}{D}_{q_{j_1}}$ express the influence of the second-order terms, and $\overset{\lambda^{i_o}}{E}_{q_{j_1}, q_{j_2}}$ the influence of the cross-coupling of the first-order terms.

On equating the coefficients of the expansions of Equations 3.83 and 3.86 and differentiating, one obtains

$$\frac{d}{d\tau}\overset{\lambda^{i_o}}{S}(\tau) = \frac{d}{d\tau}\overset{\lambda^{i_o}}{S}(\tau)$$

$$\frac{d}{d\tau}\left\{\overset{\lambda^{i_o}}{S}_{x_{i_1}, y_{i_2}}(\tau)\right\} = \left(\frac{d}{d\tau}\left\{\overset{\lambda^{i_o}}{C}_{q_{j_1}}(\tau)\right\}\overset{q^{j_1}}{S}_{x_{i_1}, y_{i_2}}(\tau) + \overset{\lambda^{i_o}}{C}_{q_{j_1}}(\tau)\frac{d}{d\tau}\left\{\overset{q^{j_1}}{S}_{x_{i_1}, y_{i_2}}(\tau)\right\}\right)$$

$$\left\{\frac{d}{d\tau}\overset{\lambda^{i_o}}{S}_{x_{i_1}, y_{i_2}}(\tau)\right\} = \left(\frac{d}{d\tau}\left\{\overset{\lambda^{i_o}}{D}_{q_{j_1}}(\tau)\right\}\overset{q^{j_1}}{S}_{x_{i_1}, y_{i_2}}(\tau) + \overset{\lambda^{i_o}}{D}_{q_j}(\tau)\frac{d}{d\tau}\left\{\overset{q^{j_1}}{S}_{x_{i_1}, y_{i_2}}(\tau)\right\}\right.$$

$$+ \frac{d}{d\tau}\left\{\overset{\lambda^{i_o}}{E}_{q_{j_1}, q_{j_2}}(\tau)\right\}\overset{q^{j_1}}{S}_{x_{i_1}}(\tau)\overset{q^{j_2}}{S}_{y_{i_2}}(\tau) + \overset{\lambda^{i_o}}{E}_{q_{j_1}, q_{j_2}}(\tau)\overset{q^{j_1}}{S}_{x_{i_1}}(\tau)\frac{d}{d\tau}\left\{\overset{q^{j_2}}{S}_{y_{i_2}}(\tau)\right\}$$

$$\left. + \overset{\lambda^{i_o}}{E}_{q_{j_1}, q_{j_2}}(\tau)\frac{d}{d\tau}\left\{\overset{q^{j_1}}{S}_{x_{i_1}}(\tau)\right\}\overset{q^{j_2}}{S}_{y_{i_2}}(\tau)\right) \qquad (3.87)$$

On substituting for the derivatives of $\overset{q^{i_o}}{S}_{x_{j_1}, x_{j_2}} \ldots$ and $\overset{\lambda^{i_o}}{S}_{x_{j_1}, x_{j_2}} \ldots$

from Equation 3.85 and replacing any resultant $S^{\underline{\lambda}^{i_o}}_{x_{j_1}, x_{j_2} \cdots}$ terms

by the corresponding coefficients from Equation 3.86, one obtains

$$\left(\left\{\frac{d}{d\tau}\left\{C^{\underline{\lambda}^{i_o}}_{q_{i_1}}\right\} - G^{\underline{\lambda}^{i_o}}_{q_{i_1}} - G^{\underline{\lambda}^{i_o}}_{\lambda_{j_1}} C^{\underline{\lambda}^{j_1}}_{q_{i_1}} + C^{\underline{\lambda}^{i_o}}_{q_{j_1}} G^{\underline{q}^{j_1}}_{q_{i_1}} + C^{\underline{\lambda}^{i_o}}_{q_{j_1}} G^{\underline{q}^{j_1}}_{\lambda_{j_2}} C^{\underline{\lambda}^{j_2}}_{q_{i_1}}\right\} S^{\underline{q}^{i_1}}_{x_{\ell_1}}\right) = 0$$

$$\left(\left\{\frac{d}{d\tau}\left\{D^{\underline{\lambda}^{i_o}}_{q_{i_1}}\right\} - G^{\underline{\lambda}^{i_o}}_{q_{i_1}} - G^{\underline{\lambda}^{i_o}}_{\lambda_{j_1}} D^{\underline{\lambda}^{j_1}}_{q_{i_1}} + D^{\underline{\lambda}^{i_o}}_{q_{j_1}} G^{\underline{q}^{j_1}}_{q_{i_1}} + D^{\underline{\lambda}^{i_o}}_{q_{j_1}} G^{\underline{q}^{j_1}}_{\lambda_{j_2}} D^{\underline{\lambda}^{j_2}}_{q_{i_1}}\right\} S^{\underline{q}^{i_1}}_{x_{\ell_1}, y_{\ell_2}}\right.$$

$$+ \left\{\frac{d}{d\tau}\left\{E^{\underline{\lambda}^{i_o}}_{q_{i_1}, q_{i_2}}\right\} - G^{\underline{\lambda}^{i_o}}_{\lambda_{j_1}} E^{\underline{\lambda}^{j_1}}_{q_{i_1}, q_{i_2}} + D^{\underline{\lambda}^{i_o}}_{q_{j_1}} G^{\underline{q}^{j_1}}_{\lambda_{j_2}} E^{\underline{\lambda}^{j_2}}_{q_{i_1}, q_{i_2}} + 2E^{\underline{\lambda}^{i_o}}_{q_{i_1}, q_{j_1}} G^{\underline{q}^{j_1}}_{q_{i_2}}\right.$$

$$+ 2E^{\underline{\lambda}^{i_o}}_{q_{i_1}, q_{j_1}} G^{\underline{q}^{j_1}}_{\lambda_{j_2}} C^{\underline{\lambda}^{j_2}}_{q_{i_2}} - G^{\underline{\lambda}^{i_o}}_{q_{i_1}, q_{i_2}} - 2G^{\underline{\lambda}^{i_o}}_{q_{i_1}} C^{\underline{\lambda}^{j_1}}_{q_{i_2}} - G^{\underline{\lambda}^{i_o}}_{\lambda_{j_1}, \lambda_{j_2}} C^{\underline{\lambda}^{j_1}}_{q_{i_1}} C^{\underline{\lambda}^{j_2}}_{q_{i_2}}$$

$$\left.\left. + D^{\underline{\lambda}^{i_o}}_{q_{j_1}} G^{\underline{q}^{j_1}}_{q_{i_1}, q_{i_2}} + 2D^{\underline{\lambda}^{i_o}}_{q_{j_1}} G^{\underline{q}^{j_1}}_{q_{i_1}, \lambda_{j_2}} C^{\underline{\lambda}^{j_2}}_{q_{i_2}} + D^{\underline{\lambda}^{i_o}}_{q_{j_1}} G^{\underline{q}^{j_1}}_{\lambda_{j_2}, \lambda_{j_3}} C^{\underline{\lambda}^{j_2}}_{q_{i_1}} C^{\underline{\lambda}^{j_3}}_{q_{i_2}}\right\} S^{\underline{q}^{i_1}}_{x_{\ell_1}} S^{\underline{q}^{i_2}}_{y_{\ell_2}}\right) = 0 \qquad (3.88)$$

Since these equations are to hold for all $S^{\underline{q}^{i}}_{x_j}$ and $S^{\underline{q}^{i}}_{x_j, y_\ell}$ then each of their coefficients must be independently equal to zero. This yields the final differential equations

$$\frac{d}{d\tau} C^{\underline{\lambda}^{i_o}}_{q_{i_1}} = \left(G^{\underline{\lambda}^{i_o}}_{q_{i_1}} + G^{\underline{\lambda}^{i_o}}_{\lambda_{j_1}} C^{\underline{\lambda}^{j_1}}_{q_{i_1}} - C^{\underline{\lambda}^{i_o}}_{q_{j_1}} G^{\underline{q}^{j_1}}_{q_{i_1}} - C^{\underline{\lambda}^{i_o}}_{q_{j_1}} G^{\underline{q}^{j_1}}_{\lambda_{j_2}} C^{\underline{\lambda}^{j_2}}_{q_{i_1}}\right)$$

$$\frac{d}{d\tau} D^{\underline{\lambda}^{i_o}}_{q_{i_1}} = \left(G^{\underline{\lambda}^{i_o}}_{q_{i_1}} + G^{\underline{\lambda}^{i_o}}_{\lambda_{j_1}} D^{\underline{\lambda}^{j_1}}_{q_{i_1}} - D^{\underline{\lambda}^{i_o}}_{q_{j_1}} G^{\underline{q}^{j_1}}_{q_{i_1}} - C^{\underline{\lambda}^{i_o}}_{q_{j_1}} G^{\underline{q}^{j_1}}_{\lambda_{j_2}} C^{\underline{\lambda}^{j_2}}_{q_{i_1}}\right)$$

$$\frac{d}{d\tau}E^{\underline{\lambda}^{i_o}}_{q_{i_1},q_{i_2}} = \Big(G^{\underline{\lambda}^{i_o}}_{\lambda_{j_1}} E^{\underline{\lambda}^{j_1}}_{q_{i_1},q_{i_2}} - D^{\underline{\lambda}^{i_o}}_{q_{j_1}} G^{\underline{q}^{j_1}}_{\lambda_{j_2}} E^{\underline{\lambda}^{j_2}}_{q_{i_1},q_{i_2}} - 2E^{\underline{\lambda}^{i_o}}_{q_{i_1},q_{j_1}} G^{\underline{q}^{j_1}}_{q_{i_2}} - 2E^{\underline{\lambda}^{i_o}}_{q_{i_1},q_{i_2}} G^{\underline{q}^{i_1}}_{\lambda_{j_2}} C^{\underline{\lambda}^{j_2}}_{q_{i_2}}$$

$$+ G^{\underline{\lambda}^{i_o}}_{q_{i_1},q_{i_2}} + 2G^{\underline{\lambda}^{i_o}}_{q_{i_1},\lambda_{j_1}} C^{\underline{\lambda}^{j_1}}_{q_{i_2}} + G^{\underline{\lambda}^{i_o}}_{\lambda_{j_1},\lambda_{j_2}} C^{\underline{\lambda}^{j_1}}_{q_{i_1}} C^{\underline{\lambda}^{j_2}}_{q_{i_2}} - D^{\underline{\lambda}^{i_o}}_{q_{j_1}} G^{\underline{q}^{j_1}}_{q_{i_1},q_{i_2}}$$

$$- 2D^{\underline{\lambda}^{i_o}}_{q_{j_1}} G^{\underline{q}^{j_1}}_{q_{i_1},\lambda_{j_2}} C^{\underline{\lambda}^{j_2}}_{q_{i_2}} - D^{\underline{\lambda}^{i_o}}_{q_{j_1}} G^{\underline{q}^{j_1}}_{\lambda_{j_2},\lambda_{j_3}} C^{\underline{\lambda}^{j_2}}_{q_{i_1}} C^{\underline{\lambda}^{j_3}}_{q_{i_2}} \Big) \tag{3.89}$$

The equation defining the coefficients of the first-order terms which represent the linearized control law is the same Riccati equation as the one developed in Section 3.1 but with coefficients depending on the trajectory about which the expansion is constructed. Thus if the linearized control problem has indeed an optimum and its control matrix is bounded, then so is $C^{\underline{\lambda}^{i_o}}_{q_j}$. The second-order terms affect the control law in the same way as the first-order terms so that $D^{\underline{\lambda}^{i_o}}_{q_j}$ and $C^{\underline{\lambda}^{i_o}}_{q_j}$ are proportional to each other. The coefficients of the cross-coupling terms $E^{\underline{\lambda}^{i_o}}_{q_j, q_\ell}$ are governed by a linear differential equation with time-varying coefficients depending on $C^{\underline{\lambda}^{i_o}}_{q_j}$ and $D^{\underline{\lambda}^{i_o}}_{q_j}$ as well as on the higher-order derivatives of $G^{\underline{x}^{i_o}}$. Provided these are all bounded, then so is $E^{\underline{\lambda}^{i_o}}_{q_j, q_\ell}$ on any finite time interval. Examination of the process of deriving Equation 3.89 reveals the form of the equations defining the coefficients of the terms of higher order. Thus all of the two-dimensional arrays of coefficients are governed by the same Riccati equation and all higher-order coefficients by linear equations with coefficients involving only the elements of coefficient array of lower order and the derivatives of $\underline{G}$.

Thus if the next set of terms in the expansion of Equation 3.86 is

$$+\dots K^{\underline{\lambda}^{i_o}}_{q_{j_1}} S^{\underline{q}^{j_1}}_{a_{j_2}, b_{j_3}, c_{j_4}} \Delta \underline{a}^{j_2} \Delta \underline{b}^{j_3} \Delta \underline{c}^{j_4} + M^{\underline{\lambda}^{i_o}}_{q_{j_1}, q_{j_2}} S^{\underline{q}^{j_1}}_{a_{j_3}, b_{j_4}} S^{\underline{q}^{j_2}}_{c_{j_5}} \Delta \underline{a}^{j_3} \Delta \underline{b}^{j_4} \Delta \underline{c}^{j_5}$$

$$+ N^{\underline{\lambda}^{i_o}}_{q_{j_1}, q_{j_2}, q_{j_3}} S^{\underline{q}^{j_1}}_{a_{j_4}} S^{\underline{q}^{j_2}}_{b_{j_5}} S^{\underline{q}^{j_3}}_{c_{j_6}} + \dots \qquad (3.90)$$

then $K^{\underline{\lambda}^{i_o}}_{q_{j_1}}$ is governed by the same equation as $C^{\underline{\lambda}^{i_o}}_{q_{j_1}}$ and $D^{\underline{\lambda}^{i_o}}_{q_{j_1}}$, whereas $M^{\underline{\lambda}^{i_o}}_{q_{j_1}, q_{j_2}}$ is governed by the same equation as $E^{\underline{\lambda}^{i_o}}_{q_{j_1}, q_{j_2}}$.

The array $N^{\underline{\lambda}^{i_o}}_{q_{j_1}, q_{j_2}, q_{j_3}}$ is defined by a new linear differential equation which in an abbreviated notation is

$$\begin{aligned}
\frac{d}{d\tau} N^{\underline{\lambda}}_{qqq} = \Big(& G^{\lambda}_{\lambda} N^{\underline{\lambda}}_{qqq} - 3N^{\underline{\lambda}}_{qqq} G^{q}_{q} - 3N^{\underline{\lambda}}_{qqq} G^{q}_{\lambda} C^{\lambda}_{q} - K^{\underline{\lambda}}_{q} G^{q}_{\lambda} N^{\lambda}_{qqq} + G^{\underline{\lambda}}_{qqq} \\
& + 3G^{\underline{\lambda}}_{q\lambda} E^{\underline{\lambda}}_{qq} + 3G^{\underline{\lambda}}_{qq\lambda} C^{\underline{\lambda}}_{q} - K^{\underline{\lambda}}_{q} G^{q}_{qqq} - 3M^{\underline{\lambda}}_{qq} G^{q}_{qq} - 3K^{\underline{\lambda}}_{q} G^{q}_{qq\lambda} C^{\lambda}_{q} \\
& + 3G^{\underline{\lambda}}_{\lambda\lambda} C^{\lambda}_{q} E^{\lambda}_{qq} + 3G^{\underline{\lambda}}_{q\lambda\lambda} C^{\lambda}_{q} C^{\lambda}_{q} + G^{\underline{\lambda}}_{\lambda\lambda\lambda} C^{\lambda}_{q} C^{\lambda}_{q} C^{\lambda}_{q} - 3K^{\underline{\lambda}}_{q} G^{q}_{q\lambda} E^{\lambda}_{qq} \\
& - 3M^{\underline{\lambda}}_{qq} G^{q}_{\lambda} E^{\lambda}_{qq} - 6M^{\underline{\lambda}}_{qq} G^{q}_{q\lambda} C^{\lambda}_{q} - 3M^{\underline{\lambda}}_{qq} G^{q}_{\lambda\lambda} C^{\lambda}_{q} C^{\lambda}_{q} - \\
& - 3K^{\underline{\lambda}}_{q\lambda\lambda} G^{q}_{q} C^{\lambda}_{q} C^{\lambda}_{q} - 3K^{\underline{\lambda}}_{q} G^{q}_{\lambda\lambda} C^{\lambda}_{q} E^{\lambda}_{qq} - K^{\underline{\lambda}}_{q} G^{q}_{\lambda\lambda\lambda} C^{\lambda}_{q} C^{\lambda}_{q} C^{\lambda}_{q} \Big)
\end{aligned}$$

(3.91)

If the control law is known at $\tau = T$, for example, if the natural boundary conditions are imposed so that

$$\underline{\lambda}(T) = \underline{S}(\,T, \underline{q}(T)\,) = \underline{0} \qquad (2.92)$$

then each of the terms in the expansion of Equation 3.86 is known at $\tau = T$. The solutions of Equations 3.89 and 3.91 can then be propagated backward in time, that is, for τ running from T toward t, thereby calculating the coefficients of the control law about the point $\underline{q}^*(t)$ at time t.

As an illustration consider the example, already studied in Section 3. 2, which is described by the Euler equations

$$q_1' = -\,q_1 + m \qquad \mathcal{P}'(m) = 2\lambda_1 \qquad \lambda_1' = \lambda_1' - \lambda_2$$

$$q_2' = q_1 \qquad \lambda_2' = q_2 \qquad (3.93)$$

In this case the penalty function used is

$$\mathcal{P}(m) = \frac{\cosh(n_c m) - 1}{\cosh(\,n_c\,) - 1} \qquad (3.94)$$

for it has more convenient differentiability properties than m^r. With this penalty function the Euler equations become:

$$G^{\underline{q}^1} = -\,q_1^* + \frac{1}{n_c}\sinh^{-1}\Big(\frac{2\lambda_1^*}{n_c}(\cosh(n_c) - 1)\Big)$$

$$G^{\underline{q}^2} = q_1^*$$

$$G^{\underline{\lambda}^1} = \lambda_1^* - \lambda_2^*$$

$$G^{\underline{\lambda}^2} = q_2^* \qquad (3.95)$$

The first-order derivatives are

$$G^{\underline{q}^1}_{q_1} = -1 \quad G^{\underline{q}^1}_{q_2} = 0 \quad G^{\underline{q}^1}_{\lambda_1} = \frac{(2\cosh(n_c)-2)/n_c^2}{\sqrt{1+\left(\frac{2\lambda_1^*}{n_c}(\cosh(n_c)-1)\right)^2}} \quad G^{\underline{q}^1}_{\lambda_2} = 0$$

$$G^{\underline{q}^2}_{q_1} = 1 \quad G^{\underline{q}^2}_{q_2} = 0 \quad G^{\underline{q}^2}_{\lambda_1} = 0 \quad G^{\underline{q}^2}_{\lambda_1} = 0$$

$$G^{\underline{\lambda}^1}_{q_1} = 0 \quad G^{\underline{\lambda}^1}_{q_2} = 0 \quad G^{\underline{\lambda}^1}_{\lambda_1} = 1 \quad G^{\underline{\lambda}^1}_{\lambda_2} = -1$$

$$G^{\underline{\lambda}^2}_{q_1} = 0 \quad G^{\underline{\lambda}^2}_{q_2} = 1 \quad G^{\underline{\lambda}^2}_{\lambda_1} = 0 \quad G^{\underline{\lambda}^2}_{\lambda_2} = 0 \tag{3.96}$$

The elements of the third set of coefficients are all zero except for

$$G^{\underline{q}^1}_{\lambda_1,\lambda_1} = -\frac{(2\cosh(n_c)-2)^2}{n_c^3}\;\frac{\frac{2\lambda_1^*}{n_c}(\cosh(n_c)-1)}{\left(1+\frac{2\lambda_1^*}{n_c}((\cosh(n_c)-1))^2\right)^{3/2}} \tag{3.97}$$

and the coefficients of the cubic terms are also all zero except

$$G^{\underline{q}^1}_{\lambda_1,\lambda_1,\lambda_1} = \frac{(2\cosh(n_c)-2)^3}{(n_c)^4}\left\{\frac{3\left(\frac{2\lambda_1^*}{n_c}(\cosh(n_c)-1)\right)^2}{\left(1+\left(\frac{2\lambda_1^*}{n_c}(\cosh(n_c)-1)\right)^2\right)^{5/2}} - \frac{1}{\left(1+\left(\frac{2\lambda_1^*}{n_c}(\cosh(n_c)-1)\right)^2\right)^{3/2}}\right\} \tag{3.98}$$

The Taylor series expansion will be developed around the trajectory

$$\underline{q}^*(\tau) = \underline{0}$$

$$\underline{\lambda}^*(\tau) = \underline{0} \qquad t \leq \tau < T \tag{3.99}$$

which does satisfy the Euler equations. The Riccati equation for the matrix of coefficients $[C]$ is

$$\frac{d}{d\tau}\begin{bmatrix} C \end{bmatrix} = \begin{bmatrix} 0 & 0 \\ 0 & 1 \end{bmatrix} + \begin{bmatrix} 1 & -1 \\ 0 & 0 \end{bmatrix}\begin{bmatrix} C \end{bmatrix} - \begin{bmatrix} C \end{bmatrix}\begin{bmatrix} -1 & 0 \\ 1 & 0 \end{bmatrix} - \begin{bmatrix} C \end{bmatrix}\begin{bmatrix} k & 0 \\ 0 & 0 \end{bmatrix}\begin{bmatrix} C \end{bmatrix} \tag{3.100}$$

where $k = \dfrac{2\cosh(n_c) - 2}{(n_c)^2}$ and $k' = -\dfrac{(2\cosh(n_c) - 2)^3}{(n_c)^4}$

Since all the forcing terms of the equation defining $E^{\underline{\lambda}^{i_o}}_{q_{i_1}, q_{i_2}}(\tau)$ involve second-order derivatives of $\underline{G}$ which are all zero at $\underline{\lambda}^* = \underline{0}$ and because $E^{\underline{\lambda}^{i_o}}_{q_{i_1}, q_{i_2}}(T)$ is initially zero, then $E^{\underline{\lambda}^{i_o}}_{q_{i_1}, q_{i_2}}(\tau)$ remains zero for all τ. That this has to be so follows also from the fact that the control law is bound to be an antisymmetric function, in this example. The equation for the coefficients of the third-order term reduces to

$$\begin{aligned} \frac{d}{d\tau} N^{\underline{\lambda}^{i_o}}_{q_{i_1}, q_{i_2}, q_{i_3}} = \Bigg(& G^{\underline{\lambda}^{i_o}}_{\lambda_{j_1}} N^{\underline{\lambda}^{j_1}}_{q_{i_1}, q_{i_2}, q_{i_3}} - 3N^{\underline{\lambda}^{i_o}}_{q_{i_1}, q_{i_2}, q_{j_1}} G^{\underline{q}^{j_1}}_{q_{i_3}} \\ & - 3N^{\underline{\lambda}^{i_o}}_{q_{i_1}, q_{i_2}, q_{j_1}} G^{\underline{q}^{j_1}}_{\lambda_{j_2}} C^{\underline{\lambda}^{j_2}}_{q_{i_3}} - C^{\underline{\lambda}^{i_o}}_{q_{j_1}} G^{\underline{q}^{j_1}}_{\lambda_{j_2}} N^{\underline{\lambda}^{j_2}}_{q_{i_1}, q_{i_2}, q_{i_3}} \\ & - C^{\underline{\lambda}^{i_o}}_{q_{j_1}} G^{\underline{q}^{j_1}}_{\lambda_{j_2}, \lambda_{j_3}, \lambda_{j_4}} C^{\underline{\lambda}^{j_2}}_{q_{i_1}} C^{\underline{\lambda}^{j_3}}_{q_{i_2}} C^{\underline{\lambda}^{j_4}}_{q_{i_4}} \Bigg) \end{aligned} \tag{3.101}$$

since all the other terms vanish. Taking further advantage of the symmetry properties of Equation 3.89 and Equation 3.91, one concludes that

$$C_2^1 = C_1^2$$

$$N_{112}^1 = N_{121}^1 = N_{211}^1 \qquad N_{112}^2 = N_{121}^2 = N_{211}^2$$

$$N_{221}^1 = N_{212}^1 = N_{122}^1 \qquad N_{221}^2 = N_{212}^2 = N_{122}^2$$

(3.102)

where superscript λ and subscript q have been dropped to abbreviate the notation further. Substituting the numerical values in the equations defining the remaining coefficients, one obtains

$$\frac{d}{d\tau} C_1^1 = -kC_1^1 C_1^1 + 2C_1^1 - 2C_2^1$$

$$\frac{d}{d\tau} C_2^1 = -kC_1^1 C_2^1 + C_2^1 - C_2^2$$

$$\frac{d}{d\tau} C_2^2 = -kC_2^1 C_2^1 + 1$$

$$\frac{d}{d\tau} N_{111}^1 = 4N_{111}^1 - 3N_{112}^1 - 4kN_{111}^1 C_1^1 - k'(C_1^1)^4$$

$$\frac{d}{d\tau} N_{111}^2 = 3N_{111}^2 - 3N_{112}^2 - 3kN_{111}^2 C_1^1 - kN_{111}^1 C_2^1 - k'C_2^1(C_1^1)^3$$

$$\frac{d}{d\tau} N_{112}^1 = N_{112}^1 - N_{112}^2 - 3kN_{111}^1 C_2^1 - kN_{112}^1 C_1^1 - k'C_2^1(C_1^1)^3$$

$$\frac{d}{d\tau} N_{112}^2 = -3kN_{111}^2 C_2^1 - k'(C_1^1 C_2^1)^2$$

$$\frac{d}{d\tau} N_{221}^1 = 4N_{221}^1 - N_{221}^2 - 3N_{222}^1 - 4kN_{221}^1 C_1^1 - k'(C_1^1 C_2^1)^2$$

$$\frac{d}{d\tau} N_{221}^2 = 3N_{221}^2 - 3N_{222}^2 - 3kN_{221}^2 C_1^1 - kC_2^1 N_{221}^1 - k'C_1^1(C_2^1)^3$$

$$\frac{d}{d\tau} N^1_{222} = N^1_{222} - N^2_{222} - 3kN^1_{221}C^1_1 - kC^1_1 N^1_{222} - k'C^1_1(C^1_2)^3$$

$$\frac{d}{d\tau} N^2_{222} = -3kN^2_{221}C^1_2 - kN^1_{222}C^1_2 - k'(C^1_2)^4 \qquad (3.103)$$

The control law in the neighborhood of $\underline{q}(t) = \underline{0}$ is

$$m(t) = \frac{1}{n_c} \sinh^{-1}\left\{\frac{(2\cosh(n_c) - 2)}{n_c}\left(q_1(t)C^1_1 + q_2(t)C^1_2 + (q_1(t))^3 N^1_{111} + (q_1(t))^2 q_2(t) N^1_{112} + q_1(t)(q_2(t))^2 N^1_{221} + (q_2(t))^3 N^1_{222}\right)\right\} \qquad (3.104)$$

Equation 3.108 was solved on a digital computer for $n_c = 1$ with τ running backward from $\tau = T$ to $T - 60$. The coefficients are shown plotted in Figures 3.28 and 3.29. Their steady-state values

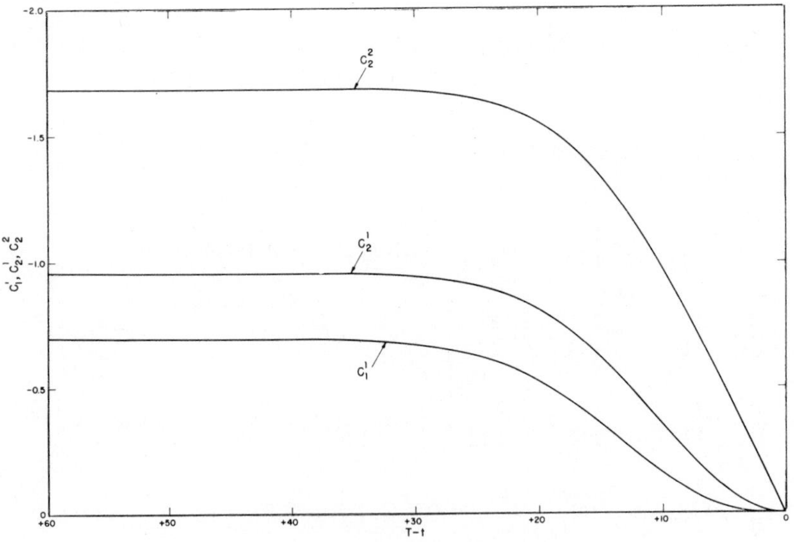

Fig. 3.28. Coefficients of the linear terms in the control law

representing the control law for $T - t \to \infty$ are

$C^1_1 = -.696$ $\qquad$ $C^2_1 = -.959$

$C^1_2 = -.959$ $\qquad$ $C^2_2 = -1.684$

$$N^1_{111} = -.1123 \qquad\qquad N^2_{111} = -.1829$$

$$N^1_{112} = N^1_{121} = N^1_{211} = -.1627 \qquad N^2_{112} = N^2_{121} = N^2_{211} = -.2219$$

$$N^1_{221} = N^1_{212} = N^1_{122} = -.2170 \qquad N^2_{221} = N^2_{212} = N^2_{122} = -.2717$$

$$N^1_{222} = -.2270 \qquad\qquad N^2_{222} = -.2898 \tag{3.105}$$

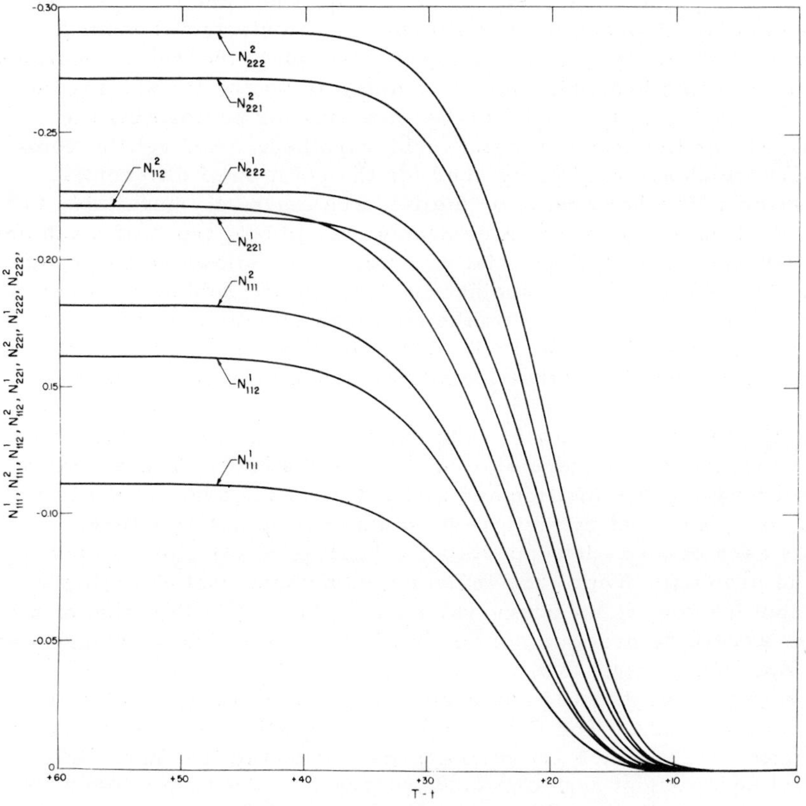

Fig. 3.29. Coefficients of the cubic terms in the control law

The Taylor series expansion developed in this section is a very useful way of representing, computing, and studying the optimum control law. Storing the coefficients of this expansion is often more efficient than storing a table of values. The coefficients themselves are governed by differential equations which are to be solved as an initial-value problem, and not as a boundary-value problem. Thus the process of computing them is not an iterative one. The control law represented in the form of a power series can be synthesized out of adding and multiplying circuits more readily than a general nonlinear function of n variables. The size of the higher-order terms is an indication of whether a linear control law may suffice and whether one can profit through nonlinear control.

3.5. Spatial Boundary-Value Problem Solvers

The previous sections emphasized the use of a general-purpose digital computer for solving the Euler equations and the associated boundary-value problems, but alternately, an electronic analog computer could have been employed to simulate the Euler equations. Possibly some hybrid combination using an analog for solving the differential equations and a digital machine for performing the auxiliary arithmetic and logic would work best. And yet the computers which are commonly used for the solution of differential equations, whether analog or digital, are inherently unsuitable for the solution of boundary-value problems. In both types of machines the solution unrolls sequentially in time as an initial-value problem. For the solution of a two-point boundary-value problem it is necessary to impose conditions on the solutions simultaneously at two points in the solution interval. Thus time cannot be used as the independent variable; rather a quantity such as distance must be employed.

In the theory of structures the deflection of a beam is described by a fourth-order differential equation in distance. The boundary conditions are the position and inclination of the beam at the two supports, hence at two different points in the solution interval. Thus each beam as it supports a load solves a two-point boundary-value problem. There are in nature many such spatial analog computers solving boundary-value problems. It is this kind of a boundary-value problem solver that is needed for the calculation of the optimum control law.

An easily constructed and readily adjustable spatial analog is an electric network. The Euler difference equations as expressed in Equation 2.17, which are also approximations to the Euler differential equations of Equation 2.18, represent a set of simultaneous algebraic equations. These equations can at times be simulated by the mesh or modal equations of an electric network.[22]

Consider the linearized form of these equations as represented by Equation 2.52 , where $[M]$ is given by Equation 2.51 . It represents the modal equations of a network for which $[M]$ is the admittance matrix, $q]$ are the mode potentials, and $\Gamma]$ represents the externally supplied driving currents. This will be a bilateral network since $[M]$ is symmetric, but it need not be a passive network; therefore a question arises as to whether it is stable or not.

If an active network is stable, then on the average it must dissipate power, that is, its admittance matrix must be positive definite. But, as was shown in Section 2.2, if $\mathcal{P}$ does have an optimum, then $[M]$ is definite. By multiplying Equation 2.52 by -1 if necessary, it can be made positive definite. Thus if the solution of Equation 2.52 does indeed represent an optimum trajectory, then the network analog is stable. Conversely, if the network is unstable, this indicates that the Euler equations define only a stationary saddle point. The same arguments show that a nonlinear network simulating Equation 2.17 is bilateral and that it is stable at least in some neighborhood of the optimum trajectory. As an example consider optimization of

$$\mathcal{P} = \int_t^T \Big\{\gamma\big(q_2(\tau) - i(\tau)\big)^2 + \big(m(\tau)\big)^2 + 2\lambda_1(\tau)\big(q_1'(\tau) - aq_1(\tau) - \beta q_2(\tau) - m(\tau)\big) + 2\lambda_2(\tau)\big(q_2'(\tau) - q_2(\tau)\big)\Big\}\, d\tau \qquad (3.106)$$

or its finite difference form

$$\mathcal{P} = \sum_{k=t}^{T-\Delta} \Delta\Big\{\gamma\big(q_2(k) - i(k)\big)^2 + \big(m(k)\big)^2 + 2\lambda_1(k)\Big(\frac{\triangleright}{\Delta} q_1(k) - aq_1(k) - \beta q_2(k) - m(k)\Big) + 2\lambda_2(k)\Big(\frac{\triangleright}{\Delta} q_2(k) - q_1(k)\Big)\Big\} \qquad (3.107)$$

subject to the boundary conditions

$$\begin{aligned} q_1(t) &= q_1(t) \qquad & q_1(T) &= 0 \\ q_2(t) &= q_2(t) \qquad & q_2(T) &= i(T) \end{aligned} \qquad (3.108)$$

The Euler difference equations are

$$m(k) = \lambda_1(k) \qquad k = t, t+\Delta, \ldots T-\Delta$$

$$q_1(k+\Delta) = (1+\Delta a)q_1(k) + \Delta\beta q_2(k) + \Delta\lambda_1(k) \qquad k = t, t+\Delta, \ldots T-\Delta$$

$$q_2(k+\Delta) = \Delta q_1(k) + q_2(k) \qquad k = t, t+\Delta, \ldots T-\Delta$$

$$\lambda_1(k-\Delta) = (1+\Delta\alpha)\lambda_1(k) + \Delta\lambda_2(k) \qquad k = t+\Delta, t+2\Delta, \ldots T-\Delta$$

$$\lambda_2(k-\Delta) = \Delta\beta\lambda_1(k) + \lambda_2(k) + \gamma\Delta\left(i(k) - q_2(k)\right) \qquad k = t+\Delta, t+2\Delta, \ldots T-\Delta$$

(3.109)

in terms of the $[M]$ matrix they become

$$\left[\begin{array}{ccccccccc|c} a & -b & c & & & & & & & q_2(t+2\Delta) \\ -b & a & -b & c & & & & & & q_2(t+3\Delta) \\ c & -b & a & -b & c & & & & & q_2(t+4\Delta) \\ & c & -b & a & -b & c & & & & q_2(t+5\Delta) \\ - & - & - & - & - & - & & & & ---- \\ & & & & c & -b & a & -b & c & q_2(T-5\Delta) \\ & & & & & c & -b & a & -b\ \ c & q_2(T-4\Delta) \\ & & & & & & c & -b & a\ \ -b & q_2(T-3\Delta) \\ & & & & & & & c & -b\ \ a & q_2(T-2\Delta) \end{array}\right] = \left[\begin{array}{l} \gamma i(t+2\Delta)+(b-c)q_2(t)+\Delta b q_1(t) \\ \gamma i(t+3\Delta)-cq_2(t) - \Delta c q_1(t) \\ \gamma i(t+4\Delta) \\ \gamma i(t+5\Delta) \\ ---- \\ \gamma i(T-5\Delta) \\ \gamma i(T-4\Delta) \\ \gamma i(T-3\Delta) - cq_2(T) + \Delta c q_1(T) \\ \gamma i(T-2\Delta)+(b-c)q_2(T)-\Delta b q_1(T) \end{array}\right]$$

(3.110)

where

$$m(t) = \frac{1}{\Delta^2}\left(q_2(t+2\Delta) - 2q_2(t+\Delta) + q_2(t)\right) - \frac{\alpha}{\Delta}\left(q_2(t+\Delta) - q_2(t)\right) - \beta q_2(t)$$

(3.111)

and

$$a = \frac{6}{\Delta^4}(1+\alpha\Delta) + \frac{2}{\Delta^2}(\alpha^2 - \beta - \Delta\alpha\beta) + \beta^2 + \gamma$$

$$b = \frac{4}{\Delta^4}(1+\alpha\Delta) + \frac{1}{\Delta^2}(\alpha^2 - 2\beta - \Delta\alpha\beta)$$

$$c = \frac{1}{\Delta^4}(1+\alpha\Delta) - \frac{\beta}{\Delta^2} \qquad (3.112)$$

Equation 3.110 in turn describes the node voltages in a network shown in Figure 3.30. In it the boundary conditions are imposed by the voltage sources, and desired outputs are introduced by the current sources. The values of the admittances are

$$Y_{cc} = - c = - \left(\frac{1 + \Delta\alpha - \Delta^2\beta}{\Delta^4}\right)$$

$$Y_c = b = \frac{4(1 + \alpha\Delta)}{\Delta^4} + \frac{1}{\Delta^2}(\alpha^2 - 2\beta - \Delta\alpha\beta)$$

$$Y_s = a - 2Y_c - 2Y_{cc} = \beta^2 + \gamma \tag{3.113}$$

It should be pointed out that the value of Y_{cc} is negative, so that the Y_{cc}'s represent negative conductances which need be synthesized

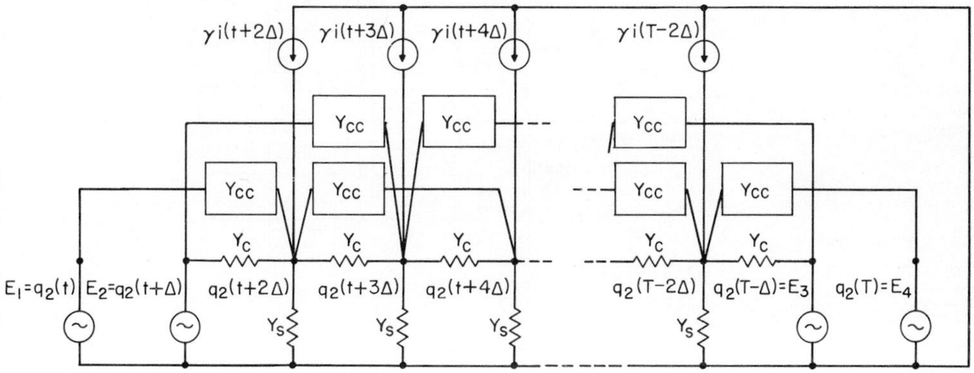

Fig. 3.30. Spatial analog network

out of active circuits. The entire network is nevertheless stable since it simulates the Euler equations which do define an optimum of $\mathcal{P}$ rather than just a saddle point.

Construction of accurate and drift-free negative conductances is rather difficult. It is usually more convenient to simulate such a network on an analog computer. If one considers the network as having stray capacitance C between each node and the common-ground terminal, then its behavior is described by the set of differential equations

$$C\frac{d}{d\tau} q] + [M]q] = \Gamma] \tag{3.114}$$

Equation 3.114 is readily set up on an analog computer, as shown in Figure 3.31. Each coefficient of the matrix corresponds to a transmission path between two integrators, and the coefficients on the diagonal correspond to feedback paths around the integrators. Once more, the system will be stable since $[M]$ is positive definite.

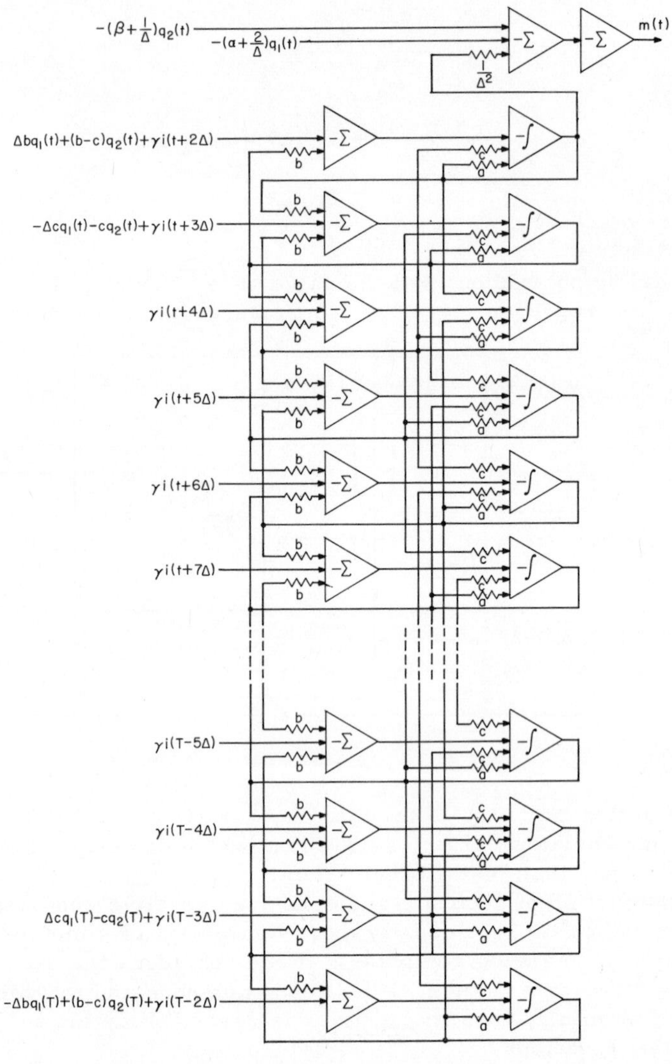

Fig. 3.31. Analog computer boundary-value problem solver

If [M] was negative definite, one would have introduced a variable change $\hat{q}] = -q]$. The steady-state values of q] are the solution of the two-point boundary-value problem defining the optimum trajectory.

Examination of the coefficients of the matrix [M] represented in Equations 3.110 and 3.112 reveals the salient difficulty with the above technique. In order that the Euler difference equation be a good approximation to the differential equation, one requires that

Δ be small. But as Δ decreases, those of the elements which have a factor $\frac{1}{\Delta^4}$ grow more rapidly than the others. Thus as Δ decreases, Y_{cc}, Y_c, and Y_s all become insensitive to α, so that very accurate components are required for these conductances to represent the contribution of α. And yet it is known that α does affect the solution of the boundary-value problem. Thus a balance must be achieved between errors due to coarseness of quantization of time and the errors due to component inaccuracies which increase as Δ decreases.

It is often possible to circumvent this problem by expressing the Euler equations in terms of $\underline{m}$ rather than $\underline{q}$. If $\underline{q}(k)$ can be expressed by a convolution sum

$$q(k)] = q(t)] + \sum_{\ell = t}^{k-\Delta} \Delta[\phi(k, \ell + \Delta]\, m(\ell)] \tag{3.115}$$

then, as shown in Section 2.4, the Euler equations can be written as

$$\nabla_m F(k, \underline{q}(k), \underline{m}(k))] + \sum_{\ell=k+\Delta}^{T-\Delta} \Delta \left\{ [\phi(\ell, k+\Delta]^T \nabla_q F(\ell, \underline{q}(\ell), \underline{m}(\ell))] \right\} = 0] \tag{3.116}$$

On a linearized basis these become

$$[F_{mm}(k)]m(k)] + \sum_{\ell=t}^{k-\Delta} \Delta \left\{ [F_{mq}(k)][\phi(\ell, k+\Delta)])^T m(\ell)] \right\}$$

$$+ \sum_{\ell=k+\Delta}^{T-\Delta} \Delta \left\{ ([F_{mq}(\ell)][\phi(k, \ell+\Delta)]m(\ell)] \right\}$$

$$+ \sum_{\ell=k+\Delta}^{T-\Delta} \sum_{j=t}^{\ell-\Delta} \Delta^2 \left\{ [\phi(\ell, k+\Delta)]^T [F_{qq}(\ell)][\phi(\ell, j+\Delta)]m(j)] \right\} =$$

$$- [F_{mq}(k)]q(t)] - \sum_{\ell=k+\Delta}^{T-\Delta} \Delta \left\{ [\phi(\ell, k+\Delta]^T [F_{qq}(\ell)]q(t)] \right\} \tag{3.117}$$

Equation 3.117, when written out in terms of the $[M]$ matrix, is shown in Figure 3.32. The matrix $[M]$ is symmetric, and since $\underline{m}[M]m$ represents the incremental $\mathcal{D}$, it is definite if the Euler equations do indeed define an optimum. The equation represented in Figure 3.32 can therefore be simulated using an electric network or an analog computer. Its advantage over the previous formulation is that as the number of meshes increases and Δ decreases, the diagonal terms remain constant while the off-diagonal terms decrease, so that the matrix becomes better conditioned. Furthermore, all the off-diagonal terms are of comparable size, and since many of them contribute to counterbalancing the term on the diagonal, the accuracy requirements on the components are relaxed. Its disadvantage is that now all of the coefficients are present in the matrix, and so more components are required for its realization.

The spatial boundary-value problem solvers described so far have been solving the linearized Euler equations. In many cases the nonlinear equations can be simulated in the same way. For example, if the problem is a linear one except for a nonlinear penalty function on $\underline{m}$ simulating a saturation, then Equation 3.116 is linear except for the nonlinear function $\nabla_m F$. The $[M]$ matrix then is the same as shown in Figure 3.32 except that the diagonal elements are not constant. In terms of a network, this results in an introduction of a nonlinear resistor between each node and the common ground. In terms of an analog computer network, this represents a nonlinear feedback element around each integrator.

No general procedure can be suggested for analoging every nonlinear problem. In the worst case, one can use this in connection with the second technique described in Section 2.3. The network analog would solve the linearized boundary-value problem about a starting trajectory and add some fraction of the linearized solution to the old trajectory, evaluate new linearized coefficients, and repeat the process. The entire procedure may be going on continuously in time, provided the coefficient adjustment is on a slower time scale than the relaxation of the linearized network.

The spatial analogs described above are the cheapest form of a boundary-value problem solver. Relatively unsophisticated circuitry can solve essentially instantaneously a problem which may tax the capabilities of a large digital machine. They therefore represent the most practical scheme for synthesizing an on-line computer for calculating the control law.

A control system utilizing a network boundary-value problem solver as the controller is shown schematically in Figure 3.33. The inputs to such a network are the current system state, $\underline{q}(t)$ and the system input $\underline{v}(t)$ processed so as to yield the future values of disturbances or estimates thereof, controlling the current sources. The network itself settles to a steady-state

$$
\begin{bmatrix}
\begin{matrix}[F_{mm}(t)] \\ + \sum_{i=t+\Delta}^{T-\Delta} \Delta^2 [\phi(i,t)]^T [F_{qq}(i)][\phi(i,t)]\end{matrix} &
\begin{matrix}\Delta\left([F_{mq}(t+\Delta)][\phi(t+\Delta,t)]\right) \\ + \sum_{i=t+2\Delta}^{T-\Delta} \Delta^2 [\phi(i,t)]^T [F_{qq}(i)][\phi(i,t+\Delta)]^T\end{matrix} &
\begin{matrix}\Delta\left([F_{mq}(t+2\Delta)][\phi(t+2\Delta,t)]\right)^T \\ + \sum_{i=t+3\Delta}^{T-\Delta} \Delta^2 [\phi(i,t)]^T [F_{qq}(i)][\phi(i,t+2\Delta)]\end{matrix} & \cdots \\
\\
\begin{matrix}\Delta[F_{mq}(t+\Delta)][\phi(t+\Delta,t)] \\ + \sum_{i=t+2\Delta}^{T-\Delta} \Delta^2 [\phi(i,t+\Delta)]^T [F_{qq}(i)][\phi(i,t)]\end{matrix} &
\begin{matrix}[F_{mm}(t+\Delta)] \\ + \sum_{i=t+2\Delta}^{T-\Delta} \Delta^2 [\phi(i,t+\Delta)]^T [F_{qq}(i)][\phi(i,t+\Delta)]\end{matrix} &
\begin{matrix}\Delta\left([F_{mq}(t+2\Delta)][\phi(t+2\Delta,t+\Delta)]\right)^T \\ + \sum_{i=t+3}^{T-\Delta} \Delta^2 [\phi(i,t+\Delta)]^T [F_{qq}(i)][\phi(i,t+2\Delta)]\end{matrix} & \cdots \\
\\
\begin{matrix}\Delta[F_{mq}(t+2\Delta)][\phi(t+\Delta,t)] \\ + \sum_{i=t+3\Delta}^{T-\Delta} \Delta^2 [\phi(i,t+2\Delta)]^T [F_{qq}(i)][\phi(i,t)]\end{matrix} &
\begin{matrix}\Delta[F_{mq}(t+2\Delta)][\phi(t+2\Delta,t+\Delta)] \\ + \sum_{i=t+3\Delta}^{T-\Delta} \Delta^2 [\phi(i,t+2\Delta)]^T [F_{qq}(i)][\phi(i,t+\Delta)]\end{matrix} &
\begin{matrix}[F_{mm}(t+2\Delta)] \\ + \sum_{i=t+3\Delta}^{T-\Delta} \Delta^2 [\phi(i+2\Delta)]^T [F_{qq}(i)][\phi(i,t+2\Delta)]\end{matrix} & \cdots \\
\\
\cdots & \cdots & \cdots &
\end{bmatrix}
\begin{bmatrix} m(t) \\ \\ m(t+\Delta) \\ \\ m(t+2\Delta) \\ \\ \cdots \end{bmatrix}
=
\begin{bmatrix}
\begin{matrix}-[F_{mq}(t)]\,q(t) \\ - \sum_{i=t+\Delta}^{T-\Delta} \Delta [\phi(i,t)]^T [F_{qq}(i)]\,q(t)\end{matrix} \\
\\
\begin{matrix}-[F_{mq}(t+\Delta)]\,q(t) \\ - \sum_{i=t+2\Delta}^{T-\Delta} \Delta [\phi(i,t+\Delta)]^T [F_{qq}(i)]\,q(t)\end{matrix} \\
\\
\begin{matrix}-[F_{mq}(t+2\Delta)]\,q(t) \\ - \sum_{i=t+3\Delta}^{T-\Delta} \Delta [\phi(i,t+2\Delta)]^T [F_{qq}(i)]\,q(t)\end{matrix} \\
\\
\cdots
\end{bmatrix}
$$

Fig. 3.32. The [M] matrix represented by Equation 3.117

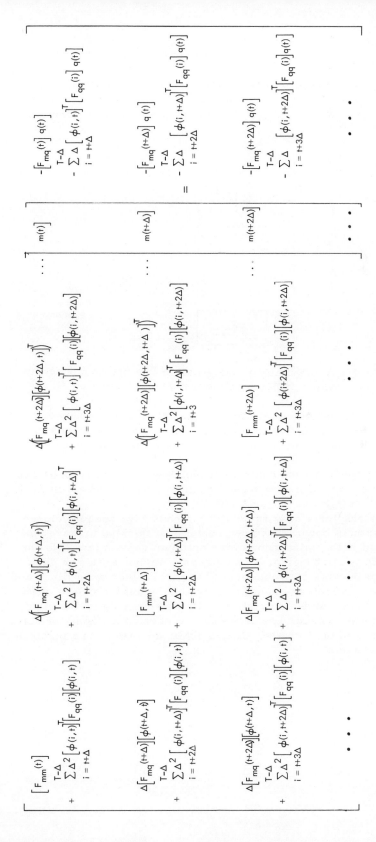

condition solving the boundary-value problem and yielding the optimum control effort as a potential on one or more nodes. For a given value of q(t) and v(t), the rate at which an equilibrium is

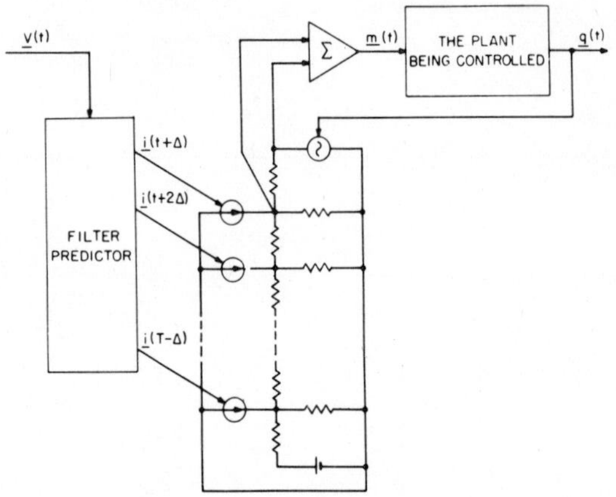

Fig. 3.33. A schematic representation of a network boundary-value problem solver used as a controller

reached depends only on the stray capacitances in the network and is normally much faster than changes in q(t) or v(t). Thus the controller generates the optimum control effort continuously with time.

No examples of such controllers which were actually built are presented here. This has been done in companion research work reported on in References 42 and 58.

In this chapter a wide variety of methods have been developed for solution of boundary-value problems of the kind that are encountered in the calculation of the optimum control law. No one technique is far superior to the others. Each has its own place in a certain class of problems. These techniques were illustrated on simple examples—examples to which the answers were often obvious, so as to demonstrate that they do indeed give the right answers. An attempt has been made to develop methods for solving a class of cases rather than to obtain an answer to a particular design problem.

Chapter 4

CONTROL IN THE PRESENCE OF STOCHASTIC DISTURBANCES

4.1. Statistical Information Needed for Control

It is characteristic of the control problem that invariably some of the parameters entering into its description are indeterministic. The system description may be inaccurate, the measurements of the state variables or state functions may be in error or even unobtainable, and the disturbances acting on the system are usually stochastic. The inputs available to the system are only statistically related to these disturbances, the statistical correlation being assumed more or less fully known. Under such circumstances the controller is required to optimize the expected value of the performance criterion, where the average is taken over the entire ensemble of functions that the stochastic parameters can take, conditional on the input $\underline{v}(t)$. Thus the performance criterion is

$$\mathcal{P} = \underset{\underline{u}(\tau),t\le\tau<T \mid \underline{v}(t)}{E} \left\{ \int_t^T F(\tau,T,\underline{q}(\tau),\underline{m}(\tau),\underline{u}(\tau))\,d\tau \right\}$$

$$= \sum_{\substack{\text{over all sample functions}\\ \underline{u}(\tau),t\le\tau<T}} \left\{ P(\underline{u}(\tau),t\le\tau<T \mid \underline{v}(t)) \int_t^T F(\tau,T,\underline{q}(\tau),\underline{m}(\tau),\underline{u}(\tau))\,d\tau \right\}$$

$$= \int_{-\infty}^{\infty} p(\underline{u}(\tau),t\le\tau<T \mid \underline{v}(t)) \left\{ \int_t^T F(\tau,T,\underline{q}(\tau),\underline{m}(\tau),\underline{u}(\tau))\,d\tau \right\} d(\underline{u}(\tau),t\le\tau<T) \tag{4.1}$$

where $\underline{m}(\tau)$ and $\underline{q}(\tau)$ are related by

$$\frac{d}{d\tau}\underline{q}(\tau) = \underline{G}(\tau,\underline{q}(\tau),\underline{m}(\tau),\underline{u}(\tau)) \tag{4.2}$$

As mentioned previously, the notion of a conditional probability density of a function rather than a variable is a delicate mathematical concept. In this context it is implied that the sample functions are completely characterized by a finite set of coefficients each of which is a random variable. The probability density of a function is then the joint probability density of its characterizing coefficients.

In the above formulation it is assumed that $p(\underline{u}(\tau), t \leq \tau < T \mid \underline{v}(t))$ is known, that it is not a function of the control law to be chosen, and that it is independent of $\underline{m}(\tau), t \leq \tau < T$. Under such circumstances the optimum control effect $\underline{m}(\tau), t \leq \tau < T$ is a deterministic time function. This is in contrast to the truly adaptive situation in which $p(\underline{u}(\tau), t \leq \tau < T \mid \underline{v}(t))$ is itself a random function whose value becomes progressively better known as the process continues.[46] The problem treated is even further removed from the more advanced adaptive or learning process in which $p(\underline{u}(\tau), t \leq \tau < T \mid \underline{v}(t))$ may depend on the control policy pursued. Such a learning process must take into account the balance which exists between the desire to pursue a policy which currently optimizes $\mathcal{P}$ and one which provides the most information about $p(\underline{u}(\tau), t \leq \tau < T \mid \underline{v}(t))$, thereby raising a hope of optimizing $\mathcal{P}$ more effectively in the future. On this scale the problem treated here can be considered as being the zeroth stage of adaptation.[8]

In the problems to be considered it is convenient to divide the disturbance functions $\underline{u}(\tau), t \leq \tau < T$, into two classes: the disturbances proper, which affect the relation between $\underline{m}$ and $\underline{q}$, and the "desired output" functions $\underline{i}(\tau), t \leq \tau < T$, which are those components of $\underline{u}$ that enter F, but not $\underline{G}$. The distinction arises from the fact that if $\underline{i}$ are the only random parameters entering the control problem, then both the optimum $\underline{m}(\tau)$ and the optimum $\underline{q}(\tau)$ are deterministic. If there are disturbances proper ($\underline{u}$ entering $\underline{G}$), then the optimum $\underline{q}(\tau)$ is a random time function.

Initially, let us consider that the randomness is introduced into the control problem only by $\underline{i}(\tau), t \leq \tau < T$. In the optimization of

$$\mathcal{P} = \underset{\underline{i}\mid\underline{v}}{E}\left\{\int_t^T \left\{F(\tau, T, \underline{q}(\tau), \underline{m}(\tau), \underline{i}(\tau)) + \underline{\lambda}(\tau)\left(\underline{q}'(\tau)\right] - \underline{G}(\tau, \underline{q}(\tau), \underline{m}(\tau))\right)\right]\right\} d\tau \tag{4.3}$$

one considers its finite difference approximation, differentiates it with respect to the deterministic quantities $\underline{q}$, $\underline{m}$, $\underline{\lambda}$, and sets the derivatives to zero to obtain the Euler equations ($\underline{m}$ and $\underline{q}$ are deterministic, and so is the relationship between them; thus $\underline{\lambda}$ is also a deterministic quantity).

It is known that the expectation and integration operators commute.[21] Furthermore, the expectation and differentiation operators commute, in that

$$\frac{d}{dy} \underset{x}{E}\left\{f(x,y)\right\} = \underset{x}{E}\left\{\frac{\partial f(x,y)}{\partial y}\right\} \tag{4.4}$$

where x is a random variable and y is deterministic. One should note that y, even if it is defined by an equation such as

$$\underset{x}{E}\left\{\frac{\partial f(x,y)}{\partial y}\right\} = 0 \tag{4.5}$$

is still a deterministic quantity. Equation 4.5 makes it a function of the statistical averages of x, which in themselves are deterministic quantities, but it is independent of any one particular sample function x.

Thus the Euler equations defining the optimum $\mathcal{P}$ of Equation 4.3 can be written as

$$\begin{aligned} \underline{q}' &= \underline{G}(\tau,\underline{q},\underline{m}) \\ \lambda'] &= \underset{\underline{i}|\underline{v}}{E}\left\{\nabla_q F(\tau,T,\underline{q},\underline{m},\underline{i})]\right\} - [J_q(\underline{G})]^T \lambda] \\ [J_m(\underline{G})]^T \lambda] &= \underset{\underline{i}|\underline{v}}{E}\left\{\nabla_q F(\tau,T,\underline{q},\underline{m},\underline{i})]\right\} \end{aligned} \tag{4.6}$$

Even before the two-point boundary-value problem associated with the Euler equations is solved, Equation 4.6 indicates what statistical properties of $i(\tau), t \leq \tau < T$ need be known for the design of the controller. Specifically, it is required that the expected values of $\nabla_q F(\tau,T,\underline{q}(\tau),\underline{m}(\tau),\underline{i}(\tau))]$ and $\nabla_m F(\tau,T,\underline{q}(\tau),\underline{m}(\tau),\underline{i}(\tau))]$ conditional on $\underline{v}(t)$ be known, with τ, T, $\underline{q}(\tau)$, and $\underline{m}(\tau)$ as parameters. No more information about $\underline{i}(\tau), t \leq \tau < T$ is needed, and no more information can be used to advantage.

Thus the filtering and prediction involved in obtaining $\underset{\underline{i}|\underline{v}}{E}\left\{\nabla_q F]\right\}$ and $\underset{\underline{i}|\underline{v}}{E}\left\{\nabla_m F]\right\}$ are effectively decoupled from dynamic optimization and consequent solution of a two-point boundary-value problem. Once these statistical averages are computed or measured, Equation 4.6 remains as a deterministic set of differential equations, and the solution of the two-point boundary-value problem is carried out as in the deterministic case. Of course the above derivation does not indicate how one should measure or compute either $p(\underline{i}(\tau), t \leq \tau < T \,|\, \underline{v}(t))$ or the averages $\underset{\underline{i}|\underline{v}}{E}\left\{\nabla_q F]\right\}$ and $\underset{\underline{i}|\underline{v}}{E}\left\{\nabla_m F]\right\}$; this is the entire field of filtering and prediction. Some examples of how this could be accomplished are presented in Section 4.2.

The knowledge of $p(\underline{i}(\tau), t \leq \tau < T \,|\, \underline{v}(t))$ represents all the statistical information about $\underline{i}(t)$ that may ever be available. One should note that the conditional averages $\underset{\underline{i}|\underline{v}}{E}\left\{\nabla_q F]\right\}$ and $\underset{\underline{i}|\underline{v}}{E}\left\{\nabla_m F]\right\}$ represent a more modest requirement. For example, if $\nabla_q F]$ and $\nabla_m F]$ are polynomials of $\underline{i}$, then only a finite number of conditional moments would be required. If $\underline{i}$ enters F only as a term $\cosh(q_1(\tau) - i(\tau))$, then only the statistical average

$\underset{i(\tau),t \le \tau < T \mid v(t)}{E} \left\{ \sinh(a - i(\tau)) \right\}$ with a as a free parameter need be known. If, as is often the case, $(q_1(\tau) - i(\tau))^2$ is the only stochastic term in F, then only the expected value of $i(\tau), t \le \tau < T$ conditional on $\underline{v}(t)$, $\underset{i(\tau), t \le \tau < T \mid v(t)}{E} \left\{ i(\tau), t \le \tau < T \mid v(t) \right\}$, is needed; this is so even if the element being controlled is nonlinear and other portions of F are nonquadratic.

As an example, consider the optimization of

$$\mathcal{P} = \underset{\gamma, i(\tau), t \le \tau < \infty \mid v(t)}{E} \left\{ \int_t^\infty \left\{ \gamma(m(\tau))^{n_c} + (q(\tau) - i(\tau))^2 + \lambda(\tau)(q'(\tau) - m(\tau)) \right\} d\tau \right\} \tag{4.7}$$

where γ is a constant but random variable and $i(\tau)$ is a square wave with amplitude of 1 or -1 and Poisson-distributed zero crossings with an average frequency a. The current input $v(t)$ and the current desired output $i(t)$ are related by

$$v(t) = i(t) + n(t) \tag{4.8}$$

where $n(t)$ is a noise with amplitude of less than 1. The Euler equations are derived as

$$q'(\tau) = m(\tau) \quad \lambda(\tau) = E\left\{\gamma\right\} n_c(m(\tau))^{(n_c - 1)} \quad \lambda'(\tau) = q(\tau) - E\left\{i(\tau)\right\} \tag{4.9}$$

The expected value of γ is a constant $\overline{\gamma}$. The expected value of $i(\tau)$ conditional on $v(t)$ is simply

$$\underset{i(\tau), t \le \tau < \infty \mid v(t)}{E} \left\{ i(\tau) \right\} = \text{sign}(v(t)) e^{-2a(\tau - t)} \tag{4.10}$$

so that Equation 4.9 becomes

$$q'(\tau) = m(\tau) \quad \lambda(\tau) = n_c \overline{\gamma}(m(\tau))^{(n_c - 1)} \quad \lambda'(\tau) = q(\tau) - \text{sign}(v(t)) e^{-2a(\tau - t)} \tag{4.11}$$

The solution to what is essentially this control problem has been developed in Section 3.2 for the case when $\overline{\gamma} = 1$, $n_c = 8$, and $a = .5$ and it is displayed in Figure 3.23. The function m versus q for $T - t = \ln(1/.025) = 3.70$ represents the control law for the problem treated in this section for $\underset{\underline{i} \mid \underline{v}}{E} \left\{ i(\tau) \right\} = e^{-(\tau - t)}$. This is plotted in Figure 4.1.

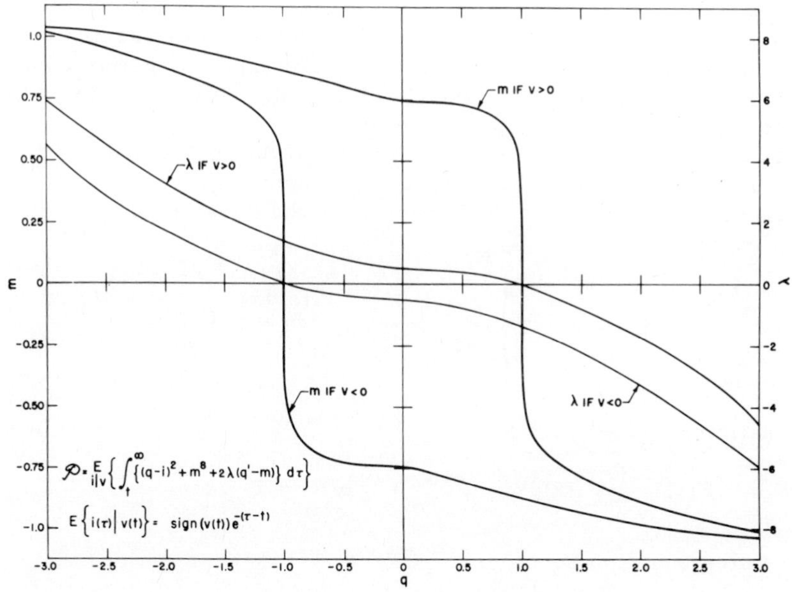

Fig. 4.1. The control law when E $\{i(\tau)\}$ = sign $(v(t))\, e^{-(\tau - t)}$

The branch for v<0 is obtained by symmetry. If the expected value of $i(\tau)$ was 2 sign $(v(t))\, e^{-(\tau - t)}$, the control law could be obtained from Figure 3.23 for $T - t = \ell n(2/.025) = .438$. This is displayed in Figure 4.2.

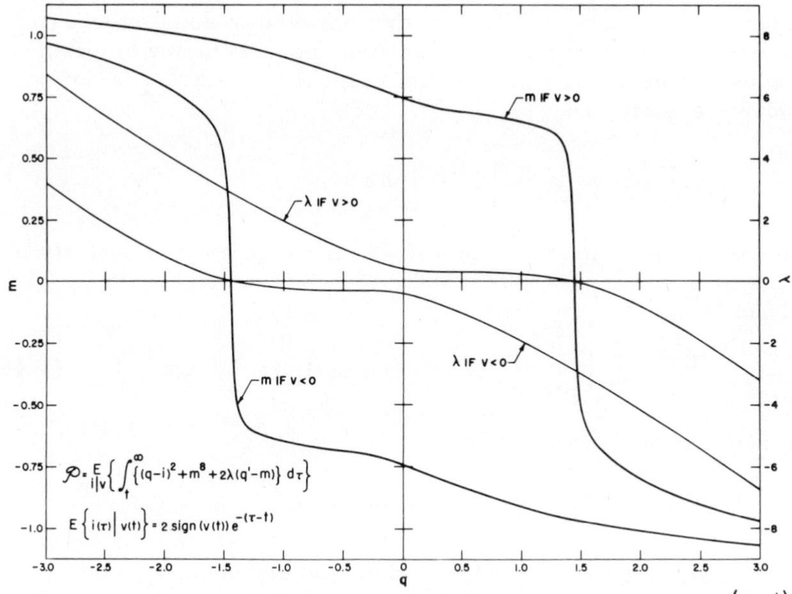

Fig. 4.2. The control law when E $\{i(\tau)\}$ = 2sign $(v(t))\, e^{-(\tau - t)}$

This figure illustrates a situation in which the system is incapable of following $i(\tau)$ because of a limitation on the amplitude of its control input. The control law is seen to command a negative control effort even when $q = 1.5$ and $E\left\{i(t)\right\} = 2$, relying on its estimate that $E\left\{i(\tau)\right\} < 1.5$ for some $\tau > t$.

As a further demonstration, the third problem of Appendix E will be treated again, assuming that the demand curve $f(\tau)$, $t \leq \tau < T$ is stochastic. As shown in Section 3.2, the performance criterion can be written as

$$\mathscr{P} = \underset{f(\tau),\, t \leq \tau < T}{E} \left\{ \sum_{\ell=1}^{N} \Delta q(\ell) \int_t^{q(\ell)} f(x)dx - \int_0^{T-t} \int_t^{y} f(x)dx\, dy \right\} \tag{4.12}$$

On defining

$$F(y) = \int_t^y f(x)dx \qquad q(0) = t \qquad q(N) = T \tag{4.13}$$

the Euler equation becomes

$$\triangleleft\, q(\ell)\, E\left\{f(\,q(\ell)\,)\right\} = \triangleright E\left\{F(\,q(\ell)\,)\right\} \qquad \ell = 1, 2, \ldots N-1 \tag{4.14}$$

It can be solved in the same way as was done in Section 3.2, but using $E\left\{f(x)\right\}$ and $E\left\{F(x)\right\}$ in place of $f(x)$ and $F(x)$.

Now let us consider the case in which there are disturbances proper, which make the relationship between $\underline{m}$ and $\underline{q}$ stochastic. One can no longer derive the conditions necessary for an optimum by considering the variations with respect to $\underline{q}$ since $\underline{q}$ is now a random variable and

$$d \underset{x}{E}\left\{f(x)\right\} \neq \underset{x}{E}\left\{\frac{\partial f(x)}{x}\right\} dx \tag{4.15}$$

One can treat the problem only if $\mathscr{P}$ can be expressed entirely in terms of $\underline{m}$.

Thus if

$$\mathscr{P} = E\left\{ \int_t^T \left\{ F(\,\tau, T, \underline{q}(\tau), \underline{m}(\tau), \underline{u}(\tau)\,)\right\} d\tau \right\} \tag{4.16}$$

and $\underline{q}(\tau)$ can be expressed as

$$q(\tau)] = q(t)] + \int_t^T [\phi(\tau,\xi\,)]\, m(\xi\,)]\, d\xi \tag{4.17}$$

where $[\,\phi(\tau,\xi\,)]$ may also be random and depend on $\underline{u}$, one can derive the Euler equation

$$E\left\{\nabla_m F(\tau, T, q(t)] + \int_t^{T} [\phi(\tau,\xi)] m(\xi)] \, d\xi, m(\tau)], u(\tau)])]\right.$$

$$\left. + E\left\{ \int_\tau^{T} [\phi(\xi, \tau)]^T \nabla_q F(\xi, T, q(t)] + \int_t^{\xi} [\phi(\xi, \eta)] m(\eta)] \, d\eta, m(\xi)], u(\xi)])] \, d\xi\right\} = 0 \qquad (4.18)$$

As before, this Euler equation shows what statistical properties of $\underline{u}(\tau), t \leq \tau \leq T$ and $[\phi(\xi, \eta)], t \leq \xi, \eta < T$ need be known for the design of the controller. It also shows what statistical function of the initial state $\underline{q}(t)$ is to be used in the control law. Therefore in this formulation one takes into account not only the stochastic nature of the desired outputs, but also the random fluctuations or imperfect knowledge of the description of the element being controlled and the noisiness of the measurements or estimates of system state.

For example, if F is quadratic in $\underline{q}$ and $\underline{m}$ and the plant is linear, one needs to know only the expected value of the impulse response and its covariance, that is,

$$E\{[\phi(\xi, \eta)]\} \text{ and } E\{[\phi(\xi, \tau)]^T [\phi(\xi, \eta)]\} \quad \text{for } t \leq \xi, \eta, \tau < T.$$

In measuring the system state for use by the controller, one need only estimate its expected value $E\{q(t)]\}$. If system state or some of its components cannot be measured, but must be predicted or estimated from indirect measurements, then one needs to obtain its expected value rather than some other statistical properties. Of course, if F is nonquadratic or the system is nonlinear, more complicated statistics would be required.

If one considers the location of the poles and zeros of the transfer function describing the plant, rather than the shape of the impulse response itself as being the stochastic quantities, one can determine which of their statistical properties are needed by expressing the impulse response in terms of the parameters specifying the pole locations. For example, if the element to be controlled has a transfer function $\frac{s + \alpha}{s(s + \beta)}$, then its impulse response is

$$q(\tau) = q(t) + \frac{q'(t)}{\beta}\left(1 - e^{-\beta(\tau - t)}\right) + \int_t^{\tau} \left(\alpha + (\beta - \alpha) e^{-\beta(\tau - \xi)}\right) \frac{m(\xi)}{\beta} \, d\xi \qquad (4.19)$$

If the performance criterion is

$$\mathscr{P} = \underset{\alpha, \beta, \gamma}{E}\left\{ \int_t^{T} \left\{ \gamma m^2(\tau) + (q(\tau) - i(\tau))^2 \right\} d\tau \right\} \qquad (4.20)$$

then the Euler equation becomes

$$E\{\gamma\}\ m(\tau) + \int_\tau^T \int_t^T \left\{ E\left\{\left(\frac{\alpha}{\beta} + \frac{\beta-\alpha}{\beta} e^{-\beta(\xi-\tau)}\right)\left(\frac{\alpha}{\beta} + \frac{\beta-\alpha}{\beta} e^{-\beta(\xi-\eta)}\right)\right\} m(\eta)\right\} d\eta\, d\xi$$

$$+ q(t) \int_\tau^T E\left\{ \frac{\alpha}{\beta} + \frac{\beta-\alpha}{\beta} e^{-\beta(\xi-\tau)}\right\} d\xi$$

$$+ q'(t) \int_\tau^T E\left\{\left(\frac{\alpha}{\beta} + \frac{\beta-\alpha}{\beta} e^{-\beta(\xi-\tau)}\right)\left(\frac{1}{\beta} - \frac{1}{\beta} e^{-\beta(\xi-\tau)}\right)\right\} d\xi$$

$$= E\left\{ \int_\tau^T \left(\frac{\alpha}{\beta} + \frac{\beta-\alpha}{\beta} e^{-\beta(\xi-\tau)}\right) i(\xi) d\xi\right\} \qquad (4.21)$$

indicating that if α, β, and γ are statistically independent, then the statistical averages needed are

$$E\{\gamma\},\ E\{\alpha\},\ E\{\alpha^2\},\ E\left\{\frac{1}{\beta}\right\},\ E\left\{\frac{1}{\beta^2}\right\},\ E\left\{\frac{1}{\beta} e^{-\beta x}\right\},\ \text{and}\ E\left\{\frac{1}{\beta^2} e^{-\beta x}\right\}$$

for all nonnegative values of x. It is interesting to note that β, which specifies the location of the pole, enters into Equation 4.21 in a much more complicated manner than α, which specifies the location of the zero.

One should not despair when the above procedure requires the knowledge of some statistical averages which one just does not know. Although one may not know it exactly, invariably one can estimate it. The performance of the resultant system will of course depend on how shrewd this estimate was. Any scheme which purports not to require statistical information about the random parameters does in effect make an assumption of its own about their statistical properties. This assumption need be reasonable for a wide class of cases, and so for a particular problem at hand one invariably can make a better estimate. The derivations in this section indicate just which of the statistical properties of the stochastic disturbances one needs to measure or estimate.

It was shown in this section how the presence of stochastic disturbances affects the design of the optimum control law. This formulation indicates what statistical averages of the disturbances are needed for the computation of the control law; once these are known, the computation is the same as in the deterministic case. Thus the control problem is separated from the filtering and prediction problems. In this way stochastic variations in the performance criterion can be treated, and if $\mathcal{P}$ can be expressed in terms of $\underline{m}$, variations in system description and uncertainty of the measurements of the state variables can also be considered.

4.2. Filtering and Prediction in the Control Problem

The treatment of stochastic disturbances in the control problem requires the knowledge of the conditional probability density of these disturbances, conditional on the system inputs, $p(\underline{u}(\tau), t \leq \tau < T \mid \underline{v}(t))$, or of some statistical averages of $\underline{u}$. Such averages will be denoted abstractly as $\underset{\underline{u}(\tau), t \leq \tau < T \; \underline{v}(t)}{E} \left\{ \underline{f}(\underline{u}(\tau), \underline{x}(\tau)) \right\}$ for some parameters $\underline{x}$. The problem of determining $p(\underline{u}|\underline{v})$ or $\underset{\underline{u}|\underline{v}}{E} \left\{ \underline{f}(\underline{u}, \underline{x}) \right\}$ constitutes the entire field of filtering, detection, and prediction. It is an asset of the formulation of Section 4.1 that it allows the decoupling of these two problems, each of which is difficult in its own right.

Both $p(\underline{u}|\underline{v})$ and $\underset{\underline{u}|\underline{v}}{E} \left\{ \underline{f}(\underline{u}, \underline{x}) \right\}$ represent a considerably greater amount of statistical information than is normally sought in filtering theory, and somewhat special techniques must be devised for obtaining them. In this section will be presented several methods which have not been commonly employed, but which have been found useful for obtaining $p(\underline{u}|\underline{v})$ and $\underset{\underline{u}|\underline{v}}{E} \left\{ \underline{f}(\underline{u}, \underline{x}) \right\}$ in control problems. It is not proposed to develop a complete theory of filtering and prediction.

Probably the most basic way of evaluating $p(\underline{u}|\underline{v})$ is through measurement. If one considers $\underline{u}(\tau), t \leq \tau < T$ as being characterized by r parameters $c_1, c_2, \ldots c_r$, then by taking a sufficient number of samples from the ensemble of $\underline{u}(\tau), t \leq \tau < T$ and $\underline{v}(t)$, one can form the frequency table and compute $p(\underline{u}|\underline{v})$ as

$$p(\underline{u}(\tau), t \leq \tau < T \mid \underline{v}(t)) = p(c_1, c_2, \ldots c_r \mid \underline{v}(t)) = \lim_{\substack{N \to \infty \\ \epsilon_i \to 0 \\ i=1,2,\ldots r}} \frac{N_\Delta(N, \underline{v}^*(t), \epsilon; c_i^*, \epsilon_i, i=1, 2, \ldots r)}{N(\underline{v}^*(t), \epsilon) \prod_{i=1, r} \epsilon_i} \tag{4.22}$$

where $N(\underline{v}^*(t), \epsilon)$ is the number of samples for which

$$\|\underline{v}(t) - \underline{v}^*(t)\| < \epsilon \tag{4.23}$$

and $N_\Delta(N, \underline{v}^*(t), \epsilon; c_i^*, \epsilon_i, i=1, 2, \ldots r)$ is the number of samples out of the N for which

$$|c_i - c_i^*| < \epsilon_i \quad i = 1, 2, \ldots r \tag{4.24}$$

The conditional probability density $p(\underline{u}|\underline{v})$ can be approximated by

$$\frac{N_\Delta}{N \prod_{i=1, r} \epsilon_i}$$

to an arbitrary degree of accuracy by taking N sufficiently large and ϵ, ϵ_i, $i = 1, 2, \ldots r$ sufficiently small.

$$\underset{\underline{u}(\tau),\, t \le \tau \le T \,|\, \underline{v}(t)}{E} \left\{ \underline{f}(\underline{u}(\tau), \underline{x}(\tau)) \right\} = \lim_{N \to \infty} \frac{\sum_{i=1}^{N} \underline{f}(\underline{u}_{(i)}(\tau), \underline{x}(\tau))\, \delta^{\underline{v}(t)}_{\underline{v}^*(t)}}{N(\underline{v}^*(t))} \tag{4.25}$$

where $\underline{u}_{(i)}(\tau)$ are the successive sample functions and

$$\delta^{\underline{v}(t)}_{\underline{v}^*(t)} = \begin{cases} 1 & \text{if } \| \underline{v}(t) - \underline{v}^*(t) \| < \epsilon \\ 0 & \text{if } \| \underline{v}(t) - \underline{v}^*(t) \| \ge \epsilon \end{cases} \tag{4.26}$$

Also, $\underset{\underline{u}|\underline{v}}{E} \left\{ \underline{f}(\underline{v}, \underline{x}) \right\}$ can be approximated to an arbitrary degree of accuracy by

$$\frac{1}{N} \sum_{i=1}^{N} \underline{f}(\underline{u}_{(i)}, \underline{x})\, \delta^{\underline{v}}_{\underline{v}^*}$$

by taking a sufficiently large N and a sufficiently small ϵ. Just such a measurement procedure for the evaluation of $\underset{\underline{u}(t)|\underline{v}(t)}{E} \left\{ \underline{u}(t) \right\}$ where $\underline{v}(t)$ are coefficients characterizing $\underline{u}(\tau)$, $-\infty < \tau \le t$ has been systematized in References 14 and 68.

Needless to say, such measurements are generally impractical because the number of samples required is astronomical. This is the same difficulty as is encountered in trying to obtain a description of a general nonlinear dynamic system from measurements of its input and output time functions. An alternative which has been used to obtain descriptions of the elements being controlled, and which can be used to obtain a description of the statistical properties of the disturbances, is to postulate a model for the mechanism involved based on the knowledge of the physics of the situation and engineering judgment. Any unknown parameters in the model can be evaluated from experimentation and measurements on the environment the model is to represent. Once the model for the generation of the disturbances has been obtained, their statistical description can be derived from it.

As an illustration, let us consider the case in which $i(k)$ is generated at discrete time intervals $k = \ldots t-\Delta, t, t+\Delta, \ldots$ by a Markovian process and $v(k)$, which also is measured at discrete time intervals, is composed of $i(k)$ and an additive and independent noise $n(k)$:

$$v(k) = i(k) + n(k) \tag{4.27}$$

If i(k) has L discrete levels $i^1, i^2, \ldots i^L$, then a model for its generation is a Markov chain described by a transition matrix $[P(\, i(k+\Delta) | i(k)\,)]$:

$$[P(\, i(k+\Delta) | i(k)\,)] = \begin{bmatrix} P_k(1|1) & P_k(1|2) & \cdots & P_k(1|L) \\ P_k(2|1) & P_k(2|2) & \cdots & P_k(2|L) \\ \vdots & \vdots & \cdots & \vdots \\ P_k(L|1) & P_k(L|2) & \cdots & P_k(L|L) \end{bmatrix} \tag{4.28}$$

so that

$$P(\, i(k+\Delta)\,)] = [P(\, i(k+\Delta) | i(k)\,)]\ P(\, i(k)\,)] \tag{4.29}$$

where the ℓth component of $P(\, i(k)\,)]$ is the probability that $i(k) = i^{\ell}$. As one lets the quantization become finer and finer, then in the limit $P(\, i(k)\,)]$ becomes a density function $p(\, i(k)\,)$ and $[P(\, i(k+\Delta) | i(k)\,)]$ an operator* $\int_{-\infty}^{\infty} p(\, i(k+\Delta) | i(k)\,)\,(\quad)\, di(k)$, so that

$$p(\, i(k+\Delta)\,) = \int_{-\infty}^{\infty} p(\, i(k+\Delta) | i(k)\,)\, p(\, i(k)\,)\, di(k) \tag{4.30}$$

The noise n(k) is statistically independent of i(k), and its successive samples are statistically independent of each other. Thus

$$p_{i_k, n_\ell}(\xi_k, \eta_\ell) = p_{i_k}(\xi_k)\, p_{n_\ell}(\eta_\ell) \quad \text{for all } k \text{ and } \ell$$

$$p_{n_k, n_\ell}(\xi_k, \eta_\ell) = p_{n_k}(\xi_k)\, p_{n_\ell}(\eta_\ell) \quad \text{for all } k \neq \ell \tag{4.31}$$

In Equation 4.31 and in the following, the subscript under the "p" will be used to indicate which of the density functions is being considered. In such a case ξ and η are dummy variables. Thus $p_{i_k}(\xi)$ and $p_{i_{k+1}|i_k}(\xi|\eta)$ will be used to denote $p(\, i(k)\,)$ and

---

* The probability density function as used here admits impulses, and i(k) may change in discrete levels. It would have been more rigorous to have used the probability distribution functions, but densities are used for convenience. It is understood that $p(\xi)d\xi$ stands for $dP(\xi \leq \xi)$ and $p(\xi|\eta)d\xi$ stands for $dP(\xi \leq \xi | \eta = \eta)$ and that the Stieltjes integral is used.

$p(\ i(k+\Delta)|\,i(k)\ )$, respectively.

From this model representing the generation of $i(k)$ and $v(k)$, one would wish to derive the probability density $p(\ i(\ell), k\leq\ell<\infty|\,\underline{v}(k)\ )$ where $\underline{v}(k) = v(k), v(k-\Delta), v(k-2\Delta), \ldots$. One need not, however, tabulate this conditional density as a function of all the components of $\underline{v}(k)$. As shown in Appendix F, it is possible to define a memory function $W_{k-1}(\xi)$, which in itself stores all the information gained from $v(k-\Delta), v(k-2\Delta), \ldots$ that is pertinent to prediction of $i(k), i(k+\Delta), i(k+2\Delta), \ldots$, so that $p(\ i(\ell), k<\ell\infty|\,\underline{v}(k)\ )$ can be expressed as a function of $W_{k-1}(\xi)$ and $v(k)$. The function $W_{k-1}(\xi)$ itself is given by a recursion relation involving the previous memory function $W_{k-2}(\xi)$ and $v(k-\Delta)$. As shown in Appendix F,

$$W_{k-1}(\xi_k) = \int_{-\infty}^{\infty} p_{i_{k-1}|i_k}(\xi_{k-1}|\,\xi_k)p_{n_{k-1}}(\ v(k-\Delta) - \xi_{k-1}\ )\,W_{k-2}(\xi_{k-1})d\xi_{k-1} \tag{4.32}$$

and

$$p(\ i(k)|\,\underline{v}(k)\ ) = p_{i_k|v_k, v_{k-1},\ldots}(\ i(k)|\,\underline{v}(k)\ ) = \frac{W_{k-1}(\ i(k)\ )p_{n_k}(\ v(k) - i(k)\ )p_{i_k}(\ i(k)\ )}{\int_{-\infty}^{\infty} W_{k-1}(\xi)p_{n_k}(\ v(k) - \xi\ )p_{i_k}(\xi)d\xi} \tag{4.33}$$

For $\ell>k$, $p(\ i(\ell)|\,\underline{v}(k)\ )$ is then given as

$$\begin{aligned} p(\ i(\ell)|\,\underline{v}(k)\ ) = &\int_{-\infty}^{\infty} p_{i_\ell|i_{\ell-1}}(i(\ell)|\,\xi_{\ell-1}) \int_{-\infty}^{\infty} p_{i_{\ell-1}|i_{\ell-2}}(\xi_{\ell-1}|\,\xi_{\ell-2})\ldots \\ &\int_{-\infty}^{\infty} p_{i_{k+2}|i_{k+1}}(\xi_{k+2}|\,\xi_{k+1}) \\ &\int_{-\infty}^{\infty} p_{i_{k+1}|i_k}(\xi_{k+1}|\,\xi_k)p(\ \xi_k|\,\underline{v}(k)\ )d\xi_k d\xi_{k+1}\ldots d\xi_{\ell-2}d\xi_{\ell-1} \end{aligned} \tag{4.34}$$

Equations 4.32, 4.33, and 4.34 define a filter for estimating $p(\ i(\ell), k\leq\ell<\infty|\,\underline{v}(k)\ )$ and therefore the mean, the mode, the expected value, or any other statistical average of $i(\ell)$, $k\leq\ell<\infty$ conditional on $\underline{v}(k)$, according to what is essentially a recursive formulation of Baye's rule. The formulation is very general, for the only assumptions about the model were the Markovian nature of the signal and the statistical independence of the additive noise. The probability distributions of the noise and the signal are arbitrary and need not be stationary. Although the signal was considered Markovian, it was not necessary to assume that it have a finite number of amplitude states. Therefore the expressions apply for a signal generated by a discrete time dynamic system excited by a white noise of arbitrary probability distribution. Thus if

$$i(k+\Delta) = \phi i(k) + x(k) \tag{4.35}$$

where $x(k)$ is a white noise, then

$$p_{i_k | i_{k+1}}(\xi_k | \xi_{k+1}) = |\phi| p_{x_k}(\xi_{k+1} - \phi\xi_k) \tag{4.36}$$

and

$$p_{i_k}(\xi_k) = \int_{-\infty}^{\infty} p_{x_k}(\xi_k - \phi\xi_{k-1}) \left|\frac{1}{\phi}\right| p_{i_{k-1}}\left(\frac{\xi_{k-1}}{\phi}\right) d\xi_{k-1} \tag{4.37}$$

so that knowing $p_{x_\ell}(\xi)$, $\ell = \ldots k-1, k, k+1, \ldots$ and $p_{i_\ell}(\xi)$ for some one value of ℓ, the transition probability of the Markovian process is known, and $p_{i_k}(\xi)$ can be computed recursively. In a similar manner, the nonlinear signal generator

$$\frac{\triangleright}{\Delta} i(k) = G(k, i(k)) + x(k) \tag{4.38}$$

can be treated.

An interesting check on the validity of Equations 4.32 and 4.33 is possible. It is known that if the signal and the additive noise are Gaussian, the optimum mean-square filter is a linear operator on $v(\ell)$, $\ell \le k$.

From Equation 4.33 one can obtain the expectation operator which is the optimum mean-square filter as

$$\underset{i(k)|\underline{v}(k)}{E}\left\{i(k)\right\} = \frac{\int_{-\infty}^{\infty} \xi W_{k-1}(\xi) p_{n_k}(v(k) - \xi) p_{i_k}(\xi) d\xi}{\int_{-\infty}^{\infty} W_{k-1}(\xi) p_{n_k}(v(k) - \xi) p_{i_k}(\xi) d\xi} \tag{4.39}$$

Since $p_{n_k}(\xi)$ and $p_{i_{k-1}|i_k}(\xi | \eta)$ are both normal distributions and because $W_{k-1}(\xi)$ is a convolution of these, it is also a normal distribution. Hence $\underset{i(k)|\underline{v}(k)}{E}\left\{i(k)\right\}$ has the form

$$\underset{i(k)|\underline{v}(k)}{E}\left\{i(k)\right\} = \frac{\int_{-\infty}^{\infty} \xi \exp(a v(k)^2 + b\xi v(k) + Q(\xi)) d\xi}{\int_{-\infty}^{\infty} \exp(a v(k)^2 + b\xi v(k) + Q(\xi)) d\xi} \tag{4.40}$$

for some constants a, b, and a quadratic function $Q(\xi)$. After canceling $e^{av(k)^2}$ and substituting s for $-bv(k)$, one notices that

$$\underset{i(k)|\underline{v}(k)}{E}\left\{i(k)\right\} = \frac{\frac{d}{ds}\exp(\hat{Q}(s))}{\exp(\hat{Q}(s))} = \frac{d}{ds}\hat{Q}(s) \tag{4.41}$$

where $\exp(\hat{Q}(s))$ is the Fourier transform of $\exp(Q(\xi))$. Thus $\hat{Q}(s)$ is a quadratic in s; $\frac{d}{ds}\hat{Q}(s)$ is linear in s and therefore in v(k). Thus the complicated-looking filter of Equation 3.49 turns out to be linear.

To illustrate the technique of this section by a simple example, let us consider a signal which is a square wave with amplitude of ±1 and the zero crossing Poisson-distributed with an average frequency α. The noise has a Gaussian probability distribution with variance σ^2 and zero mean.

In this case the signal has only two levels, so that one needs to operate with transition matrices rather than integral operators. The memory function would consist of impulses at only two values of the argument at ±1, so it too can be treated as a finite dimensional vector. Equation 4.32 then becomes

$$\begin{bmatrix} w_k(1) \\ w_k(-1) \end{bmatrix} = g(k) \begin{bmatrix} \left(\frac{1+e^{-2\alpha\Delta}}{2}\right) & \left(\frac{1-e^{-2\alpha\Delta}}{2}\right) \\ \left(\frac{1-e^{-2\alpha\Delta}}{2}\right) & \left(\frac{1+e^{-2\alpha\Delta}}{2}\right) \end{bmatrix} \begin{bmatrix} \exp\left(-\frac{(v(k)-1)^2}{2\sigma^2}\right) & 0 \\ 0 & \exp\left(-\frac{(v(k)+1)^2}{2\sigma^2}\right) \end{bmatrix} \begin{bmatrix} w_{k-1}(1) \\ w_{k-1}(-1) \end{bmatrix} \tag{4.42}$$

where g(k) is such that $w_k(1) + w_k(-1) = 1$. The conditional expected value $\underset{i(k)|\underline{v}(k)}{E}\left\{i(k)\right\}$, which shall be denoted by $\mathcal{E}(k)$, is

$$\mathcal{E}(k) = \frac{w_{k-1}(1)\exp\left(\frac{v(k)}{\sigma^2}\right) - w_{k-1}(-1)\exp\left(-\frac{v(k)}{\sigma^2}\right)}{w_{k-1}(1)\exp\left(\frac{v(k)}{\sigma^2}\right) + w_{k-1}(-1)\exp\left(-\frac{v(k)}{\sigma^2}\right)} \tag{4.43}$$

Equation 4.43 can then be manipulated and combined with Equation 4.42 to yield a recursion relation entirely in terms of $\mathcal{E}(k)$:

$$\mathcal{E}(k) = \frac{e^{-2\alpha\Delta}\mathcal{E}(k-\Delta) + \tanh\left(\frac{v(k)}{\sigma^2}\right)}{1+e^{-2\alpha}\mathcal{E}(k-\Delta)\tanh\left(\frac{v(k)}{\sigma^2}\right)} \tag{4.44}$$

and for $\ell \geq k$:

$$\mathcal{E}(\ell) = \frac{e^{-2a\Delta}\mathcal{E}(k-\Delta) + \tanh\left(\frac{v(k)}{\sigma^2}\right)}{1+e^{-2a\Delta}\mathcal{E}(k-\Delta)\tanh\left(\frac{v(k)}{\sigma^2}\right)} e^{-2a(\ell-k)} \tag{4.45}$$

Equation 4.45 represents the best possible mean-square predictor filter. It is a nonlinear device, since the signal was not Gaussian, but it is simply realizable, as shown in Figure 4.3.

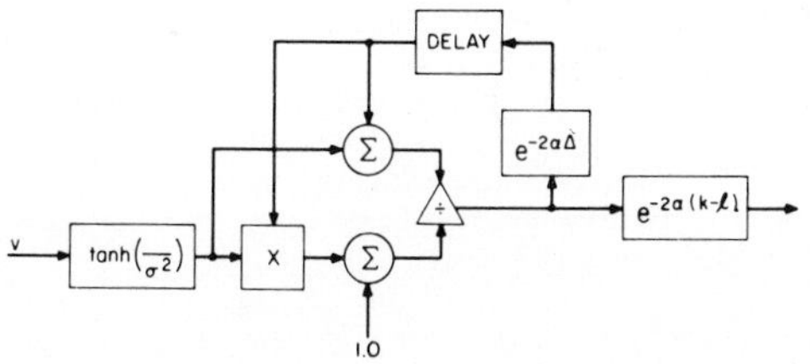

Fig. 4.3. Schematic representation of the nonlinear predictor-filter

Presented in this section was a rather powerful method of designing devices to perform the filtering and prediction of stochastic signals required to yield the data needed for the optimizing controller. Its success is based on the concept of creating a model for the environment generating the signal and deriving the required statistical averages from it. It is not a solution to all problems of filtering and prediction, but it does represent a useful approach in the situation encountered in control system design.

Chapter 5

SUMMARY AND CONCLUSIONS

In this work, control system synthesis was treated as a problem in dynamic optimization. The controller was considered to be a device which manipulates the inputs to the element being controlled in accordance with a control law specifying the values of the manipulated variables as a function of system state and the available information about the externally generated disturbances acting on the system. The problem treated was that of finding the control law which makes the over-all system behavior in some sense best, that is, one which optimizes a preassigned performance criterion measuring the degree of success with which the plant being controlled accomplishes its task. The problems associated with the implementation of the laws so found, in terms of practical hardware, were not considered. Furthermore, it was assumed that a mathematical description of the plant and of the surroundings interacting with it was available. When the surroundings affected the plant through stochastic disturbances, it was considered that there was given a description of the statistical relation between these disturbances and the measurable parameters which are the information inputs to the controller.

The general performance criterion considered was the expected value (over the sample space of the stochastic disturbances) of an integrand over some future time of a function of plant inputs and outputs. The time τ, over which the performance was to be weighed, was from the current time t to some future time T, where T could be finite or infinite, or it could be specified as that value of time at which system outputs satisfy a prescribed condition. The termination time was allowed to enter into the integrand of the performance criterion, and an auxiliary profit or penalty as a function of system conditions at the termination time also could be included. This general performance criterion is shown in Equations 2.4 and 2.5 and can represent any one of the commonly used measures of system performance.

System description was assumed given in terms of nonlinear difference or differential equations expressing the system state transitions. In the case of distributed parameter systems, the description used was in terms of partial differential equations specifying the rates of change of state functions. This method of characterizing system behavior in terms of state transitions is explained in

Appendix C and contrasted with the impedance viewpoint expounded in Appendix B.

The properties which the controller must have in order to result in optimum system behavior were derived in Section 2.1. It was shown that the optimum control inputs $\underline{m}(t)$ depend on a set of parameters $\underline{\lambda}(t)$, which, together with the current system state $\underline{q}(t)$, are the initial conditions of the Euler-Lagrange differential equations and where $\underline{\lambda}(t)$ are to be chosen such that the solutions of the Euler-Lagrange equations, $(\underline{q}, (\tau), \underline{\lambda}(\tau), t \leq \tau < T)$, satisfy the prescribed boundary conditions at the future time T. Thus the optimum control law was shown to be specified by a solution of a two-point boundary-value problem associated with the Euler-Lagrange equations and the optimum controller, a two-point boundary-value problem solver. This result was derived in Section 2.1 for plants described by ordinary difference or differential equations. In Sections 2.4 and 2.5 it was extended to other forms of system description and to distributed parameter systems. In all cases the optimum control law is a solution of a two-point boundary-value problem. In Section 2.3 the general properties of the Euler-Lagrange equations were investigated. It was shown that they are always unstable whether propagated forward or backward in time. The ways in which the Euler equations become modified when some of the variables are limited in range were discussed in Section 2.6.

The properties of the optimum control law derived in Section 2.1 are only the necessary conditions. Further tests are needed to determine whether the control law found does indeed yield an optimum rather than what is merely a stationary point of the performance criterion. Tests specifying the sufficiency conditions were described in Section 2.2.

The solution of two-point boundary-value problems and the calculation of the control law are difficult. Seldom are analytic solutions possible, and in general, recourse to numerical techniques became necessary. Analytic solutions were obtained in situations in which the plant is described by ordinary linear constant-coefficient differential equations and in which a quadratic performance criterion weighed over a semi-infinite future time interval is used. These solutions were presented in Section 2.7. When the coefficients in system description and in the performance criterion are time-varying, when the performance is weighed over a finite time and linear boundary conditions are imposed at the termination time, a systematic, semi-analytic solution is still possible, as was shown in Section 3.1. In nonlinear problems, it was found, one had to rely on numerical techniques alone.

For the numerical solution of two-point boundary-value problems encountered in the synthesis of optimum control laws, two different approaches were used. In the first method, which was described in Section 3.2, the control law was obtained by flooding, that is, by tabulating the solutions at a number of points in the domain of the control law. The peculiar instability properties of the Euler-Lagrange equations made this method possible and, indeed, very successful. In the second method, described in Section 3.3, one sought to find a solution for a particular point in the control law domain. This was done iteratively either by varying $\underline{\lambda}(t)$ until one found a solution of the Euler equations which matched the boundary conditions or by varying trajectories which satisfy the boundary conditions until a solution was found which satisfied the Euler equations.

In Section 3.4 it was shown that if the control law can be expanded in a Taylor series about a known optimum trajectory, then it is possible to derive differential equations governing the coefficients of the expansion. If the control law is known at one value of time, then it can be obtained for other values of time by solving these equations. The coefficients of the linear terms were shown to be governed by a matrix Riccati differential equation and the coefficients of the higher-order terms by linear differential equations.

Section 3.5 demonstrated how the Euler-Lagrange equations can be simulated using an electric network or an analog computer in such a way that the successive meshes correspond to successive instants of time, so that the analogous quantity to time becomes a spatial dimension. In such an analog, boundary conditions can be imposed at different meshes corresponding to boundary conditions on the Euler equations at different instants of time. Thus a two-point boundary-value problem is solved by the analog essentially instantaneously. It was shown how such an analog can be used as an optimizing control computer.

In the various methods for computing the control law which were presented in Chapter 3, it was assumed that the plant disturbances were known deterministic time functions. In Chapter 4 it was shown that when the disturbances are stochastic, the control law is still given as a solution of a boundary-value problem; but in the Euler equations, instead of the disturbance functions, there enter deterministic functions which are the various moments of the probability density of the disturbances conditional on the information inputs to the controller. The problem of measuring or determining conditional moments of random functions is beyond the scope of this work. Nevertheless, in Section 4.2 some techniques were presented which have been found useful in this aspect of the control problem.

Throughout the work the various techniques proposed were tested on what were considered to be simplified but typical control problems. These problems are described in Appendix E.

The numerical techniques for the calculation of optimum controls, which were developed in Chapter 3, were programmed for use on an IBM 709 digital computer in such a way that they can be used on general control programs. These programs are described in Appendix G.

This work presented a general approach to the synthesis of control systems or, more precisely, to the calculation of the control law in accordance with which the control system should operate. The method is applicable to what is a rather general class of systems and performance criteria. No less important than the formulation of the problem and specification of the necessary and sufficient conditions for the optimum control law is the development of practical techniques for computing these control laws. A number of solution techniques were developed and applied successfully. The numerical techniques have been programmed for a digital computer so that the solutions can be obtained essentially automatically Thus synthesis of optimizing control laws have been brought into th realm of practical procedures. It is hoped that these methods will now find application in control system design.

Appendix A

NOMENCLATURE

An attempt has been made to keep the nomenclature and symbolism consistent throughout this report and in conformance with common usage. Some departures were necessary where the work touches two fields in which the same symbol is used with different meanings. These departures and some uncommon or controversial usage are described in this appendix.

Underlined quantities, such as $\underline{y}$ and $\underline{G}$, or those with an arrow above them, for example $\vec{y}$ and $\vec{G}$, denote vectors with components $y_1, y_2, \ldots,$ and $G_1, G_2, \ldots,$ respectively. These quantities may be functions of one or more variables which are themselves either vectors or scalars, or both, for example $y(\tau)$, $y(\underline{x})$, $y(\tau, \underline{x})$. When a vector is to be treated as a column matrix it is written as $y]$, or $\lfloor y \rfloor$ when it is to be a row matrix. The null and unit vectors are $\underline{0}$ and $\underline{1}$, respectively.

The derivative of y with respect to its argument (a single scalar argument is denoted by y', and the nth derivative is indicated by $y^{(n)}$. Thus

$$y' = y'(\tau) = \frac{d}{d\tau} y(\tau) = \frac{d}{d\xi} y(\xi)$$

$$\underline{y}' = y_1', y_2', \ldots = \frac{d}{d\tau} y(\tau) = \frac{dy_1(\tau)}{d\tau}, \frac{dy_2(\tau)}{d\tau}, \ldots \quad \text{(A. 1)}$$

The partial derivatives of a scalar function of a vector variable are denoted by the symbol ∇. If there are several vector arguments, a subscript on ∇ denotes the variable with respect to which the derivative is taken. Thus

$$\nabla f(\underline{y}) = \frac{\partial f}{\partial y_1}, \frac{\partial f}{\partial y_2}, \ldots$$

$$\nabla_x f(\underline{x}, \underline{y}) = \frac{\partial f}{\partial x_1}, \frac{\partial f}{\partial x_2}, \ldots \quad \text{(A. 2)}$$

Since the gradient is a vector, it may at times be written as $\nabla f]$ or $\underline{\nabla f}$ to emphasize that it is to be treated as a column or a row matrix. A norm of a vector $\underline{y}$ is denoted by $\|\underline{y}\|$.

Matrices are distinguished by square brackets; for instance, $[A]$. The zero and unit matrices are denoted by $[0]$ and $[I]$, respectively. The transpose of a matrix is indicated by $[A^T]$ or $[A]^T$ and the inverse by $[A^{-1}]$ or $[A]^{-1}$. The symbol $(A)_{i,j}$ denotes the coefficient of the ith row and j^{th} column of the matrix $[A]$. Either $|A|$ or $|[A]|$ indicates the determinant of $[A]$. The Jacobian matrix is represented as $J(\ )$, and a subscript on J denotes the variable with respect to which the partial derivatives are to be taken, if there are several of them. Thus

$$J(\underline{G}(\underline{y})) = \begin{bmatrix} \frac{\partial G_1}{\partial y_1} & \frac{\partial G_1}{\partial y_2} \cdots \\ \frac{\partial G_2}{\partial y_1} & \frac{\partial G_2}{\partial y_2} \cdots \\ \vdots & \vdots \end{bmatrix} \qquad J_x(\underline{G}(\underline{x}, \underline{y})) = \begin{bmatrix} \frac{\partial G_1}{\partial x_1} & \frac{\partial G_2}{\partial x_2} \cdots \\ \frac{\partial G_2}{\partial x_1} & \frac{\partial G_2}{\partial x_2} \cdots \\ \vdots & \vdots \end{bmatrix} \tag{A. 3}$$

To emphasize its matrix character the Jacobian may be written with square brackets, for example $[J(\underline{G}(\underline{y}))]$ or $[J_x(\underline{G}(\underline{x}, \underline{y}))]$.

When operating with derivatives of higher orders, the following notation is used:*

$$S^{\underline{i}}_{y_j} = \frac{\partial S_i}{\partial y_j} \quad \begin{matrix} i = 1, 2, \ldots \\ j = 1, 2, \ldots \end{matrix} \qquad S^{\underline{i}}_{x_j, y_\ell} = \frac{\partial^2 S_i}{\partial y_\ell, \partial x_j} \quad \begin{matrix} i = 1, 2, \ldots \\ j = 1, 2, \ldots \\ \ell = 1, 2, \ldots \end{matrix}$$

$$S^{\underline{i}}_{x_j, y_\ell, \ldots z_r} = \frac{\partial^{\cdots} S_i}{\partial z_r \ldots \partial y_\ell, \partial x_j} \quad \begin{matrix} i = 1, 2, \ldots \\ j = 1, 2, \ldots \\ \ell = 1, 2, \ldots \\ \cdots\cdots\cdots \\ r = 1, 2, \ldots \end{matrix} \tag{A. 4}$$

* This is in fact the conventional tensor notation using underlined superscripts to indicate covariant components and subscripts to indicate contravariant components of the tensor quantities.

The order of the subscripts, in reverse, denotes the order of differentiation. When the subscripts and superscripts are letters, the symbol denotes the entire array with the literal subscripts and superscripts taking on all of their possible values. With this convention

$$y^{i} = \underline{y} = y_1, \; y_2, \; \dots \qquad G^{i}_{x_j} = [\, J_x(\, G(\underline{x})\,)] = \begin{bmatrix} \dfrac{\partial G_1}{\partial x_1} & \dfrac{\partial G_1}{\partial x_2} & \dots \\ \dfrac{\partial G_2}{\partial x_1} & \dfrac{\partial G_2}{\partial x_2} & \dots \\ \vdots & \vdots & \end{bmatrix} \tag{A. 5}$$

Large brackets, when used with this notation, indicate summation over all possible values of the indices appearing as both subscripts and superscripts.* Thus

$$\left(S^{i}_{j,k} \; A^{j}_{\ell,r} \; B_i \right) = \sum_i \sum_j \left\{ \frac{\partial^2 S_i}{\partial x_k \partial x_j} \; \frac{\partial^2 A_j}{\partial x_r \partial x_\ell} \; \frac{\partial B}{\partial x_i} \right\} \tag{A. 6}$$

δ^{i}_{j} or $\delta^{i}_{j,\ell}$ is the Kroneker delta symbol. It equals 1 when $i = j$ and when $i = j = \ell$, respectively, and 0 otherwise.

The symbol δ itself denotes the variation operator, or more precisely the weak variation of a functional with respect to its argument function. If there are several arguments, a literal subscript indicates the one with respect to which the variation is to be taken. Thus

$$\delta F(\, f(\tau)\,) = \frac{\partial F}{\partial f}\, \delta f(\tau) = \lim_{\epsilon \to 0} \frac{\partial F}{\partial \epsilon}(\, f(\tau) + \epsilon \delta f(\tau)\,) \delta f(\tau)$$

$$\delta_f F(\, f(\tau), g(\tau)\,) = \frac{\partial F}{\partial f}\, \delta f(\tau) = \lim_{\epsilon \to 0} \frac{\partial F}{\partial \epsilon}(\, f(\tau) + \epsilon \delta f(\tau), g(\tau)\,) \tag{A. 7}$$

---

* This is the conventional notation for tensor contraction.

The letter s represents the complex variable of the Laplace transform domain. It is also used as the imaginary variable, the argument of the Fourier transform. The symbol $\mathcal{L}(\,f(\tau)\,)$ denotes the Laplace transform of $f(\tau), 0 \leq \tau < \infty$ and $\mathcal{F}(\,f(\tau)\,)$ represents the Fourier transform of $f(\tau), -\infty < \tau < \infty$. The so-called double-sided Laplace transform is not used in this work. $\mathcal{Z}(\,f(k)\,)$ is the "z" transform of a function $f(k)$, $k = t, t+\Delta, t+2\Delta, \ldots$. The complex variable of the Z transform domain is z.

In operations with finite differences $\triangleright$ is used as the forward difference, $\triangleleft$ as the backwards difference, and Σ as the central difference operator. The symbol Z denotes the delay operator, and Δ denotes the increment with respect to which differencing takes place.

E is the expectation operator indicating the ensemble average over the sample space of the random function or variable in its argument. If there are several such functions or variables, those with respect to whose sample spaces the expectation operator is to be taken are shown underneath the symbol E, for example $\underset{x}{E}$ or $\underset{x(\tau)}{E}$.

A function $\underline{f}(\underline{x})$ is said to be of class C^i if $\dfrac{\partial^i f_\ell}{\partial x_{j_1}\,\partial x_{j_2} \cdots \partial x_{j_i}}$ are all continuous. The function $\underline{f}(\underline{x})$ is of class D^i if

$\dfrac{\partial^i f_\ell}{\partial x_{j_1}\,\partial x_{j_2} \cdots \partial x_{j_i}}$ are all continuous except on a set of zero area where, however, both the left and right-hand limits exist.

The symbol $\Rightarrow$ means "implies."

The generalized control problem is shown in Fig. 1.1 of Chapter 1. The plant referred to there represents the element being controlled. The controller is that part of the system which generates the control input, and the surroundings are that part of the world which generates the disturbances and provides information about them in the form of the command input. The plant is described by equations

$$\frac{d}{d\tau}\underline{q}(\tau) = \underline{G}(\,\tau, \underline{q}(\tau), \underline{m}(\tau), \underline{u}(\tau)\,)$$

$$\underline{y}(\tau) = \underline{H}(\,\tau, \underline{q}(\tau), \underline{u}(\tau)\,) \qquad (A.8)$$

if it operates continuously in time, or by

$$\frac{\triangleright}{\Delta}\,\underline{q}(k) = \underline{G}(\,k, \underline{q}(k), \underline{m}(k), \underline{u}(k)\,)$$

$$\underline{y}(k) = \underline{H}(\,k, \underline{q}(k), \underline{u}(k)\,) \qquad \text{(A. 9)}$$

if it operates only at discrete times k = t, t+Δ, t+2Δ, ... The generalized performance criterion is

$$\mathscr{P} = \underset{\underline{u}(\tau)}{E}\left\{\int_t^T \hat{F}(\,T, \tau, \underline{y}(\tau), \underline{m}(\tau), \underline{u}(\tau)\,)d\tau\right\} \qquad \text{(A. 10)}$$

or, if the function $\underline{H}$ is incorporated in $\hat{F}$, then

$$\mathscr{P} = \underset{\underline{u}(\tau)}{E}\left\{\int_t^T F(\,T, \tau, \underline{q}(\tau), \underline{m}(\tau), \underline{u}(\tau)\,)d\tau\right\} \qquad \text{(A. 11)}$$

In the case of a process acting at discrete times, this becomes

$$\mathscr{P} = \underset{\underline{u}(\tau)}{E}\left\{\sum_{k=t}^{T-\Delta} F(\,T, k, \underline{q}, (k), \underline{m}(k), \underline{u}(k)\,)\right\} \qquad \text{(A. 12)}$$

The variable assignment used throughout this report is as follows:

c_i, i = 1, 2, ...	Coefficients characterizing system input signal
c_i^*, i = 1, 2, ...	Coefficients characterizing system output signal
$\underline{\mathscr{C}}$	Control law function
$[\mathscr{C}]$	Control law matrix
F	Integrand of the performance criterion, a function of the state variables
$\hat{F}$	Integrand of the performance criterion, a function of system outputs
$\underline{g}$	Function specifying trajectory terminating conditions
$\underline{G}$	State transition function
[G]	Matrix of state transition coefficients

$[G_m]$	Matrix of coefficients relating control input to the state transitions
$[G_q]$	Matrix of state transition coefficients
H	Function specifying system outputs in terms of system states
h	System impulse response
i	Desired system outputs
k	Running time variable in discrete time case
ℓ	Running distance variable when distance is quantized
L	Lipschitz constant
$\underline{m}$	Control inputs
n	The order of the system, the dimensionality of its state vector
n_m	The number of components of the control input vector
p	Probability density
P	Probability
[P]	Coefficient matrix in the linear Euler equations
$\mathcal{P}$	Penalty function
$\mathscr{P}$	Performance criterion
$\underline{q}$	The state vector
[Q]	Coefficient matrix in the linear Euler equations
[R]	Coefficient matrix in the linear Euler equations
$\mathcal{R}$	Region of applicability of the optimization procedures

t	Current time
T	Time at which the control problem terminates
$\underline{u}$	System disturbances
$[U]$	Nodal matrix
$\underline{v}$	System inputs
V	Lyapunov function
w	System function or functional
W	System impedance function
x	Continuous distance variable
$\underline{y}$	System outputs
$[\phi]$	System matrix impulse response
τ	Running time

Appendix B

SYSTEM DESCRIPTION — THE IMPEDANCE VIEWPOINT

From the control viewpoint, system description is a specification of the relationship between the time histories of its inputs and outputs. As represented in Figure B.1, the time functions at the

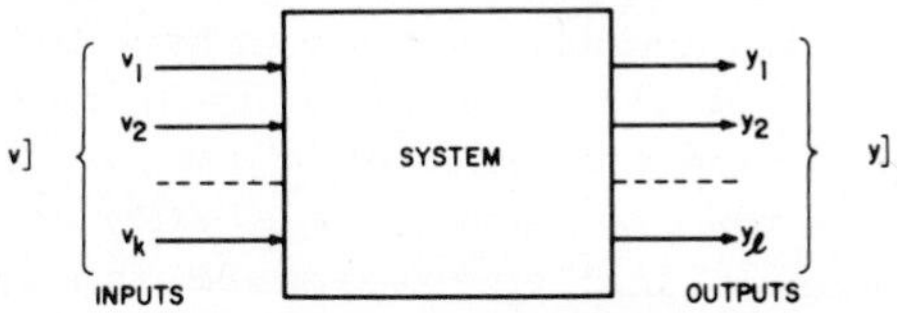

Fig. B.1. Representation of system inputs and outputs

various inputs, $v_1(t), v_2(t), \ldots v_k(t)$, and those at the outputs $y_1(t), y_2(t), \ldots y_\ell(t)$, will be treated as the components of an input vector $\underline{v}(t)$ and an output vector $\underline{y}(t)$, respectively.

A "no-memory" system is one in which the output at time t is a function of the input at time t and possibly of t itself.

$$\underline{y}(t) = \underline{w}(\, t, v(t)\,) \tag{B.1}$$

A dynamic system is one in which the output $\underline{y}(t)$ depends not only on t and $\underline{v}(t)$ but also on the entire past of $\underline{v}(t)$, that is $\underline{v}(\tau)$, $-\infty<\tau\leq t$ and so is described by a functional

$$\underline{y}(t) = \underline{w}(t; \underline{v}(\tau), -\infty<\tau\leq t) \tag{B.2}$$

If $\underline{w}$ has the property that

$$\underline{w}(t; \underline{v}_A(\tau) + \underline{v}_B(\tau), -\infty<\tau\leq t) = \underline{w}(t; \underline{v}_A(\tau), -\infty<\tau\leq t) + \underline{w}(t; \underline{v}_B(\tau), -\infty<\tau\leq t) \tag{B.3}$$

for all t and $\underline{v}$, then $\underline{w}$ is termed a linear functional, and the system is called linear; otherwise it is called nonlinear. If $\underline{w}$ has the property that

$$\lim_{T\to\infty} \underline{w}(t_1; \underline{v}(\tau-t_1), t_1-T<\tau\leq t_1) = \lim_{T\to\infty} \underline{w}(t_2; \underline{v}(\tau-t_2), t_2-T<\tau\leq t_2) \tag{B.4}$$

for all t_1, t_2, and $\underline{v}$, then the functional is said not to involve time explicitly, and the system is called time-invariant; otherwise it is called time-varying.

The notion of a functional as a means of describing dynamic system behavior is an extension of the familiar notion of a function or a transformation. One restricts the possible inputs to a certain class and defines a set of coefficients $c_1, c_2, \dots$ which completely characterize any one of the possible functions $\underline{v}$ in this class. In general, there will be an infinite number of coefficients, and a finite set $c_1, c_2, \dots c_N$ characterizes $\underline{v}$ only approximately. If we define $\underline{w}_N$ as the transformation which assigns to each point in the $(t, c_1, c_2, \dots c_N)$ space a value of $\underline{y}(t)$, then the functional $\underline{w}$ is the limit of $\underline{w}_N$ as $N \to \infty$ in such a way that the domain of $\underline{w}_N$ becomes the entire infinite dimensional space $(t, c_1, c_2, \dots)$. To talk about the convergence of $\lim_{N\to\infty} \underline{w}_N$ in a mathematically rigorous manner, one would have to define an ordering for the set $c_1, c_2, \dots$ and specify in what sense $c_1, c_2, \dots c_{N*}$ is a better characterization of $\underline{v}$ than $c_1, c_2, \dots c_N$ when $N* > N$, and in what sense $\underline{w}_{N*}$ is a better approximation to $\underline{y}(t)$ than $\underline{w}_N$. In terms of mathematical rigor, this is a rather difficult problem.[73] In engineering terms, the above notation claims that in a physical situation the input time function has a set of properties which in a given system serve to determine the output. If some of these properties are specified, the output can be determined approximately, and as more and more properties are taken into account a more accurate determination of the output is possible. For engineering purposes this explanation is sufficient.

In certain special cases the above notions have been made precise. For example,[14,16] in the case of a single-input, single-output, continuous dynamic system, if $c_1(t), c_2(t), \dots$ are the Laguerre coefficients of $v(\tau)$, $-\infty < \tau < t$ (assuming they exist), then there is a $w(t, c_1(t), c_2(t), \dots c_N(t))$ such that

$$\lim_{\substack{N\to\infty \\ T\to\infty}} \frac{1}{2T} \int_{-T}^{T} \left(w_N(t, c(t), c_2(t), \dots c_N(t)) - y(t)\right)^2 dt = 0 \tag{B.5}$$

or if v is an ergotic random variable,

$$E\left\{\left(w_N(t, c(t), c_2(t), \dots c_N(t)) - y(t)\right)^2\right\} = 0 \tag{B.6}$$

E is the expectation operator, and a dynamic system is termed continuous if for every $\epsilon_2 > 0$ there is an $\epsilon_1 > 0$ such that if $|v_A(\tau) - v_B(\tau)| < \epsilon_1$, for $-\infty < \tau \leq t$, then $|y_A(t) - y_B(t)| < \epsilon_2$. Similar results were obtained for more general measures of the goodness of approximation and more general notions of continuity.[16, 28, 73, 75]

The functional commonly used to describe the behavior of a linear dynamic system is the convolution integral

$$y(t)] = \int_{-\infty}^{t} [\phi(t, \tau)]\ v(\tau)]\ d\tau \tag{B.7}$$

where $[\phi(t, \tau)]$ is the system impulse response. Here the set of characterizing coefficients $c_1(t), c_2(t), \ldots$ is a dense set composed of the values of $\underline{v}(\tau), -\infty<\tau\leq t$. It also has been shown that the functional describing a nonlinear continuous system can be expressed as a sum of multiple convolution integrals.[70] Thus for a single-input, single-output system

$$y(t) = \int_{-\infty}^{t} h_1(t, \tau)v(\tau)d\tau + \int_{-\infty}^{t}\int_{-\infty}^{t} h_2(t, \tau_1, \tau_2)v(\tau_1)v(\tau_2)\ d\tau_1\ d\tau_2$$

$$+ \int_{-\infty}^{t}\int_{-\infty}^{t}\int_{-\infty}^{t} h_3(t, \tau_1, \tau_2, \tau_3)v(\tau_1)v(\tau_2)v(\tau_3)d\tau_1\ d\tau_2\ d\tau_3 + \ldots \tag{B.8}$$

When the description of one or more dynamic elements is given in this form, it is possible to obtain a corresponding expansion of the system obtained by connecting the component elements in parallel, cascade, or feedback arrangements.[16,28,75]

This form of system description is particularly useful when the system is nearly linear, for then the higher-order integrals can be considered as correction terms. Its chief disadvantage is that it is next to impossible to calculate the higher-order kernels h_2, h_3, . . . from the physical description of the process.

The notion of an impedance is but a logical extension of the concept of a functional. Instead of describing system output $\underline{y}(t)$ at one time instant t, one considers the entire time function $\underline{y}(\tau), t\leq\tau<T$ for some $T>t$ or a set of coefficients $c_1^*(t, T), c_2^*(t, T)$, . . . which characterize $\underline{y}(\tau), t\leq\tau<T$. The impedance is an operator defining the transformation from the space of coefficients $c_1(T), c_2(T), \ldots$ characterizing $\underline{v}(\tau), -\infty<\tau<T$ into the space of coefficients $c_1^*(t, T), c_2^*(t, T), \ldots$ characterizing $y(\tau), t\leq\tau<T$:

$$c_1^*(t, T), c_2^*(t, T), \ldots = \underline{W}(t, c_1(T), c_2(T), \ldots) \tag{B.9}$$

and therefore the relationship between $\underline{v}(\tau), -\infty<\tau<T$ and $\underline{y}(\tau), t\leq\tau<T$:

$$\underline{y}(\tau), t\leq\tau<T = \underline{W}(t, \underline{v}(\tau), -\infty<\tau<T) \tag{B.10}$$

As defined above, $\underline{W}$ is the generalized impedance describing the dynamic system behavior. If $c_1, c_2, \ldots$ and $c_1^*, c_2^*, \ldots$ are taken to be the Fourier coefficients of the inputs and outputs, respectively, with $T\to\infty$, then for a linear system $\underline{W}$ becomes the familiar impedance operator. Since the Fourier coefficients are defined by linear operations on the corresponding time functions, then for a linear system the impedance is a linear transformation from $c_1, c_2, \ldots$ to $c_1^*, c_2^*, \ldots$. Expanding in terms of Fourier coefficients has the advantage that for a time-invariant system (when $c_1, c_2, \ldots$ and $c_1^*, c_2^*, \ldots$ are treated as complex numbers) the transformation is diagonal. If a different expansion was used, in terms of the Laguerre coefficients for example, the transformation would not be diagonal; similarly, if the Fourier expansion was used in a time-varying problem, the transformation matrix would no longer be diagonal.

Time-varying impedances have been used to a considerable extent in control and filtering theory,[54] and the functionals of Equation B.8 can be considered as impedance operators in which only one c^* is used and that one is equal to $y(t)$. The convolution integral when written in the form

$$y(\tau) = \int_{-\infty}^{\infty} h(\tau, \xi)v(\xi)d\xi \qquad \text{(B.11)}$$

can be considered as an impedance operator, with $c_1, c_2, \ldots$ being a dense set composed of values of $v(\xi)$, $-\infty < \xi < \infty$ and $c_1^*, c_2^*, \ldots$ being a dense set of values of $y(\tau)$, $-\infty < \tau < \infty$.

The describing function is a prime example of a nonlinear impedance based on an expansion in terms of Fourier coefficients. In its elementary form it is taken to be a nonlinear but diagonal transformation:[45]

$$c_i^* = W_i(c_i) \qquad i = 1, 2, \ldots \qquad \text{(B.12)}$$

It can be applied successfully to predict c_i^* when c_i is the predominant generator of c_i^*. Somewhat more sophisticated treatments attempt to consider the cross-coupling effects between the various harmonics. The describing function approach to the description of nonlinear systems has been used successfully in control systems stability studies and in the analysis of modulation, detection, and frequency conversion circuits.

The description of dynamic systems in terms of their impedances has been used extensively in electrical engineering. It has been eminently successful in the analysis and synthesis of linear networks, and considerable progress has been made in applying it to nonlinear problems. However, this is not the only approach possible, and in the work reported on here the state transitions method of analysis has been found more useful. This method is described in Appendix C.

Appendix C

SYSTEM DESCRIPTION — THE STATE TRANSITIONS VIEWPOINT

An alternative to describing a dynamic system in terms of its impedance is the so-called "state transitions" approach presented in this appendix. Except for the part dealing with the Taylor series expansion of solutions and the derivation of equations for evaluating coefficients in this series, the methods and results are not original. They are presented here because this material is nowhere available in a collected form and because it is used extensively throughout this work.

The state transitions method of description of dynamic systems is based on the hypothesis that there exists a set of parameters $q_1, q_2, \ldots$ such that at time $t+\Delta$ the output of a dynamic system, $\underline{y}(t+\Delta)$, depends only on $\underline{v}(\tau), t<\tau \leq t+\Delta$ and $q_1(t), q_2(t), \ldots$. This implies that all the information about the past of the input, $\underline{v}(\tau), -\infty<\tau\leq t$, of significance in determining the future system behavior, is stored in terms of the parameters $q_1(t), q_2(t), \ldots$, which is what was known about $\underline{v}(\tau), -\infty<\tau\leq t$, to yield $q_1(t+\Delta), q_2(t+\Delta), \ldots$. Thus the system output $\underline{y}(t+\Delta)$ can be considered to be dependent on $q_1(t+\Delta), q_2(t+\Delta), \ldots$.

The set of parameters $q_1, q_2, \ldots$ are called the state variables and are said to define the state of the system. The rule for forming $q_1(t+\Delta), q_2(t+\Delta), \ldots$ from $q_1(t), q_2(t), \ldots$ and $\underline{v}(\tau), t<\tau\leq t+\Delta$ is the state transition functional

$$q_1(t+\Delta), q_2(t+\Delta), \ldots = w(t; q_1(t), q_2(t), \ldots; \underline{v}(\tau), t<\tau\leq t+\Delta) \tag{C.1}$$

The output can be expressed as a function of the current input and system state:

$$\underline{y}(t+\Delta) = \underline{H}(t+\Delta; \underline{v}(t+\Delta); q_1(t+\Delta), q_2(t+\Delta), \ldots) \tag{C.2}$$

It should be noted that in contrast to the impedance approach one need not assume that the infinitely remote past of the input has no influence on the system output,[15] so that one can treat systems exhibiting hysteresis.

If $q_1, q_2, \ldots$ has but a finite number of components, $q_1, q_2, \ldots q_n$, it can be considered an n-dimensional vector $\underline{q}$. In such a case the system will be called a lumped parameter system. If, in addition, $\underline{q}$ is allowed to change only at discrete times $k = t, t+\Delta, t+2\Delta, \ldots$ and $\underline{v}$ also changes only at $k = t-\epsilon, t+\Delta-\epsilon, t+2\Delta-\epsilon, \ldots$ (as $\epsilon \to 0$), then the state transitions can be described by a difference equation

$$\frac{\triangleright}{\Delta}\underline{q}(k) = \underline{G}(\ k, \underline{q}(k), \underline{v}(k)\ ) \tag{C.3}$$

If changes in state occur continuously in time, not just at discrete time intervals, then one can consider the system as being subject to state transitions occurring at time instants separated by infinitesimal time increments, and therefore by Equation C.3 in the limit as $\Delta \to 0$ and k varies over a continuum of values τ, $t \leq \tau$

$$\lim_{\Delta \to 0} \left\{ \frac{\triangleright}{\Delta}\underline{q}(k) = \underline{G}(\ k, \underline{q}(k), \underline{v}(k)\ ) \right\} \tag{C.4}$$

If $\lim_{\Delta \to 0} \underline{G}(\ k, \underline{q}(k), \underline{v}(k)\ )$ exists, this becomes

$$\frac{d}{d\tau}\underline{q}(\tau) = \underline{G}(\ \tau, \underline{q}(\tau), \underline{v}(\tau)\ ) \tag{C.5}$$

Thus the system is described in terms of its infinitesimal state transitions by a differential equation. If the limit does not exist, as would be the case if $\underline{q}(\tau)$ were capable of instantaneous change, then Equation C.5 may still be made meaningful by allowing $\underline{G}$ to contain impulse functions. However, in such a case this must be viewed only as convenient symbolism for representing the limiting process of Equation C.4.

If it takes an infinite set of parameters $(q_1, q_2, \ldots)$ to describe the state of a system, then it is termed a distributed parameter system. The difference equation describing its state transitions can be written as

$$\frac{\triangleright}{\Delta}q_i(k) = G_i(\ k; q_1(k), q_2(k), \ \ldots\ ; \ \underline{v}(k)\ ) \qquad i = 1, 2, \ldots \tag{C.6}$$

In the majority of the distributed parameter systems that are of practical interest, such as those involving transport lags and convection or wave-propagation phenomena, the set $(q_1, q_2, \ldots)$ represents the distribution of one or more variables over a space of one or more dimensions. For example, in a description of heat transfer by convection in a porous bed, $q_1, q_2, \ldots$ may represent the temperature at various points in the bed. The state of the system is therefore described by the entire distribution, and the state transition as expressed by Equation C.6 is the transition from one distribution to another. In these cases the value of the state at a particular point of the distribution depends only on the values of its immediate neighbors, its own and their immediate past, and the externally applied inputs at that point. If $q_1(k), q_2(k), \ldots$ represents the distribution along spatial dimensions $x_1, x_2, \ldots x_r$, it can be represented as $\underline{q}(k, x_1, x_2, \ldots x_r)$ or more compactly as $\underline{q}(k, \underline{x})$. If the distribution in some region $\check{X}_i \leq x_i \leq \hat{X}_i$, $i = 1, 2, \ldots r$ can be specified by the values at discrete points $\ell_i = \check{X}_i, \check{X}_i + \Delta_i, \check{X}_i + 2\Delta_i, \ldots$; $i = 1, 2, \ldots r$, then $\underline{q}(k, \underline{x})$ can be written as $\underline{q}(k, \underline{\ell})$. The dependence of $\underline{q}(k, \underline{\ell})$ on its neighbors is specified as

$$\frac{\Delta}{\Delta}\underline{q}(k, \underline{\ell}) = \underline{G}\Big(k, \underline{\ell}, \underline{v}(k, \underline{\ell}); \underline{q}(k, \underline{\ell}); \underline{q}(k, \ell_i + \delta_j^i \Delta_j, \; i = 1, 2, \ldots r),$$

$$\underline{q}(k, \ell_i - \delta_j^i \Delta_j, \; i = 1, 2, \ldots r), \; j = 1, 2, \ldots r\Big) \tag{C.7}$$

Thus the system is described in terms of the state distribution $\underline{q}(k, \underline{\ell})$ by a partial difference equation in $r + 1$ independent variables. If the state is considered as a continuous distribution over $\underline{x}$, one takes the limit as $\Delta_i \to 0$, $i = 1, 2, \ldots r$. If the changes in state occur continuously in time, then one lets $\Delta \to 0$ as well and the state transitions are described by a partial differential equation

$$\frac{\partial}{\partial \tau}\underline{q}(\tau, \underline{x}) = \underline{G}\left(\tau, \underline{x}, \underline{v}(\tau, \underline{x}); \underline{q}(\tau, \underline{x}); \frac{\partial \underline{q}(\tau, \underline{x})}{\partial x_i}, \frac{\partial^2 \underline{q}(\tau, \underline{x})}{\partial x_i^2} \; i = 1, 2, \ldots r\right) \tag{C.8}$$

Cases in which some of the time-space dimensions are to be treated as continuous and others as taking on discrete sets of values are also encountered, as for example in the description of a distillation column. Then the state transitions are described by a difference-differential equation.

In the preceding discussion, system description in terms of difference equations was given pre-eminence, and the description in terms of differential equations was introduced only as a limiting case. One can argue that on a sufficiently fine scale all processes are a sequence of discrete events and that a difference equation is therefore more basic. Furthermore, a difference equation is an explicit statement of the cause and effect relation which exists in a physical system, the basic criterion of physical realizability. The solution of a difference equation describing a physical system can always be computed. Solutions of differential equations are seldom known; to obtain a numerical solution one usually needs to find a difference equation whose solution approximates that of the differential equation. On the other hand, from a difference equation description of a physical system, one can always obtain the differential equation by taking the limit as $\Delta \to 0$. There are, of course, difference equations, arising in other connections, whose solution is never a good approximation to the limiting differential equation no matter how small Δ is made. For example, the solution of

$$\frac{\triangleright}{\Delta} y(k) = y^2(k) \qquad y(0) = y_o < 0 \quad k = 0, \Delta, 2\Delta, \ldots \tag{C.9}$$

remains finite for all $\Delta > 0$, for every $k < \infty$, whereas the solution of

$$\frac{d}{d\tau} y(\tau) = y^2(\tau) \qquad y(0) = y_o < 0 \qquad \tau \geq 0 \tag{C.10}$$

becomes infinite at $\tau = 1/y_o$.

For ordinary differential equations there exists a criterion for determining when they can be approximated by the difference equation obtained by replacing $d/d\tau$ by $\triangleright/\Delta$. No similar test is known in the case of partial differential equations. It can be shown (Appendix D) that if $\underline{q}_A(\tau)$ is a solution of the differential equation

$$\frac{d}{d\tau} \underline{q}(\tau) = \underline{G}(\tau, \underline{q}(\tau)) \tag{C.11}$$

with the property that in some compact region $\mathcal{R}$ of the $(\tau, \underline{q}(\tau))$ space the inequality

$$\| \underline{G}(\tau, \underline{q}_X(\tau)) - \underline{G}(\tau, \underline{q}_Y(\tau)) \| < \| \underline{q}_X(\tau) - \underline{q}_Y(\tau) \| L \tag{C.12}$$

holds for an $L < \infty$ (the Lipschitz condition), and if $\underline{q}_C(k)$ is the solution of the difference equation

$$\frac{\triangleright}{\Delta} \underline{q}(k) = \underline{G}(k, \underline{q}(k)) \qquad k = t, t+\Delta, t+2\Delta, \ldots \tag{C.13}$$

with $\underline{q}_C(t) = \underline{q}_A(t)$, and if

$$\underline{q}_B(\tau) = \underline{q}_C(k), \quad k \leq \tau < k+\Delta, \quad k = t, t+\Delta, t+2\Delta, \ldots \tag{C.14}$$

then for every $\epsilon > 0$ there is a $\Delta > 0$ such that

$$\| \underline{q}_A(\tau) - \underline{q}_B(\tau) \| < \epsilon \tag{C.15}$$

for all $t \leq \tau$ and τ, $\underline{q}_A(\tau)$, $\underline{q}_B(\tau)$, in $\mathcal{R}$.

A difference equation is in itself a representation of its solutions inasmuch as it defines a formula for numerically evaluating these solutions. By virtue of the above theorem, it can also serve for the calculation of an arbitrarily good approximation to the solution of a differential equation. It may not be the one used in practice, for there may be more efficient numerical methods of solution;[29, 31, 63] but it does demonstrate the feasibility of such a calculation.

As a rule, when attempting to solve a differential equation one requires, not a particular solution, but rather a more general knowledge of the properties of the solutions and how they change as system parameters are varied. For example, one may wish to know whether or not the system is stable. It is an important advantage of the state transition approach that, even when an analytic solution is unobtainable, an examination of the differential equation can still shed light on such problems.

In discussing system stability one is faced with the problem of defining precisely what is meant by a stable system, since in common usage the word "stable" invokes three different notions: that the system output is bounded, that it does not change abruptly with small changes in system parameters, and that if its state was perturbed the system would return to its equilibrium position. These three system properties are classified below under the headings of boundedness, stability or continuity, and asymptotic stability.

Let $\underline{q}(\tau, \underline{q}(t), \underline{v}(\tau))$, $t \leq \tau$ represent the output of a system described by

$$\underline{q}' = \underline{G}(\tau, \underline{q}(\tau), \underline{v}(\tau)) \tag{C.16}$$

for a specified input $\underline{v}(\tau)$, $t \leq \tau$ and starting from an initial state $\underline{q}(t)$ at time t. A system is termed bounded if there is an $\epsilon > 0$ and a $B < \infty$ such that

$$\| \underline{q}_A(t) - \underline{q}_B(t) \| < \epsilon \Longrightarrow \| \underline{q}(\tau, \underline{q}_A(t), \underline{v}(\tau)) - \underline{q}(\tau, \underline{q}_B(t), \underline{v}(\tau)) \| < B \tag{C.17}$$

for all $\tau \geq t$. If need be, one can specialize this further by defining boundedness in the large, uniform boundedness, and boundedness with respect to perturbations of $\underline{v}(\tau)$ as well as $\underline{q}(t)$. A system is termed stable if for every $\epsilon_1 > 0$ there is an $\epsilon_2 > 0$ such that

$$\| \underline{q}_A(t) - \underline{q}_B(t) \| < \epsilon_2 \Longrightarrow \| \underline{q}(\tau, \underline{q}_A(t), \underline{v}(\tau)) - \underline{q}(\tau, \underline{q}_B(t), v(\tau)) \| < \epsilon_1 \tag{C.18}$$

for all $t \leq \tau$. In standard mathematical terms a system is stable if the output for all $\tau \geq t$ is a continuous function of the initial conditions. It is a crucial point in this definition that ϵ_2 is independent of τ. A system is termed asymptotically stable if it is bounded and there is an $\epsilon_1 > 0$ such that for every $\epsilon_2 > 0$ there is a T such that

$$\| \underline{q}_A(t) - \underline{q}_B(t) \| < \epsilon_1 \Longrightarrow \| \underline{q}(\tau, \underline{q}_A(t), \underline{v}(\tau)) - \underline{q}(\tau, \underline{q}_B(t), \underline{v}(\tau)) \| < \epsilon_2 \tag{C.19}$$

for every $\tau > t+T$. A system is termed equiasymptotically stable if T is independent of $\underline{q}_A(t)$ and $\underline{q}_B(t)$ and uniformly asymptotically stable if T is also independent of t. Similar definitions for asymptotic stability in the large can be written.[35,40,41]

One may note in passing that a linear constant coefficient system is either uniformly asymptotically stable (in the large), if the poles of its transfer function are in the left half of the complex s plane, or only stable (uniformly), if it has simple poles on the jw axis, or else unbounded. The finer subdivisions show up only among non-linear and time-varying systems.[35,40]

The most basic approach to the study of system stability short of obtaining an analytic expression for the solutions is Lyapunov's direct or second method.[40] It is described below for the treatment of continuous time systems. A corresponding theory exists for the treatment of discrete time systems.[41] To test for system stability about a trajectory $\underline{q}_o(\tau, \underline{q}_o(t), \underline{v}(\tau))$, $\tau \geq t$, one introduces the change of variables $\hat{\underline{q}} = \underline{q} - \underline{q}_o$ and tests for stability in terms of $\hat{\underline{q}}$ about trajectory $\underline{0}$. To test for stability of a system

$$\underline{q}' = \underline{G}(\tau, \underline{q}) \qquad \text{(C.20)}$$

about the trajectory $\underline{0}$, Lyapunov's theorem provides the following criterion. If there exists a scalar function $V(\underline{q}, \tau)$ of class C^1, bounded from below and above by monotonic nondecreasing functions $\alpha(||\underline{q}||)$ and $\beta(||\underline{q}||)$, respectively, such that $\alpha(||\underline{0}||) = 0 = \beta(||\underline{0}||)$ and $\alpha(||\underline{q}||) \to \infty$ as $||\underline{q}|| \to \infty$ (see Figure C.1) with the property that

$$\frac{d}{d\tau} V(\underline{q}, \tau) = \frac{\partial V}{\partial \tau} + \nabla_{\underline{q}} V \underline{q}'] = \frac{\partial V}{\partial \tau}\ \nabla_{\underline{q}} V \underline{G}(\tau, \underline{q})] \qquad \text{(C.21)}$$

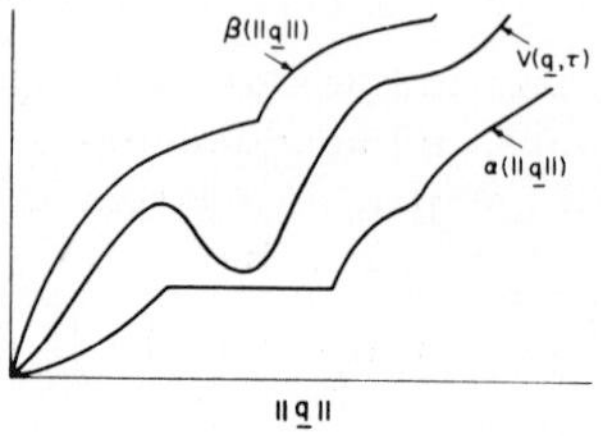

Fig. C.1. Lyapunov function

is less than zero except at $\underline{q} = \underline{0}$ when it equals 0, then the system is uniformly asymptotically stable.[40] To the various weakened forms of stability there correspond weakened Lyapunov conditions. Thus for asymptotic stability the requirement that $\alpha(||\underline{q}||) \to \infty$ as $||\underline{q}|| \to \infty$ is unnecessary and for just stability $\frac{d}{d\tau} V(\underline{q}, \tau)$ must be equal to or less than zero, $V(\underline{0}, \tau)$ must be 0 but $V(\underline{q}, \tau)$ need not have an upper bound $\beta(||\underline{q}||)$. Lyapunov function V represents a quantity akin to the energy stored in a system. Just as a dissipative physical system is characterized by a negative net rate of change of stored energy, so a stable system is characterized by a negative rate of change of its Lyapunov function.

For example, consider the first-order system

$$q' = G(\tau, q) \qquad \text{(C.22)}$$

The function $V(q, \tau) = q^2$ is a suitable Lyapunov function, and since

$$\frac{dV}{d\tau} = 2qG(\tau, q) \qquad \text{(C.23)}$$

the system is uniformly stable about $q = 0$ everywhere in the region where

$$\operatorname{sign}(\ G(\tau, q)\ ) = -\operatorname{sign}(q) \tag{C.24}$$

and is uniformly asymptotically stable in the region where in addition $G(\tau, q) \neq 0$ unless $q = 0$. As a more complicated example,[40] consider the system

$$q_1' = q_2 - aq_1(q_1^2 + q_2^2) \qquad q_2' = -q_1 - aq_2(q_1^2 + q_2^2) \tag{C.25}$$

Choosing

$$V = q_1^2 + q_2^2 \tag{C.26}$$

one verifies that

$$\frac{d}{d\tau} V = -2a(q_1^2 + q_2^2)^2 = -2aV^2 \tag{C.27}$$

Thus the system is uniformly asymptotically stable in the large if $a > 0$ and at least uniformly stable in the large if $a = 0$.

The Lyapunov test is only a sufficient condition for stability. Although it has been shown that for every stable or asymptotically stable system there exists a corresponding Lyapunov function,[57] it may not be known what this function is. If one Lyapunov function fails to demonstrate stability, there may yet be another which will prove the system stable. Although considerable experience has been acquired in constructing useful Lyapunov functions, no general procedure exists, which limits the applicability of this method.

To discuss the influence of initial conditions on system output in more quantitative terms, consider again the description in terms of the difference equation

$$\frac{\triangleright}{\Delta}\underline{q}(k) = \underline{G}(\ k, \underline{q}(k), \underline{v}(k)\ ) \tag{C.28}$$

For a given $\underline{v}(k)$, $k = t, t+\Delta, t+2\Delta, \ldots T$ and an initial state $\underline{q}(t)$ one can compute the number $\underline{q}(T)$ numerically. If one wants to determine $\underline{q}(T)$ as a function of $\underline{q}(t)$, one needs to evaluate the entire function $\underline{S}(\ T, \underline{q}(t)\ )$:

$$\underline{q}(T) = \underline{S}(\ T, \underline{q}(t)\ ) \tag{C.29}$$

If $\underline{q}_o(T)$ is the solution resulting from an initial condition $\underline{q}_o(t)$, then one can express $\underline{q}(T)$ in the neighborhood of $\underline{q}_o(T)$ by L_o terms of a finite Taylor series with a remainder

$$\underline{q}(T) = S^{\underline{i}_o}(T, \underline{q}(t)) = S^{\underline{i}_o}(T, \underline{q}_o(t)) + \sum_{\ell=1}^{L_o} \left(S^{\underline{i}_o}_{i_1, i_2, \ldots i_\ell}(T, \underline{q}_o(t)) \prod_{j=1,\ell} \frac{\Delta q^{\underline{i}_j}(t)}{\ell!} \right)$$

$$+ \left(S^{\underline{i}_o}_{i_1, i_2, \ldots i_{L_o+1}}(T, \underline{\eta}(t)) \prod_{j=1, L_o+1} \frac{\Delta q^{\underline{i}_j}(t)}{(L_o+1)!} \right) \quad \text{(C.30)}$$

where $\Delta q^{\underline{i}}(t) = q^{\underline{i}}(t) - q_o^{\underline{i}}(t)$ and $\underline{\eta}(t)$ is some vector such that each of its components has some value between those of the corresponding components of $\underline{q}(t)$ and $\underline{q}_o(t)$. In the above the shortened notation for the derivatives (explained in Appendix A) is used, so that

$$S^{\underline{i}_o}_{i_1, i_2, \ldots L_o}(T, \underline{q}_o(t)) = \frac{\partial^\ell S_{i_o}(T, \underline{q}_o(t))}{\partial q_{i_\ell} \partial q_{i_{\ell-1}} \ldots \partial q_{i_1}} \qquad i_o = 1, 2, \ldots n$$

(C.31)

and $\left(\right)$ indicates summation over all possible values of the indices repeated within the brackets both as subscripts and as superscripts. $S^{\underline{i}_o}(T, \underline{q}_o(t))$, the term for $\ell = 0$ in the general expansion, is the vector $\underline{q}(T)$. The coefficient of the term for $\ell = 1$ is the Jacobian matrix

$$S^{\underline{i}_o}_{i_1}(T, \underline{q}(t)) = [J_{\underline{q}(t)}(\underline{S}(T, \underline{q}(t)))] \quad \text{(C.32)}$$

The remaining coefficients are higher-order derivatives, each of which is an array of $n^{\ell+1}$ terms. It will be shown that each of these arrays can be evaluated as a solution of a difference equation.

The original difference equation defines the term for $\ell = 0$. The solution of

$$\frac{\triangleright}{\Delta}\underline{q}(k) = \underline{G}(k, \underline{q}(k)) \qquad k = t, t+\Delta, t+2\Delta, \ldots \quad \text{(C.33)}$$

can be written as

$$S^{\underline{i}_o}(T, \underline{q}(t)) = \underline{q}(T) = \underline{q}(t) + \sum_{k=0}^{T-\Delta} \Delta G^{\underline{i}_o}(k, \underline{q}(k), \underline{v}(k))$$

(C.34)

Taking the differential of both sides with respect to the initial conditions, one obtains

$$\left(S^{i_o}_{i_1}(T, \underline{q}(t))\, dq^{i_1}(t) \right) = \left(\delta^{i_o}_{i_1} dq^{i_1}(t) + \sum_{k=0}^{T-\Delta} \Delta G^{i_o}_{j_1}(k, \underline{q}(k), \underline{v}(k))\, q^{j_1}_{i_1}(k)\, dq^{i_1}(t) \right) \tag{C.35}$$

Since the above has to hold for all differentials, it has to hold for the coefficients of each differential. On equating coefficients and noticing that

$$S^{i}_{j}(k, \underline{q}(t)) = q^{i}_{j}(k) \tag{C.36}$$

one obtains

$$S^{i_o}_{i_1}(T, \underline{q}(t)) = \delta^{i_o}_{i_1} + \sum_{k=0}^{T-\Delta} \Delta G^{i_o}_{j_1}(k, \underline{q}(k), \underline{v}(k))\, S^{j_1}_{i_1}(k, \underline{q}(t)) \tag{C.37}$$

By analogy with Equation C.34, one sees that this represents the solution of a difference equation in $S^{i_o}_{i_1}$:

$$\frac{\triangleright}{\Delta} S^{i_o}_{i_1}(k, \underline{q}(t)) = \left(G^{i_o}_{j_1}(k, \underline{q}(k), \underline{v}(k))\, S^{j_1}_{i_1}(k, \underline{q}(t)) \right) \qquad k = t, t+\Delta, t+2\Delta, \ldots \tag{C.38}$$

with initial conditions $S^{i_o}_{i_1}(t, \underline{q}(t)) = \delta^{i_o}_{i_1}$. In matrix notation, Equation C.38 is

$$\frac{\triangleright}{\Delta} [J_{q(t)}(\underline{S}(k, \underline{q}(t)))] = [J_{q(k)}(\underline{G}(k, \underline{q}(k), \underline{v}(k)))] [J_{q(t)}(\underline{S}(k, \underline{q}(t)))] \tag{C.39}$$

To obtain the coefficients of the next term in the Taylor series expansion one takes the differential of both sides of Equation C.37 to obtain

$$\left(S^{i_o}_{i_1, i_2}(T, \underline{q}(t))\, dq^{i_2}(t) \right) = \left(\sum_{k=0}^{T-\Delta} G^{i_o}_{j_1, j_2}(k, \underline{q}(k), \underline{v}(k))\, q^{j_2}_{i_2}(k)\, dq^{i_2}(t) \right.$$

$$\left. + G^{i_o}_{j_1}(k, \underline{q}(k), \underline{v}(k))\, q^{j_1}_{i_1, i_2}(k)\, dq^{i_2}(t) \right) \tag{C.40}$$

which leads to a difference equation

$$\frac{\triangleright}{\Delta} S^{\underline{i}_o}_{i_1, i_2}(k, \underline{q}(t)) = \left(G^{\underline{i}_o}_{j_1}(k, \underline{q}(k), \underline{v}(k)) S^{\underline{j}_1}_{i_1, i_2}(k, \underline{q}(t)) + G^{\underline{i}_o}_{j_1, j_2}(k, \underline{q}(k), \underline{v}(k)) S^{\underline{j}_1}_{i_1}(k, \underline{q}(t)) S^{\underline{j}_2}_{i_2}(k, \underline{q}(t)) \right) \tag{C.41}$$

In this way by taking the differentials of both sides of the difference equations, one obtains in succession equations for all of the coefficients of the Taylor series expansion. If the equation describing system behavior is a differential equation, then one takes the limit as $\Delta \to 0$ and obtains differential equations defining the successive coefficients. The equations for the first few coefficients are listed in Table C.1. It should be noted that each equation represents n^ℓ separate n-dimensional vector equations to determine $n \times n^\ell$ components of an array $S^{\underline{i}_o}_{i_1, \ldots i_\ell}$. Each equation is a linear differential equation (except for $\ell = 0$) with coefficients dependent only on $G^{\underline{i}_o}_{j_1}$, that is, on the Jacobian $[J(\underline{G}(\tau, \underline{q}(\tau)))]$ and forcing terms dependent on $S^{\underline{i}_o}_{i_1, \ldots i_{\ell-1}}$ and the various partial derivatives of $\underline{G}$ of orders up to and including the ℓth. The terms in the Taylor series expansion can be evaluated only as far as differentiability of $\underline{G}(\tau, \underline{q}(\tau), \underline{v}(\tau))$ with respect to $\underline{q}(\tau)$ allows. If $\underline{G}$ is analytic with respect to $\underline{q}(\tau)$ about a trajectory $\underline{q}_o(\tau)$, then so is $S^{\underline{i}_o}(\tau, \underline{q}(t))$; thus the system is termed analytic.

The Taylor series expansion indicates that $S^{\underline{i}_o}(\tau, \underline{q}(t))$, $\tau \geq t$ is a continuous function of $\underline{q}(t)$ in some neighborhood of $\underline{q}_o(t)$, that is, the system is stable, if $S^{\underline{i}_o}_{i_1}(\tau, \underline{q}_o(t))$ and $S^{\underline{i}_o}_{i_1, i_2}(\tau, \underline{\eta}(t))$, $t \leq \tau$ are bounded for all $\underline{\eta}(t)$ in that neighborhood. $S^{\underline{i}_o}_{i_1}(\tau, \underline{q}_o(t))$ and $S^{\underline{i}_o}_{i_1, i_2}(\tau, \underline{\eta}(t))$, $t \leq \tau$ in turn are bounded if either the linear equation

$$\frac{d}{d\tau} y^{\underline{i}_o}(\tau) = \left(G^{\underline{i}_o}_{j_1}(\tau, \underline{\eta}(\tau), \underline{v}(\tau)) y^{\underline{j}_1}(\tau) \right) \tag{C.42}$$

is asymptotically stable and $G^{\underline{i}_o}_{j_1, j_2}(\tau, \underline{\eta}(\tau), \underline{v}(\tau))$, $t \leq \tau$ is bounded for all $\underline{\eta}(t)$ in the neighborhood and the resultant $\underline{\eta}(\tau)$, $t \leq \tau$, or if it is only stable but in addition $G^{\underline{i}_o}_{j_1, j_2}(\tau, \underline{\eta}(\tau), \underline{v}(\tau))$ approaches 0 as $\tau \to \infty$ at least exponentially.* To guarantee asymptotic stability of the system the condition

$$\lim_{\tau\to\infty} S^{i_o}_{i_1}(\tau, \underline{\eta}(t)) = 0 \qquad \lim_{\tau\to\infty} S^{i_o}_{i_1, i_2}(\tau, \underline{\eta}(t)) = 0 \quad (C.43)$$

must be satisfied for all $\underline{\eta}(t)$ in a neighborhood of $S^{i_o}(\tau, \underline{q}_o(t))$. This is guaranteed if Equation C.42 is asymptotically stable and $G^{i_o}_{j_1, j_2}(\tau, \underline{\eta}(\tau), \underline{v}(\tau))$, $t \leq \tau$ is bounded. Thus system stability is seen to depend on the stability of the linearized equation, that is, on the properties of the Jacobian matrix as evaluated about a specified trajectory. (Tests for stability of linear systems will be presented subsequently.) It should be emphasized that this expansion gives information about local stability, that is, about stability in a sufficiently small neighborhood about the specified trajectory.

If a system is linear, the Taylor series breaks off after $\ell = 1$. In the equation for $\ell = 2$, for example, $S^{i_o}_{i_1, i_2}$ is zero initially, and since $G^{i_o}_{j_1, j_2}$ vanishes then so does the entire right-hand side; therefore $S^{i_o}_{i_1, i_2}$ remains zero. In such a case S^{i_o} and $S^{i_o}_{i_1}$ completely specify the linear affine transformation from $(t, \underline{q})$ into the $(T, \underline{q})$ space, and the first two entries from Table C.1 provide a means of calculating it.

In the linear case it is customary to choose $\underline{q}_o(\tau) = \underline{0}$ and call $S^{i_o}_{i_1}(t, \underline{q}_o(t))$ a matrix $[\phi(\tau, t)]$. Instead of writing $\underline{G}(\tau, \underline{q}(\tau), \underline{v}(\tau))$, one expands it as

$$G(\tau, \underline{q}(\tau), \underline{v}(\tau))] = [J_q(\underline{G}(\tau, \underline{q}(\tau), v(\tau)))] + \hat{v}(\tau)] \quad (C.44)$$

and in the abbreviated form as

$$G(\tau, \underline{q}(\tau), v(\tau))] = [G(\tau)]\, q(\tau)] + \hat{v}(\tau)] \quad (C.45)$$

In general $[G(\tau)]$ is a function of time and depends on the input $\underline{v}(\tau)$. But $\hat{v}(\tau)]$ is only that portion of $\underline{v}(\tau)$ which does not enter multiplicatively with the state variables. With these abbreviations the first two entries of Table C.1 become

$$q'(\tau)] = [G(\tau)]\, q(\tau)] + \hat{v}(\tau)] \quad (C.46)$$

$$\frac{\partial}{\partial \tau}[\phi(\tau, t)] = [G(\tau)][\phi(\tau, t)] \qquad [\phi(t, t)] = [I] \quad (C.47)$$

In many control problems $[\phi(\tau, t)]$ is independent of $\underline{v}$. Knowing $[\phi(\tau, t)]$, it is then of interest to find $q(\tau)]$ for all possible $\hat{v}(\tau)]$.

---

* These are not the weakest possible conditions.

Table C.1

Coefficient	Initial Conditions	Defining Equation
0	$S^{\underline{i}_o}(t, \underline{q}(t)) = \underline{q}(t)$	$\frac{d}{d\tau} S^{\underline{i}_o}(\tau, \underline{q}(t)) = G^{\underline{i}_o}(\tau, \underline{q}(\tau), \underline{v}(\tau))$
$\ell = 1$	$S_{i_1}^{\underline{i}_o}(t, \underline{q}(t)) = \delta_{i_1}^{\underline{i}_o}$	$\frac{dS_{i_1}^{\underline{i}_o}}{d\tau} = \left(G_{j_1}^{\underline{i}_o} S_{i_1}^{\underline{j}_1}\right)$
$\ell = 2$	$S_{i_1, i_2}^{\underline{i}_o}(t, \underline{q}(t)) = 0$	$\frac{dS_{i_1, i_2}^{\underline{i}_o}}{d\tau} = \left(G_{j_1}^{\underline{i}_o} S_{i_1, i_2}^{\underline{j}_1} + G_{j_1, j_2}^{\underline{i}_o} S_{i_1}^{\underline{j}_1} S_{i_2}^{\underline{j}_2}\right)$
$\ell = 3$	$S_{i_1, i_2, i_3}^{\underline{i}_o}(t, \underline{q}(t)) = 0$	$\frac{dS_{i_1, i_2, i_3}^{\underline{i}_o}}{d\tau} = \left(G_{j_1}^{\underline{i}_o} S_{i_1, i_2, i_3}^{\underline{j}_1} + G_{j_1, j_3}^{\underline{i}_o} S_{i_3}^{\underline{j}_3} S_{i_1, i_2}^{\underline{j}_1} + G_{j_1, j_2}^{\underline{i}_o} S_{i_1}^{\underline{j}_1} S_{i_2, i_3}^{\underline{j}_2} + G_{j_1, j_2}^{\underline{i}_o} S_{i_1, i_3}^{\underline{j}_1} S_{i_2}^{\underline{j}_2} + G_{j_1, j_2, j_3}^{\underline{i}_o} S_{i_1}^{\underline{j}_1} S_{i_2}^{\underline{j}_2} S_{i_3}^{\underline{j}_3}\right)$

Table C.1 (continued)

Coefficient	Initial Conditions	Defining Equation
$\ell = 4$	$S^{\underline{i}_o}_{i_1,i_2,i_3,i_4}(t, \underline{q}(t)) = 0$	$\frac{dS^{\underline{i}_o}_{i_1,i_2,i_3,i_4}}{d\tau} = \Big(G^{\underline{i}_o}_{j_1} S^{\underline{j}_1}_{i_1,i_2,i_3,i_4} + G^{\underline{i}_o}_{j_1,j_3} S^{\underline{j}_3}_{i_3} S^{\underline{j}_1}_{i_1,i_2,i_4} + G^{\underline{i}_o}_{j_1,j_2} S^{\underline{j}_1}_{i_1} S^{\underline{j}_2}_{i_2,i_3,i_4}$ $+ G^{\underline{i}_o}_{j_1,j_2} S^{\underline{j}_1}_{i_1,i_3,i_4} S^{\underline{j}_2}_{i_2} + G^{\underline{i}_o}_{j_1,j_4} S^{\underline{j}_4}_{i_4} S^{\underline{j}_1}_{i_1,i_2,i_3}$ $+ G^{\underline{i}_o}_{j_1,j_2} S^{\underline{j}_1}_{i_1,i_4} S^{\underline{j}_2}_{i_2,i_3} + G^{\underline{i}_o}_{j_1,j_2} S^{\underline{j}_1}_{i_1,i_3} S^{\underline{j}_2}_{i_2,i_4} + G^{\underline{i}_o}_{j_1,j_3} S^{\underline{j}_1}_{i_1,i_4} S^{\underline{j}_3}_{i_3,i_4}$ $+ G^{\underline{i}_o}_{j_1,j_3,j_4} S^{\underline{j}_4}_{i_4} S^{\underline{j}_3}_{i_3} S^{\underline{j}_1}_{i_1,i_2} + G^{\underline{i}_o}_{j_1,j_2,j_4} S^{\underline{j}_4}_{i_4} S^{\underline{j}_1}_{i_1} S^{\underline{j}_2}_{i_2,i_3}$ $+ G^{\underline{i}_o}_{j_1,j_2,j_4} S^{\underline{j}_4}_{i_4} S^{\underline{j}_1}_{i_1,i_3} S^{\underline{j}_2}_{i_2} + G^{\underline{i}_o}_{j_1,j_2,j_3} S^{\underline{j}_1}_{i_1} S^{\underline{j}_2}_{i_2} S^{\underline{j}_3}_{i_3,i_4}$ $+ G^{\underline{i}_o}_{j_1,j_2,j_3} S^{\underline{j}_1}_{i_1} S^{\underline{j}_2}_{i_2,i_4} S^{\underline{j}_3}_{i_3} + G^{\underline{i}_o}_{j_1,j_2,j_3} S^{\underline{j}_1}_{i_1,i_4} S^{\underline{j}_2}_{i_2} S^{\underline{j}_3}_{i_3}$ $+ G^{\underline{i}_o}_{j_1,j_2,j_3,j_4} S^{\underline{j}_1}_{i_1} S^{\underline{j}_2}_{i_2} S^{\underline{j}_3}_{i_3} S^{\underline{j}_4}_{i_4} \Big)$

If $[\phi(\tau, t)]$ is known, the solution of Equation C.46 for the case when $\hat{v}(\tau)] = 0]$ can be written down as

$$q(\tau)] = [\phi(\tau, t)]q(t)]$$

This is but a consequence of the definition of $S_{\underset{1}{i}}^{\underset{-}{i}o}$. Similarly, if $\hat{v}(\tau)] = \rho(\tau, \ell)1]$ and $q(t)] = 0]$ where

$$\rho(\tau, \ell) = \lim_{\Delta \to 0} \begin{cases} = 1 & \text{if } \ell \leq \tau < \ell + \Delta, \quad \ell = t, t+\Delta, t+2\Delta, \ldots \\ = 0 & \text{otherwise} \end{cases} \quad \text{(C.48)}$$

the solution can be written as

$$q(\tau)] = \lim_{\Delta \to 0} \begin{cases} = \Delta[\phi(\tau, \ell + \Delta)]1] & \tau \geq \ell \\ = 0] & \tau < \ell \end{cases} \quad \text{(C.49)}$$

To write down the entire solution, one notes that $\hat{v}(\tau)], t \leq \tau$ can be represented as

$$\hat{v}(\tau)] = \lim_{\Delta \to 0} \sum_{\ell = t}^{\tau - \Delta} \rho(\tau, \ell)\hat{v}(\ell)] \quad \ell = t, t+\Delta, t+2\Delta, \ldots, \tau \quad \text{(C.50)}$$

In view of the fact that in a linear system superposition holds, one obtains the solution of Equation C.46 due to $\hat{v}(\tau)], t \leq \tau$ as

$$q(\tau)] = \lim_{\Delta \to 0} \sum_{\ell = t}^{\tau - \Delta} \Delta[\phi(\tau, \ell + \Delta)]\hat{v}(\ell)] \quad \text{(C.51)}$$

which is

$$q(\tau)] = \int_t^\tau [\phi(\tau, \xi)]\hat{v}(\xi)]\,d\xi \quad \text{(C.52)}$$

Relying once more on superposition to incorporate the solution due to $q(t)]$, one can write the general solution of Equation C.46 as

$$q(\tau)] = [\phi(\tau, t)]q(t)] + \int_t^\tau [\phi(\tau, \xi)]\hat{v}(\xi)]\,d\xi \quad \text{(C.53)}$$

For a difference equation, the general solution* is

$$q(k)] = [\phi(k, t)]q(t)] + \sum_{\ell = t}^{k - \Delta} \Delta[\phi(k, \ell + \Delta)]\,\hat{v}(\ell)] \quad \text{(C.54)}$$

One can compute $[\phi(\tau, t)]$ by numerically solving Equation C.47. There are also cases in which an analytic solution is possible, of

* It is to be noted that $[\phi(k, \ell)] = [I]$ when $k = \ell$ and $[\phi(k, \ell)] = [0]$ for $k < \ell$.

which the most important one is that for $[G(\tau)] = [G]$, a constant matrix. Equation C.45, defining $S_{i_1}^{i_0}$, can be rewritten in matrix form as

$$[\phi(T,t)] = [I] + \sum_{\ell=t}^{T-\Delta} \Delta[G(\ell)][\phi(\ell,t)]$$

$$= \Big([I] + \Delta[G(t)]\Big) + \Delta[G(t+\Delta)]\Big([I] + \Delta[G(t)]\Big)$$
$$+ \Delta[G(t+2\Delta)]\Big([I] + \Delta[G(t)] + \Delta[G(t+\Delta)]\Big([I] + \Delta[G(t)]\Big)\Big) + \ldots$$
$$= \prod_{i=0}^{N-1}\Big([I] + \Delta[G(t+i\Delta)]\Big) \qquad (C.55)$$

where $N = \frac{T-t}{\Delta}$. If $[G(\tau)]$ is a constant matrix $[G]$, then

$$[\phi(T,t)] = \Big([I] + \Delta[G]\Big)^N = \sum_{i=0}^{N} \frac{N!\ \Delta^i}{i!\,(N-i)!}[G]^i \qquad (C.56)$$

and for a discrete time process this is the answer. In a continuous time problem, in the limit as $\Delta\to 0$ while $N\Delta \to T-t$ one obtains

$$\lim_{\substack{\Delta\to 0\\ N\to\infty\\ N\Delta\to T-t}} [\phi(T,t)] = \lim_{\substack{\Delta\to 0\\ N\to\infty\\ N\Delta\to T-t}} \sum_{i=0}^{N} \frac{N!\,(\Delta)^i}{(N-i)!\,i!}[G]^i$$

$$= \lim_{\substack{\Delta\to 0\\ N\Delta\to T-t\\ N\to\infty}} \sum_{i=0}^{N} \frac{N^N\Delta^i}{i!\,(N)^{N-i}}[G]^i \qquad (C.57)$$

so that in the limit

$$[\phi(\tau,t)] = \sum_{i=0}^{\infty} \frac{([G]\,(\tau-t))^i}{i!} = \exp([G](\tau-t)) \qquad (C.58)$$

Equation C.58 is simplified if $[G]$ happens to be diagonal, for then each term in the series and therefore $[\phi(\tau,t)]$ is also diagonal:

$$(\phi(\tau,t))_{i,j} = \delta_i^j \exp((G)_{i,i}(\tau-t)) \qquad (C.59)$$

If the matrix $[G(\tau)]$ in Equation C.46 is a matrix of constant coefficients $[G]$, Equation C.46 can be reduced to a form in which

[G] is diagonal by premultiplying both sides by a nonsingular matrix [U] such that $[U][G][U]^{-1}$ is diagonal. Thus

$$[U]q'] = [U][G][U]^{-1}[U]q] + [U]\hat{v}] \tag{C.60}$$

With the change of variables

$$\check{q}] = [U]q] \qquad \check{v}] = [U]\hat{v}] \qquad [D_G] = [U][G][U]^{-1} \tag{C.61}$$

where the D signifies that $[D_G]$ is diagonal, Equation C.46 becomes

$$\frac{d}{d\tau}\check{q}] = [D_G]\check{q}] + \check{v}] \tag{C.62}$$

and its solution is

$$\check{q}_i(\tau) = q_i(t)\exp\left((D_G)_{i,i}(\tau - t)\right) + \int_t^\tau \exp\left((D_G)_{i,i}(\tau-\xi)\right)\check{v}_i(\xi)d\xi$$

$$i = 1, 2, \ldots n \tag{C.63}$$

In the above, [U] is the matrix of characteristic vectors of [G], that is, the modal matrix. $(D_G)_{i,i}$, $(i = 1, 2, \ldots n)$ are the characteristic numbers of [G], that is, the roots of the nth degree polynomial in s :

$$|[G] - s[I]| = 0 \tag{C.64}$$

It is seen from Equation C.63 that the system described by Equation C.46 is asymptotically stable (uniformly in the large) if all the characteristic roots have negative real parts, and only stable if some of the roots, which are not repeated, have zero real parts. Thus stability of a linear time-invariant system depends on the values of the real parts of the roots of its characteristic polynomial. Fortunately, there are tests available, for example the Routh criterion, which allows one to determine whether the characteristic roots have negative, zero, or positive real parts without solving for their actual values. In contrast to Lyapunov's direct method, this test provides the necessary and sufficient stability conditions.

No similar test for stability exists if $[G(\tau)]$ is time-varying. It is known, however, that if $[G(\tau)]$ and $\hat{v}(\tau)]$ are bounded on some finite time interval, the solution $q(\tau)]$ will remain bounded on that interval. In contrast to nonlinear problems, there cannot be a finite escape time. Thus if $[G(\tau)]$ is bounded and

$$\lim_{\tau\to\infty}[G(\tau)] = [G] \tag{C.65}$$

exists, the system is stable if and only if [G] yields a stable system.

In the description of a plant, one of the properties of interest is controllability.[36] If one lets $\underline{m}$ be those of its inputs $\underline{v}$ which can be manipulated by the controller and $\underline{u}$ those that cannot, then the describing equation becomes

$$\underline{q}'(\tau) = \underline{G}(\ \tau, \underline{q}(\tau), \underline{m}(\tau), \underline{u}(\tau)\ ) \tag{C.66}$$

The plant is termed completely controllable at time t if there exists a bounded function $\underline{m}(\tau), \tau \geq t$ such that it changes $\underline{q}$ from $\underline{q}_o$ to $\underline{q}_1(t+T)$ for some $T<\infty$ and for any $\underline{q}_o$ and $\underline{q}_1$ in a region $\mathcal{R}$. (A local controllability can also be defined.) In physical terms this means that the control effort must be capable of influencing each and every component of the state vector independently. Whereas in the vast majority of cases this condition is satisfied, or else the control problem is incorrectly formulated, in developing an abstract treatment of control theory it is necessary to know which of the possible functions $\underline{G}$ represent a physically reasonable control situation, i.e., which ones represent a controllable plant.

A linear discrete time plant can be described by

$$\frac{\triangleright}{\Delta} q(k)] = [G_q(k)]q(k)] + [G_m(k)]m(k)] \qquad k = t, t+\Delta, t+2\Delta, \ldots \tag{C.67}$$

where $\underline{u}(k), t \leq k$ is incorporated in the time-dependent variation of $[G_q(k)]$ and $[G_m(k)]$. If $m]$ is to be capable of producing every change in state in a finite number of steps, that is, for the plant to be controllable, it is necessary (and sufficient) that for some $T<\infty$ the output vectors

$$\Delta[\phi(T, t+\Delta)]\,[G_m(t)]m(t)], \quad \Delta[\phi(T, t+2\Delta)]\,[G_m(t+\Delta)]m(t+\Delta)], \ \ldots$$

$$\Delta[\phi(T, T)][G_m(T-\Delta)]m(T-\Delta)] \tag{C.68}$$

span* the space of $\underline{q}$, where

$$[\phi(T, T)] = [I] \qquad [\phi(T, \ell)] = \prod_{i=0}^{N-1}\Big([I] + \Delta[G_q(\ell+i\Delta)]\Big) \ N = \frac{T-t}{\Delta} \tag{C.69}$$

This in turn is so if the matrix $[M]$

$$[M] = \sum_{\ell=t}^{T-\Delta} \Big([\phi(T, \ell+\Delta)][G_m(\ell)]\Big)^T \Big([\phi(T, \ell+\Delta)][G_m(\ell)]\Big) \tag{C.70}$$

is nonsingular (positive definite). In the continuous time case $[M]$

---

* A set of vectors span a space if every vector in the space can be represented as a linear combination of the members of the set.

is defined as

$$[M] = \int_t^T \left([\phi(T,\tau)]\,[G_m(\tau)]\right)^T \left([\phi(T,\tau)]\,[G_m(\tau)]\right) d\tau \tag{C.71}$$

Since $[\phi(t,\tau)]$ is nonsingular and since

$$[\phi(t,\tau)] = [\phi(t,T)]\,[\phi(T,\tau)] \tag{C.72}$$

$[M]$ is nonsingular if and only if $[M^*]$ is nonsingular where

$$[M^*] = [\phi(t,T)]\,[M]^T\,[\phi(t,T)]^T = \int_t^T [\phi(t,\tau)][G_m(\tau)][G_m(\tau)]^T\,[\phi(t,\tau)]^T\,d\tau \tag{C.73}$$

The significance of $[M^*]$ is that the control input generated according to the law

$$m(\tau)] = -\,[G_m(\tau)]^T\,[\phi(t,\tau)]\,[M^*]^{-1} q(\tau)]$$

transfers the system state from $\underline{q}(t)$ at time t to $\underline{0}$ at time T.[39]

The above is a review of the basic notions of the state transitions approach used throughout this work for the analysis of dynamic systems.

Appendix D

DIFFERENCE APPROXIMATIONS TO DIFFERENTIAL EQUATIONS

Theorem. Let $\underline{y}_C(\tau, \underline{y}_o(t)),\ t \leq \tau$ be the solution of the differential equation

$$\underline{y}'(\tau) = \underline{G}(\tau, \underline{y}(\tau)) \tag{D.1}$$

and $\underline{y}_D(k, y_o(t)),\ k = t,\ t+\Delta, t+2\Delta, \ldots$ be the solution of the difference equation

$$\frac{\triangleright}{\Delta}\underline{y}(k) = \underline{G}(k, \underline{y}(k)) \tag{D.2}$$

It is required to show that if $\underline{G}(\tau, \underline{y}_A(\tau)),\ t \leq \tau$ is of class D^0 for $\underline{y}_A(\tau)$ in a compact region $\mathcal{R}$ of the $(\tau, \underline{y})$ space and

$$|| \underline{G}(\tau, \underline{y}_A(\tau)) - \underline{G}(\tau, \underline{y}_B(\tau)) || < || \underline{y}_A(\tau) - \underline{y}_B(\tau) || L \tag{D.3}$$

for some $L < \infty$ and all $\underline{y}_A(\tau)$ and $\underline{y}_B(\tau)$ in $\mathcal{R}$, then

$$\lim_{\substack{\Delta \to 0 \\ k \to \tau}} || \underline{y}_D(k, \underline{y}_o(t)) - \underline{y}_C(\tau, \underline{y}_o(t)) || = 0 \tag{D.4}$$

for all $\underline{y}_D$, $\underline{y}_C$ and τ in $\mathcal{R}$

Proof. Let $\epsilon(k) = ||\underline{y}_C(k) - \underline{y}_D(k)||$ and $\delta(k)$ be a function such that

$$\delta(k) = \begin{cases} 1 \text{ if } \underline{G}(\xi, \underline{y}(\xi)) \text{ is not continuous for } k \leq \xi < k+\Delta \\ 0 \text{ if } \underline{G}(\xi, \underline{y}(\xi)) \text{ is continuous for } k \leq \xi < k+\Delta \end{cases}$$

Let B be a bound on $||\underline{G}||$ and let B_D be a bound on its derivative with respect to time, when it exists.

The difference equation can be written as

$$\underline{y}_D(k+\Delta) = \underline{y}_D(k) + \Delta\underline{G}(k, \underline{y}_D(k)) \tag{D.5}$$

and the differential equation as

$$\underline{y}_C(k+\Delta) = \underline{y}_C(k) + \Delta\underline{G}(k+\xi_i, \hat{\underline{y}}_C(k)) + \Delta\delta(k)\underline{f}(k, \underline{y}_C(k)) \tag{D.6}$$

where ξ_i are some values such that $0 \leq \xi_i < \Delta$ (with $\xi_i = 0$ if $\delta(i) = 1$), $\hat{\underline{y}}_C(k)$ is some value of $\underline{y}_C(\tau)$ for $k \leq \tau < k+\Delta$, and $\underline{f}(k, \underline{y}_C(k))$ is the correction term when $\underline{G}$ is not continuous. By subtracting the two equations, one obtains a difference equation for a bound on $\epsilon(t+i\Delta)$:

$$0 \leq \epsilon(k+\Delta) \leq \epsilon(k) + \Delta \| \underline{G}(k+\xi_i, \hat{\underline{y}}_C(k)) - \underline{G}(k, \underline{y}_D(k)) \| + \Delta\delta(k) \| \underline{f}(k, \underline{y}_C(k)) \|$$

$$\begin{aligned} 0 \leq \epsilon(k+\Delta) \leq \epsilon(k) + \Delta \Big\{ & \| \underline{G}(k+\xi_i, \hat{\underline{y}}_C(k)) - \underline{G}(k+\xi_i, \underline{y}_C(k)) \| \\ & + \| \underline{G}(k+\xi_i, \underline{y}_C(k)) - \underline{G}(k, \underline{y}_C(k)) \| \\ & + \| \underline{G}(k, \underline{y}_C(k)) - \underline{G}(k, \underline{y}_D(k)) \| \\ & + \delta(k) \| \underline{f}(k, \underline{y}_C(k)) \| \Big\} \end{aligned} \tag{D.7}$$

$$0 \leq \epsilon(k+\Delta) \leq \epsilon(k) + \Delta \Big\{ B\Delta L + \Delta B_D + L\epsilon(k) + \delta(k)B \Big\} \tag{D.8}$$

Thus

$$\epsilon(k+\Delta) \leq (1+\Delta L)\epsilon(k) + \Delta^2 B_o + \Delta\delta(k)B \tag{D.9}$$

where $B_o = BL + B_D$. On solving this equation, one obtains the bound

$$\epsilon(k) \leq \epsilon_B(k) = \sum_{j=0}^{i-1} (1+\Delta L)^{i-1-j} (\Delta^2 B + \Delta B \delta(j)) \tag{D.10}$$

where $i = (k-t)/\Delta$. In the limit as $\Delta \to 0$

$$\lim_{\substack{\Delta\to 0 \\ k\to\tau}} \epsilon_B(k) = \epsilon_B(\tau) = \lim_{\substack{\Delta\to 0 \\ \Delta i\to\tau \\ i\to\infty}} \sum_{j=0}^{i-1} (1+\Delta L)^{i-1-j} (\Delta^2 B + \Delta B\delta(j))$$

$$= \Delta \int_t^\tau e^{L(\tau-\xi)} B \, d\xi + \epsilon_o \tag{D.11}$$

Since $\underline{G}$ is discontinuous only at a finite number of points, that is, on a set of zero area, $\epsilon_o = 0$. Therefore,

$$\epsilon(\tau) = \lim_{\substack{\Delta\to 0 \\ k\to\tau}} \epsilon(k) = 0 \tag{D.12}$$

for all $\tau < \infty$.

The above proof is of note because it does not require $\underline{G}(\tau, \underline{y}(\tau))$ to be continuous with respect to its explicit time variations. The requirement that it be Lipschitz of course implies that $\underline{G}$ is continuous with respect to $\underline{y}(\tau)$ in $\mathcal{R}$.

Appendix E

DESCRIPTION OF CONTROL PROBLEMS USED AS DEMONSTRATIVE EXAMPLES

The methods of dynamic optimization and controller synthesis developed in this work are demonstrated on several examples representative of various control situations. These problems are specified in this appendix.

E. 1. Positional Servomechanism

The most familiar control problem is the positional servomechanism, illustrated in Figure E. 1.

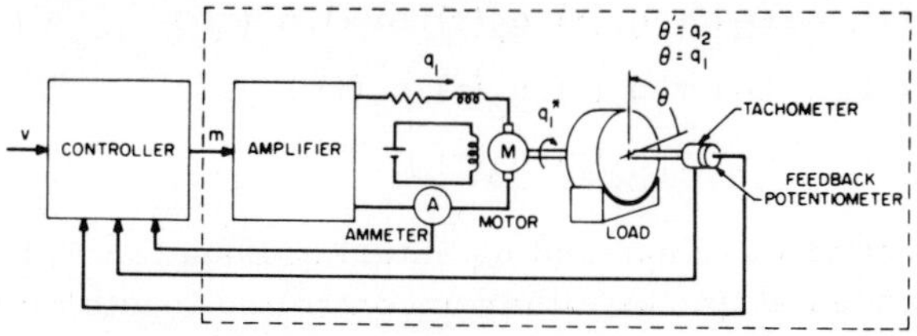

Fig. E. 1. Pictorial representation of a positional servomechanism

The following is a qualitative description of how the mechanism works, illustrating the cause and effect relationship between the various quantities and how this is used to determine the form of the model.

The control input m instantly results in an amplifier output voltage q_0; q_0 causes q_1', the rate of change of armature current q_1 of a D. C. shunt motor. The motor torque q_1^* depends on q_1 and is transmitted instantaneously to the load, causing q_2', a rate of change of its velocity q_2. Next q_3', the rate of change of position q_3, is a result of the velocity q_2. The flow of current in turn causes a voltage drop which affects the rate of change of current.

The motor velocity generates a potential influencing q_1' as well as a friction torque acting on q_2'. This set of causal relationships is represented in Figure E. 2.

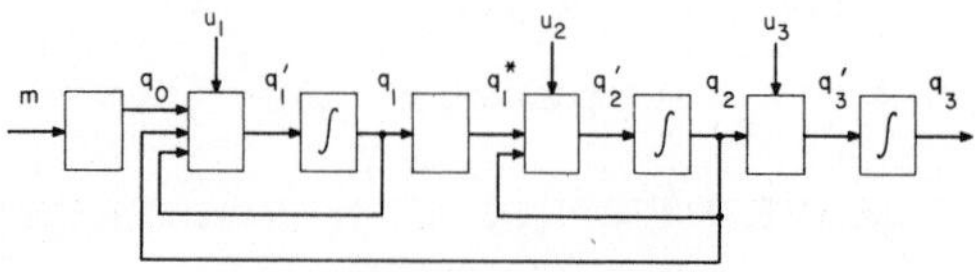

Fig. E. 2. Cause and effect relations in a positional servomechanism

Since there are three integrations in the system, the output $q_3(\tau), t \leq \tau$ depends not only on $m(\tau), t \leq \tau$ but also on three quantities, for example $q_1(t)$, $q_2(t)$, and $q_3(t)$ (but $q_1(t)+k$, $q_2(t)+q_3(t)$, and $q_1(t)+q_3(t)$ would do just as well). These quantities can be considered as the state variables of the system. A differential equation describing this set of causal relationships is

$$
\begin{aligned}
q_1'(\tau) &= G_1(\tau, q_1(\tau), q_2(\tau), m(\tau), u_1(\tau))\\
q_2'(\tau) &= G_2(\tau, q_1(\tau), q_2(\tau), u_2(\tau))\\
q_3'(\tau) &= G_3(\tau, q_2(\tau), u_3(\tau))
\end{aligned}
\qquad \text{(E. 1)}
$$

The functions u_1, u_2, and u_3 entering Equation E. 1 represent the disturbances acting as either uncontrolled inputs or changes in system parameters. If all the elements in Figure E. 1 are considered as representing additions and multiplications by constants, as is done in elementary analysis of such mechanisms, then G_1, G_2, and G_3 are linear functions, and Equation E. 1 can be written in vector notation as

$$q'(\tau)] = [G_q]q(\tau)] + [G_m]m(\tau)] \qquad \text{(E. 2)}$$

where $\underline{q}(\tau) = q_1(\tau), q_2(\tau), q_3(\tau)$ and $\underline{m}(\tau) = m(\tau)$, while

$$[G_q] = \begin{bmatrix} k_{11} & k_{12} & 0 \\ k_{21} & k_{22} & 0 \\ 0 & k_{32} & 0 \end{bmatrix} \qquad [G_m] = \begin{bmatrix} k_{10} \\ 0 \\ 0 \end{bmatrix} \qquad \text{(E. 3)}$$

where

k_{10} = (Amplifier gain)/(Armature circuit inductance)

k_{11} = -1/(Time constant of the armature circuit)

k_{12} = -(Motor torque constant)/(Armature circuit inductance)

k_{21} = (Motor torque constant)/(Load and motor polar moment of inertia)

k_{22} = -(Load and motor viscous damping)/(Load and motor polar moment of inertia)

k_{32} = 1

in an appropriate set of units. This differential equation description is equivalent to the transfer function shown in Figure E. 3.

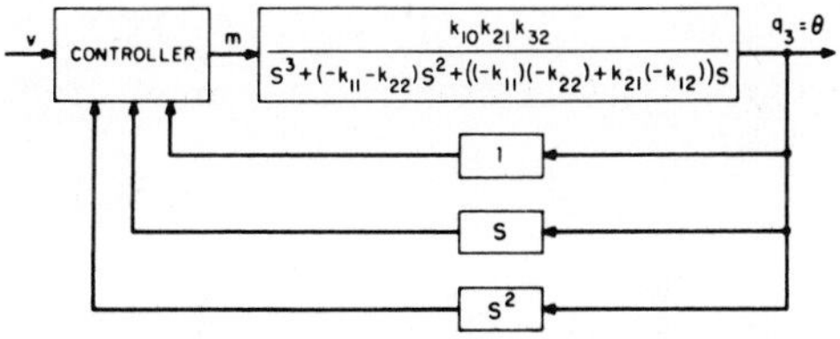

Fig. E. 3. Transfer function of a positional servomechanism

The system is to act as a positional servomechanism, that is, its output is to follow the desired output $i(\tau), t \leq \tau$ as closely as possible. The input v(t) may equal i(t) or may correspond to i(t) corrupted by noise. In any case, the controller must use present and past inputs $v(\tau), \tau \leq t$ to estimate the present and future desired output $i(\tau), \tau \geq t$. The current system state $q_3(t)$ can be measured by a potentiometer or a synchro on the output shaft, $q_2(t)$ by a tachometer, and $q_1(t)$ by an ammeter in the armature circuit. Even though direct measurement of state variables is feasible, the values are still subject to uncertainty and error so that the controller actually uses what is its estimate of system state.

A suitable measure of how well the system output is following the desired output is the expected value of the square of the error as integrated over all future time. The over-all performance criterion represents a balance between the cost of tolerating the error and the cost of doing something about it. With the application of control effort, there is associated a cost which may be just the cost of energy used or the cost of wearing out the gears and may be very small indeed; but in addition there is a limitation on the allowable amplitude of the control signal or other variables. It may be argued that these limitations are not sharp constraints, but rather represent a cost or a penalty associated with overdriving the system in an attempt to exceed the normal operating range. From this viewpoint the amplitude limitation represents a cost function in the performance criterion such that it contributes little if m is within the normal operating range, but a great deal when it tends to exceed this range. If m_ℓ and m_u are the bounds, then a suitable function might be

$$\mathcal{P}(m) = (\hat{m})^r \tag{E.4}$$

for some large even value of r, where

$$\hat{m} = \frac{m - \frac{1}{2}(m_u + m_\ell)}{m_u - m_\ell} \tag{E.5}$$

or

$$\mathcal{P}(m) = \begin{cases} k_2\hat{m}^2 + (k_2 - k_1)(1 + 2\hat{m}) & \hat{m} < -1 \\ k_1\hat{m}^2 & |\hat{m}| \leq 1 \\ k_2\hat{m}^2 + (k_2 - k_1)(1 - 2\hat{m}) & \hat{m} > 1 \end{cases} \tag{E.6}$$

for $k_2 >> k_1$. Thus a suitable performance criterion might be

$$\mathcal{P} = \underset{\substack{u(\tau),\, i(\tau) \\ \tau \geq t}}{E} \left\{ -\int_t^{\infty} \Big((q_3(\tau) - i(\tau))^2 + \mathcal{P}(m(\tau)) \Big) d\tau \right\} \tag{E.7}$$

This problem is solved to illustrate the effect of constraints, that is, nonquadratic cost functions of control effort, on linear system design. The examples illustrate cases in which $i(\tau)$, $\tau \geq t$ is deterministic and cases when it is a stochastic time function.

E.2. An Interception Problem

To illustrate the techniques in a situation in which the end point is variable, an interception problem, illustrated in Figure E.4, is considered. A rocket is to meet with and match the speed of an orbiting vehicle moving on a known path $i(\tau)$ and consume the least fuel in the process. It is required to find the control law specifying thrust $m(\tau)$ as a function of the state of the rocket and time, and therefore as a function of rocket state and the position of the orbiting vehicle. For simplicity, motion in a single dimension only will be considered.

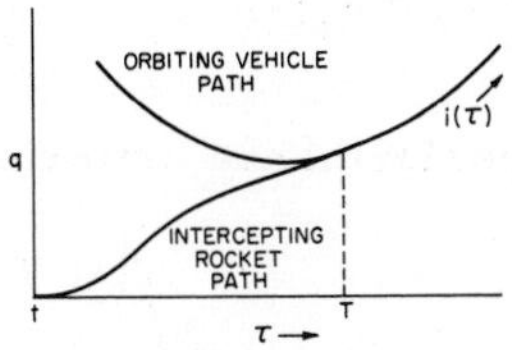

Fig. E.4. An interception problem

Rocket thrust $m(\tau)$ can be positive or negative and is related to fuel flow $f(\tau)$ by

$$m(\tau) = A(\, f(\tau)\,) \qquad\qquad f(\tau) = A^{-1}(\, m(\tau)\,) \qquad\qquad (E.8)$$

Since $f(\tau)$ is positive, A is of necessity a double-valued function of f, for example $m(\tau) = \pm\sqrt{f(\tau)}$, $f(\tau) = m^2(\tau)$. A differential equation describing rocket motion in one dimension is

$$m(\tau) = M(\tau)q''(\tau) + q'(\tau)M'(\tau) + D(\, q'(\tau), q(\tau)\,) + G(\, q(\tau)\,) \qquad (E.9)$$

where $q(\tau)$ is rocket position, $G(\, q(\tau)\,)$ is the force of gravity, for example $G_o M(\tau)/(q(\tau) + h_o)^2$, and $D(\, q'(\tau), q(\tau)\,)$ is an expression for aerodynamic drag, for example $D_o(\, q'(\tau)\,)^7/(q(\tau) + h_o)^8$. The rocket mass is $M(\tau)$, which is assumed to be an independent function of time to account, in part, for its decrease as fuel is consumed. (A more correct assumption would be to express it as

$$M(\tau) = M_o - \int_t^{\tau} f(\xi)\,d\xi$$

but this makes the problem more difficult than is desirable for the purpose of illustrating the method.)

Thus the state transition equations are

$$q_1'(\tau) = \frac{1}{M(\tau)}\Big(M'(\tau)q_1(\tau) + D(\, q_1(\tau), q_2(\tau)\,) + G(\, q_2(\tau)\,) + m(\tau)\Big) \tag{E.10}$$

$$q_2'(\tau) = q_1(\tau)$$

and the performance criterion is

$$\mathcal{P} = -\int_t^{T|\underline{g}(\,T, q(T)\,) = 0} A^{-1}(\, m(T)\,)d\tau \tag{E.11}$$

where

$$\underline{g}(\,T, \underline{q}(T)\,) = q_1(T) - i'(T),\ q_2(T) - i(T) \tag{E.12}$$

E. 3. An Inventory Problem

The following is an illustration of a discrete time problem. The demand for a given item over a time interval from t to T is known to be a function $f(\tau), t \leq \tau \leq T$. Assuming that the stock is depleted at time t and that it can be replenished at t and N - 1 other times, it is required to determine the replenishment policy so as to minimize the cost of keeping the inventory, but always be able to supply the demand. The cost is assumed to be proportional to the time integral of stock on hand, and it is assumed that stock can be replenished instantaneously, that is, without any time lag between the decision to increase stock and the time when the replenishment arrives. The replenishing is to be done at most N times.

Let $t = \tau_0, \tau_1, \tau_2, \ldots \tau_{N-1}, \tau_N = T$ be the replenisnment times and $F(\tau)$ be the cumulative demand, that is,

$$F(\tau) = \int_t^\tau f(\xi)d\xi \tag{E.13}$$

Inasmuch as f is nonnegative, F will be monotonic nondecreasing. Since replenishment is instantaneous, one orders only when stock is depleted so that the cumulative order curve $F^*(\tau)$ is

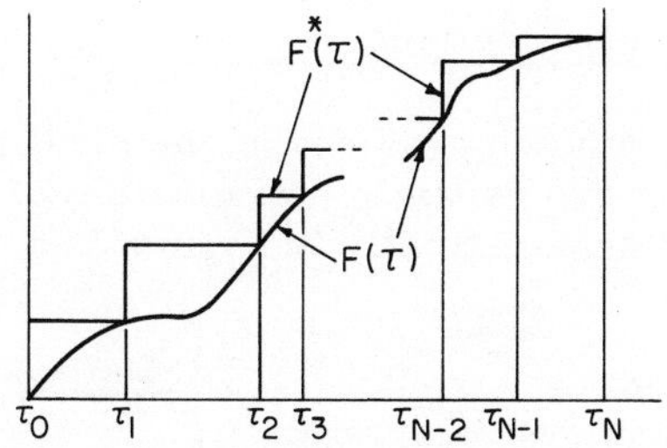

Fig. E.5. Cumulative order and demand curves

$$F^*(\tau) = F(\tau_\ell), \tau_{\ell-1} \leq \tau < \tau_\ell \tag{E.14}$$

as shown in Figure E.5, and the cost is seen to be proportional to

$$-\mathcal{P} = \sum_{\ell=1}^{N} F(\tau_\ell)(\tau_\ell - \tau_{\ell-1}) - \int_t^T F(\tau)d\tau \tag{E.15}$$

Thus finding the replenishment policy can be reduced to finding the ordering times $\tau_0, \tau_1, \ldots \tau_{N-1}$.

Let $q(\tau)$ be a function such that

$$q(t+\ell\Delta) = \tau_\ell \qquad \ell = 0, 1, 2, \ldots N \tag{E.16}$$

where $\Delta = (T-t)/N$. Equation E.15 becomes

$$\mathcal{P} = \int_t^T F(\tau)d\tau - \sum_{\ell=1}^{N} F(\, q(t+\ell\Delta)\,) \triangleright q(t+\ell\Delta) \tag{E.17}$$

This is now a matter of finding the function $q(k)$, $k = t, t+\Delta, t+2\Delta, \ldots$ to optimize the performance criterion of Equation E.17. This is the class of problems treated in this work. It will be solved first assuming $f(\tau), t \leq \tau \leq T$ to be deterministic and then considering stochastic variations in the demand curve.

E. 4. A Stirred-Tank Chemical Reactor

A relatively common problem in chemical process control is the stabilization and dynamic optimization of a stirred-tank reactor, depicted schematically in Figure E. 6.

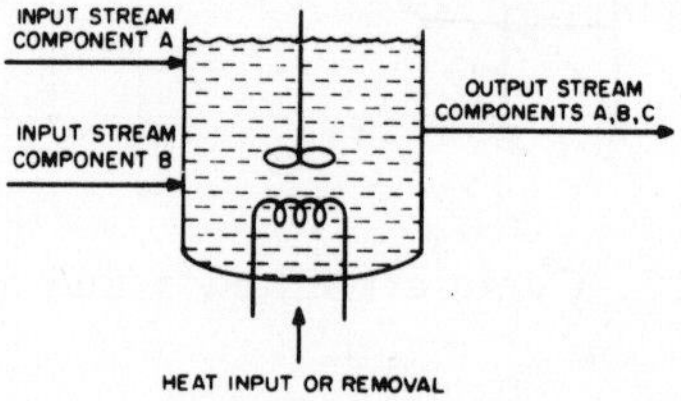

Fig. E. 6. A stirred-tank chemical reactor

In the reactor, two reactions take place: A → B at a rate r_1, and B → C at a rate r_2. The reactions are assumed to be molecular rearrangements so that there is no change in the molecular weight of the components. Specific heats and densities are assumed to be the same for A, B, and C.

The rate expressions are

$$r_1 = y_A \exp\left(\alpha_A - \frac{\beta_A}{T_o}\right)$$

$$r_2 = y_B \exp\left(\alpha_B - \frac{\beta_B}{T_o}\right) \tag{E. 18}$$

where T_o is the temperature in the reactor, while y_A and y_B are mole or weight fractions of components A and B. Reaction A → B is assumed exothermic, and B → C endothermic, the heats of reaction being H_A and H_B, respectively (H_A is positive, H_B is negative). The flow rates of A and B are f_A and f_B, respectively, whereas T_A and T_B are their temperatures. The rate of heat input (if positive) or heat removal (if negative) from the reactor is f_H Temperature, flow rates, and heats of reaction have all been normalized and made dimensionless. In these terms the heat and material balances are

$$
\begin{aligned}
T'_o &= H_A y_A \exp\left(\alpha_A \frac{\beta_A}{T_o}\right) + H_B y_B \exp\left(\alpha_\beta - \frac{\beta_B}{T_o}\right) \\
&\quad + f_A(T_A - T_o) + f_B(T_A - T_o) + f_H \\
y'_A &= f_A - (f_A + f_B)y_A - y_A \exp\left(\alpha_A - \frac{\beta_A}{T_o}\right) \\
y'_A &= f_B - (f_A + f_B)y_B + y_A \exp\left(\alpha_A - \frac{\beta_A}{T_o}\right) - y_B \exp\left(\alpha_B - \frac{\beta_B}{T_o}\right) \\
y'_C &= \quad - (f_A + f_B)y_C \qquad\qquad + y_B \exp\left(\alpha_B - \frac{\beta_B}{T_o}\right)
\end{aligned}
\tag{E.19}
$$

Of course $y_A + y_B + y_C = 1$.

In this problem, f_A, f_B, T_A, and T_B are assumed to be the uncontrolled but completely deterministic disturbances, and f_H is the control input. In this situation, the reactor is required to process all that it receives from other sections of the plant so that these inputs are uncontrolled, but the controlling intelligence knows what goes on in other sections of the plant and so can predict what these inputs will be for some time in the future.

The performance criterion representing the actual rate of return from this portion of the plant is of the form

$$
\begin{aligned}
\mathcal{P} = \lim_{T \to \infty} \frac{1}{T-t} \int_t^T \Big\{ & (P^o_B y_B + P^o_C y_C)(f_A + f_B) - P^i_B f_B \\
& - P^i_A f_A - \wp(f_H) \Big\} d\tau
\end{aligned}
\tag{E.20}
$$

where P^o_B and P^o_C represent the prices of B and C at the reactor outlet while P^i_A and P^i_B the prices of A and B at the reactor inlet. The control input cost function representing the heating or refrigerating cost and a limitation on the possible range of f_H is represented by $\wp(f_H)$.

Defining

$$q_1 = T_o \qquad q_2 = y_C$$

$$q_3 = y_A \qquad y_B = 1 - q_2 - q_3$$

$$m = f_H \tag{E.21}$$

the state transition equations become

$$q_1' = H_A q_3 \exp\left(\alpha_A - \frac{\beta_A}{q_1}\right) + H_B(1 - q_2 - q_3)\exp\left(\alpha_B - \frac{\beta_B}{q_1}\right)$$

$$+ f_A(T_A - q_1) + f_B(T_B - q_1) + m$$

$$q_2' = (1 - q_2 - q_3)\exp\left(\alpha_B - \frac{\beta_B}{q_1}\right) - (f_A + f_B)q_2$$

$$q_3' = f_A - (f_A + f_B)q_3 - q_3 \exp\left(\alpha_A - \frac{\beta_A}{q_1}\right) \tag{E.22}$$

and

$$\mathcal{P} = \lim_{T\to\infty} \frac{1}{T-t}\int_t^T \left\{\left(P_B{}^o(1 - q_2 - q_3) + P_c{}^o q_2\right)(f_A + f_B) - P_A{}^i q_3 - P_B{}^i(1 - q_2 - q_3) - \rho(m)\right\} d\tau \tag{E.23}$$

The above problem is a simplification of the "Williams Reactor."[74] The normalization and dimensionalization used here is shown in Reference 30, and the numbers to be used in this example are in the range of those obtained in Reference 30.

E.5. A Fixed-Bed Chemical Reactor

A number of chemical processes are carried out in cyclically operated fixed-bed reactors such as the one depicted in Figure E.7.

In a typical situation,[43] the reactants are passed through a heated bed of catalyst and/or heat-retaining material. The raw materials react when in contact with the catalyst. The reactions are heat-dependent and endothermic so that as the reactions progress, they cool the bed and as the bed cools the rates of reactions slow down. When the temperature reaches a certain lower level, the operation is stopped, the bed is reheated, and then the process is repeated. The temperature to which the bed is reheated is generally limited by catalyst degradation and the occurrence of undesirable reactions at the higher temperatures. During the make part of the cycle the temperature in the bed can be affected only by the temperature of the incoming raw materials.

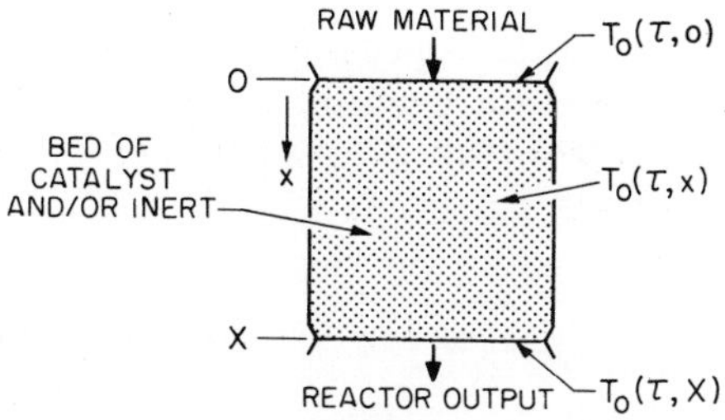

Fig. E. 7. A fixed-bed catalytic reactor

Consider a case in which a zero-order reaction takes place, that is, one with a rate dependent only on the temperature and not on reactant concentration y. Thus at any point x in the bed

$$\frac{dy}{d\tau} = \exp\left(a_o - \frac{\beta_o}{T_o(\tau, x)}\right) \tag{E. 24}$$

where $T_o(\tau, x)$ is the temperature at the point x at time τ. If one considers $T_o(\tau, x)$ as representing small variations about a mean temperature, then a good approximation of the Arhenius rate expression is

$$\frac{dy}{d\tau} = \exp(a + \beta T_o(\tau, x)) \tag{E. 25}$$

Assuming that heat transfer between the bed and the reacting fluid is so high that they are both at the same temperature and that heat transfer through the bed is predominantly by convection, the bed operation can be described by

$$\frac{\partial T_o(\tau, x)}{\partial x} + \frac{1}{V_o}\frac{\partial T_o(\tau, x)}{\partial \tau} = -\frac{h_o}{V_o}\exp\left(a + \beta T_o(\tau, x)\right) \tag{E. 26}$$

where h_o is the heat of reaction and V_o is the heat wave velocity of the bed, which depends on the ratio of heat capacities of the fluid to that of the bed as well as on fluid velocity. One should like to control the inlet temperature $T_o(\tau, 0)$ so as to optimize the performance of the bed, that is, to maximize the conversion

$$\int_0^X \exp\left(a + \beta T_o(\tau, x)\right) dx.$$

This represents the control of a distributed parameter system with state function at time t, $T_o(t, x) = q(t, x), 0 \leq x \leq X$, the control input $m(\tau) = q(\tau, 0) = T_o(\tau, x)$ and a performance criterion

$$\mathcal{P} = \int_t^T \left\{ \int_0^X \exp\left(\alpha + \beta q(\tau, x)\right) dx - \rho\left(q(\tau, 0)\right) \right\} d\tau \qquad \text{(E. 27)}$$

The above problem is a simplification of the reactor studied in References 15 and 44.

Appendix F

BAYE'S ESTIMATION FROM A MODEL FOR THE MESSAGE-GENERATING PROCESS

Consider system input v(k) given as

$$v(k) = i(k) + n(k) \qquad k = \ldots\ t-\Delta,\ t,\ t+\Delta,\ \ldots \tag{F.1}$$

where n(k) is an independent white noise with an amplitude probability density (not necessarily stationary) $p_{n_k}(\xi)$, and i(k) is a Markovian process with transition probability density $p_{i_{k+1}|i_k}(\xi_{k+1}|\xi_k)$ and total probability density $p_{i_k}(\xi)$, neither of which need to be stationary. It is required to derive a recursive expression for evaluation of the conditional probability density

$$p_{i_k|v_k, v_{k-1}, \ldots}(\eta_k|\xi_k, \xi_{k-1}, \ldots) \tag{F.2}$$

In a first-order Markovian process the knowledge of i(k) specifies the entire influence of the past history of i on i(k+Δ). If i(k) is known, the knowledge of i(k-Δ), i(k-2Δ), ... is of no extra help in predicting i(k+Δ). In mathematical terms this implies that

$$p_{i_{k+1}|i_k, i_{k-1}, \ldots}(\xi_{k+1}|\xi_k, \xi_{k-1}, \ldots) = p_{i_{k+1}|i_k}(\xi_{k+1}|\xi_k) \tag{F.3}$$

This property can also be expressed as

$$\begin{aligned} p_{i_1, i_2, \ldots i_k}(\xi_1, \xi_2, \ldots \xi_k) &= p_{i_1}(\xi_1) \prod_{\ell=1,k-1} p_{i_{\ell+1}|i_\ell}(\xi_{\ell+1}|\xi_\ell) \\ &= p_{i_k}(\xi_k) \prod_{\ell=1,k-1} p_{i_\ell|i_{\ell+1}}(\xi_\ell|\xi_{\ell+1}) \\ &= \prod_{\ell=1,k-1} p_{i_\ell, i_{\ell+1}}(\xi_\ell, \xi_{\ell+1}) \end{aligned} \tag{F.4}$$

The noise n(k) is statistically independent of i(k), and its successive samples are statistically independent of each other. Thus

$$p_{i_k, n_\ell}(\xi_k, \eta_\ell) = p_{i_k}(\xi_k)p_{n_\ell}(\eta_\ell) \quad \text{for all } \ell \text{ and } k$$

$$p_{n_k, n_\ell}(\eta_k, \eta_\ell) = p_{n_k}(\eta_k)p_{n_\ell}(\eta_\ell) \quad \text{for } \ell \neq k \tag{F.5}$$

Since i and n are additive and independent, the distribution of their sum is the convolution of their distributions, so that

$$p_{v_1, v_2, \ldots v_k}(\xi_1, \xi_2, \ldots \xi_k) = \int_{-\infty}^{\infty} p_{n_k}(\xi_k - \eta_k) \ldots \int_{-\infty}^{\infty} p_{n_2}(\xi_2 - \eta_2)$$

$$\int_{-\infty}^{\infty} p_{n_1}(\xi_1 - \eta_1) p_{i_1, i_2, \ldots i_k}(\xi_1, \xi_2, \ldots \xi_k) d\eta_1 d\eta_2 \ldots d\eta_k \tag{F.6}$$

or in another form

$$p_{v_1, v_2, \ldots v_k}(\xi_1, \xi_2, \ldots \xi_k) = \int_{-\infty}^{\infty} p_{i_k}(\eta_k) p_{n_k}(\xi_k - \eta_k)$$

$$\int_{-\infty}^{\infty} p_{i_{k-1}|i_k}(\eta_{k-1}|\eta_k) p_{n_{k-1}}(\xi_{k-1} - \eta_{k-1}) \ldots$$

$$\int_{-\infty}^{\infty} p_{i_1|i_2}(\eta_1|\eta_2) p_{n_1}(\xi_1 - \eta_1)\, d\eta_1 d\eta_2 \ldots d\eta_k \tag{F.7}$$

which reduces to

$$p_{v_1, v_2, \ldots v_k}(\xi_1, \xi_2, \ldots \xi_k) = \int_{-\infty}^{\infty} p_{i_k}(\eta_k) p_{n_k}(\xi_k - \eta_k) p(\xi_1, \xi_2, \ldots \xi_{k-1}|\eta_k) d\eta_k \tag{F.8}$$

By defining

$$W_{k-1}(\eta_k) = p(\xi_1, \xi_2, \ldots \xi_{k-1}|\eta_k) \tag{F.9}$$

one can express the joint probability of $v(\ell)$, $\ell = 1, 2, \ldots k$ as

$$p_{v_1, v_2, \ldots v_k}(\xi_1, \xi_2, \ldots \xi_k) = \int_{-\infty}^{\infty} W_{k-1}(\eta_k) p_{n_k}(\xi_k - \eta_k) p_{i_k}(\eta_k) d\eta_k \tag{F.10}$$

and obtain a recursion relationship for $W_k(\eta_k)$:

$$W_{k-1}(\eta_k) = \int_{-\infty}^{\infty} p_{i_{k-1}|i_k}(\eta_{k-1}|\eta_k) p_{n_{k-1}}(\xi_{k-1} - \eta_{k-1}) W_{k-2}(\eta_{k-1}) d\eta_{k-1} \tag{F.11}$$

Multiplying both sides of Equation F.9 by $p_{i_k}(\eta_k)$, one obtains

$$p_{v_1, v_2, \ldots v_{k-1}, i_k}(\xi_1, \xi_2, \ldots \xi_{k-1}, \eta_k) = W_{k-1}(\eta_k) p_{i_k}(\eta_k) \quad \text{(F.12)}$$

from which there immediately follows an expression for the probability density of i_k conditional on all the past measurements of v,

$$|v_i, v_2, \ldots v_{k-1}(\eta_k | \xi_1, \xi_2, \ldots \xi_{k-1}) = \frac{p_{v_1, v_2, \ldots v_{k-1}, i_k}(\xi_1, \xi_2, \ldots \xi_{k-1}, \eta_k)}{p_{v_1, v_2, \ldots v_{k-1}}(\xi_1, \xi_2, \ldots \xi_{k-1})}$$

$$= \frac{W_{k-1}(\eta_k) p_{i_k}(\eta_k)}{\int_{-\infty}^{\infty} W_{k-1}(\xi) p_{i_k}(\xi) d\xi} \quad \text{(F.13)}$$

To take into account the most recent measurement v(k), one considers

$$p_{v_{k-1}, v_{k-2}, \ldots i_k, i_k}(\xi_{k-1}, \xi_{k-2}, \ldots, \hat{\eta}, \check{\eta})$$

$$= p_{v_{k-1}, v_{k-2}, \ldots i_k | i_k}(\xi_{k-1}, \xi_{k-2}, \ldots \hat{\eta} | \check{\eta}) p_{i_k}(\check{\eta})$$

$$= W_{k-1}(\hat{\eta}) p_{i_k | i_k}(\hat{\eta} | \check{\eta}) \, p_{i_k}(\check{\eta})$$

$$= W_{k-1}(\hat{\eta}) \, \delta_0(\hat{\eta} - \check{\eta}) p_{i_k}(\check{\eta}) \quad \text{(F.14)}$$

Convolving both sides with the probability distribution of n(k), one obtains

$$p_{v_k, v_{k-1}, \ldots, i_k}(\xi_k, \xi_{k-1}, \ldots \eta_k)$$

$$= \int_{-\infty}^{\infty} p_{v_{k-1} \, v_{k-2}, \ldots i_k, i_k}(\xi_{k-1}, \xi_k \ldots \eta_k, \xi) p_{n_k}(\xi_k - \xi) d\xi$$

$$= \int_{-\infty}^{\infty} W_{k-1}(\xi) p_{n_k}(\xi_k - \xi) \delta_0(\xi - \eta_k) p_{i_k}(\eta_k) d\xi$$

$$\text{(F.15)}$$

The conditional probability density is therefore

$$p_{i_k | v_k, v_{k-1}, \ldots}(\eta_k | \xi_k, \xi_{k-1}, \ldots) = \frac{\int_{-\infty}^{\infty} W_{k-1}(\xi) p_{n_k}(\xi_k - \xi) \delta_0(\xi - \eta_k) p_{i_k}(\eta_k) d\xi}{\int_{-\infty}^{\infty}\int_{-\infty}^{\infty} W_{k-1}(\hat{\eta}) p_{i_k}(\xi_k - \hat{\eta}) \delta_0(\hat{\eta} - \check{\eta}) p_{i_k}(\check{\eta}) d\hat{\eta} d\check{\eta}}$$

(F.16)

This expression in its final form is

$$p(i(k) | v(k), v(k-\Delta), \ldots) = \frac{W_{k-1}(i(k)) p_{n_k}(v(k) - i(k)) p_{i_k}(i(k))}{\int_{-\infty}^{\infty} W_{k-1}(\xi) p_{n_k}(v(k) - \xi) p_{i_k}(\xi) d\xi}$$

(F.17)

where

$$W_{k-1}(\xi_k) = \int_{-\infty}^{\infty} W_{k-2}(\xi_{k-1}) p_{n_{k-1}}(v(k-\Delta) - \xi_{k-1}) p_{i_k | i_{k-1}}(\xi_{k-1} | \xi_k) d\xi_{k-1}$$

(F.18)

Appendix G

THE BVPS SYSTEM

G.1 (MAIN) Program

In this work a number of numerical techniques were developed for the solution of two-point boundary-value problems of the kind arising in dynamic optimization theory. These have all been programmed for use on an IBM 709 computer in such a way that they can be used to obtain the solutions to a general class of control problems with a minimum of programming. These programs are referred to collectively as the BVPS System. A simplified description of these programs follows.

The BVPS programs are written for use on an IBM 709 computer with a 32 K core memory and equipped with tapes logical 2, 4, 9, and 10 as well as CRT output. The programs are to be run by a MONITOR System or an equivalent. A majority of the variables used by more than a single subprogram are stored in COMMON storage. Table G.1 is a partial list of these variables and the role in which they are commonly employed.

The flow chart of the (MAIN) BVPS program is shown in Figure G.1. After performing preliminary program chores, subroutine PRE, DAT, and CAL are called in succession. Subroutine PRE reads an identification record from tape 4 containing a run number, a BCD identification, and an array (NSR(I), I=1, 16) The variables NSR are the steering variables for the program, specifying which subprograms are to be run and what input-output facilities will be used. The program then writes an identification on the output elements which are to be used. Data for the entire program is read in by subroutine DAT and immediately recorded on tape 2. Subprogram CAL computes combinations of parameters of frequent use in subsequent subprograms. The program then enters subroutines SOP, BPT, LNS, HCL, RLN, and RIC and performs each one if NSR(1), NSR(2), NSR(3), NSR(4), NSR(5), or NSR(6) are other than zero, respectively. After completing one or more of these subprograms or if an error exit occurs, control is transferred to FIN, which terminates the run or returns to DAT or to PRE if NSR(16) is zero, negative or positive, respectively. When the run is terminated, FIN3 writes sign-off records on the output facilities used and returns control to the MONITOR. If control is returned to DAT, the program reads data for the next run and resumes from there. If the return was to PRE, the program reads record after record from tape 4 until it meets a sign-off record whose columns

Table G.1

BVPS System Variable Assignment

Variable*	Octal Location	Commonly Assigned Function
PLUG(305)	77461	Scratch storage
K	77000	Current time increment
NT	76777	Number of time increments in solutions, plus one
NN	76776	Number of state variables
NM	76775	Number of control inputs
NA	76774	Sign of NA specifies the direction in which the solutions are propagated
NSR(16)	76760	Steering variables specifying the subprograms to be used, the form of output, and the number of sets of runs to be performed
NTT(16)	76740	Number of time increments in solutions generated by the various subprograms
ND(64)	76700	Auxiliary storage for integer constants
M(8)	76600	Initial values of $\underline{m}$
PQ(8)	76570	Initial values of $\underline{q}$
PU(8)	76560	Initial values of $\underline{\lambda}$
XN(16)	76540	Lower bound on variables manipulated by the hill-climbing programs
XM(16)	76520	Upper bound on variables manipulated by the hill-climbing programs
DA(64)	76500	Auxiliary storage for constants
C(64)	76400	Auxiliary storage for constants
DELT(16)	76160	Size of time increments in various subprograms
DELQ(16)	76140	Size of perturbations of q_i
DELU(16)	76120	Size of perturbations of λ_i
BU(32)	76100	Maximum value of q_i and λ_i expected
BL(32)	76040	Minimum value of q_i and λ_i expected
CONVA(8, 8)	76000	Matrices specifying boundary conditions or the stabilizing parameters for the solution of Euler equations to steady state
AT(64)	71500	Time scale
AF(64, 12)	71400	Array in which the solutions of Euler equations are generated
AR(64, 25)	70000	Array in which the solution of the Euler equations is stored
AA(64, 12, 12)	64700	Array in which $[\phi(\tau, t)]$ is stored

*If a variable is an array, the numbers in brackets specify its dimensions. The octal location specifies the location of its first element, that is, the highest-numbered storage cell it occupies.

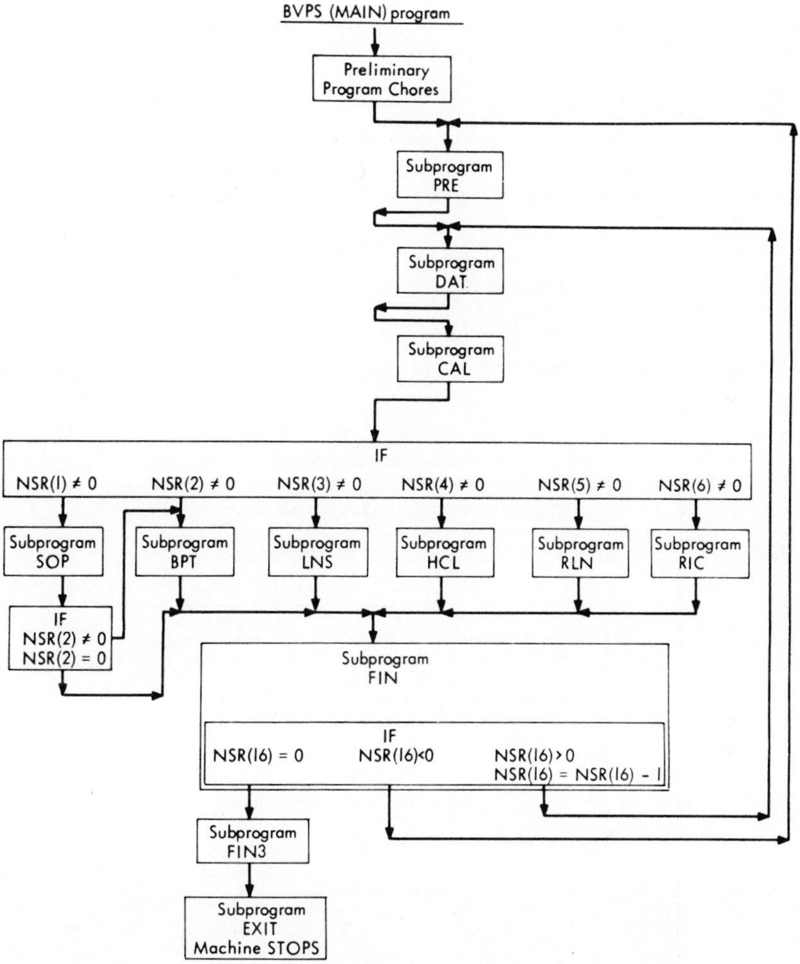

Fig. G.1. Flow chart of BVPS (MAIN) program

6 through 23, match those of the identification record, reads the next record as the new identification, and proceeds from there.

Subroutine SOP is called in to determine the steady-state system optimum, that is, the equilibrium point of the Euler equations. The computation of the control law by flooding is done by BPT. For the solution of a linear boundary problem by the matrix inversion technique, the subroutine LNS is used. The subprogram HCL yields a point solution by varying $\underline{\lambda}(t)$ to optimize an auxiliary performance criterion, while RLN does this by varying trajectories which satisfy the boundary conditions until one is found which satisfies the Euler equations. RIC obtains the coefficients of the first two terms of the Taylor series expansion of the control law by solving the Riccati equation and the linear differential equation defining the coefficients of the quadratic terms.

G.2. SOP Subprogram

Subroutine SOP computes the steady-state optimum provided NSR(1) is set to be greater than zero. If NSR(1) equals 1, the optimum is found by modifying the Euler equations so that they are stabilized and solving them to a steady-state to compute the

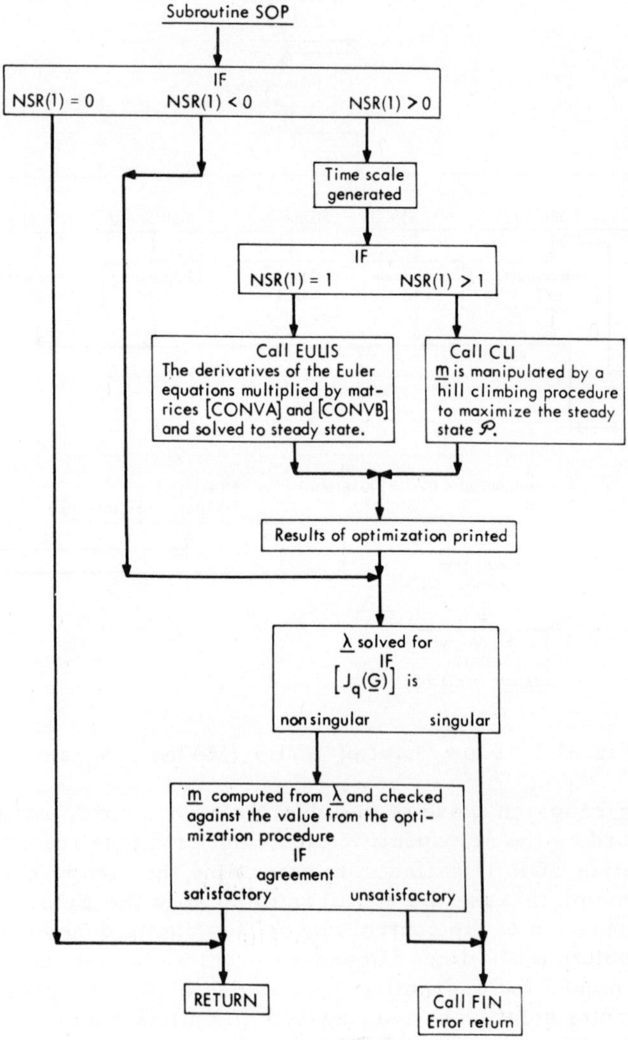

Fig. G.2. Flow chart of subroutine SOP

equilibrium point. Otherwise, a hill-climbing procedure is used to maximize the steady-state $\mathcal{P}$ with respect to $\underline{m}$. The optimum values of $\underline{\lambda}$ are found by solving the equation

$$[J_q(\underline{G})]^T \lambda\,] = \nabla_q F] \tag{G.1}$$

From this value of $\underline{\lambda}$ and $\underline{q}$, the vector $\underline{m}$ is recomputed and checked against its value as obtained in maximization of $\mathcal{P}$ If the values do not agree to within a prescribed tolerance, an error return occurs. Figure G.2 shows the subroutine's flow chart.

G.3. BPT Subprogram

Subroutine BPT generates solutions of the Euler equations backward in time. It generates an entire pattern of solutions computing trajectories and from them contours of constant $\underline{m}_i$, $i = 1, 2, \ldots n_m$, constant $\underline{\lambda}_i$, $i = 1, 2, \ldots n$, and constant $\mathcal{P}$. Its flow chart is shown in Figure G.3.

G.4. LNS Subprogram

This subroutine solves the general linear two-point boundary-value problem by the matrix inversion method, described in Section 3.1. The interval T-t is taken to be of $|NTT(3)| - 1$ steps of DELT(3) each. If NTT(3) is negative, the "shrinking time to go" problem is solved, and if it is positive, a solution to the "floating time to go" problem is obtained. If NTT(3) equals zero, the sign of the variable NA determines which of the problems is solved and a previously generated time scale is used. If the variable NSR(3) is zero, the subroutine is skipped; if NSR(3) > 0, the entire control matrix is computed; and if NSR(3) < 0, only the control vector for a single specified set of initial conditions is obtained. Whether the "floating" or the "shrinking time to go" problem is solved, the solution is computed for points from |NSR(3)| to |NTT(3)|. Figure G.4 displays the flow chart for this subprogram.

G.5. HCL Subprogram

Subroutine HCL manipulates $\underline{\lambda}(t)$ so as to optimize an auxiliary performance criterion which is a measure of how nearly the solutions of the Euler equations come to satisfying the prescribed boundary conditions. If NSR(4) = 0, the subroutine is skipped, and a time scale is generated only if NSR(3) < 0; otherwise, it is assumed to have been generated previously. The hill-climbing procedure performing the optimization is carried out for no more than |NSR(4)| steps before it is stopped and the results printed.

G.6. RLN Subprogram

Subroutine RLN solves a nonlinear boundary-value problem by

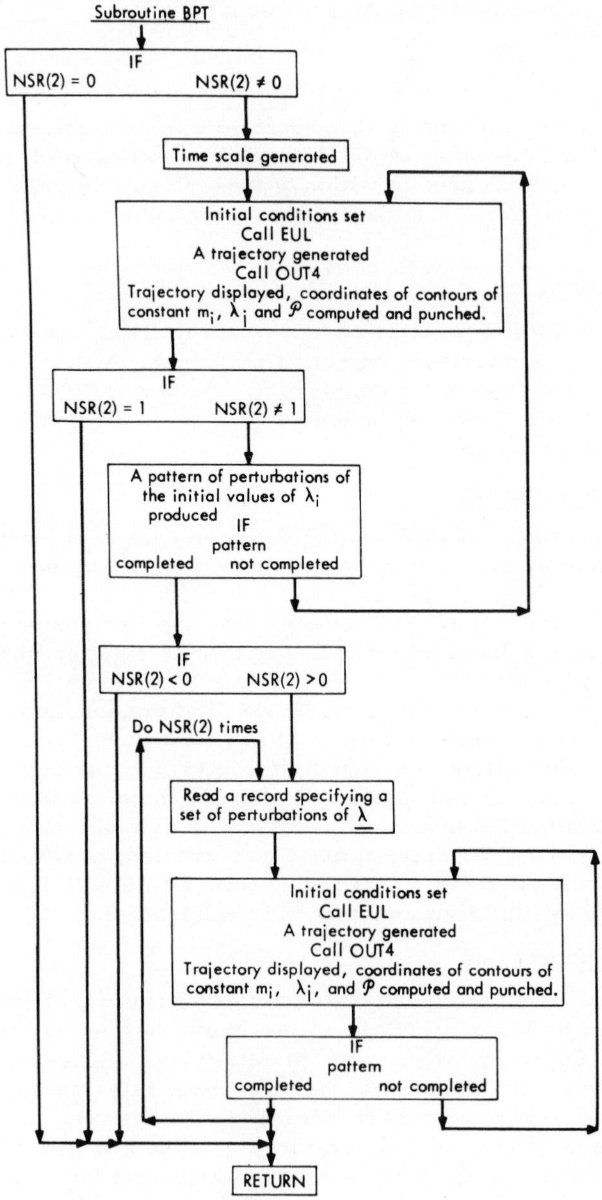

Fig. G.3. Flow chart for subroutine BPT

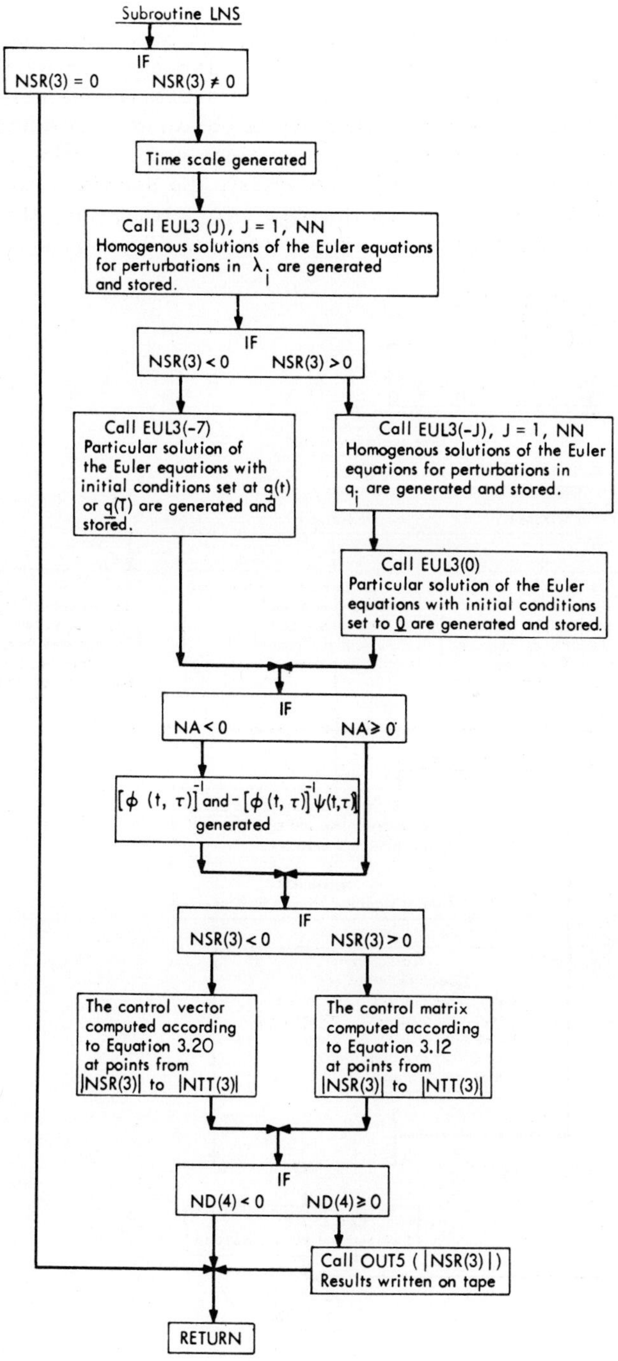

Fig. G.4. Flow chart of subroutine LNS

iterating on trajectories which satisfy the boundary conditions until they satisfy the Euler equations. The flow chart of RLN is shown in Figure G.5. If NSR(5) is zero, the subroutine is not executed. If NSR(5) > 1, the initial trajectory is obtained by reading in the derivatives of the solutions, integrating, and adjusting the trajectories to make sure that they do satisfy the boundary conditions. Setting NSR(5) < 0 signifies that the initial trajectory itself is to be read in and its derivative calculated by differencing. When

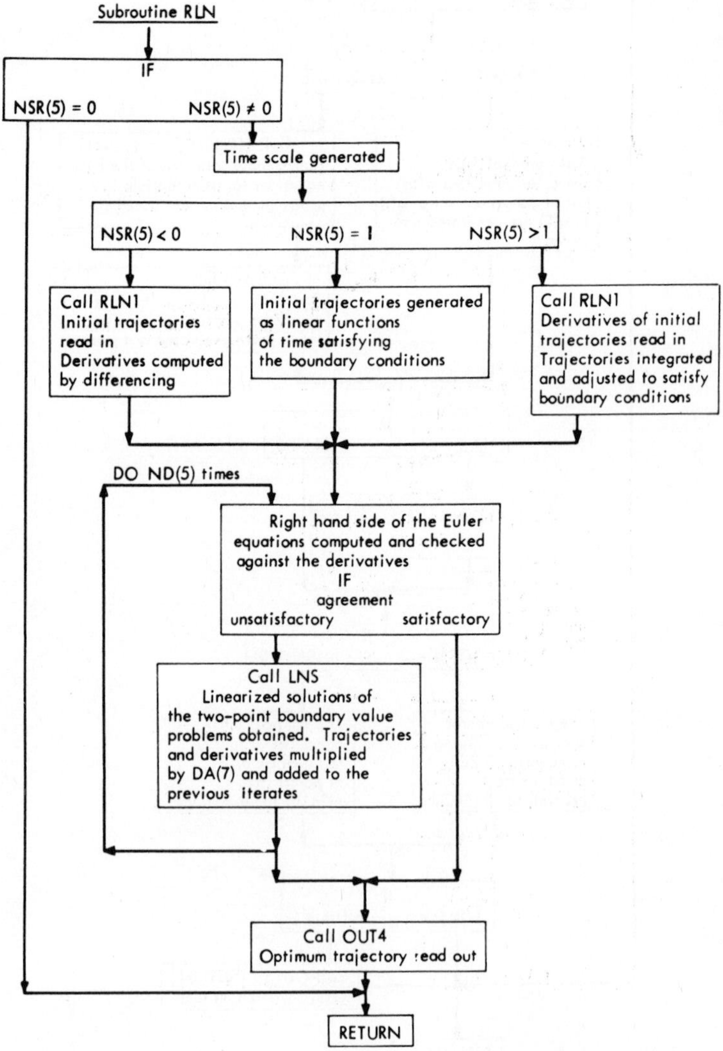

Fig. G.5. Flow chart for subroutine RLN

NSR(5) equals 1, the initial trajectory is generated internally as a linear function of time. The linearized solutions of the boundary-value problems are generated by a simplified version of LNS. At each stage the computed trajectories and their derivatives are multiplied by DA(7) and added to the trajectory of the previous iteration. This is carried out until the trajectories satisfy the Euler equations to within a prescribed tolerance, but for at most ND(5) steps.

G.7. RIC Subprogram

Subroutine RIC solves the differential equations governing the coefficients of the linearized control law and the coefficients of the quadratic terms. If NSR(6) equals 0, the subroutine is not executed; if NSR(6) < 0, only the Riccati equation for the linearized control law is solved. Otherwise, the coefficients of both the linear and the quadratic terms are evaluated. The initial conditions for the coefficients are read in from tape 4; the output is printed on tape 2.

G.8. BVPS System Listings

The listings of the programs described briefly in this appendix are available in Technical Report 112 of the Electronic Systems Laboratory of the Massachusetts Institute of Technology, entitled "Digital Computer Programs for the Solution of Two-Point Boundary-Value Problems." A more detailed description of the programs and instructions on how to use them are also presented in that report.

REFERENCES

1. Beecher, A. F., Synthesis of an Optimum Distillation Controller, Technical Report 7793-R-7, Electronic Systems Laboratory, M.I.T. (June, 1960). Also E. E. Thesis, M.I.T. Electrical Engineering Department (June, 1960).

2. Bellman, R. E., Dynamic Programming and the Computational Solution of Feedback Design Control Problems, Rand Corporation Technical Report R 115.

3. Bellman, R. E., Dynamic Programming, Princeton University Press, Princeton, N. J., 1957.

4. Bellman, R. E., I. Glicksberg, and O. A. Gross, Some Aspects of the Mathematical Theory of Control Processes, Rand Corporation Technical Report R 313 (Jan. 16, 1958).

5. Bellman, R. E., "Some New Techniques in the Dynamic Programming Solutions of Variational Problems," Quarterly of Applied Mathematics (Oct., 1958).

6. Bellman, R. E., and R. Kalaba, "Adaptive Control Processes," 1959 IRE National Convention Record, Part IV. Also IRE Transactions on Automatic Control 4, 2, 1-9 (Nov., 1959).

7. Bellman, R. E., Stability Theory of Differential Equations, McGraw-Hill, New York, 1953.

8. Bellman, R. E., Adaptive Control Processes: A Guided Tour, Princeton University Press, Princeton, N. J., 1961.

9. Bliss, G. A., Calculus of Variations, Carus Mathematical Monograph, University of Chicago Press, Chicago, 1925.

10. Bliss, G. A., Lectures on the Calculus of Variations, University of Chicago Press, Chicago, 1946.

11. Bode, H. W., Network Analysis and Feedback Amplifier Design, Van Nostrand, New York, 1945.

12. Bogner, I., and L. Kazda, "An Investigation of the Switching Criteria for Higher Order Contractor Servomechanisms," AIEE Transactions, Part II, 118 (1954).

13. Booten, R. C., Jr., "An Optimization Theory for Time Varying Linear Systems with Nonstationary Statistical Inputs," Proc. IRE, 40, 8, 977 (Aug., 1952).

14. Bose, A. G., A Theory of Nonlinear Systems, Technical Report 309, Research Laboratory of Electronics, M.I.T. (May, 1956). Also Sc.D. Thesis, M.I.T. Electrical Engineering Department (June, 1956).

15. Boyle, T. J., Optimal Operation of a Fixed Bed Cyclic Adiabatic Reactor, Technical Report 7967-R-6, Electronic Systems Laboratory, M.I.T. (Sept., 1960). Also S.M. Thesis, M.I.T. Chemical Engineering Department (June, 1960).

16. Brilliant, M. B., Theory of the Analysis of Nonlinear Systems, Technical Report 345, Research Laboratory of Electronics, M.I.T. (Mar., 1958). Also Sc.D. Thesis, M.I.T. Electrical Engineering Department (Feb., 1958).

17. Cherniak, A. E., Prediction Errors in a Class of Optimum Control Systems, S.M. Thesis, M.I.T. Electrical Engineering Department (Sept., 1958).

18. Chestnut, H., and R. W. Mayer, Servomechanisms and Regulating System Design, John Wiley & Sons, New York, 1959.

19. Coales, J., and A. Noton, "An ON-OFF Servomechanism with Predicted Changeover," IEE Proceedings, Part B (Aug., 1955).

20. Coddington, E. A., and N. Levinson, Theory of Differential Equations, McGraw-Hill, New York, 1955.

21. Davenport, W. B., Jr., and W. L. Root, An Introduction to the Theory of Random Signals and Noise, McGraw-Hill, New York, 1958.

22. Dennis, J. B., Mathematical Programming and Electrical Networks, Technology Press and John Wiley & Sons, Cambridge and New York, 1959.

23. Desoer, C. A., "The Bang-Bang Servo Problem Treated by the Variational Techniques," Information and Control, 2, 4 (Dec., 1959).

24. Flugge-Lotz, I., Discontinuous Automatic Control, Princeton University Press, Princeton, N.J., 1954.

25. Forsyth, A. R., Calculus of Variations, Cambridge University Press, Cambridge, England, 1927.

26. Fox, C., An Introduction to the Calculus of Variations, Oxford University Press, New York, 1950.

27. Freimer, M., "A Dynamic Programming Approach to Adaptive Control Processes," IRE National Convention Record, Part IV (1959).

28. George, D. A., Continuous Nonlinear Systems, Technical Report 355, Research Laboratory of Electronics, M.I.T. (1959). Also Sc.D. Thesis, M.I.T. Electrical Engineering Department (1959).

29. Gill, S., "A Process for the Step by Step Integration of Differential Equations in an Automatic Digital Computing Machine," Cambridge Philosophical Society Proceedings, 96 (1951).

30. Gould, L. A., and W. Kipiniak, "Control of a Stirred-Tank Chemical Reactor," AIEE Transactions, Part I (Communications and Electronics), 734-746 (Jan., 1961).

31. Hildebrand, F. B., Introduction to Numerical Analysis, McGraw-Hill, New York, 1956.

32. Ho, Y. C., Study of Optimal Control of Dynamic Systems, Sc.D. Thesis, Harvard University Electrical Engineering Department (Feb., 1961).

33. Howard, R. A., Dynamic Programming and Markov Processes, Technology Press and John Wiley & Sons, Cambridge and New York, 1960.

34. Kaiser, J. F., Constraints and Performance Indices in the Analytical Design of Linear Controls, Technical Report 7849-R-6 or 7967-R-1, Servomechanisms Laboratory, M.I.T. (Feb., 1959).

35. Kalman, R. E., "Physical and Mathematical Mechanisms of Instability in Nonlinear Automatic Control Systems," ASME Transactions (Apr., 1957).

36. Kalman, R. E., "General Synthesis Procedure for Computer Control of Single and Multiloop Linear Systems (An Optimal Sampled-Data System)," Proceedings of the Joint Computers in Control Systems Conference, Atlantic City, N.J. (1957).

37. Kalman, R. E., and R. W. Koepcke, "Optimal Synthesis of Linear Sampling Control Systems Using Generalized Performance Indices," ASME Paper 58-IRD-6.

38. Kalman, R. E., "A New Approach to Linear Filtering and Prediction Problems," ASME Transactions: Journal of Basic Engineering (Mar., 1960).

39. Kalman, R. E., "On the General Theory of Control Systems," Proceedings of the First International Congress on Automatic Control, Moscow (1960).

40. Kalman, R. E., and J. E. Bertram, "Control System Analysis and Design Via the Second Method of Lyapunov-I Continuous-Time Systems," ASME Transactions: Journal of Basic Engineering, 371 (June, 1960).

41. Kalman, R. E., and J. E. Bertram, "Control System Analysis and Design Via the Second Method of Lyapunov-II Discrete-Time Systems," ASME Transactions: Journal of Basic Engineering, 394 (June, 1960).

42. Kanus, K., Synthesis of a Self Optimizing Controller, S.B. Thesis, M.I.T. Electrical Engineering Department (June, 1961).

43. Kipiniak, W., Optimum Nonlinear Controllers, Technical Report 7793-R-2, Servomechanisms Laboratory, M.I.T. (Nov., 1958). Also S.M. Thesis, M.I.T. Electrical Engineering Department (June, 1958).

44. Kipiniak, W., Optimization and Control of a Cyclicly Operated Fixed Bed Catalytic Reactor, Technical Report 7793-R-6, Electronic Systems Laboratory, M.I.T. (Feb., 1960).

45. Kochenburger, R. J., "A Frequency Response Method for Analyzing and Synthesizing Contractor Servomechanisms," AIEE Transactions, 69, 270 (Mar., 1950).

46. Kramer, J. D. R., "On Control of Linear Systems with Time Lags," Information and Control, 3, 4, 299.

47. Kulikowski, R., "On Optimal Control with Constraints," Bulletin de l'Academie Polonaise des Sciences, VII, 4 (Jan., 1959).

48. Kulikowski, R., "Concerning the Synthesis of the Optimum Nonlinear Control Systems," Bulletin de l'Academie Polonaise des Sciences, VII, 4 (Apr., 1959).

49. Kulikowski, R., "Synthesis of a Class of Optimum Control Systems," Bulletin de l'Academie Polonaise des Sciences, VII, 11 (Oct., 1959).

50. Kulikowski, R., "On the Synthesis of Adaptive Systems," Bulletin de l'Academie Polonaise des Sciences, VII, 12 (Nov., 1959).

51. Kulikowski, R., "Synthesis of Optimum Control Systems with Area-Bounded Control Signal," Bulletin de l'Academie Polonaise des Sciences, VIII, 4 (Mar., 1960).

52. LaSalle, J. P., "Time Optimal Control Systems," Proc. Natl. Acad. Sci. U.S., 45, 4, 573-577 (Apr., 1959).

53. Lanczos, C., The Variational Principle of Mechanics, University of Toronto Press, Toronto, Canada, 1949.

54. Laning, J. H., Jr., and R. H. Battin, Random Processes in Automatic Control, McGraw-Hill, New York, 1956.

55. Lefschetz, S., Controls: An Application of the Direct Method of Lyapunov, Technical Report 59-8, RIAS Corporation (Dec., 1959).

56. Mesarović, M. D., The Control of Multivariable Systems, Technology Press and John Wiley & Sons, Cambridge and New York, 1960.

57. Messara, J. L., "On Lyapunov's Conditions of Stability," Annals of Mathematics, 50, 4, 705-721 (1949).

58. Meer, A., Synthesis of an Optimum Nonlinear Controller as a Spatial Analog, S.M. Thesis, M.I.T. Electrical Engineering Department (Sept., 1961).

59. Merriam, C. W., III, Synthesis of Adaptive Controls, Technical Report 7793-R-3, Servomechanisms Laboratory, M.I.T. (Feb., 1959). Also Sc.D. Thesis, M.I.T. Electrical Engineering Department (June, 1958).

60. Merriam, C. W., III, "An Optimization Theory for Feedback Control System Design," Report to the Office of Naval Research of the Department of the Navy under Contract Nonv. 1841(53), M.I.T. Electrical Engineering Department (May, 1959).

61. Merriam, C. W., III, "Computational Considerations for a Class of Optimum Control Systems," Report to the Office of Naval Research of the Department of the Navy under Contract Nonr. No. 1841(53), M.I.T. Electrical Engineering Department (June, 1959).

62. Merriam, C. W., III, "A Class of Optimum Control Systems," J. Franklin Inst., 267, 4, 277-297 (1959).

63. Milne, W. E., Numerical Solution of Differential Equations, John Wiley & Sons, New York, 1953.

64. Morse, M., The Calculus of Variations in the Large, American Mathematical Society (1934).

65. Nesline, F. W., Jr., "Optimum Response of Discontinuous Feedback Control Systems," Proceedings of the Joint Computers in Control Systems Conference, Atlantic City, N.J. (1957).

66. Newton, G. C., L. A. Gould, and J. F. Kaiser, Analytical Design of Linear Feedback Controls, John Wiley & Sons, New York, 1957.

67. Nickerson, H. K., D. C. Spencer, and N. E. Steenrod, Advanced Calculus, Van Nostrand, Princeton, N. J., 1959.

68. Singleton, H. E., Theory of Nonlinear Transducers, Technical Report 160, Research Laboratory of Electronics, M.I.T. (Aug., 1950).

69. Truxel, J. G., Automatic Feedback Control System Synthesis, McGraw-Hill, New York, 1955.

70. Volterra, V., Theory of Functionals and of Integral and Integro-Differential Equations, Dover, New York, 1959.

71. Weinstock, R., Calculus of Variations; with Applications to Physics and Engineering, McGraw-Hill, New York, 1952.

72. Whittaker, E. T., A Treatise on the Analytical Dynamics of Particles and Rigid Bodies, Dover, New York, 1944.

73. Wiener, N., Nonlinear Problems in Random Theory, Technology Press and John Wiley & Sons, Cambridge and New York, 1958.

74. Williams, T. J., and R. E. Otto, "A Generalized Chemical Processing Model for the Investigation of Computer Control," AIEE Transactions, Part I (Communications and Electronics), 79, 458-473, (Nov., 1960).

75. Zames, G., Nonlinear Operators for System Analysis, Sc.D. Thesis, M.I.T. Electrical Engineering Department (Sept., 1960).

INDEX